India's Foreign Policy

'Former foreign secretary Muchkund Dubey condenses in this book his deep insights, and his thorough and informed analysis of the most salient points of Indian foreign policy ... [Each] chapter brings [is]backed by facts and observable trends that inspire an autonomous, principled, and dynamic policy geared to the self-interest of the nation.'

Outlook

'This volume [will be of] interest to anyone who is interested in the future of India ... [it] has an impressive wealth of information and current data. The interpretation of policy and its context has also been dealt with great efficacy ... an important contribution to the current debate about the future directions of our foreign policy.'

Indian Foreign Affairs Journal

'... it is a delight to read this book. It should be read by the general public interested in foreign policy ... Scholars and practitioners of diplomacy will benefit from the book. For young diplomats in India and in other SAARC countries, it is essential reading.'

Frontline

'It is marked by a freshness of insight, balanced analysis and cogent arguments born out of experience as a participant in India's foreign policy-making and international negotiations as a career diplomat ... an important contribution to understanding India's foreign policy.'

The Daily Star

'The book is useful because it warns that foreign policy cannot exist in a vacuum; it must be related to the needs of the people. The author ... takes an enlightened view of national interest, placing equal emphasis on security and development.'

Strategic Analysis

India's Foreign Policy

Coping with the Changing World

Updated Edition with New Chapter on Pakistan

Muchkund Dubey

Orient BlackSwan

INDIA'S FOREIGN POLICY

ORIENT BLACKSWAN PRIVATE LIMITED

Registered Office
3-6-752 Himayatnagar, Hyderabad 500 029 (Telangana), India
e-mail: centraloffice@orientblackswan.com

Other Offices
Bengaluru, Chennai, Guwahati, Hyderabad,
Kolkata, Mumbai, New Delhi, Noida, Patna

First published in India by Dorling Kindersley (India) Pvt. Ltd., 2013
This updated edition © Orient Blackswan Private Limited 2016
First published 2016
Reprinted 2016
This paperback edition by Orient Blackswan Private Limited 2017
Reprinted 2018, 2025

ISBN 978-93-86392-08-4

040695

Typeset in
Bembo 10/12
by Shine Graphics, Delhi 110 094

Printed in India at
B.B. Press, Tronica City Ghaziabad (UP) 201 102

Published by
Orient Blackswan Private Limited
3-6-752 Himayatnagar, Hyderabad 500 029, Telangana, India
e-mail: info@orientblackswan.com

Dedicated to my wife

Lalita

Contents

Preface and Acknowledgements

For the past several decades, I have been conceptualizing and articulating, through my writings and speeches, my views on a large number of national and international issues. These cover a variety of subjects ranging from world order to international relations, including India's foreign policy to alternative strategies for India's social and economic development. These views are scattered in hundreds of pages of articles in journals, chapters of books and newspaper columns. Ever since I retired from the Indian Foreign Service at the end of 1991, I had been under constant pressure from my friends and well-wishers, particularly my wife, to update my published articles and papers, classify them under subject headings and get them published as separate books. There was no doubt considerable merit in this suggestion. For, articles and papers published along with those of other authors attract only divided attention, whereas a book containing the work of a single author receives more concentrated attention. Moreover, writings assembled in a single volume have a better chance of winning recognition and are likely to have a longer shelf life than those dispersed in a large number of books and journals.

At long last, drawing on my published work on foreign policy issues I was able to get my book *India's Foreign Policy: Coping with the Changing World* published in 2012. The current volume is a revised and updated version of that book including the addition of a chapter on Pakistan and Indo-Pak Relations.

This book is still not a complete text on India's foreign policy, as it leaves out India's relationships with some of its very important partners, particularly its close neighbours like Nepal, Sri Lanka, Bhutan, Maldives and Afghanistan. Another important absentee is the European Union, which is the most successful example of regional economic integration in the world and a unique model of global governance at the regional level. The book also does not separately deal with India's relations with Brazil and South Africa with which it is united in the forums of

IBSA (India, Brazil and South Africa) and BRICS (Brazil, Russia, India, China and South Africa), the groupings that constitute an important underpinning of India's global strategy. Finally, I would have liked to add to the book a chapter on India's foreign economic policy, a subject that I had got introduced as a course in the syllabus of the Jawaharlal Nehru University, and which I taught for eight years during my tenure there. There are still other subjects like security and disarmament, new regionalism, multilateralism under the United Nations (UN) and a new international economic order, which have a vital bearing on India's foreign policy and which have been dealt with at appropriate places in different chapters of the book, but which deserve separate chapters, if not separate volumes.

With the exception of the chapter on Pakistan and Indo-Pak Relations, each chapter in this book has a parentage; but as happens in real life, the progeny, that is, the current chapter, bears little resemblance with the parent, that is, the originally published work. The latter has been thoroughly updated and drastically reorganized and restructured. The only resemblance is that, in most cases, I have borrowed the titles of the original papers. In a few cases, I have also used some of the facts contained therein.

The core theme of the book is enunciated in its first chapter. This chapter broadly reflects my world view and my preferred approach and strategy for India's foreign policy. I have tried my best to make the chapter self-contained and stand alone so that this chapter by itself can make it worthwhile for the readers to reach out for a copy of the book. This chapter has been fully updated by incorporating the implications for the strategy of India's foreign policy of some of the recent game-changing developments in the world, particularly China's further rise as a world power; initiatives for negotiating the new generation of economic partnership agreements, particularly in the Asia-Pacific region; sharp decline in US–Russian relations and the resumption of the Cold War between North Atlantic Treaty Organization (NATO) countries led by the United States (US) and Russia; and the rising spiral of local wars, other violent conflicts and terrorism in the region west of India's border with Pakistan, particularly West Asia.

Those who will read this book in order to find juicy anecdotes of a retired diplomat, or get first-hand accounts of events in the making of which I have played some part or come across slices of history to which I have been a witness and which have remained buried so far, will feel betrayed and disappointed. I offer my deep apologies to them! In writing this book, I have no doubt drawn upon my experience of shaping and conducting India's foreign policy. The book, therefore, inevitably includes my reflections and insights as a participant in policymaking and international negotiations. But I have scrupulously avoided using the first person or including stuff of which memoires are made. I would, therefore, like the book to be judged on the criteria of the depth of the research that has gone into it, the rigour and soundness of the arguments marshalled in it, the freshness of the insights that it provides into events and policies, and the significance and the practicability of its policy prescriptions.

This book is not on the history of India's relations with important countries or groups thereof. A summary of the evolution of some of the important relationships is given as a backdrop. However, the main emphasis in each chapter is on the current state, future challenges and prospects of these relations, and the policies and strategies to be followed for nurturing them.

In the delineation of general relations, greater salience is given to their economic dimensions. The chapter on relationship with Bangladesh is confined to its economic aspects. In the chapter on Pakistan and Indo Pak Relations, equal if not larger space is devoted to economic aspects. Towards the end of the chapter, the importance of Indo-Pak economic relations has been brought out in greater detail than found in most other published work on the subject. The chapter also contains a whole blueprint of Indo-Pak economic cooperation that can be implemented even without their being a paradigmatic shift in Pakistan's state ideology which determines its attitude towards India. A full chapter is devoted to China's tryst with globalization. This is because the spectacular success of China's embrace of globalization has transformed the entire global political equation with far-reaching implications for the foreign policy of all major powers, including that of India.

I hope that this revised and updated version of the book would commend itself to and fully come up to the expectations of the academic community, policy makers and general readers.

In acknowledgement, I would like to single out Orient BlackSwan, particularly Mimi Choudhury, Publisher, Higher Academic Social Sciences, for their bold decision to publish this revised and updated version of the book only three years after it was originally published. I owe a special debt of gratitude to Nilanjana Majumdar, senior editor, for her very gentle but effective proddings to adhere to the schedule for revising the manuscript, and to Aldeena Raju for her editorial effort which has undoubtedly improved the quality of the book. The task of updating and revising the book would have been more painstaking and time consuming but for the unsparing assistance extended by Akhil Alha, my colleague in the Council for Social Development. I really appreciate his assiduousness in collecting the bulk of the additional data and redoing the Notes to each chapter. Some of the important additional data I have used in this volume have been provided by Dr Sachin Chaturvedi, Director General, and Professor Ram Upendra Das of the Research and Information System for Developing Countries (RIS). I am most grateful to them and their RIS colleagues for this. I also owe a debt of deep gratitude to Dr Biswajit Dhar for the time he found for discussing some of the economic issues analyzed in this volume and for filling the data gap. I also sincerely appreciate the assistance extended by Dr Sheel Kant Sharma, my colleague in the Indian Foreign Service, in verifying facts and clarifying concepts about which I had doubts. In view of my repeatedly demonstrated incapacity to use the computer, the project of this book would not have materialized but for the tireless and unhesitating secretarial assistance provided by Harpal Singh, my executive assistant and friend. My debt to him is, therefore, immense. Finally, I must also recognize the contribution of the Council for Social Development, as it provided the perfect working condition for writing this book.

My wife, Lalita, relieved me from all the worries of household chores to enable me to work single-mindedly on the book. She kept insisting that I must drastically reduce my other engagements in order to concentrate on the book which would be the only durable legacy of my thoughts, beliefs and perceptions. Nobody was happier than she in seeing this book published originally and I know that she would be equally elated to see it published in its revised and amplified form. It is to her, therefore, that this volume is dedicated.

Abbreviations

ADB	Asian Development Bank
AIIB	Asian Infrastructure Investment Bank
AFTA	ASEAN Free Trade Agreement
AMRO	ASEAN+3 Macro Research Office
APEC	Asia and Pacific Economic Cooperation
ARC	Asian Relations Conference
ARF	ASEAN Regional Forum
ASAT	anti-satellite weapons
ASEAN	Association of Southeast Asian Nations
ASER	Annual Status of Education Report
BAKSAL	Bangladesh Krishak Shramik Awami League
BCIM	Bangladesh, China, India and Myanmar
BDCA	Border Defence Cooperation Agreement
BDR	Bangladesh Rifles
BHEL	Bharat Heavy Electricals Limited
BIMSTEC	Bay of Bengal Initiative for Multi-Sectoral Technical and Economic Cooperation
BJP	Bharatiya Janata Party
BMD	Ballistic Missile Defence
BPO	Business Process Outsourcing
BRAC	Bangladesh Rural Advancement Committee
BRIC	Brazil, Russia, India and China
BRICS	Brazil, Russia, India, China and South Africa
CARIFTA	Caribbean Free Trade Association
CD	Conference on Disarmament
CECA	Comprehensive Economic Cooperation Agreement
CENTO	Central Treaty Organization
CEPA	Comprehensive Economic Partnership Agreement
CHT	Chittagong Hill Tracts
CII	Confederation of Indian Industry

CMI	Chiang Mai Initiative
CMIM	Chiang Mai Initiative Multilateralization
CPN	Communist Party of Nepal
CRA	Contingency Reserve Arrangement
CSD	Council for Social Development
CSTO	Collective Security Treaty Organization
CTBT	Comprehensive Nuclear-Test-Ban Treaty
DAP	diammonium hydrogen phosphate
DEP	Digital Equalization Programme
DPJ	Democratic Party of Japan
DTTI	Defence Technology and Trade Initiative
ECOSOC	Economic and Social Council
EU	European Union
EXIM	Export Import Bank of India
FAO	Food and Agriculture Organization
FAQ	Frequently Asked Questions
FATA	Federally Administered Tribal Areas
FDI	Foreign Direct Investment
FICCI	Federation of Indian Chambers of Commerce and Industry
FMCT	Fissile Material Cut-off Treaty
FOCAC	Forum of China–Africa Cooperation
FTA	Free Trade Agreement
FTAAP	Free Trade Area of the Asia-Pacific
GATT	General Agreement on Tariffs and Trade
GATS	General Agreement on Trade in Services
GDP	Gross Domestic Product
GEP	Group of Eminent Persons
Global-INK	Global Indian Network of Knowledge
GNP	Gross National Product
GPA	Agreement on Government Procurement
GSP	Generalized System of Preferences
GSTP	Global System of Trade Preferences
HIV/AIDS	Human immunodeficiency virus infection and acquired immune deficiency syndrome
HRMPA	Human Resource Mobility Partnership Agreement
IAEA	International Atomic Energy Agency
IBSA	India–Brazil–South Africa Dialogue Forum
ICBM	Intercontinental Ballistic Missile
ICM	Indian Centre for Migration

ICNND	International Commission on Nuclear Non-Proliferation and Nuclear Disarmament
ICT	Information and Communication Technology
ICWF	Indian Community Welfare Fund
IDA	International Development Association
IDPL	Indian Drugs and Pharmaceuticals Limited
IFC	International Finance Corporation
IGNOU	Indira Gandhi National Open University
IMF	International Monetary Fund
IMR	Infant Mortality Rate
INF	Intermediate-Range Nuclear Forces (Treaty)
IPR	Intellectual Property Rights
IRBM	Intermediate-Range Ballistic Missile
ISFTA	India–Sri Lanka Free Trade Agreement
ISI	Inter-Services Intelligence
ISIS	Islamic State of Iraq and Syria
ISRO	Indian Space Research Organisation
IT	information technology
ITA	Information Technology Agreement
ITEC	Indian Technical and Economic Cooperation
IWTT	Inland Water Transit and Trade
JEC	Joint Economic Commission
JI	Jamaat-e-Islami
JRC	Joint River Commission
KKNPP	Kudankulam Nuclear Power Plant
LAC	Line of Actual Control
LAFTA	Latin American Free Trade Association
LDP	Liberal Democratic Party
MIRV	Multiple Independently Targetable Re-entry Vehicle
MFA	Multi-Fibre Agreement
MFN	Most-Favoured Nation
MMR	Maternal Mortality Rate
MMTC	Mineral and Metal Trading Corporation
MOIA	Ministry of Overseas Indian Affairs
MoU	memorandum of understanding
MRBM	Medium-Range Ballistic Missile
MTCR	Missile Technology Control Regime
NAFTA	North American Free Trade Agreement
NATO	North Atlantic Treaty Organization
NDA	National Democratic Alliance

NDB	New Development Bank
NDPG	National Defence Programme Guidelines
NGO	Non-Governmental Organization
NHRC	National Human Rights Commission
NPT	Non-Proliferation Treaty
NRI	non-resident Indian
NSG	Nuclear Suppliers Group
NTPC	National Thermal Power Corporation
NWFP	North-West Frontier Province
NWFZ	Nuclear-Weapon-Free Zone
OCI	Overseas Citizenship of India
OECD	Organisation for Economic Co-operation and Development
OFDI	Outbound Foreign Direct Investment
OIFC	Overseas Indian Facilitation Centre
ONGC	Oil and Natural Gas Corporation Limited
OWRC	Overseas Workers Resource Centre
PIO	Persons of Indian Origin
PLA	People's Liberation Army
PML(NS)	Pakistan Muslim League (Nawaz Sharif)
PPP	Pakistan Peoples Party
RIC	Russia, India and China
RBI	Reserve Bank of India
RCEP	Regional Comprehensive Economic Partnership
RTI	Right to Information
SAARC	South Asian Association for Regional Cooperation
SAFTA	South Asian Free Trade Area
SAGQ	South Asia Growth Quadrangle
SALT	Strategic Arms Limitation Talks
SAPTA	South Asian Preferential Trading Arrangement
SCO	Shanghai Cooperation Organisation
SDF	Self Defence Forces
SDR	Special Drawing Rights
SEATO	Southeast Asia Treaty Organization
SED	Strategic Economic Dialogue
SOE	state-owned enterprise
SSA	Social Security Agreement
START	Strategic Arms Reduction Treaty
TISA	Trade in Services Agreement
TPP	Trans-Pacific Partnership

TRIMs	Agreement on Trade-Related Investment Measures
TRIPS	Agreement on Trade-Related Aspects of Intellectual Property Rights
TTIP	Transatlantic Trade and Investment Partnership
TTP	Tehrik-i-Taliban Pakistan
TVE	Township and Village Enterprise
UK	United Kingdom
UN	United Nations
UNCTAD	United Nations Conference on Trade and Development
UNICEF	United Nations Children's Fund
UPA	United Progressive Alliance
US	United States
USSR	Union of Soviet Socialist Republics
USTR	United States Trade Representative
VAT	Value-Added Tax
WMD	weapons of mass destruction
WTO	World Trade Organization

ONE India's Foreign Policy

Underlying Principles, Strategies and Challenges Ahead

Basic Assumptions

The fundamental purpose of India's foreign policy—and for that matter of any other nation's—is to promote its national interest. But national interest is not as simple a concept as it may appear superficially. There is, first, a hierarchy of national interests and it is not easy to establish the right priority or to strike the right balance among them. Besides, the way national interest is pursued in a particular domain influences, in a far-reaching manner, both in the positive and negative sense, the national interest in other domains. In the hierarchy of national interests, security occupies the pre-eminent position. It is the foremost duty—nay, the very raison d'être—of a state to meet threats emanating from any quarters to its security, to repel aggression and to safeguard the sovereignty and territorial integrity of the nation. The state, therefore, must possess the military wherewithal, either alone or in alliance with other countries, to thwart military threats to its security. For, there can be no peace and prosperity in a nation without ensuring its physical survival.

Every country has equal right to security and to take all possible measures to safeguard it. However, in doing so, it must ensure that the national interests of other countries or global peace and security are not affected adversely. Besides, security is very much a national perception. Others cannot impose their perception of security on a state, as their perception is very frequently shaped by their own vested interests.

In the modern world, security has both military and non-military dimensions. What concerns a modern state is not only military security but also economic security, energy security, environmental security, food security etc. The fabric of a nation today is threatened not only by open aggression but also by subversions, interventions or interferences in various forms from abroad, and by strifes, contentions and conflicts from within. Multifaceted internal threats to security include economic instability, persistence of social inequalities, inability to meet the basic needs of the people, persistence of large-scale poverty, marginalization of large sections of the population and the denial of basic human rights to the people. Whereas averting military threats is an indispensable condition for safeguarding national security, it is not a sufficient condition. In order to remain secure and stable, apart from military preparedness, a nation must be able to meet the challenge of subversion and interferences from abroad as well as home-grown threats to its unity and cohesion. An all-round failure of security on non-military fronts can push a nation into the category of 'a failed state', exposing it to external interventions of myriad kinds.

A major way in which foreign policy today serves a country's interest is by contributing to its economic and social progress. This has made foreign policy increasingly development-oriented. Until the mid-1980s, before the onset of the current phase of globalization, it mainly involved facilitating the flow of foreign development assistance, enhanced access to foreign markets and securing the transfer of appropriate technologies. It also involved working together with other nations to bring about a change in the international economic environment in order to make it supportive of development. This called for taking initiatives for changing regimes, rules and regulations of the international economic system and putting in place new ones to provide adequate elbow room to developing countries to pursue their development policies. The development-oriented foreign policy was required to be pursued simultaneously at the multilateral, regional and bilateral levels. It is easier to achieve quick results at the bilateral level rather than at the regional and multilateral levels. On the other hand, developing countries have a better bargaining position at the multilateral level than at the regional or bilateral levels. In order to optimize gains, each country has to strike its own balance in concentrating its limited diplomatic and other resources at one or the other of these three levels of engagement with foreign countries.

An important aim of the foreign policy of any country, including that of India, is to contribute to world peace and prosperity and play an active role in the establishment of a just, fair and equitable world order. At times, the pursuit of this objective may appear in the short run as a negative sum game, because it can annoy the nations which matter in the world, and thus harm India's national interest. For example, India's earlier stand against the use of nuclear weapons, its advocacy of a nuclear weapon-free world and its refusal to be a party to the discriminatory Nuclear Non-Proliferation Treaty of 1968 was then perceived by the nuclear weapon powers as militating against their interest. Similarly, its non-endorsement of the stand of the North Atlantic Treaty Organization (NATO) powers on the 1998–99 Kosovo conflict and of the attack by the United States (US) and its allies against Iraq (2003) may not have been taken kindly by these powers, and therefore, have had a negative effect in the short run on India's foreign policy. However, in the medium- and long-term, these seemingly negative sum games become positive sum games. This is because India's national interests are best served in a world free from discrimination and arbitrary action, and one based on equity, justice and fair play. For, in the long run, the very sustainability of the world order and the very survival of humankind depend on its ability to establish a just and equitable world order, free from weapons of mass destruction (WMD).

India's foreign policy was inspired by the ideals and vision of the leaders of its independence movement and reflected the finest elements of its cultural and philosophical heritage. It started taking shape during the independence movement itself. Leaders like Mahatma Gandhi, Jawaharlal Nehru, Subhas Chandra Bose and Rammanohar Lohia were principally responsible for providing its philosophical and intellectual content. Some of its major tenets were articulated by Jawaharlal Nehru, India's first prime minister, at the Asian Relations Conference held in Delhi in March 1947. This foreign policy combined national interest with the broader objective of establishing a just and equitable world order. It was deeply anchored in the ideals of truth, non-violence, tolerance, the notion of global governance and the world as a single family of humankind. These essential principles were also embodied in the Constitution of India.

The sheet anchor of India's foreign policy was non-alignment—not as a negative or neutral concept of keeping out of the rival power blocs which dominated the period following the Second World War, but as a positive concept of exercising independence of judgement and action in matters of foreign policy, judging each issue on its merits, and not just toeing the line laid down by others or, as Nehru said, becoming the 'play-thing of the others'.[1] These axioms constitute the thread of continuity in India's foreign policy. No government of India can abdicate independence of judgement and action in matters of foreign policy or in its conduct, compromise with the basic values enshrined in the

Constitution, without jeopardizing national interest. This is a view widely shared in the country.

The most significant strivings of the Non-Aligned Movement (NAM)—of which India, under Nehru, was one of the founding members—have been in the areas of development, peace, disarmament, decolonization, the establishment of a just and equitable world order and the strengthening of multilateralism under the United Nations (UN). The pursuit of the development goal through NAM was necessary for giving substance to India's hard-won freedom. This called for, apart from national effort, international assistance and a propitious international environment. India, therefore, made NAM a platform for seeking larger flows of external resources under favourable terms and conditions, greater access for its exports in the markets of the developed countries, and restructuring of the international trading, financial and monetary systems in order to make them supportive of development.

For India, the maintenance of peace was not only a moral imperative but also a prerequisite for pursuing development. In India's perception, the rivalry between the two power blocs for hegemony over the world and their pursuit of the doctrine of nuclear deterrence had, by triggering an unprecedented nuclear arms race, brought the world to the brink of nuclear war and was threatening humankind's very right to live. India, therefore, utilized the NAM platform to raise its voice against the nuclear arms race, worked for the prevention of nuclear war and called for the elimination of nuclear weapons. India also believed that its own independence would not be complete until all the peoples living in territories still under colonial domination gained their freedom. Decolonization thus became an unfinished agenda of India's own national movement for freedom and NAM's principal agenda during its earlier phase.

The UN has always been at the centre of India's global vision and a preferred instrumentality for serving its foreign policy ends. India, therefore, actively supported the UN and took initiatives from time to time to strengthen the multilateral system underpinned by it. The UN Charter's principle of the sovereign equality of states and its provision of non-interference in domestic affairs ideally suited India's interest and that of other NAM countries which wanted to be treated as equals and which were very watchful of their newly acquired sovereignty. The UN was the most important arena for India and other NAM countries to project and assert their sovereignty at the international level.

For many years after independence, this foreign policy admirably served India's national interest. It contributed to its pursuit of development.

It gave India an international profile larger than was warranted by its economic strength and military power. India's efforts to defuse the Korean crisis were duly recognized when in 1953, following the Korean Armistice, India was appointed the Chairman of the Neutral Nations Repatriation Commission. India also played a dominant role behind the scenes in bringing about the 1954 Geneva Agreements on peace in Indo-China. As a recognition of its contribution, India was asked to chair the International Control Commission set up under the Agreement. Throughout this period, India's opinion on global issues was eagerly awaited. And India was almost universally regarded as the most important leader of NAM. On several occasions, India helped in lowering tensions between the rival power blocs and pulling them back from the brink so as to enable the world to gain the urgently needed breathing space for resolving disputes. India also needed an environment free from conflict in order to pursue its goals of economic development and political consolidation. The policy of non-alignment made it possible for it to maintain normal relations with all the major powers of the world in varying degrees of warmth and intimacy and enlist their help in the pursuit of its development goals.

Both external and internal factors combined in the later years of the Nehru era and after, to deprive this policy of some of its elan and effectiveness. Externally, India's defeat at the hands of China in 1962 proved to be a major setback, and the relationship of near permanent hostility with Pakistan exercised a disabling effect on the conduct of its foreign policy. Internally, India was increasingly seen as a country that could not live up to the expectations aroused by it in the economic field, nor could it graduate to the status of a major military power, as China did.

By the mid-1960s, most of the promises held out by India, both to its own people and to the outside world, were belied. Several developing countries, particularly in Asia, which were far behind India at the time of its independence, forged ahead. During the next three decades, they registered much higher rates of growth than India.[2] They achieved notable success in building infrastructure and in accumulating and improving human capital. This became the springboard for further acceleration of growth. This enabled them to diversify their economies, build a strong export base and virtually eradicate poverty. For example, the headcount poverty rate in China decreased from 30.7 per cent in 1978 to 14.3 per cent in 1987. It was down to 3.2 per cent in 2001.[3] In Indonesia, the proportion of the population in poverty (based on estimates of expenditure) dropped from 41.1 per cent to 17.4 per cent between 1976 and 1987. It further dropped to 11.3 per cent in 1996.[4] India, on the other hand, remained mired in poverty and tied down by a prolonged spell of very low growth.[5] There was, in fact, an accentuation of poverty in India during this period. The country experienced acute famine conditions in the second half of the 1960s. It still remains among countries with the largest number of underprivileged, illiterate and malnourished persons in the world. In the immediate post-colonial period, even some of the African countries outperformed India in attaining higher levels of literacy and making health services available to larger sections of their populations. In 1960, the Infant Mortality Rate (IMR) per 1,000 live births in India was 159.3, in Indonesia 128.9, in the Republic of Korea 100.9 and in Malaysia, 70. By 2010, India was able to reduce its IMR to 48.2, but the other Asian countries mentioned reduced it to much lower levels—Indonesia to 22.72, the Republic of Korea to 4.2 and Malaysia to 2.54. China's IMR in 1968 was 86.6, but by 2010, it was down to 15.8.[6] Famine conditions were by and large beyond the pale of the experience of these countries. Nearer home, Sri Lanka outperformed India along most indicators of social development and achieved a much higher per capita income. Pakistan's rate of growth in the 1960s was much higher than that of India, though there might have been questions about the quality of this growth.

All these factors accounted for a substantial lowering of India's stature in the comity of nations, particularly among developing countries. This situation continued till the early 1990s, when, following the Gulf War, India got engulfed in an acute balance-of-payment crisis and found itself on the verge of defaulting on the payment of its external debt. This had an adverse effect on the effectiveness of India's foreign policy. Nothing brought out this relative impotence of India's foreign policy more dramatically than the crushing defeat inflicted on India by Japan in the election to one of the Asian non-permanent seats in the UN Security Council in 1995. So chastised was India by this defeat that it was not until 2008 that it was able to muster the confidence to put up its candidature again for election to a non-permanent seat in the Security Council. In 2010, India managed to get elected to the Security Council for the two-year term of 2011–12.

The situation with regard to India's foreign policy has taken a turn for the better since the mid-1990s. This has been mainly because of the positive impact on India's international standing, of the relatively high rate of growth—on an average, about 5 per cent per annum during the 1980s, approximately 6 per cent during the 1990s and between 7 and 8 per cent during the first decade of the new century. Trend growth rates in India during the 1980s (1980–89) was 5.65, during the 1990s (1990–99), it was 6.02 per cent, and between 2000 and 2010, 7.85 per cent.[7] On the basis of a linear projection of this trend of growth, it was predicted in the beginning of 2003 that India would emerge as the world's third largest economy by 2050. The fact that such projections were made by multinational companies like Goldman Sachs and PricewaterhouseCoopers, which were very prestigious and influential at that time, carried a great deal of weight. After that, predictions regarding India's position in the world economy in the coming decades were made by Indian think tanks and independent experts, painting even a rosier picture. It was stated by several of them that if India's size, its pivotal position in Asia, its growing youth population, its strong scientific and technology base and its open society with a long tradition of individuality and innovation are taken into account, then its prospects in the long run are even better than that of China. Some experts and writers on strategic issues argued that India had already become a First World economic power and it was, therefore, necessary for it to jettison its Third World baggage in the formulation and conduct of its foreign policy. The new dynamism acquired by the Indian economy was fuelled in large part by an impressive improvement in the competitiveness of India's manufacturing sector and a very robust rate of growth in export, led by the computer software sector. This created vastly expanded demands for foreign private capital, technologies, goods and services. The Indian economy and market, particularly that for consumer goods for a middle-class population of some 300 million with rising per capita incomes, is now coveted by most of the major economic powers of the world.

India's rising stature in the global community has also been partly due to the emergence of India as a de facto nuclear weapon power after its testing of nuclear weapons in 1998. It is debatable if this alone would have sufficed to enhance India's international standing. It may even be argued that in a stagnant and adverse economic situation, India's going public on the possession of nuclear weapons could have landed it in greater trouble and increased its vulnerability to pressure for applying standstill on and to roll back the production of nuclear arms. Thus, the newly acquired dynamism of the Indian economy played a decisive role in enhancing India's standing in the world, lending a much higher profile to its foreign policy, and in getting the major world powers reconciled to India's status as a nuclear weapon power.

This high profile is reflected in the almost incessant visits of Heads of States and Governments of major powers to India for clinching big commercial deals and for entering into agreements for jointly meeting threats of a transnational character like terrorism, drug trafficking, natural disasters and HIV/AIDS. There has also been a veritable scramble on their part to elevate their relations with India to a strategic level.

This change in the attitude of major powers is also reflected in the new salience acquired by Sino-Indian relations—in the dramatic expansion of Indo-Chinese trade in the last few years and the initiation of dialogue between the two countries on a variety of issues, particularly those figuring in multilateral economic negotiations. Till a few years ago, China's response to overtures by India to have a dialogue on the nuclear issue was one of total indifference, on the ground that India, being a non-nuclear power, had no locus standi to have such a dialogue with China. But today, discussions on strategic issues have become an integral part of the Sino-Indian Strategic and Cooperative Partnership.

In spite of the high profile it has acquired recently, India's foreign policy remains constrained by such domestic factors as poor infrastructure, poor performance on the social front, particularly health and education, socio-economic inequality, social exclusion and marginalization, regional disparity and the abysmally poor state of governance. There is a growing credibility gap between the masses and the elite who run the state. India is still struggling to live up to the social contract embodied in its Constitution. It has not been able to cope effectively with ethnic aspirations and the primordial urge to preserve cultural identities. As a result, there is simmering discontent at various levels which often erupts into conflict and violence, and there is a near insurgency situation in the north-east and the state of Jammu and Kashmir. According to the government's own admission, 125 out of a total of 640 Indian districts spread over 12 states are in the grip of Naxalite violence,[8] and in a good number of these districts, the dictate of the state does not prevail. It is the dismal state of governance in the country, coupled with the denial of justice and unmet socio-economic needs and cultural aspirations, which is mainly responsible for the eruption of violence and terrorist attacks in different parts of the country. Frequent attempts by India's political class to divert attention from these factors, for which they are mainly responsible, by attributing these acts of violence and terror to the designs and actions of foreign intelligence agencies, have only served the purpose of exacerbating the prevailing tensions in India's relations with its neighbours.

Impact of Major Changes between 1980 and 1995

End of the Cold War

The end of the Cold War during the dying years of the 1980s brought about changes of seismic proportions in the world situation. Its most dramatic manifestation was the disintegration of the Communist system led by the Soviet Union and the headlong rush by Russia, East European countries and many of the countries which were part of the erstwhile Soviet Union, towards ushering in a democratic system in some form or the other, giving maximum scope to the free play of market forces and integration with the capitalist system. With the disintegration of the Soviet Union and Russia's compulsion, mainly due to domestic developments, to abdicate its status as a superpower and its decision to withdraw from its commitment to security overseas, the US emerged as the only superpower in the world, mainly by virtue of its overwhelming military and economic superiority. In the early 1990s, the US was universally regarded as the only super-power, a 'hyper power' as the then French foreign minister called it and the 'ultimate hegemon'. The absence of a countervailing power against the US created complications for the foreign policy of almost all countries, including India.

The end of the Cold War, in the short and medium term, had several positive sides to it. It led to an unprecedented progress in resolving some of the chronic and seemingly intractable regional conflicts and restoring to the UN its legitimate role in the field of peace and security. It proved to be the most important factor in the achievement of the Namibian independence in 1990. It saw the then President F. W. de Klerk of South Africa liquidating the apartheid regime in his country by 1993, for which he was awarded the Nobel Peace Prize. Peace at long last dawned in Cambodia in 1991. The longstanding problems of Mozambique and Angola were resolved. And democracy was restored in Nicaragua and El Salvador. The UN started playing an active role in the pacific settlement of disputes, preventive diplomacy and peacekeeping because, for the first time, the permanent members of the Security Council were able to act together.

There was also spectacular progress in arms control and disarmament. The two largest nuclear weapon powers of the world—the then Soviet Union and the US—agreed through the Intermediate-Range Nuclear Forces (INF) Treaty of 1987, to eliminate all their land-based intermediate range missiles, and two-thirds of their strategic nuclear weapons. They also took unilateral action to eliminate their tactical and short range nuclear weapons. The North Atlantic Treaty Organization (NATO) and the member countries of the now-defunct Warsaw Pact agreed to slash their conventional arms by almost half. And an unprecedented convention was signed by nations across the globe to ban, under strict verification, the development, production, stock-piling, deployment and use of chemical weapons, which constitute an important category of weapons of mass destruction (WMD). The negotiations on the Comprehensive Nuclear-Test-Ban Treaty (CTBT) were completed and the Treaty was endorsed by the UN General Assembly in 1996. It was signed by several nations, but it could not come into force because of the insertion into it of an 'Entry into Force' clause which required that all 44 nuclear capable countries sign the Treaty before September 1999 for it to become operational.

Although militarily the US emerged as the only superpower, in terms of economic power the world still remained multi-polar. Three main centres of economic power emerged in the immediate post-Cold War period—North America, dominated by the US; Europe, dominated by unified Germany; and the Asia and the Pacific region, dominated by Japan. These centres were in competition with one another for the world market, raw materials and the political influence that goes with economic power.

In spite of inter se competition in the economic field, the major military and economic powers pursued a common strategic objective, and that was to maintain the status quo in the world power structure. This is because they saw the main threat to their security coming from the rise of new powers, particularly in the Third World. Thus, instead of two rival power blocs contending for hegemony, as in the Cold War era, there emerged a new alliance striving to establish its supremacy. This alliance consisted of both the East, the West and Japan, against the rest of the world, particularly the Third World. China too was a member, albeit an informal one, of the new alliance. For developing countries like India, this multi-polarity presented an uncertain and complex global environment which did not offer many new opportunities, but certainly increased their vulnerability.

The main interest of the new alliance lay in preserving the status quo in the global balance of economic and political power. It, therefore, worked for the retention and use of nuclear weapons by the nuclear weapon powers alone, preventing the proliferation of WMDs to Third World countries and forestalling the emergence of any of these countries as a big power on the world scene. For this purpose, Third World countries were expected not only to give up their ambitions to acquire WMDs but also substantially reduce their expenditure on conventional arms. As the countries of the new alliance saw the real threat to their security coming from the Third World, they wanted to establish a cordon sanitaire against the developing countries. For this reason, soon after the end of the Cold War, US think tanks and policy makers propounded the theory of discriminate deterrence, that is, not a pre-fixed deterrence as during the Cold War, but one that can be used discriminately and flexibly against any power that threatens to upset the status quo. The US decision, supported by most of its allies, to build a defensive weapon system against nuclear weapons was, according to their public declarations, also directed against Third World countries.

The new alliance put in place a number of exclusive discriminatory regimes which had the purpose of freezing the level and structure of the development of developing countries. These included the Australia Group (for chemical weapons), the Missile Technology Control Regime (for missile technology) and the London Club (for nuclear weapons), which later became the Nuclear Suppliers Group—all designed to control the export of dual-purpose substances, material and technologies in the respective areas. The lists of substances, materials and technologies which are prohibited or controlled under these regimes are so wide-ranging and open-ended as to enable the countries applying these regimes to determine the level and sophistication of the chemical and engineering industries of the Third World countries. Through these regimes, the access of developing countries to advanced and frontier technologies can be blocked and they can be virtually prevented from competing with developed countries in these areas. Thus, the members of the new alliance had strategic as well as commercial and economic reasons behind establishing these regimes and enacting commensurate national legislations to give effect to them.

Some of the environmental regimes established at that time, like the Montreal Protocol, required developing countries to phase out the production of substances the use of which could have an adverse effect on the environment. In the areas where such regimes applied, the developed countries had a technology lead of at least 25 to 50 years over developing countries, but the latter were given a margin of just a few years—say five to ten years—to phase out the production of such substances. These countries did not have the technologies to produce these substances or their substitutes in an environmentally friendly way. Such technologies developed by industrially advanced countries were available at exorbitantly high prices, which developing countries could ill afford. On the other hand, doing without these substances had adverse implications for the industry as a whole. Among the World Trade Organization (WTO) agreements, the Agreement on Trade-Related Aspects of Intellectual Property Rights (TRIPS) had the effect of freezing the technological development of the vast majority of developing countries at their current levels and establishing a regime whereby the industrially advanced countries would be the main source of generating technologies and manufacturing products using these and developing countries would provide the markets for such products.

The end of the Cold War also coincided with the increasing acceptance of democracy as a form of government. The values of fundamental freedoms and basic human rights came to be almost universally acclaimed even though only infrequently adhered to in practice. Moreover, country after country all over the world opted for development strategies designed to give the fullest possible play to free market forces and to integrate themselves with the world economy. Such a strategy is predicated on increased reliance on foreign markets, capital and technology. It has, therefore, pronounced foreign policy implications. Among others, it enhanced the dependence of developing countries like India on major economic powers. It also gave a new salience to economic diplomacy.

India found a lot in these changes to rejoice about. It was particularly happy to see the powerful assertion of the popular will all over the world in favour of democracy, freedom and human rights. In its own neighbourhood, democracy was restored in Nepal and Bangladesh in the early 1990s after decades of authoritarian rule. Most of the East European countries opted for a democratic form of government based on a multiparty system. A number of countries in Africa were also swept along in the same tide. These developments were very much in accord with India's own democratic ethos.

The end of the division of the world into two rival power blocs, which was the source of many conflicts in the world and the paralysis of the UN, came as a sort of nirvana for the Non-Aligned Movement, of which India was a great champion. The reduction of tension all around and the restoration of order in the conflict areas created an environment in which India was most comfortable pursuing its development objectives. The substantial reductions in the global nuclear arsenal was undoubtedly a vindication of India's stand on nuclear disarmament. India also had reasons to be gratified with the increasing evidence at that time of the UN coming into its own in the field of security.

Unfortunately, these developments proved to be very short-lived and the great promises of the end of the Cold War were belied or remained unfulfilled. International relations, after a brief period following the end of the Cold War, entered an uncharted terrain. India made several adaptations and changes in its foreign policy in order to cope with the post-Cold War situation. The most important among them was its policy towards the major Western powers, particularly the US. India tried to discard the ideological baggage of the past in dealing with these countries and explore new avenues of convergence of interest.

Decline of Multilateralism

India has, in the past, successfully used the UN for projecting its national personality on the international scene and for promoting its interests in the areas of peace, disarmament and development. Jawaharlal Nehru regarded the UN as an embryonic form of world government.

Starting from the early 1980s, multilateralism under the UN suffered a serious setback. The hopes aroused in the immediate post-Cold War period, that with the possibility of unanimity among the permanent members of the Security Council, the UN would start playing its due role in the field of peacekeeping, peace-making and preventive diplomacy, were soon belied. After a brief spurt of activities under Chapters VI and VII of the Charter during 1989–93, the UN was again reduced to a residual role in peacekeeping and peace-building. The permanent members of the Security Council reached an informal understanding to retain the discretion of acting on their own, in the pursuit of their interests, in all major situations of threat to peace, breach of peace or acts of aggression. This is what happened in Bosnia and Yugoslavia (1992), Kosovo and Iraq. These countries were among the few that opted out of the world order that found almost universal acceptance after what was hailed as the triumph of capitalism following the end of the Cold War. The main purpose of the assault mounted against these countries by the US and its allies was to flatten them into conformity with this world order. One of the main reasons for preserving and bolstering the NATO even after the demise of the Warsaw Pact was to use it for intervention in pursuit of this objective. The mandate of the NATO was expanded in order to allow it to intervene in countries falling outside the geographic region of the North Atlantic.

These powers turned down all proposals designed to strengthen the capacity of the UN in the peacekeeping and peace-making areas. They rejected the proposal made by several commissions and panels set up to make recommendations on UN reforms, to create a Rapid Deployment Force of the UN. They also rejected the then UN Secretary General's recommendation in his report 'Agenda for Peace' submitted in 1992, for the creation of a Peace Endowment Fund, the interest from which could be used to finance peacekeeping operations as and when they became necessary, without waiting for contributions by member States. The US, by withholding the payment of its assessed shares of both peacekeeping and the regular budgets of the UN, frequently drove the Organization to the brink of bankruptcy and in the process, considerably weakened its role in peacekeeping and other areas.

On the economic side, the Charter functions of the UN in the area of global economic policymaking, particularly in the fields of money, finance and trade, were transferred to the International Monetary Fund (IMF), World Bank and WTO. The UN was prevented from playing any role in discussing and making recommendations on the macroeconomic policies of developed countries. The entire economic agenda of the UN was turned upside down. According to the new agenda, the UN was asked to concentrate on social, human rights and humanitarian issues and relief operations. On the economic side, the UN's role was confined to prescribing self-help kits to developing countries. It was also turned into a forum for promoting and inculcating the virtues of free market forces—deregulation, privatization and opening up of markets for foreign goods and services.

Even the IMF ceased to discharge in any significant manner, its statutory function of surveillance over the economies of developed countries. Nor was the World Bank any longer discharging its statutory function of being an intermediary in transferring a significant portion of the world's surplus resources to those who were in need of them, under affordable terms and conditions. The new international financial architecture that was taking shape by the early 1990s, mainly at the behest of the major economic powers, was basically of a status quoist and discretionary character. In this, the developed countries would remain outside the IMF's surveillance. There was to be no increase in the liquidity at the IMF's disposal, through the creation of additional Special Drawing Rights (SDR). No international regulation was envisaged of the massive flows of capital for speculative purposes, which were known to have devastating effect worldwide, particularly on the economies of developing countries. Proposals such as the Tobin Tax for regulating such flows were not even looked at seriously at the intergovernmental level. The IMF was either unable, because of paucity of resources at its disposal, to bail out economies in distress, or prevented on political grounds from doing so. Consequently, bailouts of economies in crises were left to the discretion of countries disposing of resources for this purpose.

All the proposals made by major developed countries for reforming the UN were and have since then been intended to downsize and weaken it. The Organization has been enfeebled beyond recognition, mainly through denial of funds; and the threat to deny funds has been used as a basis for further reducing its powers and functions. The historic opportunity that became available after the end of the Cold War to build the international security and economic system on the basis of a new paradigm, that is, a new, dynamic multilateralism under the UN, was missed almost irretrievably.

The member states of the UN could no longer rely on the collective security system of the Organization nor on the protection of international law. They were, by and large, left to fend for themselves. They were also not free to build their own capacity to safeguard their security as perceived by them. They were thus obliged to take shelter behind the inadequate and leaking security umbrella of major powers belonging to the new alliance, thereby mortgaging their independence and sovereignty.

Globalization

A material change in the world situation was brought about by the current phase of the process of globalization, starting from the early 1980s. This was the result of the objective factor of the modern technological revolution as well the policies imposed on the rest of the world by major economic powers. Modern technological revolution has been most prominently evident in the fields of microelectronics, informatics, robotics, communications, biotechnology, space and new material sciences. It has, among others, led to the globalization of the process and pattern of production, consumption, trade and distribution. It has also emerged as the most powerful driver of growth.

Globalization has also been promoted through economic pressure and political and security leverages. Liberalization has been the principal policy prescription used to pave the path of globalization. It has been pressed home through bilateral and multi-lateral conditionalities. The IMF, World Bank and WTO are the principal international institutions used to promote it. The structural adjustment programmes of the IMF and the World Bank and WTO regimes like TRIPS, the Agreement on Trade-Related Investment Measures (TRIMs) and the General Agreement on Trade in Services (GATS) were basically designed to serve this purpose. Thus, globalization came not only as a process but also as a project.

There is no doubt that globalization opened up immense opportunities for countries like India to accelerate development by linking to the world economy. Integration with the major economies of the world provided vastly enhanced access to their markets, capital and technology. It could also help in upgrading skills, standards and technologies, thus making the weaker economies more competitive. It was, therefore, not surprising that India also became a part of the process of globalization. The opportunities opened up by globalization also defined broadly the areas of concentration of modern development-oriented foreign policy. In India's foreign economic policy, there is now greater emphasis on attracting more foreign direct investment, including foreign institutional investment; facilitating Indian investment and joint ventures abroad; enhancing earnings from services, particularly in the areas of tourism, media, entertainment, healthcare and education; and working in tandem with the private sector in the pursuit of India's economic interest abroad.

The development strategy based on the globalization paradigm was predicated on export orientation and reliance on foreign capital and technologies. This has the effect of enhancing dependence, at least in the short and medium run, on major economic powers of the world. This can come in the way of a country so dependent, following a genuinely independent foreign policy. This is particularly true of the smaller and economically weaker nations of the world. Though India does not fall in this category, it is still vulnerable to external pressures and influences. Instances abound of India's enhanced reliance on the markets and capital of the major economic powers having been used to influence its foreign policy, particularly in relation to the nuclear and the Kashmir issues.

As globalization has progressed, its negative sides, generally referred to as its discontents, have come to the fore. It is now universally recognized that globalization has accentuated inequity between and within nations. It also favours the economically stronger over the weaker and further marginalizes those who are already at the margins of the economy. Besides, globalization closes options of macroeconomic policymaking, limits and blunts instruments of monetary and fiscal policy, and engenders inertia and encourages soft options in these domains of macroeconomic policymaking. Thus, conditions created by globalization can drive economies in crisis to utter ruin. This was demonstrated in the case of the meltdown of the economies of the South-East Asian countries in 1997 and the economic disaster in Russia in 1998.

Therefore, the challenge that globalization poses for foreign policy is not only to help in taking advantage of the opportunities opened up by it, but also in coping with its discontents. In this context, a major challenge of foreign policy today is to recover the policy space already surrendered and to keep options open in vital areas of policymaking. These objectives have to be pursued in the negotiations on the establishment of new regimes, rules and regulations, which have become a principal task in the conduct of foreign policy today. Foreign policy has also to be deployed for seeking revisions in the regimes, rules and regulations which have been negotiated recently, but which, in retrospect, have turned out to be grossly unequal and unbalanced.

Decline of the Nation State

A development of major concern to a country like India is the trend of the erosion of the authority of the nation state. The nation states that disintegrated during the period between 1980 and 1995 are the Soviet Union, Czechoslovakia, Ethiopia and Yugoslavia. The nation state today is much weaker and much less in control of affairs at home and abroad than it was until the early 1980s. The state today has very little control over the information that flows to its citizens and over the violence that takes place in its territory. It is also constantly under the pressure of and interference from, powerful human rights groups functioning outside its territory and often receiving more than tacit support of the governments of the countries where they are located. There is no doubt that many developing countries have come to this pass also because they have failed to provide the minimum needs to most of their population, denied their citizens justice and basic human rights, and because they have been hijacked by the elite which has used the state for private gains and in the process, indulged in the grossest forms of corruption, exploitation and injustice.

The erosion of the authority of the nation state has, in large part, been brought about by the same factors that have contributed to the process of globalization. A decisive shift in the policies of Western powers, relating to the post-World War international order, has also contributed to this phenomenon. Being assured of their own national integrity, underpinned by their military power or that of their allies, and their relative political stability and economic prosperity, governments of Western countries, backed by their think tanks and academics who have provided the theoretical justification, have been espousing causes and championing principles calculated to encourage fissiparous forces in developing countries, where the economic and political situation is far from satisfactory or stable.

An important element of the post-Second World War international order was the sanctity of international borders existing and established after the war. This is no longer the case now. Whenever it has suited their purpose, countries of the West have openly encouraged the redrawing of post-World War borders, as in the case of Yugoslavia, Czechoslovakia and Ethiopia. This has posed a potential threat to the unity and cohesion of all nation states that have pluralistic societies.

Similarly, until the early 1980s, there was a consensus that the concept of self-determination should not be applied to a part of the territory of a sovereign state but only to territories under colonial occupation. This consensus has also collapsed as ethnic groups within a sovereign territory have been actively encouraged by governments of Western countries and global Non-Governmental Organizations (NGOs) based therein, to claim self-determination. This is proving to be a major source of instability and turmoil in state after state in the Third World.

Finally, major powers and their allies have, for some time, been working for the recognition of a new doctrine—the doctrine of intervention, including armed intervention, by the UN or outside powers, in the internal affairs of a nation state on so-called humanitarian grounds. They have argued that there is a strong case for such intervention, in a situation of a large-scale violation of human rights over a prolonged period of time.

The UN Charter explicitly prohibits interventions in the internal affairs of member states unless there is a breach of peace, threat to peace or act of aggression under Chapter VII of the Charter. The alleged violations of humanitarian laws or human rights generally do not pose a threat to the peace and security of the intervening powers, let alone to global peace and security, calling for action under Chapter VII of the Charter. Moreover, the decision on whether there has been such a violation is taken by the intervening powers, which generally act in furtherance of their national interests and not necessarily for preventing the violation of human rights. This happens even if the intervention is undertaken directly or authorized by the UN Security Council. Initiatives for intervention by the Security Council are generally taken by major powers which use their economic and political leverage to get a decision taken in their favour. Thus, interventions on humanitarian grounds have often taken place in a discriminatory and selective manner, taking advantage of the vulnerability of the country concerned, and have been designed to advance the foreign policy interests and the global strategy of the powers seeking or undertaking intervention. In spite of these pitfalls, the UN General Assembly in 2005 took a decision in favour of intervention on humanitarian grounds, in exercise of the international 'responsibility to protect'.

New Regionalism

Regional economic groupings in the form of Customs Unions or Free Trade Areas are permitted to be set up, under Article XXIV of the General Agreement on Tariffs and Trade (GATT). There is no doubt that their immediate consequence is trade discrimination against countries outside such groupings, which is against Article 1 of GATT providing for Most-Favoured Nation (MFN) treatment. Nevertheless, a departure from Article 1 was permitted in the belief that the trade-diverting effect of regional groupings will be more than compensated by their trade-creating effects. A free trade area, by enlarging the market of the member countries, can bring about several economic benefits. The enlarged market can enable the member countries of the grouping to reap economies of scale. It can also facilitate larger inflow of foreign capital and restructuring of their economies on a cost-efficient basis. These can lead to higher growth, creating additional import demands. Besides, important political considerations have also gone behind the creation of such groupings in the post-Second World War period.

In the late 1980s and early 1990s, several new mega-sized groupings came into being. These mega groupings comprised both developed and developing countries and instead of being geographically contiguous, brought together countries from different continents and from across oceans. Examples of such mega groupings include the vastly enlarged European Union (EU), the North American Free Trade Agreement (NAFTA) and the Asia and Pacific Economic Cooperation (APEC). The APEC, however, is an example of open regionalism, as it is not a preferential trading arrangement. Trade concessions negotiated under the APEC have been extended to non-member countries on an MFN basis.

The new regionalism is competition-driven and hence, a direct product of the phenomenon of globalization, one of the defining features of which is gaining competitive advantage. The idea is to place the countries concerned, through an enlargement of the market and the pooling of resources for undertaking large-scale research and development activities, in a better competitive position vis-à-vis their rivals. We have thus been witnessing the phenomena of mergers and takeovers of firms at the micro-level and the merger of markets at the macro-level—both designed to acquire a competitive edge over rivals. These mega groupings are also in a better position to strike strategic bargains in trade negotiations, which now go well beyond exchanges of trade concessions and are aimed at the establishment of new trade regimes and new rules of the game. Some of these regional groupings, particularly the APEC, have been sought to be used as a springboard for seeking worldwide liberalization of trade.

In response to the challenges of the mega groupings, older groupings have been revived and imparted greater momentum, and new groupings created. This includes the revival of the Caribbean Free Trade Associ-ation (CARIFTA), the creation of MERCOSUR[9] and the establishment of the ASEAN (Association of Southeast Asian Nations) Free Trade Agreement (AFTA). These initiatives are important enough in themselves. But they are also intended to place the member countries of the groupings in a stronger bargaining position in their bid to join one or the other mega grouping or seek other forms of association with them.

The immediate implication of the phenomenon of mega groupings for a country like India was discrimination against its trade in the markets of member countries of these groupings and further weakening, in relative terms, of its bargaining position in negotiations on trade. The option for India was to join as many of these mega groupings as possible and at the same time, to strengthen the regional grouping to which it belonged, that is, South Asian Association for Regional Cooperation (SAARC). However, neither of these options proved feasible. In the early 1990s, India approached APEC and ASEAN for membership, but its applications in these fora are still pending. Apparently these groupings were not prepared to admit a country of India's size and strategic importance, as it could have changed their very character and the balance of power within them. There was also not much prospect for strengthening SAARC, as it remained bogged down because of political factors. One of the manifestations of new regionalism has been a scramble for entering into bilateral Free Trade Agreements (FTAs), for minimizing losses arising out of mega groupings and gaining increased market access.

A major challenge for foreign policy at that time was, and still is, to cope with the phenomenon of new regionalism. For, the future prosperity and security of the nation was going to depend, to a considerable extent, on the ability of the government to take advantage of various opportunities of entering into bilateral and regional FTAs, to establish an inter se priority among them and minimize the losses and maximize the gains while negotiating them.

Growing Divergence between the Interests of the State and the People

The task of pursuing national interests through the conduct of foreign policy has been rendered very difficult and complex because of the recent perception of a growing divergence between the interests of the state and that of the people. Today, people in many parts of the world, particularly in the developing countries, perceive the state as their greatest enemy. The state is seen as being engaged primarily in protecting and promoting the interests of the elite which controls it. This creates foreign policy problems which need not arise, like the waging of unnecessary wars; committing unwarranted aggression; projecting power, which, by provoking similar actions by other nations, create tensions; raising the spectre of external threats even where they do not exist; and incurring excessive military expenditure to meet largely imagined threats to security. There is also a perception among large sections of the people in several countries that the state, in collusion with the elite, indulges in actions such as compromise with law and order, suppression of human rights and pursuit of an elitist development strategy in which the vast number of the poor do not participate and are increasingly marginalized, all of which create domestic threats to security. Though the situation in this regard is not as bad in India as in many other Third World countries, India is by no means an exception to this trend.

Those who conduct the foreign policy of a nation cannot demand an ideal domestic situation to be able to pursue their calling. Nor are they in a position to influence domestic policies that are inimical to a large section of the people or to the national interest in general. But there is no doubt that the prevalence of the distortions of the kind mentioned here results in a shrinkage of the very narrow margin on which foreign policy operates. For example, if, because of the upsurge of majoritarian communalism, the Indian state decides to compromise its basic principle of secularism or treats its minorities virtually, if not legally, as second-class citizens, it puts India's foreign policy to a more severe test than would be warranted otherwise. This is apart from its adverse implications for the unity, cohesion and prosperity of India.

Changes since the Mid-1990s

In the early 1990s after the official closure of the Cold War, the US was universally recognized as the only superpower in the world. It was way ahead of other major powers in technological and military prowess.

And there was no contender to it in sight at that time in the economic field. The powers informally constituting the 'new alliance' implicitly accepted its pre-eminent position. It is significant that during the first half of the 1990s, Russia and China did not veto a single resolution that the US pressed for adoption by the UN Security Council, calling for enforcement action under Chapter VII of the Charter.

Russian rivalry to US power steadily receded into the background as its economy continued to shrink and as it was obliged, under economic pressure, to carry out unilateral disarmament measures. A major objective that the Western powers pursued during this period was to ensure that Russia did not emerge as a rival power again for a long, if not all, time to come. For this purpose, they facilitated Russia's unilateral disarmament by providing appropriate assistance, actively sought to remodel its political system into a Western style democracy and assisted in transforming its economy in line with their neo-liberal theology.

Russia's servility to the West under President Boris Yeltsin is reflected in the fact that in April 1993, it received an aid package of $1.6 billion from the US, which included a direct grant, supply of food grains, funds for encouraging the private sector and for carrying out a programme to build house units to re-settle demobilized Russian troops. At about the same time, the G-7 announced a grant of $28.4 billion, out of which $4 billion were set aside to finance the conversion of state-run industries into private ownership.

While publicly proclaiming its intention to bury the vestiges of the Cold War, the George H. W. Bush administration went ahead with a concerted policy of encircling Russia and disabling its military power. It set up new military bases in Eastern Europe and Central Asian Republics which before the end of the Cold War were an integral part of the Soviet Union. It admitted as members of NATO the erstwhile Soviet Republics of Estonia and Lithuania and started negotiating NATO membership for Ukraine and Georgia. The Bush administration also announced its highly ambitious plan to develop and deploy a Ballistic Missile Defence (BMD) system, which would have the potential to enable the US to launch a nuclear first strike against Russia without fear of retaliation. As a part of its global missile defence system, the US announced its plan to deploy missile interceptors in Poland and radars in the Czech Republic. In the economic field, it remained a silent witness and was even complicit in the drift of the Russian economy to disaster in 1997–98.

These measures forced Russia to make a number of retaliatory moves. The Russian government, under President Vladimir Putin, suspended

Russian compliance with the provisions of the Treaty on Conventional Armed Forces in Europe, threatened to withdraw from the process of the implementation of the INF treaty and to deploy the newly developed tactical missile, Iskander I, along its western borders close to Poland. The Bush administration's policy also drove Russia closer to China. The latter took advantage of the transformation in its bilateral relationship with Russia to acquire its technologies to modernize and build its military strength.

China and Russia also took the initiative of establishing the Shanghai Cooperation Organisation (SCO) consisting of, apart from these two powers, the Central Asian countries of Kazakhstan, Kyrgyzstan, Tajikistan and Uzbekistan, and designed mainly to reduce the influence of the US in Central Asia. At its 2005 summit conference, the SCO adopted a declaration calling upon the US to set a deadline for the withdrawal of its air bases from Kyrgyzstan and Uzbekistan. Uzbekistan subsequently obliged the US to wind up its base in the country. However, the SCO is not a military alliance and hence, poses no military threat to any outside power, including the US.

Towards the end of the Bush administration, it appeared that a new Cold War was about to begin between the US and Russia. The new US President Barack Obama promised to reverse the trend and reset the relations between the two countries. Very soon after being sworn in as President, he decided to withhold the US plan to deploy a missile defence network in Eastern Europe and not to pursue NATO membership for Georgia and Ukraine. In response, Russia announced the postponement of the deployment of the Iskander missiles from its western borders. However, the US, even under the Obama administration, remains committed to developing and deploying a global missile defence system. It has also not responded positively to the Russian invitation to jointly develop such a system if the desire is to meet threats emanating from the so-called rogue countries in the region. Russia, therefore, feels that its offensive weapons system, the only guarantee of its security, is still in danger of being rendered ineffective. Without an understanding on this critical issue, it is unlikely that there would be any real progress towards restoring confidence and resetting the relations between the two largest military powers in the world.

During the decade and a half after the mid-1990s, there has been a major shift in global power equations. The US is nowhere near becoming the ultimate hegemon in the world and its reputation as a superpower stands severely dented. The limits of its military powers were exposed in the wars it waged in Iraq and Afghanistan. In spite of its massive use of force, it has not had its way in either of these theatres of war. Its exit from Iraq was ignominious, as it left the country in a terrible political mess and immersed in ever spiralling violence.

In spite of the billions of dollars spent by the US in raising, equipping and training it, the Iraqi Army could not withstand the onslaught in 2014 of the forces of the newly carved out Islamic State of Iraq and Syria (ISIS) and had to surrender vast territories including the important cities of Mosul and Ramadi. The ISIS forces were knocking at the door of the capital city of Baghdad before it became possible to halt their march. But they are still firmly entrenched in large swathes of adjoining territories of Iraq and Syria, have the Syrian city of Raqqa under their control and have been pushing forward to expand further. The problem the US faces in Iraq today is how to safeguard the territorial integrity of the country against this onslaught. In a sense, the US has already staged a comeback to Iraq by deploying thousands of military advisers and regularly carrying out air strikes against enemy positions. But is it sufficient to meet the challenge it faces in Iraq?

The US finds itself in an equally difficult situation in Syria where it has been assisting an assortment of rebel groups, including some elements of the Al-Qaeda, in their fight to oust President Bashar al-Assad from power in the Syrian Arab Republic. At one stage, on the issue of the Syrian government's alleged use of chemical weapons against the rebels, the US was contemplating an armed strike in Syria. It, however, changed its course and agreed to spare Syria in lieu of its accepting the Russian mediated deal of September 2013, to accede to the UN Convention on Chemical Weapons and destroy all its stockpiles of such weapons. When this deal was faithfully implemented by the Syrian government, the international community heaved a sigh of relief because West Asia narrowly escaped another military conflagration led by a big power. At the same time, it rejoiced over the unprecedented achievement of getting rid of one of the largest stockpiles of a category of WMDs by any state in the world. This monumental development instead of bringing laurels to the Obama administration compounded his problems in Syria. Israel and Arab countries led by Saudi Arabia were deeply disappointed by the reversal of US decision to strike Syria. The US remains committed to seeking a regime change in Syria and to its support to the motley group of the rebels who share the same objective. On the other hand, the US needs the cooperation of the Bashar al-Assad government to eliminate the Al-Qaeda and ISIS forces in Syria and that of the Iranian government, to fight them in Iraq. Iran is a logical source to turn to for this purpose because of its stake in the survival of the Shia-majority government in Iraq. It is, perhaps, because of this consideration that US seems to have extended its tacit support to Iran's assistance to the Iraqi government both in an advisory capacity and in the fighting on the ground. Iran has been invited to participate in the next round of the peace talks on Syria under the UN-sponsored Geneva process. This would not have been possible without US consent.

A big game changer in this context has been the interim nuclear deal struck between Iran and the P5+1[10] on confining Iran's nuclear programme to peaceful uses and stripping it of all its elements to convert it into a nuclear weapon programme. However, in exploiting the potentiality of this agreement for bringing about far-reaching positive changes in West Asia with Iran's cooperation, the US finds itself pitted against its Arab allies as well as its longest-time friend, Israel. They are strongly opposed to any expansion of Iran's influence in the region. They are also not happy with the nuclear deal. An indication of the resentment of these Arab States against the deal was the unprecedented absence of most of the Heads of Governments of the Arab countries from a meeting in Camp David convened by President Obama to explain the nuclear deal. As a gesture to these Arab allies, the US is supporting the military operation in Yemen led by Saudi Arabia against the Houthis rebels who enjoy the support of Iran, assisting the operation by providing military intelligence and warning Iran against interference in the internal affairs of Yemen.

In spite of its massive military intervention in Afghanistan, the Al-Qaeda is still active there and poses a grave threat to the homeland security of the US. Nor has the US been able to rid Afghanistan of the Taliban who have come to control a much larger part of the country than the government in power. In recent months, acts of violence and destruction perpetrated by Taliban in Afghanistan have become more frequent. They are hitting civilian and military targets at their will. One cannot rule out the possibility of their overrunning the country and taking over power soon after the completion of the US withdrawal. The US is banking on Pakistan to assist in providing stability to the present government there headed by President Mohammad Ashraf Ghani. For the same purpose, it is also engaged clandestinely in negotiations with some elements of the Taliban or the so-called good Taliban. The main goal of the US in Afghanistan is to save its face domestically and internationally by not giving the impression that it is leaving the place as a defeated power. To this end, it wants to ensure that whatever it claims to have been achieved in Afghanistan is not completely destroyed after its withdrawal. This US design in Afghanistan bristles with all kinds of contradictions. Pakistan's role in the unfolding events in Afghanistan is at best unpredictable. Besides, even the so-called good Taliban are unlikely to cooperate unless the semblance of democracy that the US is seeking to leave behind in Afghanistan, is stamped out. For more than a decade now, the US has proved either unwilling to or impotent in prevailing upon Israel to engage in a meaningful negotiation for peace with the Palestinians. Thus, the peace process in that region has remained at a virtual standstill since the Clinton Peace Plan proved abortive 14 years ago. This has been a major factor undermining the credibility of the US in the Islamic world.

Never in the history of US–Israeli relations have the two countries drifted as far apart as they have done during the period when President Obama has been in power in the US and Prime Minister Benjamin Netanyahu in Israel. The differences between them started mainly on the issue of Israeli settlements when the Netanyahu government spurned repeated efforts of the Obama administration to prevent the building of additional settlements in the occupied territory, thereby pre-empting possibilities of an eventual solution to the Palestinian issue. But the crunch came on the issue of American decision not to launch its contemplated military strike against Syria and on the nuclear deal with Iran. Against the Iranian nuclear deal, Prime Minister Netanyahu made an appeal to the US Congress over the head of the President of the country. He even managed to get invited by a group of pro-Israeli Congressmen belonging to both the Democratic and Republican parties, to address the Congress on the Iranian nuclear deal, without the consent of President Obama. Israel does not trust the Iranians to implement the provision of the deal with sincerity. It also firmly believes that the deal will pave the way for the Iranians to become a nuclear weapon power. Israeli's preference right from the beginning has been to pre-emptively strike the Iranian nuclear facilities. The US to start with had not excluded any possibility. In the light of this, the deal has come as a great disappointment to Prime Minister Netanyahu and has become one of the greatest security concerns of Israel.

The shock treatment of liberalization and privatization administered to the Russian economy during the Yeltsin era resulted in its collapse in 1997–98. It started recovering from the shock only after Putin set it on a different course of development. Under him, Russia succeeded in reasserting the state power and regaining its vastly eroded national self-confidence. High oil prices, coupled with state-orchestrated macroeconomic policies, put the Russian economy back on the path of growth. Having regained economic health and political stability, Russia started challenging US policies calculated to harm its interests. It has so far successfully prevented the NATO from granting membership to Ukraine and Georgia. It also succeeded in pressurizing the US to withhold, till the latest resurrection of Cold War between the two powers, the deployment of missile defence in Russia's close vicinity. At the same time, it launched a plan for the expansion and modernization of its offensive nuclear force. Russia has also demonstrated its will to use force to safeguard its interest in its close neighbourhood.

The situation has changed drastically after the Russian takeover of Crimea in 2014 following the political turmoil in neighbouring Ukraine. The overthrow of the duly elected pro-Russian President in Ukraine by illegal means, seizure of power by a coalition of political groups including Nazi elements, harsh measures taken against the Russian minorities in the country, the belligerent attitude of the new government towards Russia and finally the signing of the treaty for Ukraine to join the EU, have been perceived by Russia as a threat to its security and wider interests in the region. After the Russian occupation of Crimea, the Western media and the propaganda machinery of the US and its NATO allies have been engaged in a relentless campaign to demonize President Putin. A central point of their propaganda against him is that he is out to occupy Ukraine and other neighbouring countries in order to reunite them with Russia. Given Russia's other preoccupations demanding urgent and priority attention, this should be the farthest from the intention of any Russian leader or government. Moreover, the Russians can be expected to be aware of the risks involved in any such adventure in the 21st century and of the changes of a fundamental character that have taken place in its vicinity in Europe after the disintegration of the Soviet Union.

US and other NATO countries have applied progressively accelerated sanctions against Russia which has re-enforced the negative trends in the Russian economy set in motion by the recent dramatic decline in oil prices. The impact of the sanctions is evident, among others, in rising prices, exodus of capital, pressure on the Rouble and continued sliding down of the Russian economy. As a result of these developments, the US–Russian relations have hit a new low and there seems to be a resurrection of the Cold War between Russia on the one hand and the US and its NATO allies on the other.

Other adverse consequences of the deterioration in the US–Russia relationship have been a halt in the progress that was being made in limiting the size of the nuclear arsenals of the two super powers, the return of the US defence weapons to countries adjoining Russia and the production and deployment by both countries of highly sophisticated offensive nuclear weapon systems.

All this has made the world situation extremely tense and unstable, posing difficult foreign policy problems for other countries, including India.

In the context of its fast deteriorating relationship with US and other NATO countries, Russia has started looking East, particularly to China, for diverting its natural resources from Europe to Asia and for forging closer economic, political and defence cooperation with Asian countries. A historic initiative in this regard was the announcement on 21 May 2014 of a mega deal of a gas pipeline connecting Russia and China. Under this deal, Gazprom will supply 3.75 billion cubic feet of liquefied natural gas a day to the National Petroleum Corporation of China for 30 years starting in 2018. That will be equivalent of a quarter of Russia's export of gas to all of Europe. The agreement is worth $400 billion.

A major change during this period has been a decisive shift in the world economic power balance from Europe and the US to Asia. Important emerging Asian economies, particularly China and India, have grown up to three times faster than the US and Europe continuously for a period of nearly three decades. In 2013, Asia accounted for 31 per cent of the global GDP, up from 25.1 per cent in 2008,[11] The same year, it claimed 33.4 per cent share of the world trade,[12] up from 26.7 per cent in 2004.[13] China has emerged as a formidable rival to the US in the economic domain. It is today the largest trading nation and the second largest economy in the world. Its economy is poised to reach the size of the US economy in the not too distant future. India is also moving up the ladder of economic power fast. The Indian economy grew at the rate of 10.25 per cent in 2010. The growth rates during the next two years were relatively lower at 6.63 and 5.08 per cent, respectively. It was 6.89 per cent in 2013[14] and projected to touch the figure of 7.4 per cent in the financial year 2014–15.[15] The IMF has forecast India's growth to be 7.5 per cent in 2015, when China's growth rate will be 6.8 per cent.[16] Both India and China are today competing with the US and important European countries for access to markets, raw material and energy sources in the rest of the world, while themselves providing huge markets for the goods, services and technologies of the Western world.

The US and Europe are still reeling under the impact of the global financial and economic crisis which peaked during the year 2009. The economic recovery of these countries has been rather sluggish and patchy. Unemployment remains very high. And because of these factors, the purchasing power of the people, which generally provides momentum to recovery, remains limited. These factors, along with the contractionist economic policy measures adopted by leading European countries, have resulted in a double dip recession in several of these countries.

Imbalances in the US economy, persisting for decades, have been accentuated by the global economic crisis. In 2010, US trade deficit was close to $700 billion,[17] and its budget deficit was nearly $1.3 trillion.[18] Its total public debt, the largest in the world, had reached a staggering figure of $14 trillion in December 2010[19] out of which $1.5 trillion was owed to China.[20] There were some improvements in the trade and budget deficits in 2013 when they were $518 billion and $680 billion,[21] respectively. But the public debt situation worsened. The debt on 31 December 2013 was $17.3 trillion.[22] The US economy is back on the path of growth, but the growth rates have been low. The growth in GDP in 2014 which was relatively a good year, was 2.4 per cent.[23] Since the onset of the recession, the US has lost trillions of dollars of national output. The involvement of the US in the Iraq and Afghanistan wars has led to massive dissipation of national energy, assets and resources. The wars were largely financed by borrowed money, which is mainly responsible for the massive public debt accumulated by the US. The pursuit, under the influence of the neo-conservative ideology, of the economic laissez-faire policy, particularly in the financial sector, was a major factor leading to the economic and financial crisis. The questions that now arise are whether the US can go on living beyond its means, without putting the dollar and its economy in jeopardy, and whether it can hope to retain its global dominance on the strength of its military power alone.

The US's unipolar status did not last as long as it was expected. The year 2001 marked the beginning of the end of the unipolar moment in history. After that, there was a precipitate decline in the prestige and power of the US as compared to the situation prevailing in the early 1990s. The other factors that contributed to the decline of unipolarity were the initiatives of the emerging economies to set up groups of their own like the India–Brazil–South Africa Dialogue Forum (IBSA) and BRICS,[24] linking their economies with each other and with other developing countries by bilateral and regional FTAs and Comprehensive

Economic Cooperation Agreements (CECAs) as well as the increasing role and influence of people's movements and civil society organizations, brought about in large part by the communication revolution.

In spite of the decline in its power and status, the US still has the most powerful economy in the world and remains a powerhouse of technology. There is no rival power in sight which will be able to catch up with the US militarily, at least in the next few decades. Besides, more than any nation in the world, the US has demonstrated during the last century or so an unparalleled capacity to innovate and reinvent itself, and thereby take a headlong lead from time to time in the race for power and supremacy. Therefore, the most important bilateral relationship that any nation in today's world should have is still with the US. India cannot be an exception to it.

Strategies

Basic Approach

In recent years, the formulation and conduct of India's foreign policy has singularly suffered from the absence of long-term thinking and a holistic approach. It has been ad hoc and reactive rather than pro-active. It has also lacked in transparency. Diplomacy has been played more against India's own people than against foreign powers. On several sensitive issues, including matters of security, what has been conveyed to the Indian people has been at variance with what has transpired in discussions with major powers. What is therefore needed is long-term thinking and a holistic approach towards the formulation and conduct of India's foreign policy and greater transparency in its projection to the people and to the world at large. Transparency is needed, above all, to mobilize and build the will of the people to withstand pressures from foreign powers. For, in a democratic system no government can withstand pressures from abroad without the support of the people and without the preparedness of the people to make sacrifices. And this cannot happen unless the people are clearly told what is at stake. For this purpose, the people should be given the opportunity to participate in formulating foreign policy through open and transparent public debates both in the Parliament and outside. This was lacking on several occasions, for example, on the exercise of India's nuclear option, on the issues in the Uruguay Round of trade negotiations, particularly on TRIPS, and on the Indo-US nuclear deal. The government has actually misled the people on these issues.

In a holistic approach to the conduct of foreign policy, it is extremely important to take into account not only military threats to security but also non-military threats, and not only external, but also internal threats. It is also important to build both military and economic leverages and use them flexibly in combination or as substitutes of each other, as the need arises.

In the vastly changed and still changing world situation today, with all its uncertainties and ambiguities, the watchwords for Indian diplomacy should be flexibility and nimbleness. India can no longer remain tied to dogmas and paradigms that have become outmoded. It has to make the necessary adjustments and take new initiatives in keeping with the new situation. India will have to continue to judge each bilateral and multilateral issue on its merits and conduct its foreign policy accordingly. India is too large and too self-respecting a nation to climb on to any bandwagon of ideology or alliance. For the same reason, India cannot depend upon any other power for its security. It has to develop autonomous capability to safeguard its security. This need not and cannot be done in an autarchic fashion. It is necessary to seek the collaboration of other major powers. But here also, instead of relying exclusively on a particular power, India should keep its options open.

India straddles major civilizations of the world and has had cultural and commercial contacts with countries located far and wide. In fact, India has had close relations with all the major countries and groupings in the world. Therefore, though there is a need to set priorities, it is not desirable for India to be rigidly selective in dealing with countries or their groupings—cultivating some and neglecting others altogether. India's interest lies with great powers as well as with countries in Asia, Africa and Latin America. It has a vital stake in the evolution of SAARC as a full-fledged regional economic grouping and at the same time, it has to seek association or membership, wherever possible, of the EU, NAFTA, ASEAN, APEC and other groupings.

The traditional basis of India's relationship with the vast majority of the non-aligned countries in Asia, Africa and Latin America has become somewhat anachronistic today. India's relations with these countries were based mainly on its anti-imperialist, anti colonial and anti-racist solidarity with them. It also shared a common platform with them on peace, disarmament and development issues. Today, this solidarity has become outmoded and no longer provides a basis of enduring relations, and issues of peace, disarmament and development have become too complex to lend themselves to the formulation and adoption of readily reachable common positions.

It is, therefore, incumbent on India to build new bases of relations with non-aligned countries. An important new basis has to be the economic and commercial one. In this area, India's endeavours are too hesitant, timid and on the whole, too limited to be effective. It should be able to take bold initiatives in trade relations with its neighbours instead of persisting with the present ad hoc and incremental approach. It should substantially increase the resources earmarked for technical and economic cooperation with other countries. These resources need to be at least 10 times more than what they are today.

India should also pay far greater attention to the micro-management of its relations with individual countries. Countries, like individuals, have their own pride and idiosyncrasies and these need to be pandered to. India must build and work on the basis of past and present bonds with different countries, try to cater to their specific needs, painstakingly avoid giving any impression of neglect and causing hurt by wanton or thoughtless behaviour. Unfortunately, this is far from being the case today. Posts abroad, including that of heads of missions, are kept vacant for too long. It takes a long time to invite personalities at the policymaking levels from foreign countries. Return visits at high political levels are kept postponed for too long. Seemingly difficult bilateral problems get indefinitely mired in inter-ministerial discussions and are left unresolved for years.

Indian missions abroad are generally manned by competent and alert officers. But their reports and recommendations receive scant attention, and more often than not, elicit no response from the headquarters. The practice of not compromising on top-quality officers manning joint secretaries' posts seems to have been given up. Besides, the whole culture of functioning has undergone a change. Senior officers at the head quarters concentrate on work that brings them close to and enables them to create a better impression on the minister, as this has become necessary for improving career prospects. The ministers concentrate on matters that will enhance their popularity with the people and project a good image of them in the Parliament and the country. Responding to media reports and managing the media has become the primary pre-occupation of diplomacy. Officers are seldom able to stand up to ministers on important issues; in fact, there is a virtual collusion between ministers and senior officers in pandering to the press and in highlighting the trivia to attract publicity and to gain popularity. In the process, the nitty-gritty of international relations gets ignored and issues of vital interest to the country go unattended.

The media plays an important role in the formulation and conduct of foreign policy. A positive fallout of this role is that the government is being compelled to be more transparent and responsive to the voice of the people. On the negative side, the media forces the government to come out daily or even hourly with responses and information, which makes it extremely difficult to negotiate in secrecy, without which it is not possible to solve complex bilateral and other problems. Moreover, Indian diplomats and political leaders dealing with foreign policy, in their quest to grab media attention, often inappropriately and prematurely reveal information, take unwarranted credit and make exaggerated claims about the outcome of their efforts. These are hardly conducive to the conduct of foreign policy consistent with national interest. Finally, in the media's projection of foreign policy, the emphasis is on non-issues or peripheral issues that are the current fad among the people. This makes it extremely difficult to use the media for serious discussions on foreign policy issues and to mobilize public support for policies designed to serve the long term enlightened interests of the country.

Recently, the consensus that till lately prevailed on the essential aspects of the foreign policy of India seems to have weakened a great deal and been replaced by discordance and discontinuity. The position that both the government in power and the Opposition parties take on major foreign policy issues are based less on values, principles and enlightened long-term national interest and more on expediency. The overriding consideration behind adopting a particular position is to gain or remain in political power. In this pursuit, the government frequently misleads the people in the way it advocates a foreign policy and Opposition parties go back on the positions that they had adopted earlier, particularly when they were in the government.

A recent disconcerting trend in the formulation and conduct of foreign policy has been the desire to play up to the predilections of particular vote banks or join their bandwagons. As a result, foreign policy is losing its moorings and its articulation is becoming increasingly immoderate and shrill.

Indian diplomats are often advised by local and foreign media, strategic thinkers, other experts and foreign political leaders to think out of the box, to be bold and active, to take initiatives and demonstrate the capacity to lead in the conduct of foreign policy. Those who advocate these so-called new thrusts in foreign policy, have nothing concrete or specific to suggest. Their only measuring yard of innovation and boldness in the conduct of India's foreign policy is how rapidly India aligns its policies with those of the Western powers, particularly on the issues of human rights and democracy. These experts and strategic thinkers and political luminaries generally tend to exaggerate India's economic strength and put under the carpet the rot that prevails in many sectors of the Indian economy and sections of society, which put limits on the capacity of diplomacy to deliver the goods. Speaking at a public meeting in Chennai on 20 July 2011, the then US Secretary of State, Hillary Clinton, made some concrete suggestions regarding India's leadership role in international affairs. She suggested that such a role could be played in the South Pacific in fora like the East Asia Summit and the ASEAN Regional Forum in contributing more to maritime security and democracy promotion, in exploring a new Silk Route into Central Asia, supporting the rebuilding of Afghanistan and even helping in stabilizing Pakistan. These are indeed laudable suggestions. But India faces formidable difficulties and suffers from basic constraints in playing an effective role in all these areas. And this is not confined to the constraints of resources, but includes political and logistical problems. Nevertheless, India should play its due role in these and other areas within the limitations of its capacity, consistent with its national interest and in collaboration with the countries concerned with and more directly involved in the issue.

Working for a New World Order

The world order continues to remain unjust, inequitable and unfair to the interests of the overwhelming majority of the nations of the world. It continues to serve the interests of the dominant powers and works inexorably against those of the weaker nations. The current process of globalization and some of the regimes governing international trade and finance, established recently to promote this process, have contributed to a further widening of the gulf between the rich and poor nations. The former group of countries are determined to maintain the status quo in the existing world order and resort to any means, including the use of force, to achieve this purpose. In this endeavour, they have tried to co-opt the relatively more developed among the developing countries, like India, China, Brazil and South Africa. The designation in 2009, of the G-20, a grouping of 20 major world economies,[25] as the premier forum for international economic cooperation, was a significant move to harness the support of these emerging economies for the preservation of the main features of the existing world order.

It is in India's self-interest as well as its moral obligation to actively work for changing the status quo and establishing a new world order. In the long run, it is also in the interest of the major economic powers. India should not be diverted from this task by the temptation of sitting at the high table and being prematurely proclaimed as a major economic power. For, India is still at the receiving end of the present world order and is likely to remain so for quite some time to come in the foreseeable future.

The new paradigm on which the international system should be based is democratic and dynamic multilateralism, essentially underpinned by the UN. India missed the opportunity of presenting a blueprint for UN reforms when this subject was actively considered during the 1990s and the first five years of the current century. Moreover, India has not looked positively at some of the reform proposals designed for strengthening the role of the UN and diluting the domination of the major powers. These include the creation of a Rapid Deployment Force for the UN, special arrangements for financing its peacekeeping operations and proposals for putting the finances of the UN on an automatic and predictable basis so that it no longer remains entirely dependent on the budget provisions of member countries for contributions, which is subject to the vicissitudes of political trends and public opinion.

This negative approach is presumably because of the feeling that if the decision-making process in the UN, particularly in the Security Council, is not democratized, any strengthening of the Organization on the lines of these proposals would prove counterproductive from the point of view of developing countries like India. The strengthened UN would be used mainly against these countries, which are more vulnerable than the permanent members and their allies. Given its bilateral problems with its neighbours, India would be particularly vulnerable to interventions by the UN.

This is one of the reasons why among the proposals for strengthening the UN, India has been almost exclusively preoccupied with the issue of the expansion of the membership of the Security Council, including an increase in the number of permanent members, as a step towards democratizing the decision-making process. There is no doubt that this reform proposal is of crucial importance and that India has a very strong case for becoming a permanent member if and when a decision is taken to expand the membership of the Council. However, there are several issues relating to the process of expansion which are yet to be resolved. On the whole, there seems to be little prospect of an expansion taking place in the near future.

India cannot remain indifferent to the other proposals put forward for strengthening the multilateral system under the UN. Building on these proposals, India should take the initiative to elaborate and submit, either alone or in collaboration with leading non-aligned countries, a blueprint for reforms aimed at restoring to the UN the Charter functions it has lost during the last three decades, putting the Organization on a sounder financial basis and equipping it with the wherewithal by which it can play a more effective role under Chapter VII of the Charter. The task of garnering worldwide support for such a package is going to be difficult and time-consuming. But this initiative is very much worth undertaking and the effort to build a consensus on it, worth pursuing. This will be in keeping with the basic tenets of India's foreign policy.

Working through NAM and G-77

There is a school of thought in India which believes that after the end of the Cold War, NAM has lost its validity. The question generally asked is: after the end of the division of the world into two rival power blocs, who is there to be non-aligned with? Similarly, it is argued that after becoming a major economic power, India has outgrown the G-77, which has now turned into a liability. Therefore, the sooner India discards the baggage of belonging to the G-77, the better it would be for the conduct of its foreign policy.

There is a long history of the developed countries' endeavour to undermine and deride the G-77. Their main argument has been that because of the differences in the structures and levels of development among developing countries and the accentuation of these over time, the Group is unworkable and has, in fact, never worked. They ask: what is common between India, Indonesia and Malaysia on one hand, and the bulk of the African countries on the other. Besides, some of the more developed among these countries have never been interested in the activities of the G-77. Rather than belonging to this Group, they have been keen to join the big league, like the Organisation for Economic Co-operation and Development (OECD). Some of these countries, namely South Korea and Mexico, have, in fact, become members of the OECD, while others are knocking at its door. India itself is taking pride in being recognized by the OECD as a country with a dynamic economy and takes this as a precursor to becoming a full-fledged member of the organization.

The G-77 has faced a number of problems arising out of its structure and method of work. First, with its total current membership at 132, it has become extremely difficult and time-consuming, if not impossible, to evolve a consensus on any major issue in this forum. Second, because of their deteriorating economic conditions, most of the countries belonging to this Group have become extremely vulnerable to pressures from outside. The G-77, therefore, is left with much less clout than it commanded earlier. Finally, the main action for the G-77 was in UN fora. With the erosion of the economic functions of the UN, there has been a commensurate erosion in the role of the G-77 in negotiations in international fora.

It is true that one of the purposes of NAM was to oppose the division of the world into two power blocs, to prevent the proxy wars that the rival power blocs waged in the Third World and to ensure that rivalry between them did not escalate into a global armed conflict. NAM, therefore, worked for bringing about a thaw in the Cold War and reconciliation between the rival power groups. It also took a number of initiatives for reducing and halting the nuclear arms race. With the end of the Cold War, the possibility of a war brought about by the division of the world into two blocs receded into the background and significant progress was made in the reduction of the nuclear arsenals of the two largest nuclear powers. Thus, some of the purposes behind NAM were largely served. In that sense, it stood vindicated.

However, the struggle for hegemony in the world did not disappear with the end of the Cold War. Nor did the alliance politics. After the Cold War, a new alliance emerged, seeking to perpetuate its dominance and hegemony. Even though this new alliance is no longer as cohesive as it was during the 1990s, its members are continuing to pursue the objective of preserving the status quo in the world order. One of the major objectives of NAM was to change this status quo. This objective still remains unfulfilled. Moreover, the essence of NAM was to judge issues on their merits and not in the light of the interest of a power or power bloc. Major powers continue to impose their points of view on important issues, like trade liberalization, global financial architecture and climate change, on the rest of the world. Therefore, this essence of the Movement still remains valid.

As regards the G-77, differences among developing countries are not a new phenomenon. In fact, it is inevitable in any large grouping of countries. Such differences have been evident among the members of G-77 ever since its inception. They are also present among developed countries. But this has not prevented them from adopting common positions on international issues through fora like the OECD and the G-7.[26] What is important is not the existence of differences in a group, but whether the group has a common interest on a set of global issues, whether it can forge a common position on these and whether differences among them can be set aside while formulating such positions.

It is true that because of the increase in its size, the G-77 has become unwieldy and incapable of formulating common positions which have operational significance. This led the Group in the late 1980s and the early 1990s to set up smaller groups of more important developing countries whom the group of major developed countries, that is, the G-7, could take as a serious dialogue partner. In this context, India took the initiative of setting up the G-15 in 1989, to enable a group of politically and economically significant developing countries to hold regular consultations, coordinate their positions at the highest level on global issues and also promote economic and technical cooperation among themselves. It was hoped that the G-7 would regard this as an effective forum to do business with. Unfortunately, the G-15 could not fulfil this promise. This was mainly due to the changing power equation within the group. Some of the G-15 members were effectively co-opted by the G-7, following which they were left with no interest in working for the G-15. Other G-15 members lost their economic and political clout at the international level. They, therefore, no longer met the principal criterion of remaining in the group, that is, being economically and politically significant. On the other hand, the character of G-7 itself underwent a change on account of the emergence of countries like China, India and Brazil as important economic powers. It was realized, particularly in the context of the recent global economic crisis, that the G-7 was too limited a forum for the coordination of global macroeconomic policies. Therefore, it was decided to designate the G-20 as the premier mechanism for international economic cooperation.

Another reason why a general purpose group like the G-77 and its abbreviated version, the G-15, became less effective and relevant was the emergence of issue-specific groups like the G-20, the G-33[27] and the NAMA-6[28] in the WTO, and the very effective role they played in the negotiations in this forum.

Third, a number of smaller groups of important emerging economies appeared on the world scene with their very distinctive economic clout, complexion and agenda. These included the group of IBSA, that of Brazil, Russia, India and China (BRIC), which became BRICS upon South Africa joining it, and the group consisting of Russia, India and China (RIC). IBSA leaders have been meeting at the summit level for the past several years. BRICS has been holding regular summit conferences in which some very important initiatives have been taken recently. The group of Russia, India and China has been meeting regularly at the foreign ministers' level. These groups have a number of things in common. They consist of dynamic emerging economies with relatively high rates of growth, comfortable reserves positions and promising prospects for future growth. Each of these groups carries considerable weight in the world economy. Their mutual cooperation can make a major contribution to global peace and stability. They are also a useful counterweight to the unipolarity or hegemony of other power or powers and to their scheme of imposing their world view or ideology on the rest of the world. Moreover, there is considerable scope of functional cooperation among them, particularly in the areas of energy, infrastructure, science and technology, environment, and combating terrorism and pandemics.

IBSA

Among these smaller groups of emerging economies, IBSA is the most cohesive and a natural grouping for economic cooperation. All the members of this group are developing countries, with a substantial commonality on international economic issues. For example, they would all like to be in a position to use the WTO's TRIPS Agreement with maximum flexibility in order to ensure for their people universal access to essential drugs at affordable prices. All of them happen to be democracies with a belief in a set of universal values and with accountability to their peoples. All of them are experimenting in one form or the other, with inclusive growth, which makes it both important and possible for them to derive lessons from each other's experiences. If they evolve a united position on issues under negotiation, they can have a decisive influence in shaping the positions of the G-77 on these issues. They also have the capacity of advancing the interest of the G-77 as a whole.

IBSA has recently been overshadowed by BRICS. This is partly because in terms of membership, IBSA is included in BRICS. Moreover, mainly due to the inclusion of China, but also of Russia, BRICS has several times greater political and economic strength than IBSA. Besides, the economies of two out of the three members of IBSA, that is, Brazil and South Africa, have been going through a prolonged process of slow growth and that of the third country, that is, India, has since 2011, lost quite a bit of its dynamism. Besides, these countries are facing other economic problems. They are, therefore, hardly in a position to take any major initiative through IBSA. Nevertheless, because of the unique characteristics of IBSA that enables it to pioneer ideas for the restructuring of the world order, it needs to be revived and imparted fresh momentum.

BRIC(S)

BRIC(S) is a grouping of large-sized dynamic economies. All the members of this group belong to the G-20. They can, therefore, play a very important role in imparting sustainability and strength to the process of recovery of the world economy, which is still weak and unstable. They can also exercise considerable influence in shaping policies designed to bring about reforms in the international monetary and financial systems. In addition, they can benefit a lot by functional cooperation among themselves, particularly in the areas of trade, investment, infrastructure, energy, science and technology and agriculture.

There are, however, underlying differences among the members of the group which, for obvious political reasons, are not allowed to surface in the public. For example, both India and Brazil are concerned about the implications for their economies of the undervalued yuan and of the nature of China's economic engagement with other developing countries, particularly in Africa. Though in their summit statements issued from time to time, the BRIC leaders have called 'for a multipolar equitable and democratic world order', China's ambiguous response to the candidature of India and Brazil for permanent membership of the Security Council raises doubts as to whether it is really interested in democratizing the decision-making process in the Security Council. Similarly, though Russia has joined the other members of the group in demanding that the outcome of the forthcoming negotiations on climate change should reflect the principle of equity and common and differential treatment, it itself did not undertake any commitment under the Kyoto Protocol to reduce carbon emission. Its attitude on such commitments being undertaken on a differential basis in the final deal to be negotiated in the forthcoming Paris Conference on Climate Change is at best ambiguous.

An initiative of far-reaching significance taken by the BRICS leaders at the summit conference in Brazil in July 2014, was to establish a BRICS development bank, subsequently named as the New Development Bank (NDB), and put in place a Contingency Reserve Arrangement (CRA). The NDB will have a total capital subscription of $50 billion shared equally by the five member countries. The bank will be located in Shanghai and its first president will be an Indian, who has recently been appointed. The initial capital of the CRA will be $100 billion to be paid up on call. China will have a major share of this capital, amounting to $41 billion. The NDB will finance infrastructure and sustainable development projects of BRICS and other emerging and developing countries. The CRA will meet short-term liquidity needs of these countries. Opening the bank for access by other emerging and developing countries will strengthen the solidarity of the developing countries which is important for enhancing their bargaining power in negotiations on global economic issues. The improved infrastructure built in these countries with the support of the NDB will impact positively on the prospect for forging stronger trade and economic ties between the BRICS countries and other developing countries.

These institutions cannot, nor are intended to be, substitutes for the World Bank and the IMF, but their potential impact on the global financial architecture cannot be ignored. They will complement the World Bank, IMF and the Regional Development Banks and in the process contribute to the strengthening of the global financial architecture. They will also help the BRICS and other developing countries to strengthen their voice in the financial and monetary system and place them in a stronger position to be able to press for the long postponed reforms of the system. In view of these considerations, India has taken a very wise decision in joining the initiative for establishing these institutions and thereby becoming an active participant in shaping their organizational structure and operational guidelines.

G-20

The decision taken at the Pittsburgh summit of the G-20, to designate the group as the premier forum for international economic cooperation has been welcomed with great enthusiasm in India. There is no doubt that by virtue of this enhanced role of the G-20, India will now exercise a greater influence in decision-making on international economic issues. However, it is not really correct, as widely believed in India, that the G-20 has now replaced the G-7. The fact is that the coordination of the macroeconomic policies of the G-7 countries will continue to take place in the G-7 forum itself. Only those issues would be brought to the G-20 forum on which there can be no meaningful international cooperation without the involvement of countries like India, China and Brazil. These issues relate to the new global financial architecture; negotiations on climate change, energy security, food security and the Doha Round of trade negotiations under the WTO. They are no doubt of crucial importance. However, it is a moot point whether countries like India, China and Brazil will be able really to influence the decisions of the G-20 on these issues. The greater likelihood is that the voices of these countries will remain weak and muted in the G-20 forum. This is mainly because of the composition of the group, in which the developed countries and their camp followers from developing countries have the majority. Therefore, the G-20 is likely to be used as a forum for putting the stamp of approval of the group on decisions taken at the G-7 forum. Moreover, the G-20 will function mainly as an institution for maintaining the status quo in the international monetary and financial systems. Countries like India, Brazil, China and South Africa may play the role of a ginger group, but a reluctant and loyal one. They can be scarcely expected to demand changes of a structural nature in the world economy and in international economic relations. For example, it is very unlikely that these countries will ever use the G-20 forum for persuading the US to reduce its trade and budget deficits and stop living on borrowed money.

Starting from the Seoul summit, G-20 leaders sought to make a transition from responding to a contingent situation to deal with the structural problems of the world economy. These included the problem of development, IMF reforms, international reserve currency and financial regulation. G-20 summit deliberations since then have not led to any significant progress in any of these areas. Objectives and policy measures agreed upon in almost all major areas of concern to G-20 are platitudinal in nature, having little operational significance.

The remaining 173 members of the UN remain outside the G-20. They have equal rights to participate in the dialogue on international economic cooperation. For them, the UN is the only available forum for this purpose. It also happens to be the designated forum for this, according to international law. However, during the last three decades, the major developed countries have made a conscious, well-planned and concerted effort to deprive the UN of its functions in the economic field as provided in the Charter. The emergence of the G-20 as the premier forum for international economic cooperation is a significant institutionalization of the process of the erosion of the economic functions of the UN. Unfortunately, this has the approval of India. This is most unfortunate because the pioneer of India's foreign policy, Jawaharlal Nehru, had an abiding faith in the UN and until the end kept on insisting that a 'world government' of his vision would be built on its foundations.

In several areas, India's interests lie in cooperation within the UN through the broader forum of NAM and the G-77, rather than under the G-20. A number of shipments of generic drugs exported by India were confiscated in 2008 and 2009 without justification by developed countries which are members of the G-20, while those who joined India in opposing it were developing countries, members of the G-77. Major developed countries, members of the G-20, are hurting India's economic interest by persisting with their agricultural protectionist policies. The countries that have joined India in an effort to bring about a change in these policies during the Doha Round are the G-33 members, who are a part of the G-77. India seeks amendments to the TRIPS Agreement in order, among other things, to prevent the usurpation of its bio resources by developed countries that are members of the G-20. In this effort too, support comes only from the G-77 members. These and several other examples demonstrate that in order to safeguard its immediate and long-term interests in the international economic order, India needs the support of developing countries much more than that of developed countries that dominate the G-20.

At the same time, there is an inevitability about the empowerment of the G-20, arising out of the change in the global economic scenario. It is, therefore, not possible for India to opt out of the G-20. Hence it should continue to play its due role in the G-20 in concert with like-minded countries. But it should have no illusions that it would be possible to transform the international financial and monetary systems through cooperation in the G-20. For this, India will have to work through the G-77 and NAM, of which it should remain an active member.

Issue-based fora are proving very effective in negotiations in the WTO. For example, G-20 in the WTO played a very important role in the beginning in formulating and pushing forward the position of the developing countries in the negotiations on the key area of agriculture. This role was subsequently taken over by G-33. The group of African countries has pressed for demands in the areas of cotton, trade for aid, etc.

These issue-based groups have their umbilical link with the G-77 and derive their strength from it. The positions evolved in issue-based groups need to be endorsed periodically by the G-77 in order to lend them political weight and credibility. Finally, NAM and the G 77 have been used in the past and can still be used for floating new ideas and launching new initiatives for negotiations on behalf of the member countries.

Developing countries like India are under pressure on several fronts. They can protect their interests best by adopting common positions on crucial international issues and acting collectively to uphold these positions through NAM and the G-77. The issues to be taken up are both old and new. Some of the issues that cut across the differences among developing countries are:

- Strengthening the UN
- New international financial architecture
- Nuclear-weapon-free world
- Climate change negotiations
- Revising WTO agreements
- Financing for development

India has so far successfully used the collective bargaining power of the developing countries through NAM and the G-77 for improving the external environment of its growth. Given its domestic situation, it is far from joining any of the big leagues, at least in the near future. Even if it does join one in the long run, it is still its moral duty and in its long-term national interest to work for an equitable world order by continuing to use the leverage of NAM and the G-77.

New Regionalism and India

Not only India, but the whole of Asia remained untouched by the first wave of regionalism that swept most parts of the developing world during the 1960s and the 1970s. But Asian countries and groups thereof tried to respond to the new regionalism which started from the early 1980s by forming new groupings, injecting new vigour into the existing ones and adding fresh dimensions to them. Two significant initiatives in this direction were the formation of the APEC in 1989 and the signing of the AFTA in 1992. The APEC was a trans-Pacific mega grouping comprising the US and Canada from across the Pacific; Japan, China and South Korea from North-East Asia; all the members of ASEAN; and Australia and New Zealand. In South Asia, regional cooperation was put on an institutionalized basis only in December 1985 with the establishment of SAARC. However, until the mid-1990s, SAARC did not put cooperation in hardcore economic areas like trade, manufacturing, money and finance on its agenda.

India found itself marginalized by the new wave of regionalism. Therefore, in the early 1990s, it took the initiative of getting associated with APEC and ASEAN. It was, and still is, unrealistic for India to expect that it can become a full-fledged member of the ASEAN, which is a grouping of geographically contiguous countries in a region to which India strictly does not belong. In spite of this, it was useful for India to have sought association with this group because it could pave the way for cooperation between them and India in non-trade areas, could be politically beneficial in the context of the strategic games being played in Asia and could give a fillip to strengthening bilateral relations with the individual member countries of the group. Over time, India has succeeded in associating itself with ASEAN at various levels. It became a Sectoral Dialogue Partner of ASEAN in 1992, a full Dialogue Partner in 1995 and a member of the ASEAN Regional Forum (ARF) in 1966. In 2002, it was able to forge a summit-level partnership with ASEAN. The summit meetings were supplemented by meetings at the level of foreign ministers and those of trade and industry. Since 2005, India and ASEAN have become partners at the forum of the East Asia Summit. India is also a participant in the ongoing negotiations for the Regional Comprehensive Economic Partnership (RCEP) launched from the ASEAN platform.

Unlike AFTA, APEC is not a free trade area. It is an example of open regionalism, where trade concessions exchanged among the member states are automatically extended to outside countries on the basis of the MFN obligation assumed under WTO. Nor is APEC a grouping of contiguous countries. Because of these two factors, a membership of APEC may be possible for India, now that the freeze on the admission of new members has been lifted. But apart from political factors, this will very much depend on the ability of India to maintain the current dynamism in its development process and to catch up and keep pace with the level of liberalization achieved by APEC countries. Since APEC is an example of open regionalism, India is unlikely to derive any preferential trade benefit by joining it. However, the membership of, or association with, APEC can help it in taking advantage of the cooperation within APEC in areas like science and technology, trade facilitation and harmonization of standards.

APEC recently seems to have lost momentum in its endeavour to forge regional cooperation through collective measures. This is partly because most of its Asian members have either entered into or are in the process of negotiating bilateral FTAs between themselves. Besides, ASEAN itself is now a free trade area and has FTAs with several individual Asian countries. Finally, the recent movement, even though slow and tentative, towards forming a pan-Asian economic grouping, has been another factor responsible for the decline of APEC. Two important developments recently would seem to have imparted new relevance to APEC. The first is the US initiative to launch negotiations for the formation of the Trans-Pacific Partnership (TPP). A large number of the APEC members are participating in these negotiations which have been going on for the last few years and are expected to be concluded soon. Neither India nor China has been invited to participate in these negotiations. Another major development took place recently when at the last summit meeting of APEC in Beijing in November 2014 China's initiative to launch negotiations for a Free Trade Area of the Asia-Pacific (FTAAP) was endorsed by the summit. India is not in a position to participate in any of these two initiatives. Therefore, APEC membership no longer appears to be a priority for India.

India had taken the initiative in the early years of this century for achieving a pan-Asian economic integration with the participation, among others, of both India and China. The Indian initiative was, however, thwarted by China in the ASEAN forum at that time and the compromise was the institution in 2005 of the East Asian Summit of which India became a participant. The original Indian initiative has now, in a sense, emerged in a new form of the RCEP which was launched at the 19th Asian Summit in 2011 and the negotiations on which are continuing since then. Side by side, negotiations are also going on for establishing the TPP. India is not in a position to participate in it because its economy is not in a strong enough position for it to accept, at least during the next 15 to 20 years, the far-reaching commitments envisaged under it. India has problems in the negotiations in the RCEP also because commitments being negotiated under this forum are also very far-reaching and not compatible with India's obligation to protect its industry and the livelihood and other socio-economic interests of its vast number of economically disadvantaged people. However, there is a greater possibility of India's unique development needs to be taken into account under the negotiations for RCEP than for TPP. Therefore, RCEP is India's preferred mega grouping for regional integration.

For India and other South Asian countries, there is no substitute for SAARC becoming a full-fledged regional grouping by moving towards a free trade area, and eventually to a customs and economic union. This can go a long way towards bringing prosperity and stability to the region and endowing the members with an effective bargaining power in strategic negotiations on trade and other international issues. This can also enable the South Asian region to march in unity, and therefore, with a stronger bargaining position, towards a pan-Asian economic grouping, if and when it is established. For, the South Asian countries can link with the pan-Asian movement more effectively and meaningfully if they do it together.

SAARC moved a little closer to a free trade area when, at its Islamabad summit in 2005, it adopted a framework agreement on the South Asian Free Trade Area (SAFTA). The agreement entered into force on 1 January 2006. Unfortunately, SAFTA is a deeply flawed agreement. The time target for achieving the goal of free trade is too long. The negative lists of member countries, which are exempted from free trade, are too large and there is no commitment to phase them out within a time-bound framework. There is no commitment to eliminate non-tariff and para-tariff barriers within a set time frame. Neither is there any specific provision in the agreement to adopt measures of deeper integration. And finally, there is no roadmap for moving beyond free trade towards customs or economic union. But the biggest problem is that Pakistan has acceded to the agreement with the qualification that trade concessions granted by it under SAFTA will not be applicable to trade between India and Pakistan. Any arrangement for free trade in South Asia is of little significance if it does not include the trade between the two largest countries of the region, that is, India and Pakistan. Thus, the denial of MFN treatment by Pakistan to India is effectively coming in the way of establishing a free trade area in South Asia and thereby moving towards regional integration. Not extending MFN treatment to India has been an integral part of Pakistan's policy not to come close to India economically, commercially and culturally, in order to preserve its identity based on the two-nation theory.

During the 1990s, India tried to take or join in other initiatives to form regional groupings that did not have Pakistan as a member. These included the Bay of Bengal Initiative for Multi-Sectoral Technical and Economic Cooperation (BIMSTEC) and the Indian Ocean Rim Association for Regional Cooperation. The latter group expressly rules out preferential trade arrangements. It, therefore, mainly provides a forum to explore possibilities of bilateral or plurilateral cooperation among the member countries.

BIMSTEC includes Bangladesh, India, Myanmar, Sri Lanka, Thailand, Nepal and Bhutan. An important development in the evolution of BIMSTEC was the signing in Phuket, Thailand in February 2005 of a framework agreement for the establishment of a free trade area among the member countries. The free trade area in BIMSTEC was supposed to include the liberalization of trade in services and investment also. Under the agreement, the process of negotiating free trade was supposed to have been completed by 2005 and the regime was to have come into force from 2006. The target for achieving free trade was 2017. As it happened, the negotiations could not be completed by the scheduled dates and the entire BIMSTEC process is at a standstill.

Another alternative that India explored during this period was sub-regional cooperation in the form of the South Asia Growth Quadrangle (SAGQ) consisting of the north-eastern part of India, Bangladesh, Nepal and Bhutan. Growth triangles and quadrangles envisage project-based cooperation in a contiguous zone consisting of more than two countries or parts thereof. This kind of cooperation finesses political divergences and the politically difficult task of harmonizing macroeconomic policies. India succeeded in getting the approval of the SAARC Ministerial Council at its meeting in Delhi in the summer of 1997 for exploring the possibility of sub-regional cooperation in South Asia. As a follow-up measure, a mechanism was set up to identify projects to be commonly undertaken. But this process was interrupted because of the strong criticism against this form of cooperation mounted by the main Opposition parties in Nepal and Bangladesh and by the government and media in Sri Lanka and Pakistan which were not expected to be members of the proposed sub-grouping. In the propaganda campaign against the idea of sub-regional cooperation, it was alleged that this was an attempt by India to dominate South Asia economically by keeping important countries like Pakistan and Sri Lanka out of regional cooperation. Ultimately a compromise was reached whereby it was agreed to pursue the idea through the SAARC institutional machinery where unanimity is a requirement for taking any decision. This put an end to the entire initiative. Another suggestion for sub-regional cooperation mooted in the second half of the 1990s was the Kunming Initiative, envisaging a sub-regional grouping consisting of the Yunan province of China, the north-eastern part of India, Myanmar, Bangladesh, Laos and Thailand.

The major problem for the SAGQ was the mobilization of resources for infrastructure-building. And the Kunmin Initiative did not pick up momentum because of the over-cautious position taken by India. The Government of India is afraid that if there is an opening up between South China and the north-east, the Indian market would be swamped by Chinese goods and India's security in that part of the country would be jeopardized because of the free movement of the Chinese. These fears have not been substantiated. They are exaggerated and reflect the inferiority complex of India vis-à-vis China.

The Kunming initiative has since acquired a new form under the garb of the BCIM (Bangladesh, China, India and Myanmar) Corridor. This is designed to connect these countries through multi-model transport links and also to undertake joint economic projects. Casting aside its misplaced reservations against the Kunming initiative, India has very rightly decided to endorse the BCIM Corridor initiative. It is participating in the on-going discussions on the shape it should take as well as on individual projects.

The other alternative route to SAFTA that India has been pursuing is to have bilateral FTAs with Asian countries. India has had such arrangements with Nepal and Bhutan for a long time. In 1999, it concluded an FTA with Sri Lanka, which came into force in 2000 and turned out to be of great benefit to both countries. This encouraged the two countries to negotiate a Comprehensive Economic Partnership Agreement. This, however, has not so far been approved by the Government of Sri Lanka, mainly due to political reservations on their part. In 2007, India offered to conclude an FTA with Bangladesh, and is still waiting for the latter's response. The Indo-Sri Lanka Free Trade Agreement provides for special measures to take care of the asymmetry between the Indian and Sri Lankan economies. India will have to go farther in this direction in its FTA with Bangladesh because of the latter being a least developed country. Even a unilateral free trade arrangement with Bangladesh is likely to redound to the benefit of India in the medium and long run. India has made a decisive move in that direction by removing almost all restrictions on the entry of Bangladeshi products into the Indian market. India has now an FTA with ASEAN as well as with Indonesia and Malaysia. The latest trend is for India to enter into CEPAs which include not only an agreement for free trade in goods, but also liberalization of trade in services and of investment flows and measures of deeper integration consisting of cooperation in the areas of trade facilitation, money, finance and harmonization or mutual recognition of standards. India has CEPAs with Singapore, Japan, South Korea and is in the process of negotiating them with Australia, New Zealand, Malaysia and Indonesia.

Integrating with the World Economy at Axes of India's Choice

The kind of development strategy that India is going to pursue will have a close bearing on the nature and effectiveness of its foreign policy. If India wants to retain independence and flexibility in its foreign policy, it need not rush headlong towards integrating with the world economy. Developed countries themselves do not practise what they preach by way of liberalization and globalization. Even China, which has gone quite far in integrating itself with the world economy, has fully retained its control over the strategic sectors of its economy. Countries that did not exercise caution and rushed in headlong, like the South-East Asian countries and Russia, had to pay a heavy price for it. It is indispensable for the conduct of independent foreign policy for India not to rely excessively on foreign private investment for its development, to augment its domestic savings, to depend for its growth principally on its domestic demand, to reduce its external debt burden substantially and to retain strategic control over the economy. This also calls for the avoidance of measures like capital account convertibility, which carry the risk of sudden depletion or outflow of foreign exchange reserves, and being careful about creating import-intensive production structures or encouraging import-based consumption patterns. India should also be able to delink from the world economy selectively in its security interests and for developing new technologies on a dedicated basis. Finally, any withdrawal of the State from its indispensable role in developing the country's human resources and infrastructure and bringing the marginalized groups to the national mainstream will be at a grave peril to its growth prospects and internal security, and hence to the conduct of independent foreign policy.

Bolstering India's Military Security

India faces a direct and immediate threat to its security from Pakistan. Pakistan has sought, and to a large measure, achieved parity with India in its military build-up. Its armed forces are built, mobilized, trained and oriented to fight a war against India. Successive Pakistani governments have systematically depicted India as the enemy country and carried out a vicious propaganda against it. Pakistan has fought three wars against India and has, for several years, been waging a proxy war against it in the state of Jammu and Kashmir. Pakistan has consistently reiterated its claim over Kashmir and has never given up the option of going to war against India in order to take possession of this territory. Pakistan has established near parity with India even in the acquisition of nuclear weapons and missiles to deliver them. The latest reports indicate that it has, in fact, an edge over India in building a nuclear arsenal.

In 1999, taking advantage of a lapse in vigilance on the part of the Indian armed forces deployed in the region, Pakistan took over by force

Kargil, which constitutes a sizeable part of the territory of Jammu and Kashmir. India had to wage a war to regain this territory.

Pakistan has been harbouring, training, arming and otherwise assisting terrorist groups in its territory for carrying out terrorist activities not only in Jammu and Kashmir, but also in other parts of India. The links of these groups with Pakistan's military establishment, particularly its intelligence agency, have been established beyond doubt, through information revealed by visiting journalists, independent experts, people arrested while planning and executing terrorist activities and US investigating and intelligence agencies.

Pakistan has recently also raised the water issue with India even though the distribution of the waters of the common rivers between the two countries is governed by the Indus Waters Treaty which, according to several Indian experts, is tilted decisively in Pakistan's favour and which contains built-in provisions for dispute settlement that have until now worked to the satisfaction of both parties. Therefore, Pakistan's campaign against India, centred on the water issue, is yet another indication of the fact that it would continue to look for some excuse or the other to maintain an atmosphere of perpetual hostility against India and that the resolution of the Kashmir issue alone is unlikely to result in a normalization of relations between the two countries.

China poses the other major threat to India's security. Its armed forces are arrayed along the northern and eastern borders of India in very close proximity with Indian armed forces. China is an officially recognized nuclear weapon power and the only one today that is still actively engaged in augmenting and improving its nuclear arsenal at a hectic pace. At least a part of its medium-range nuclear missiles deployed in Tibet are aimed at targets in India. China has fought a war against India and the border dispute on which the war was fought still remains unresolved. It has also been helping Pakistan, both openly and clandestinely, in augmenting its military might by way of supplies of nuclear and missile technologies and material, the actual delivery of missiles and other weapons, and has engaged in joint collaboration with Pakistan for the production of sophisticated weapons. This is intended to keep India destabilized and bogged down in the South Asian region and prevent its emergence as a global military power. China's propensity to resort to force to safeguard what it perceives to be its national interest has been demonstrated time and again by its actions in its neighbourhood—its military actions against Vietnam, the aggressive assertion of its claim in the South China Sea and its offensive military postures against Taiwan, including the deployment of missiles targeted against this territory. It is true that India's political relations with China are presently more or less on an even keel but that is no basis to neglect these objective factors and be lulled into a position of military unpreparedness vis-à-vis China.

A third level of threat to its security that India faces is the military bases and the deployment of nuclear forces of extra-regional powers, in its close vicinity, particularly in the Indian Ocean and the Persian Gulf. Given India's current relations with these powers, there is no immediate threat to its security from these sources. However, the very presence of these bases and nuclear forces in the region constitute a potential long-term threat. In this context, it is difficult for India to forget, in the formulation of its security policy, the threat to which it was subjected by the movement of the US warship, Enterprise, to the Bay of Bengal during the 1971 Bangladesh Liberation War. Given the limitations of its economic and military power, India cannot meet this potential threat by military means. It has, however, available to it a whole range of diplomatic options to seek a reduction in and ultimately the removal of the military presence of outside powers in its neighbourhood, and to make such a presence as benign from its security point of view as possible.

Given these threats to its military security, and taking into account the current world situation, India has no alternative to bolstering its security both in the conventional and nuclear fields. In the conventional field, while looking for every opportunity to effect economy, the country will have to go in for updating its existing arsenal and acquiring new weapons. India has already gone ahead and weaponized its nuclear capability, and publicly declared itself a nuclear weapon power after more than 50 years of agonizing and after the failure of all its efforts during this period to seek security through alternative means, particularly through nuclear disarmament.

Mahatma Gandhi had described atom bombs as a 'diabolical use of science'. Nehru had called it 'an evil thing'. In the 1950s, India had taken initiatives for banning tests of nuclear weapons. In the mid-1960s, it had joined other countries to get a resolution passed by the UN General Assembly which declared that nuclear war is a 'crime against humanity'. In the early 1980s, India had taken the initiative for the international community to reach an agreement on the non-use of nuclear weapons and for a freeze on the testing, accumulation and possession of nuclear weapons. India's last major effort for nuclear disarmament was the submission of an Action Plan for a Nuclear Weapon-Free and Non-Violent World

Order by the then Prime Minister Rajiv Gandhi at the 1988 UN General Assembly.

Unfortunately, none of these efforts elicited a positive response from the officially recognized nuclear weapon powers and their allies. The US and its allies never accepted the concept of no first use or non-use of nuclear weapons on the ground that it would go against their proclaimed policy of nuclear deterrence. When the issue of the legitimacy of nuclear weapons was debated in the World Court in The Hague, these powers asserted their right to use them. Subsequently, they legitimized the division of the world into the nuclear 'haves' and 'have nots for a long time to come by getting the Nuclear Non-Proliferation Treaty extended for an indefinite period.

India's acquisition of nuclear weapons and making a public declaration to this effect in July 1998 was mainly intended to safeguard its security, which had come under threat after Pakistan acquired nuclear weapons. For all one knows, but for the acquisition of nuclear weapons by Pakistan, India would have remained content with its recessed or unweaponized deterrent. There was at least a strong body of public opinion in India which did not want the country to go overtly nuclear.

There was a very important reason why, in spite of the abhorrence of the atom bomb by leaders like Mahatma Gandhi and Jawaharlal Nehru, India did not give up the nuclear weapon option and retained its nuclear capability without converting it into weapons. This was to use it as a challenge to the division of the world into the nuclear 'haves' and 'have nots' and as a leverage to keep alive the issue of nuclear disarmament. However, the imminent threat posed to its security by the acquisition of nuclear weapons by Pakistan compelled India to go overtly nuclear. Nevertheless, soon after its declaration of having become a nuclear weapon power, India adopted a nuclear doctrine, some of the main elements of which are the pursuit of a credible minimum deterrence, no first use of nuclear weapons and continuing pursuit of nuclear disarmament.

Both Pakistan and China, from which India faces a direct threat to its security, have been busy augmenting and improving their nuclear arsenals. Pakistan does not subscribe to the no-first-use doctrine and is producing and deploying tactical weapons which can be used only for first strike. Only a few years ago, there was a sharp deterioration in the international security environment because of some of the unilateral measures adopted by the US under the Republican administration. These included the abrogation of the Anti-Ballistic Missile Treaty (1972), the launching of a highly ambitious programme for the development and deployment of a

BMD system and the military attack on Iraq without the authorization of the UN Security Council. Recently, the Cold War seems to have been revived in its full fury over the situation in Ukraine. Defensive weapons have been redeployed. The nuclear arms limitation talks have been halted and a new offensive nuclear arms race has commenced. In such a situation, India cannot afford to take too long in putting its minimum nuclear deterrent in place, and for that purpose, acquiring a full-fledged second strike capability. It must adopt a phased programme within a time-bound framework, for acquiring this capability.

There is a perception among a wide section of those who follow India's foreign and strategic policy that the government is not pursuing the objective of building a minimum nuclear deterrent with the seriousness and single-mindedness warranted by the currently prevailing global security situation and which has characterized the programmes of other nuclear weapon powers. This impression has been reinforced by India's long intervals in carrying out tests for developing a weapon system and frequent failures in meeting time targets. These lapses and acts of omission and commission themselves constitute a threat to national security.

The nuclear threat from China should be factored into the building of India's minimum nuclear deterrent. However, in doing so, India need not get involved in a nuclear arms race with China or any other nuclear weapon power. Each nuclear weapon power determines what is adequate for it as a minimum deterrent, and no two such powers maintain the same level of deterrent.

The whole issue of nuclear disarmament was derailed by the Bush administration's policy in 2003 to resume the nuclear arms race in order to bolster the US's position as the only superpower in the world. As a result, the ongoing negotiations between the US and Russia to further reduce the stockpile of strategic nuclear weapons were suspended. The US launched its BMD initiative unmindful of the fact that it would trigger a new nuclear arms race.

In his speech in Prague on 1 April 2009, President Obama signalled the US intention to reverse the process set in motion by the Republication administration and work for a nuclear-weapon-free world. This was followed by his decision to expedite the New Strategic Arms Reduction Treaty (START) negotiations, which were soon concluded and resulted in a further reduction by the two powers of their stockpiles of strategic nuclear weapons. Unfortunately Obama has not demonstrated the same zeal and purpose in pursuing the objective of eliminating nuclear weapons. The mainstream view prevailing in the US defence and foreign policy establishments as well as in the US Congress is in favour of the country maintaining its global nuclear superiority. It seems that under this pressure, Obama has diluted his vision projected in the Prague speech, of a nuclear-weapon-free world. This was reflected in his administration's decision not to bring the issue of nuclear disarmament on the agenda of the Washington Summit convened in 2010 and to confine the deliberation to the issue of nuclear safety. Even in the resolution adopted at the summit-level meeting of the Security Council held in New York on 24 September 2009, and chaired by Obama himself, the emphasis was on non-proliferation and not on nuclear disarmament, which was referred to only in one of the preambular paragraphs, as follows: 'Resolving . . . to create the conditions for a world without nuclear weapons'.[29]

India seems to have lost interest in nuclear disarmament after its emergence as a de facto nuclear weapon power following the Pokhran II tests in 1998. The National Democratic Alliance (NDA) government at that time appeared to have accepted the view of the 'realists' that there is an inherent contradiction in a policy that seeks to pursue at the same time the goals of minimum nuclear deterrence and nuclear disarmament. This thinking came sharply into focus when India announced its intention to join the Treaty on South-East Asia as a Nuclear Weapon Free Zone[30] and when the then foreign minister accorded a full-throated endorsement to the US administration's initiative for deploying a BMD system. While the former implied that India was no longer opposed to partial measures for disarmament and no longer believed that they militated against the objective of eliminating nuclear weapons, the latter meant that India was not concerned about the potentiality of BMDs to trigger a new nuclear arms race. The United Progressive Alliance (UPA) government also seemed to be under the spell of the same 'realist' school of thinking, as there was no evidence of its resiling from the position taken by the NDA government.

Disarmament is a perennial quest of humankind. It is, therefore, bound to remain an important issue on the agenda for international negotiations for a long time to come. If India is sincere in its objective of pursuing nuclear disarmament enunciated in its nuclear doctrine and does not dilute its position for opportunistic reasons, it must play an important role in the effort of the world community to realize the goal of a nuclear-weapon-free world. India has the advantage of being the only nuclear weapon power that has publicly declared its willingness to put its entire nuclear arsenal on the negotiating table. Moreover, if Indian scientists who have been involved in the development of India's nuclear weapons are to be believed, India has considerable flexibility in taking a positive view on the CTBT and in negotiations on a Fissile Material Cut-off Treaty. Both these issues are related to and are, therefore, bound to figure prominently in any negotiations in the future, on nuclear disarmament. The 'realist' view that prevails today among most policymakers in India is erroneous, dangerous and bereft of the morality that India has come to prize as one of its greatest legacies, which inspired the leaders of India's freedom movement, and which, on achieving independence, was brought to bear on the conduct of India's foreign policy.

Dealing with Major World Powers

Western Powers

One of the highest priorities of India's foreign policy should be maintaining close and friendly relations with major Western powers, particularly the US. These countries have the markets, capital and technologies that India needs for its economic development. They also have considerable influence in the IMF and the World Bank, whose assistance India may need from time to time. These countries, especially the US, can influence what happens in India's neighbourhood, particularly Pakistan. Besides, India will have no chance of succeeding in its endeavour to establish a just and equitable world order without their cooperation. Finally, the possibility of their taking direct action against India in situations of conflict of interest cannot be ruled out.

It is, therefore, important for India to maintain a continuing dialogue with these countries on both bilateral issues and issues of disarmament and security with a view to developing a common understanding. For this purpose, democratic values, basic human rights, rule of law, independent judiciary, free press and free enterprise, which bind India with these countries, should be emphasized. India can also cooperate with these countries in combating the menace of international terrorism, drug trafficking, religious and sectarian extremism and in dealing with transnational issues like pandemics and natural disasters. India's recent economic performance and the opening up of its market after the 1991 economic reforms have given these countries a stake in the Indian economy. The leverage that it provides should be used for furthering India's interests in other areas. However, India should not, in any circumstance, be a camp follower of any of these countries. It should not hesitate from taking principled positions on important issues, particularly on world order issues, and should not allow its voice to be muffled under their pressure.

In this context, India should not underestimate the strength and assets it has in dealing with these countries.

Indo-US Relations

Recently, there have been several positive developments in Indo-US relations.[31] The US is now more or less reconciled to India's informal status as a nuclear weapon State. However, it can be expected to continue its efforts to place limits on India's nuclear ambitions. The US is also unlikely to formally recognize India as a nuclear weapon power. But once India acquires what it considers to be its minimum nuclear deterrent, it does not matter very much whether or not it is formally recognized as a nuclear weapon state.

There has also been a perceptible change in the US attitude towards the Kashmir issue. Now the US can be expected to do its best to thwart attempts by Pakistan to change the Line of Control by the use of force. However, India should have no illusions that the present US position on the Line of Control is an indication of its having given up its substantive position on the Kashmir issue, that is, it is a dispute that remains to be settled and that in settling it, the wishes of the Kashmiri people must be taken into account.

The US has now come to recognize that Pakistan has strong links with international terrorist groups and that the recent pronounced lurch of its polity and society towards religious extremism poses a serious threat to the Pakistani state and regional and global peace and security. The US has made efforts to get this trend reversed but without much success. India must recognize that there are limits to what the US can do to bring about changes in Pakistan's society and politics. Therefore, the ultimate responsibility of dealing with Pakistan or coping with the situation in Jammu and Kashmir rests squarely with India. The Indian authorities tend to place too much reliance on the US to solve India's problems with Pakistan. This comes in the way of their seriously pursuing other options that lie within India's competence.

The recent positive changes in the US position on matters of concern to India have happened mainly because of the stake that the US is developing in the Indian economy. Therefore, developments in the Indian economy will be a crucial factor determining Indo-US relations in future. More than any other factor, the maintenance of dynamism in the economy will give India flexibility and leverage in dealing with the US.

During the last decade, India and the US have built a very elaborate institutional infrastructure to deal with the whole gamut of their bilateral relationship and discuss all international issues of common concern. The continuing stream of two-way high-level visits in recent years has also contributed much to the improvement in bilateral relations. The momentum generated by these visits should be sustained and the institutions created for imparting new dimensions to the bilateral relationship should not be allowed to stagnate.

Indo-Russian Relations

India's relations with Russia[32] are of vital importance. Russia's predecessor state, the Soviet Union, was a trusted friend of India and among foreign countries, contributed most vitally to India's development. India still has available to it the invaluable asset of goodwill and friendship of the Russian people, which was cultivated during the long period of the Indo-Soviet relationship. India still depends on Russia for anything between 70 to 90 per cent for the supply of arms, equipment and spare parts for its Army, Navy and Air Force.

Besides, Russia is the second largest military power in the world. It has the potentiality of emerging as a great economic power as it is endowed with rich natural resources, very advanced and sophisticated technological capacity and highly skilled manpower. Its universal literacy and wide coverage of higher education guarantee constant accretion to this manpower pool. Russia may, therefore, be expected in the not-too-distant future to resume its position as one of the greatest powers in the world. It is, therefore, necessary for India to keep alive and inject new life into all the sinews of the bilateral relationship that were built during the period of Indo-Soviet cooperation as well as those which have been put in place recently.

Indo-Chinese Relations[33]

China's rise is one of the most important phenomena of the 21st century. China's great strides in the economic realm along with the dynamism displayed by the Indian economy have been primarily responsible for bringing about a shift in the global economic power balance from the West to Asia. China and India are, therefore, destined to play a major role in international cooperation in the areas of money, finance, trade and environment.

India cannot afford to have a hostile China as its neighbour. For, it can come under all kinds of pressure if its relations with China are marred by prolonged tensions or hostility. On the other hand, normal relations with

China can free a vast amount of resources currently devoted to defence expenditure.

India should, therefore, try to keep up the improvement in its relations with China, which have taken place during the last decade. It should maintain the recent trend of high-level political visits and dialogue with China. It should build further on the recent acceleration in the two-way trade transactions and explore new avenues of cooperation in the economic and technological field to sustain and further accelerate the growth in trade. A conscious and well-planned effort should be made to attract a substantial part of the surplus resources and knowhow at the disposal of China for the development of infrastructure and industry in India. There is also considerable scope for evolving and pursuing common positions on world economic issues, particularly in the WTO. India should join all those Chinese initiatives for the development of developing countries from which it is likely to benefit and to which it is capable of making meaningful contribution.

Relations with Neighbours

In any strategy of India's foreign policy, relations with neighbours[34] should be given the highest priority. For, India is judged by the world mainly through the prism of the perception of its neighbours. Adverse relations with them are bound to pull India back in the pursuit of playing its rightful role in the comity of nations. Besides, relations with neighbours impinge directly on India's security, both military and non-military. Neighbours are also the best and natural partners for economic cooperation.

Geographical proximity, common language and culture as well as inheritance of common physical and institutional infrastructures give India a comparative advantage in trading and developing other economic links with its neighbours. Finally, India is a pluralistic society; as are most of its neighbours. What happens to any of the pluralistic societies in its neighbourhood seriously affects India's ability to hold its own pluralistic society together. India should make every possible effort to ensure that the pluralistic character of society is preserved in its neighbourhood. For this, the most important thing to do is to preserve the secular character of its own polity and society. At the same time, secular forces in neighbouring countries should receive India's full support.

India faces unique problems in dealing with its neighbours. Almost all its neighbouring countries suffer from an identity crisis vis-à-vis India.

Moreover, India's relations with its neighbours are characterized by a big-neighbour–small-neighbour syndrome. These countries, particularly the relatively smaller ones, view with suspicion most of the moves made by India for coming close to them. India, on the other hand, tends to take its neighbouring countries for granted and accords lower priority to them among its foreign policy preoccupations. Sometimes, it is overbearing in dealing with its neighbours and more often than not, its policies towards its neighbours are short-sighted, lacking in vision and courage and over-calculative of the short-term costs. Sometimes, India adopts policy measures in wanton disregard of how they might affect the interests of neighbouring countries. Finally, some political parties and groups in India tend to communalize bilateral issues with neighbours and in the process make them more complex and difficult than they already are.

Any accretion of India's military power is perceived by India's neighbours, particularly Pakistan, as a threat to their security. Even though India may have a global perspective and broader security objectives in view while pursuing its security interests, its moves are unfortunately perceived by India's neighbours as directed against them. India cannot downsize itself or ignore its larger security interests, going beyond the region, in order to remove misperceptions among its neighbours. But it can certainly go about systematically in explaining to its neighbours that its actions are not targeted against them, but designed to serve wider purposes. India should also consciously try to factor its neighbours' perception into its policymaking on major economic, political and security issues.

India should never interrupt its dialogue with its neighbours as it is likely to lead to further misapprehension and misunderstanding. The dialogue should be continuously maintained at all levels, including the highest political level. Bilateral problems should not be neglected or allowed to fester. Finally, India should constantly try to develop and maintain people-to-people contact with neighbouring countries even if it involves only a one-way traffic,that is, from the neighbouring countries to India and not vice versa.

Limits to Diplomacy

Diplomacy operates on a very thin margin of practical possibilities. In the case of India, that margin is provided by outsiders' perception of the country's strengths and weaknesses. This perception depends more on what is happening inside India than what is happening outside.

Domestic factors such as national unity, stability of the political system, economic clout and military strength are among the pre-conditions for the success of India's foreign policy. They set an absolute limit on what foreign policy can achieve. Nehru had once said: 'Foreign policy depends ultimately on internal conditions and development. Internal progress for us, therefore, becomes essential if we are to play any effective part in world affairs'.[35]

The internal situation in India leaves much to be desired. Among internal factors, the rise of communalism can have the most debilitating effect on the conduct of India's foreign policy.[36] There is a tendency among some political parties to communalize foreign policy for electoral purposes. This is particularly so with regard to issues figuring in bilateral relations with neighbouring countries, particularly the Muslim-majority neighbours. All this puts a big question mark on India's credentials as a secular state. If India's image as a secular state is tarnished, it would lose one of its unique selling points in the realm of foreign affairs. It would cast a shadow on Indian foreign policy and put Indian diplomats at a great disadvantage in the pursuit of their vocation.

Thus, in the ultimate analysis, the battle for carving out the rightful place for India in the comity of nations will be won or lost on the domestic front, and not so much on the diplomatic front.

Notes

1. Asian Relations Organization, *Asian Relations: Being a Report of the Proceedings and Documentation of the First Asian Relations Conference, New Delhi, March–April 1947* (New Delhi: Asian Relations Organization, 1948).
2. In 1960, China's Gross Domestic Product (GDP) as a proportion of world output was 1.31. In 2010, it increased to 7.84. On the other hand, India's GDP (as a proportion of world output) was 1.18 in 1960 and declined to 1.11 in 1990. It started increasing only from the 1990s. It was 1.43 in 2000 and 2.35 in 2010. In 1960, India's per capita GDP was 84.2 (in current US$) whereas those of China, the Republic of Korea and Malaysia were 92.0, 155.2 and 299.1 respectively. In 2000, India's per capita GDP increased to 453 (in current US$) whereas those of China, Republic of Korea and Malaysia increased to 949.2, 11,346.7 and 1,005.6 respectively. Thus, in the 40 years between 1960 and 2000, the increase in India's per capita GDP was over five times, but that of China was over 10 times, that of Korea over 73 times and that of Malaysia over 13 times. See World Bank, World Bank Data: World Development Indicators and Global Development Finance, http://databank.worldbank.org/ddp/home.do?Step=12&id=4&CNO=2 (accessed on 19 September 2011).

3. Rural Survey Organization, 'Poverty Statistics in China' (National Bureau of Statistics, China, September 2004).
4. Terry McKinley and Barsha Khattry, 'Slow Post-Crisis Recovery in Indonesia', in *The Macroreconomic of Poverty Reduction in Indonesia* (independent study supported by the United Nations Development Programme, 2003).
5. The headcount poverty rate in India in 1973–74 was 54.88 per cent. After a decade, in 1983–84, it was as high as 44.48 per cent. There has been further decline since then. But the headcount poverty rate in 2004–05 was still quite high, at 27.5 per cent. See Government of India, Planning Commission of India Report, March 2007.
6. World Bank, World Development Indicators and Global Development Finance.
7. United Nations Conference on Trade and Development (UNCTAD) Statistics, http://www.unctad.org/Home (accessed on 20 June 2015).
8. Government of India, 'Development Challenges in Extremist Affected Areas: Report of an Expert Group to Planning Commission' (New Delhi, April 2008).
9. MERCOSUR, or the Common Market of the South American countries, is a trading bloc consisting of Brazil, Argentina, Uruguay and Paraguay. It was established in March 1991 by the Treaty of Asunción. Venezuela became a member in 2006.
10. 'P5+1' refers to the five permanent members of the UN Security Council—China, France, Russia, the United Kingdom (UK), and the US—plus Germany.
11. International Monetary Fund, Directorate of Trade Statistics database, http://elibrary-data.imf.org/ (accessed on 6 April 2015).
12. World Bank, World Development Indicators, http://www.data.worldbank.org (accessed on 22 August 2011)
13. World Trade Organization, Statistics Database, http://stat.wto.org/Home/WSDB-Home.aspx?Language=E (accessed on 22 August 2011).
14. World Bank, World Development Indicators.
15. Press Information Bureau, 'A Growth Rate of over 8 Per Cent Expected for the Coming Year' (Government of India, 27 February 2015), http://pib.nic.in/budget2015/ecosurveyRel.aspx (accessed on 25 May 2015).
16. International Monetary Fund, World Economic Outlook, April 2015.
17. World Trade Organization, Statistics Database.
18. US Congressional Budget Office, 'The Budget and Economic Outlook: An Update' (24 August 2011), http://www.cbo.gov/ftpdocs/123xx/doc12316/08-24-BudgetEconUpdate.pdf (accessed on 22 August 2011).
19. US Department of the Treasury, 'Monthly Statement of the Public Debt of the United States' (Bureau of the Fiscal Service, 31 December 2010), http://www.treasury-direct.gov/govt/reports/pd/mspd/2010/opdml22010.pdf (accessed on 22 August 2011).

20. US Department of the Treasury, http://www.treasury.gov/resource-centre/data-chart-center/tic/Documents/mfh-his01.txt (accessed on 22 August 2011).
21. US Congressional Budget Office, 'The Budget and Economic Outlook: 2014 to 2024' (4 February 2014), https://www.cbo.gov/sites/default/files/45010-Outlook2014_Feb_0.pdf (accessed on 25 June 2015).
22. US Department of the Treasury, 'Monthly Statement of Public Debt of United States' (Bureau of the Fiscal Service, 31 December 2013), http://www.treasurydirect.gov/govt/reports/pd/mspd/2013/opdm122013.pdf (accessed on 25 June 2015).
23. US Department of Commerce, Bureau of Economic Analysis, http://www.bea.gov/newsreleases/national/gdp/gdpnewsreleases.htm (accessed on 22 April 2015).
24. BRICS is an acronym for the combined economies of five countries with major emerging markets: Brazil, Russia, India, China and South Africa.
25. G-20 is group of 20 countries, that is, Argentina, Australia, Brazil, Canada, China, France, Germany, India, Indonesia, Italy, Japan, Mexico, Russia, Saudi Arabia, South Africa, South Korea, Turkey, the UK, the US and the EU.
26. G-7 comprises Canada, France, Germany, Italy, Japan, the UK and the US.
27. G-33 is a group of developing nations in the WTO that safeguards their interest in the negotiation on agriculture in the Doha Round.
28. Nama-6 has now become NAMA-11, which is a group of developing countries set up to safeguard their interest in the negotiations on non-agricultural market access in the Doha Round of WTO.
29. UN Security Council Resolution 1887, adopted in the year 2009.
30. This could not materialize because of the provision in the treaty that only nuclear powers which are so recognized in the Non-Proliferation Treaty (NPT) can adhere to its protocol.
31. For details, see Chapters 5 and 6 of this volume.
32. For details, see Chapter 7 of this volume.
33. For details, see Chapter 8 of this volume.
34. For details, see Chapters 2 and 4 of this volume.
35. Quoted in Ministry of Information and Broadcasting, *March of India*, vol. 11 (Delhi: Publications Division, Ministry of Information and Broadcasting, Government of India, 1959) lxiii.
36. Muchkund Dubey, ed., *Communal Revivalism in India: A Study of External Implications* (New Delhi: Har Anand Publications, 1994).

TWO Dealing with Neighbours

Importance of Relations with Neighbours

In any strategy of India's foreign policy, relations with neighbours should be accorded the highest priority. For, a country is judged by the world through the prism of its neighbours' perception. And India is no exception to this. India's standing in the world very much depends on its ability to maintain good relations with its neighbours. Adverse relations with neighbours are bound to be a major constraint to India playing its rightful role in the comity of nations. For example, India's almost chronically hostile relationship with Pakistan is the biggest constraint to its realizing the objective of becoming a permanent member of the UN Security Council.

Besides, relations with neighbours impinge directly on India's security, both military and non-military. The only country that poses a direct military threat to India's security is Pakistan. India faces non-military threats to its security from almost all its neighbouring countries. These include the spillover of their domestic ethnic conflicts, large-scale illegal migration and their providing the base for terrorism directed against India. It is now well documented that Pakistan has been encouraging and assisting terrorists to cross over the Line of Control in Jammu and Kashmir and the international border to indulge in acts of terrorism in India. For this purpose, it maintains a whole infrastructure of terrorist organizations and their training camps in its territory. This is a part of its strategy to keep militancy alive in Jammu and Kashmir and generally to destabilize India.

Bangladesh for several years, before the present Awami League government put a halt to it, contributed to the destabilization of the north-eastern region of India by allowing the United Liberation Front of Asom and other militant groups to operate from its territory with a view to carrying out terrorists activities in India. These groups were provided shelter in Bangladesh, and allowed to run training centres there.

Another non-military threat to India's security from Bangladesh has been the large-scale illegal migration of its citizens to India, which has created law and order problems in the adjoining Indian states and also imposed economic and social burdens on the country. Of late, Bangladesh's policy-makers, intellectuals and think tanks have been busy building up an ostensibly plausible case justifying such migration. The arguments frequently advanced by them are that international migration is a global phenomenon, that Bangladesh does not have adequate space for its large and rising population, and that migration from Bangladesh helps the Indian economy as it meets its need for cheap labour. From both Bangladesh and Sri Lanka, India has, from time to time, faced the problem of the spillover to its territory of refugees fleeing scenes of ethnic violence, often due to the oppression of minorities in these countries. For example, India has harboured for prolonged periods Chakma and Tamil refugees fleeing Bangladesh and Sri Lanka, respectively.

The non-cooperation of Nepal in taming rivers commonly shared with India has inflicted immense damage on the latter. The consequent silting of these rivers has led to an increase in the frequency and intensity of floods in the plains of India. Nepal's non-cooperation has also deprived India of thousands of megawatts of hydropower that it needs to meet the rising demand for energy for its growing economy, and water for irrigation during the dry season in the Indo-Gangetic plains.

India's neighbours are its best and natural partners for economic cooperation. Geographical proximity, common languages, religions and consumption patterns and the inheritance of common institutional and physical infrastructures from its colonial past, confer on India, by way of reducing transaction costs, competitive advantage over countries outside the region, in trading and forging other links of economic cooperation with neighbouring countries. This was demonstrated by the emergence of India, following the trade liberalization measures adopted by Sri Lanka from 1977 and Bangladesh from 1982, as the largest exporter of goods and services to these countries. For Bangladesh, India remained the largest source of imports till 2005–06 when it was overtaken by China. For Sri Lanka, India emerged as the largest source of imports soon after the India–Sri Lanka FTA came into force in 2000, a position it has since maintained.

India's export of goods to Bangladesh went up from $43.33 million in 1982–83 to nearly $3.5 billion in 2008–09 and $5.246 billion in 2013–14.[1] It is estimated that the value of illegal imports from India into Bangladesh is about the same as that of legal imports.[2] This pushes the figure of India's legal exports to Bangladesh into the range of $10–11 billion. To this should be added earnings from services, mostly from Bangladeshis coming to India for education and medical treatment. In spite of the fact that Pakistan does not extend MFN treatment to India and permits the export of only those goods that are included in the list established by it, the value of India's exports to Pakistan increased from $164.3 million in 2001–02 to $1,795.5 million in 2007–08, and to $2247.6 million in 2013–14.[3] Various estimates have been made of India's exports to Pakistan through informal and illegal channels, mainly via Singapore and Dubai and through smuggling across the border. These range between $1 billion and $2 billion.[4] It has been conservatively estimated that if Pakistan starts extending MFN treatment to India and if restrictions on trade are removed by both the countries, the total trade between the two countries has the potential of reaching $10 billion within five years.[5]

Our neighbours acquire an added importance for us because of the pluralistic nature of our society. For what happens in the neighbourhood affects our ability to hold our own pluralistic society together. For example, flagrant and large-scale violation of the rights of the minorities in Bangladesh and Pakistan can, through a chain reaction, trigger communal violence in India, putting in jeopardy the life and safety of our minorities. The reverse is also true. If pluralism is under threat in India, as has happened several times during communal riots in this country, particularly during the demolition of the Babri Masjid in Ayodhya in 1992, it puts tremendous strain on the ability of our neighbours to manage their own pluralistic societies. The brunt of it is borne by the minority communities in these countries.

Unique Problems in Dealing with Neighbours

Identity Crisis

India faces unique problems in dealing with its neighbours. This arises, first and foremost, because almost all of them suffer, in varying degrees, from identity crisis vis-à-vis India. For, practically everything they can claim as their own or identify themselves with, that is, their history, language, religion, art, architecture, mores, customs, legends and folklore, is their heritage from the former Indian subcontinent. In any direction they turn to express their national identity, they find themselves under India's looming shadow. This is especially true in case of India's relations with Pakistan.

They, therefore, have often resorted to various artificial and unusual means of distinguishing themselves from India. For example, in their textbooks, they distort history and established facts and figures to set themselves apart from India. They claim as exclusively belonging to them, cuisines, dresses, music, dance forms and other common heritages which are quintessentially subcontinental. They put restrictions on the import of films, cassettes, videos and other cultural goods from India and on the visits of Indian cultural troupes, lest these swamp the identities they are seeking to carve out in these domains. In spite of this, cultural exchanges do take place when India's relations with these countries warm up from time to time.

Two important qualifications must be made while analyzing the pathology of the identity crisis. First, there are influential political elements and vested cultural interests in India too, which try to project Indian history and culture in a monolithic and chauvinistic manner. Second, the restrictions imposed in this field by our neighbours are also designed to serve the legitimate purpose of protecting their nascent entertainment industries.

India faces problems arising out of the identity crisis with almost all its neighbours, but these are particularly acute in the case of its relations with Pakistan. This is largely because in Indo-Pak relations, the problem is compounded by Pakistan's belief in the two-nation theory. Leaders like Muhammad Ali Jinnah who worked for the creation of Pakistan, argued that the Hindus and Muslims constituted two separate nations and therefore, there was no way for them to live together. The logical corollary of this idea was that there must be two separate states for them. Eventually, Pakistan was created on the basis of the two-nation theory, while secularism became the foundation of the Indian State. Pakistan perceived secular India as an intrinsic and standing threat to its raison d'être based on the two-nation theory. It, therefore, adopted a policy of perpetual hostility towards India as the sine qua non of its existence as a separate Muslim state. It tried to build its identity as being not only different from that of India, as other neighbours did, but also in anti-Indian terms. It not only distorted the collective subcontinental history and culture in an attempt to create an identity of its own, but also went on a frontal attack on India's secularism. It mounted a concerted propaganda to depict India as a Hindu state and Indian secularism as a sham. Pakistan acted in this fashion out of the fear that if Indian secularism emerged triumphant, the two-nation theory would be discredited, thus delegitimizing the Pakistani State based on this theory. The splitting in 1971 of Bangladesh from Pakistan primarily on cultural and economic grounds made a heavy dent on the two-nation theory. But in spite of this, the Pakistani State continues to justify its raison d'être and operate on the basis of this theory.

Pakistan's claim on Kashmir has been an extension of the same theory. Pakistani political leaders at the highest level have often asserted that Kashmir is the 'unfinished agenda of the Partition'. They have gone about inculcating the belief in the country that Pakistan as a state will not be complete until Kashmir becomes a part of it. The logic of this argument is derived from the fact that Kashmir, particularly the valley, is a Muslim-majority state. This logic has horrendous implications for the future of the Muslim population in other parts of India. Besides, the separation of Bangladesh from Pakistan in 1971 convincingly demonstrated the hollowness of this logic.

Another fallout of the two-nation theory impinging on Indo-Pak relations has been the Pakistani ruling class's inordinate and demonstrative interest in what happens to the Muslim population in India. Pakistan not only takes up bilaterally with the Government of India cases of real or alleged denial of human rights to, and harassment of, Muslims in India, but also raises such cases in international fora. This is partly designed to placate public opinion back home and partly to debunk Indian secularism and bolster the two-nation theory. Pakistan's interventions in matters involving the Muslim community in India generally works against the latter's interest as it has the effect of alienating its members from the mainstream of national life. But Pakistan disregards this implication and continues to intervene in these matters.

There are several instances in the world of states adopting religion as their organizing principle. These need not necessarily be antagonistic to states that are based on a different organizing principle. What is pernicious about the two-nation theory is the compulsion it imposes on the nation based thereon to maintain a relationship of hostility towards the nation not following this principle. Moreover, as a part of the practice of the two-nation theory, successive rulers of Pakistan have consciously fostered, supported and relied on extremist religious groups which have spread their tentacles so widely and deeply in Pakistan's polity and society that they are now threatening to devour the state itself. Having won his case for Pakistan on the basis of the two-nation theory, Jinnah, the founder of the nation, had intended to build secular institutions and practise secular norms in Pakistan. One wonders whether Pakistan would not have been better off, with greater chances of survival as a Muslim State, following Jinnah's precept.

Big-Neighbour–Small-Neighbour Syndrome

Another unique problem that India faces in dealing with its neighbours arises from what has frequently been referred to as the 'big-neighbour–small-neighbour syndrome'. This syndrome influences policies negatively on both sides, that is, India as well as its neighbours. Because of this syndrome, most of the moves made and initiatives taken by India to come closer to its neighbours are viewed with suspicion by the latter. The negative aspects of such initiatives are singled out and exaggerated. Many of the woes that befall these countries due to natural circumstance or their own actions are attributed to machinations by India. For example, most of the social and economic distress prevailing in the riverine areas in Bangladesh is attributed by the Bangladeshi media to the increase in the salinity of the water of their rivers, caused by the withdrawal of water by India at the Farakka barrage. Smuggling across the border is depicted as Indians stealing Bangladesh's wealth. Floods in Bangladesh are claimed to be caused by India's actions in the upper reaches of the common rivers. Similarly, inflation in Nepal is projected by the Nepali media as a spillover of inflation in India or being deliberately caused by India's denial of essential supplies to Nepal.

India, on the other hand, takes its smaller neighbours for granted and does not pay much attention to their problems, aspirations and expectations from it. These countries, with the exception of Pakistan, do not figure prominently in India's foreign policy priority. High-level Indian policymakers have advocated a policy of benign neglect of smaller neighbours without realizing that the latter take such a policy as an insult. Stagnation or breakdown in relations with smaller neighbours always translates itself into adverse relationships. Our neighbours perceive it as a conspiracy against them. During the period when relations are allowed to stagnate, the sinews of cooperation painstakingly built over the years start breaking down one by one, with the result that anti-India forces in these countries become stronger and pro-Indian forces are on the retreat.

The apprehension of loss of identity and the fear of threat to their sovereignty emanating from the bigger neighbour is often so great that the smaller neighbours do not want to come close to India even if it is clearly in their interest to do so. They do not want to do even those things with India which must be done on merit. This has been a major factor behind Bangladesh's reluctance to supply natural gas to India, accord India transit facilities through its territory or take up large-scale joint venture projects. This also, at least partly, explains Nepal's reluctance over the past few decades to undertake large-scale projects with India for harnessing the waters of common rivers, and Pakistan building a high-cost industrial structure based on more expensive imports from countries outside the region instead of opting for a more competitive industrial structure based on cheaper imports from India.

Governments in neighbouring countries regard being pro-India as a political liability. The Bangladesh Nationalist Party's (BNP's) depiction of rival Sheikh Hasina and her party Awami League as pro-India was a factor behind Hasina's defeat in the Bangladesh general elections in 1999. That is why in the period following the elections, she strongly tried to play down this pro-India image to the extent of forging an alliance, even though temporarily, with an element of the Bangladesh Jamaat-e-Islami, the diehard religious party in Bangladesh. The Nepali Congress reached the pinnacle of popularity in 1990, when it played the principal role in restoring democracy in Nepal. After that it steadily declined till very recently, partly because of its pro-India image. Prominent political groups and individuals in the neighbouring countries, therefore, do not want to be depicted as pro-India. They prefer to give vent to their pro-Indian sentiments in private rather than in public. This makes it difficult to take our relationship with the neighbouring countries to the optimal level even when more friendly governments are in power.

The manner in which India deals with its neighbours also leaves much to be desired. We are often overbearing in dealing with them. We fail to give their representatives the importance and respect they deserve. We are also over-calculative of the short-term costs of accepting their proposals or striking deals with them. When Nepal, during the course of the negotiations on the Mahakali project in the early 1990s, asked India for the payment of royalty for the use of the water of the river downstream after it was released from the proposed dam in Nepal, India rejected it on the ground that going by its obligations under international law, it was not required to make such a payment. In doing so, India might have been on a sound legal footing, but it failed to calculate the tremendous benefits that would have accrued to the country, had the concession by way of royalty enabled India to clinch the deal on the Mahakali project. Similarly, several times in the past we turned down Bangladesh's requests for providing expanded access for their exports to our market, for fear of the imaginary havoc it might inflict on our domestic industries, particularly in the states adjoining Bangladesh. In the process, we have ignored the long-term benefits of enhancing Bangladesh's import capacity and the positive political outcome of our providing a greater space in our market for its exports.

India generally adopts economic policy measures in total disregard of how they might affect the interests of its neighbours. Sometimes the macroeconomic policies we adopt on taxation, pricing, interest rates and exchange rates can have far-reaching implications for the economies of our neighbours which are more closely linked with our economy through free trade arrangements, investment, credit and joint projects. But we seldom consult these countries or consciously factor their interests into our macroeconomic policymaking.

Neighbours' Exaggerated Perception of Threats from India

As an emerging global power, India often has to take actions to project its power globally, in order to serve global strategic purposes and to meet threats emanating from sources outside the region. Unfortunately, these are perceived by its neighbours as directed against them and therefore, as a threat to their security. This is how neighbours have viewed India's decision to keep its nuclear option open after the Nuclear Proliferation Treaty (1970) came into force; its large-scale acquisition, from time to time, of sophisticated conventional weapons and the expansion of its naval force. Pakistan's perception of threat to its security from India's global strategic pursuits has been a major factor triggering an arms race between the two countries and the nuclearization of South Asia.

India's neighbours, including Pakistan, do not appreciate that India may have broader strategic purposes or security objectives in view while taking these steps. These include getting access to raw material and other strategic supplies; keeping open sea lanes which carry India's trade; meeting threats from China; protecting its sea coast; power projection beyond the region, designed to serve its strategic interests, such as in the Indian Ocean; and enhancing its bargaining power in multilateral and bilateral negotiations with countries other than its neighbours.

Role of Domestic Factors

Our neighbours' perception of and attitude towards us also depends to a great extent on what is happening in our own country. This is true of our relations with other countries also, but with neighbours, it acquires a greater salience. In the early post-Independence period, coinciding with Jawaharlal Nehru's helmsmanship of the nation, India was perceived by its neighbours and other countries as having a strong and stable government, effective leadership and sturdy democratic institutions.

It had evolved and was implementing a development strategy which, in several ways, was uniquely its own and later came to be adopted, with suitable modifications, by many other developing countries. It had an international stature that was much higher than that justified by its economic and military power. These attributes considerably influenced our neighbours' attitude towards us, which was one of admiration and envy at the same time, sometimes expressed publicly, but most of the time, entertained privately.

This changed by the mid-1960s, when Pakistan decided to go to war against India. Between the mid-1960s and the end of the 1980s, the country witnessed an all-round decay of its democratic institutions and a deterioration in its political, economic and social situation. During this period, India, though still stronger in several respects than its neighbours, was reduced to the common denominator of the subcontinent in terms of economic and social progress, quality of governance and moral stature. It was seen as a blundering and fumbling country which had failed to live up to the high expectations it had aroused after independence and to the social contract it had entered into with its citizens in its Constitution. In 1975, with the declaration of emergency, the Indian democracy came to the verge of being extinguished. In the meantime Sri Lanka forged ahead of India in economic and social fields. And democracy, even if flawed and sporadic, made its appearance in most of our neighbouring countries.

From the early 1990s, there have been spells of weak and unstable governments in India. The leaders of these governments remained largely preoccupied with the problem of their political survival. They were, therefore, incapable of mustering the courage and vision for solving long-standing bilateral problems or evolving long-term strategies for improving relations with neighbours. The only exception to this was the signing of the agreement for sharing the waters of the Ganga at Farakka (known as the Ganges Water Sharing Treaty) with Bangladesh in December 1996 by the then United Front government. This happened because of the combination of three unique factors—the Awami League government under Sheikh Hasina being in power in Bangladesh; the personal effort of the then Foreign Minister I. K. Gujral, who, among all the foreign ministers of India, had the most enlightened attitude towards neighbours; and the active involvement in the negotiations of the West Bengal government, under the forward-looking leadership of the late Jyoti Basu.

After the demolition of the Babri Masjid in Ayodhya in 1992 by Hindu fanatics and the subsequent ascendancy of communal forces in the Indian politics, the country's image as a secular state came to be severely dented. Some of the issues in India's relations with neighbouring countries were communalized. For example, the Bharatiya Janata Party took the position that Hindus entering India illegally from Bangladesh should be treated as refugees, but Muslims in a similar situation should be treated as illegal immigrants. They also grossly exaggerated the problem of illegal migration from Bangladesh, proclaiming it as a threat to India's sovereignty and stability. When out of power, they adopted intransigent positions on several issues figuring in Indo-Pak relations. This made the already complex problem of dealing with neighbours even more difficult.

Problems Posed by Neighbours' Policy Postures

The way India is perceived by its neighbours, influenced by the latters' identity crisis and the big-neighbour–small-neighbour syndrome, has led them to adopt policy measures that pose major problems for India in dealing with them. There is, first, a tendency to multilateralize bilateral problems with India. This was manifested in Bangladesh's effort to involve Nepal in the negotiations on the distribution of the waters of the Ganga at Farakka. The involvement of Nepal could not but have delayed a solution to the problem and made it more difficult than it already was.

The other device adopted by our neighbours has been to involve outside countries, mainly bilateral donors and aid agencies like the World Bank, in bilateral negotiations, either in the capacity of mediators or advisors. India has consistently rejected such outside involvement, mainly because such agencies are often prone to political influence by their major contributors, which themselves have vested interests in the region, either directly or in the pursuit of their global strategic objectives. They can, therefore, be scarcely expected to be impartial in playing a mediatory or advisory role. In fact, there is a greater chance of their going against the interests of India, either out of sympathy for its smaller neighbours or as a nemesis for a real or imagined grievance against India. In spite of this, we should understand our neighbours' reluctance to accept at face value facts adduced and arguments advanced by us in relation to bilateral issues and the desire to get them verified by third parties. We should, therefore, accept the involvement of third parties as advisors if our neighbours insist upon it and if it inspires confidence in them.

There is also a tendency on the part of the smaller neighbours to gang up against India for extracting concessions from it or reducing its influence in the region. This was at least partly the motive behind the initiative taken by President Ziaur Rahman of Bangladesh for creating SAARC. For, the smaller neighbours believe that what they cannot wrest from India bilaterally, without making reciprocal concessions, can be obtained multilaterally as a right under SAARC. They have, therefore, used the SAARC forum from time to time for this purpose, with only limited success so far, largely because of the vigilance exercised by India. However, in the process, India has often found itself in embarrassing positions. Through this device, its smaller neighbours have succeeded in getting some of their bilateral technical cooperation programmes with India multilateralized under SAARC. At one stage, the Bangladesh delegation, with the support of other SAARC members, had tried without success to pressurize India to share, under the aegis of SAARC, the research findings from its Antarctica missions. Nepal and Bhutan, with the support of other smaller member countries, have used the SAARC forum to put pressure on India to provide transit through Indian territory to trade with Bangladesh, and to the ports of Chittagong and Mongla for their trade with other countries. But they have not in this context, considered it fit to press, at the same time, for the acceptance of India's demand for transit for its products through the Bangladesh territory to the north-eastern region of India, and through the Pakistan territory to Afghanistan. Other examples of their combined efforts to whittle down and counterbalance India's legitimate role and influence in SAARC is their advocacy for external financing of regional funds created under SAARC and their undue and extraordinary interest in granting observer and associate membership status in SAARC to major outside countries and entities like the US, Japan, China and the EU.

Finally, in most neighbouring countries, the government propaganda machinery, the media and a large section of the academic and intellectual community deliberately portray India as a hegemon. Even government leaders and officials make such allegations from time to time. In doing so, they derive inspiration from think tanks and scholars in Western countries, particularly the US and the UK. They are also reinforced in this campaign by the Chinese government, scholars and media which, for their own purpose, swing into action from time to time, depicting India as a hegemon or a bully in South Asia. It goes without saying that this portrayal of India is motivated and seldom based on facts. The oft-quoted examples in journalistic and academic writings, both in the neighbouring countries as well as in the West, are India's so-called annexation of Sikkim (1975), trade blockade against Nepal (1989–90), the despatch and operation of the Indian Peace Keeping Force (IPKF) in Sri Lanka

(1987–90) and the naval assistance to the Maldives when it was facing a piracy threat from a group of dissidents (1988).

In all these instances, India had very strong reasons to act as it did. India never imposed a trade blockade against Nepal nor deprived it of essential supplies for which it was dependent on India. It simply closed down a few border posts, while keeping most of them still open, as an expression of displeasure against certain unilateral measures taken by the then Nepalese government which, according to India's perception, represented a departure from the past practice and militated against its interest. These included the erosion of preferences to imports from India by granting preferences to a third country, imposition of surcharges and switching from ad valorem to specific rates of duties on imports of certain items from India, and discrimination against Indian citizens working in Nepal. When, in spite of repeated assurances, Nepal did not remove these restrictions and discriminatory measures, India held back the formal renewal of the bilateral agreements on trade and transit, which still remained operational in practice. India also thought that the purchase of arms made at that time by Nepal from China, without consulting India, was in contravention of the relevant provisions of the Indo-Nepal Treaty of 1950.

The IPKF was despatched at the request of the government of Sri Lanka on the basis of a formal agreement signed between the two countries at the highest level. Far from being a hegemonic intervention in the domestic affairs of Sri Lanka, it was a courageous and highly risky venture undertaken by India for protecting the territorial integrity and in the interest of peace, stability and democracy in Sri Lanka. As a part of the package, India persuaded the then President of Sri Lanka to agree on a autonomy package for Sri Lankan Tamils, which was more far-reaching than any ever granted to this community by a Sri Lankan government. It is a different matter that this package came unstuck because of subsequent political developments in Sri Lanka, over which India had only limited control.

India's naval despatch in support of the Maldives government was also in response to a request made by the then President of the Maldives. This was not against any popular uprising within the country. The pirates against whom this action was taken were a tiny group of conspirators who had hardly any support within the country. The Indian intervention was highly appreciated by the Maldives government. It helped in preventing the destabilization of the government and contributed to imparting a new momentum to the bilateral relationship.

Policy Prescriptions

Sensitivity to Psychological Factors

The analysis of the special problems we face in dealing with our neighbours shows that we must take special precautions and keep in mind certain broad considerations while conducting relations with them. Psychological factors play an equally—and sometimes, even more—important role as objective factors in dealing with neighbours. And perceptions often play a greater role than the reality on the ground. Therefore, it is important to be extremely sensitive to the perceptions and feelings of our neighbours while dealing with them. We should treat them as equals in all respects, and make them feel important. While considering their proposals and responding to their actions and reactions, we should always try to put ourselves in their position. We should never ignore them or make them feel ignored. There is, therefore, no place in this discourse for the often invoked prescription of 'benign neglect' or 'allowing them to stew in their own juice'. What we may regard as benign neglect is very often seen as an insult or humiliation by our neighbour.

Our neighbours are very sensitive about their identity and sovereignty, particularly while confronting India. They go out of the way to assert their identity and take every available opportunity to reiterate their sovereignty. We should show appreciation for their sentiments instead of resenting them or taking their assertions as unfriendly. We must be very careful in saying and doing things which even implicitly question their identity. We should eschew the tendency, too frequently on display among Indians, of rubbing in commonalities or overstating them. We should generally leave it to them to highlight their commonalities with us. We should also, to the maximum extent possible, avoid taking actions that may be perceived by them as an affront to their sovereignty.

Of course, in its relations with neighbours, India cannot help acting in pursuit of its legitimate national interest, as perceived by it. But in doing so, it must have an enlightened view of its national interest. For example, the unilateral air-dropping of relief supplies in the Tamil-populated areas of Sri Lanka in 1987 could have been avoided. For, it was perceived not only by the government but also by the people at large in Sri Lanka as an assault on the nation's sovereignty. This rankled the Sri Lankans for decades, and even now, the ill feeling generated by this adventure has not been totally obliterated. The unilateral withdrawal of water by India in 1975 at Farakka, after the completion of the construction of the barrage on that site, was projected by the Bangladesh government and perceived by many Bangladeshis, as an affront to their sovereignty. Having constructed the barrage, India had perhaps no alternative to taking this action in pursuit of its national interest. But it could have explained more effectively and persuasively than it did, that this action had to be taken as the last resort, after the failure of all efforts made to arrive at an agreement.

No Interruption of Dialogue

We should maintain dialogue with our neighbours on a regular basis at all levels, including the highest. In any case, we should not be the ones to interrupt the dialogue or allow an unduly long hiatus to appear in the dialogue process. At the regional level, India has been responsible on more than one occasion for the postponement of SAARC summits. This has left other SAARC countries unhappy and resentful. Bilaterally, India suspended the Indo-Pakistan Composite Dialogue following the terrorist attack on Mumbai on 9 November 2008, planned and mounted from Pakistan's territory. Even if there was a justification for putting a freeze on this dialogue for a while because of the pressure of public opinion, there was no justification for its non-resumption for a very long time.

Former Prime Minister P. V. Narasimha Rao kept postponing an official visit to Bangladesh, ultimately not paying such a visit during his entire five-year tenure from 1991 to 1996. The reason for this, given by him privately, was that the Bangladesh government would raise the issue of the distribution of water at Farakka during the visit, which would put him in an embarrassing situation because he had no solution to offer. But this was hardly convincing. We are destined to have difficult, and at times, seemingly intractable, bilateral problems with our neighbours. This cannot be a valid excuse for abjuring or keeping in abeyance summit-level contacts and dialogues that have come to be recognized as an effective means of removing mistrust and suspicion and laying the basis for resolving bilateral issues. If there were any diplomatic designs behind these postponements of dialogue, they were never articulated explicitly and publicly. They, therefore, did not serve any purpose except being viewed as instances of India's arbitrary and overbearing demeanour.

Our relations with neighbours cannot stand still for any length of time. If they are not imparted fresh impetus every now and then, they tend to deteriorate rapidly. In the long run, prolonged stagnation in relations and the interruption of dialogue with neighbours goes against India's interest. In the absence of an exchange of views on controversial issues through multi-level dialogues, the neighbours start attributing all kinds of evil designs to India in relation to these issues, thus further complicating their resolution. They sometimes also take desperate measures in anticipation of wrongly assumed evil designs by India. These can create major problems for both India and its neighbours. A long hiatus in normal contacts results in an alienation of public opinion in the neighbouring countries. It takes a long time after the resumption of contacts to move back to the status quo ante.

India should take a long-term view of its relations with neighbours and should not be thwarted by setbacks or adverse situations that are bound to arise from time to time. While grappling with existing problems, we should not lose sight of the ultimate objective of removing suspicions, restoring confidence, building trust and laying the foundations for a dynamic, vibrant and cooperative relationship.

Not Permitting Stagnation in Bilateral Problems

Bilateral problems between India and its neighbours should never be allowed to fester. There has been a tendency on the part of policymakers in India to let bilateral issues with neighbours simmer so long as the status quo suits India. And when they flare up, the tendency is to find patchwork solutions or somehow manage, rather than to resolve them. Experience shows that bilateral problems, if left unresolved for long, get more complicated with the passage of time. There is also often a recurring opportunity cost of leaving a problem unresolved. Moreover, complacency about a bilateral problem is often a rationalization of a leadership's lack of vision or its incapacity to muster courage and take risks to solve the problem.

In a democratic system, while dealing with a bilateral problem, governments have to often look over the shoulder of the Opposition which may not cooperate, and to show sensitivity to the vote banks which may turn against it if it makes sacrifices in the short run to resolve a problem with its neighbour. It requires assiduous efforts to persuade the Opposition and extraordinary courage to decide on a course of action that may not be popular with a section of the electorate. Very few governments are capable of mustering such courage. Hence, the preference is not to bestir themselves to solve the problem until it acquires crisis proportions.

This complacency, at best, is a sub-optimal choice and at its worst, can be a recipe for disaster in the long run. It is, therefore, incumbent on us to be constantly on the lookout for an opportune moment to solve a problem with our neighbour and to grab it when it comes our way.

This happened when the agreement to resolve the issue of distributing the water of the Ganga at Farakka between India and Bangladesh was reached. Consequently, a major cause of tension in Indo-Bangladesh relations was removed. Farakka has already enjoyed a relatively long shelf life of more than a decade, as a resolved bilateral issue.

India's neighbours often put the onus of solving bilateral problems on India. As the bigger neighbour, India definitely has the responsibility of taking the initiative for solving such problems and as the stronger and more capable party, it is expected to show a degree of magnanimity in its approach towards finding a solution. However, this cannot be an entirely unilateral affair. In most cases, there can be no solution without neighbours recognizing India's compulsions and imperatives and adjusting their positions accordingly.

Making Short-Term Sacrifices for Long-Term Gains

In dealing with its neighbours, India should make sacrifices in the short and medium term for long-term gains. India should consciously, and in a planned manner, invest in the prosperity and stability of its neighbours. Over the past few decades, a number of specific suggestions have been made in this regard. The most important among them was the unilateral extension of duty-free and quota-free access to the Indian market for the exports of its least developed neighbours, particularly Bangladesh, as the other least developed neighbours, that is, Nepal and Bhutan, already enjoy such access. With Sri Lanka, India already has an FTA. This leaves out only Pakistan. There is a strong case for India extending at an appropriate moment, free trade facility to Pakistan too. This would have a positive political impact in the short run and far-reaching economic benefits to both countries in the medium and long run.

Another suggestion, made at the time when there were severe limitations on the amount of resources that Indian companies could invest in neighbouring countries, was to permit convertibility of the Indian rupee on capital account for the limited purpose of investment in the neighbouring countries. Yet another idea advanced has been that India should extend large-size grants and soft-term credits for the development of the physical infrastructure and human resources of the neighbouring countries. This could be done either bilaterally or within the framework of the South Asian Free Trade Agreement (SAFTA). The SAARC Eminent Persons Group, in its report, had suggested the creation of a large-size fund on the lines of the EU Development Fund, to finance projects designed to expand export production capacity of the least developed member countries. Going by the criterion of capacity to pay, India would be required to contribute more than 70 per cent of the total resources of such a fund. So far as Nepal is concerned, India should have provided enough financial and other economic incentives in order to persuade it to agree to undertake major water resources development projects which have been under negotiation for the past several decades without any noticeable progress.

Importance of Non-Reciprocity

India should not, in dealing with neighbours, expect reciprocity from them, at least in the short and medium run. When I. K. Gujral was at the helm of India's foreign policy in 1996–98, non-reciprocity was the principal element of what then came to be known as the Gujral Doctrine. Non-reciprocity makes such an eminent sense for serving India's enlightened self-interest vis-à-vis its neighbours that there is hardly any need for it to be underpinned by a doctrine. For example, greater access to the Indian market through one-way free trade facilities to Bangladesh will enhance the import capacity of Bangladesh. In the present context of the liberalized import regime of Bangladesh and in view of India's comparative advantage over third-country suppliers to Bangladesh, a large part of the increase in imports is likely to be sourced from India.

Besides, at the international level, the doctrine of non-reciprocity in favour of the least developed countries has been accepted in the WTO. During the course of the Doha Round of Trade Negotiations in December 2005 at the Hong Kong Ministerial Meeting, it was agreed that developed countries and similarly placed developing countries that opt to do so, should grant duty-free and quota-free access in their markets to all manufactured exports from the least developed countries. As more developed among developing countries, India is no doubt 'similarly placed' and has, therefore, the moral obligation to extend such treatment at least to its neighbouring least developed countries, particularly to Bangladesh. India has, no doubt, recognized this obligation. But it took more than three years after the Hong Kong agreement to do so and that too in a qualified manner. India has taken an exception from granting free trade treatment for those products that are in the negative list under SAFTA. India applies a sort of non-reciprocity in its trade relations with Pakistan too, in that it extends MFN treatment to imports from Pakistan without the latter according similar treatment to imports from India. However, as already mentioned, in its enlightened self-interest, India could have moved a step forward and offered unilateral free trade treatment to Pakistan also without much damage to its industry.

A policy of non-reciprocity on the part of India is also called for in its cultural relations with neighbours. Due to their identity problem and also for protective purposes, neighbouring countries tend to restrict cultural exchanges with India. In Pakistan, imports of cultural goods like films, videos and CDs from India are banned, while in other neighbouring countries, these are traded under severe restrictions. Moreover, some of the neighbours have, from time to time, imposed an absolute ban on Indian cultural shows or performances in their countries. This has at times provoked Indian policymakers to retaliate by banning or putting restrictions on the visits of individual artists and cultural ensembles from neighbouring countries. This is short-sighted and counter-productive. It only weakens the secular and democratic elements in the cultural community of these countries, who look up to India for inspiration, nourishment of their creative talent and the fullest possible realization of their potential. It thus leaves the cultural space open for domination by fundamentalist, obscurantist and extremist elements. In the long run, this engenders cultural isolation and increases the cultural distance between India and its neighbours. As culture and politics are inextricably linked, a policy of cultural isolation influences the political stance of these countries towards India in a negative way.

Maintaining People-to-People Contacts

India should, under all circumstances, seek to maintain and expand people-to-people contacts with its neighbours. These contacts should not normally be allowed to be subjected to the vicissitudes of bilateral political relations. As a relatively more open society, India has little to fear from enhanced flows of people and ideas from the neighbouring countries. On the other hand, people-to-people contacts offer India an opportunity to influence societies in these countries in wholesome, pluralistic and democratic directions. It was because of these considerations that at the Bangalore SAARC Summit in 1986, India took the initiative of proposing and getting accepted a number of proposals for enhancing people-to-people contact among the SAARC members. These were:

- Launching a South Asian Broadcasting Programme covering both radio and television
- Taking concrete steps to facilitate tourism in the region, including facilities for limited convertibility of national currencies for tourists from SAARC countries

- Establishment of a SAARC Documentation Centre for students, scholars and researchers to have ready access to reliable and up-to-date information on technical, scientific and developmental matters
- Institution of SAARC Scholarships, SAARC Fellowships and SAARC Chairs
- Establishment of a Youth Volunteer Programme in SAARC, under which volunteers from one country would be able to work in other countries in the fields of agriculture and forestry extension

Security concerns have been a major obstacle to enhancing the flow of people and ideas, and even goods and services, between India and its neighbours. It is, to some extent understandable, given the conflictual nature of the political relations we often have with our important neighbours. But the threats to security that our policymakers perceive as emanating from neighbouring countries are often exaggerated. In any case, they do not justify the draconian measures that we have put in place to restrict the movement of people and ideas from these countries. It goes without saying that our neighbours put equally, if not more, severe restrictions. Thus, it becomes a vicious circle, widening the already existing distance between India and the neighbouring country concerned.

Safeguarding Basic Interests

There are, however, limits to India acting unilaterally in favour of its neighbours and making sacrifices without seeking reciprocity. India also has its national interest to safeguard in dealing with its neighbours. Democratically elected governments in India have to take into account public opinion on bilateral issues and pacify domestic lobbies that may perceive their interests to be threatened by India's grant of concessions to its neighbours. India may, in the long-term perspective, eschew reciprocity, but it has to insist on mutuality of interests, which is the basis for any sustainable bilateral relationship. For example, in an FTA with a neighbour, India may extend unilateral free trade treatment to its neighbour, particularly if it happens to be a least developed country; but this will have to be subject to the condition of the latter agreeing to join the process of liberalization at a subsequent stage, say, after five years, and generally to commit itself to eventually freeing its market for India in order for the FTA to be a reality within a finite period of time, as mandated under Article XXIV of GATT (1994). Similarly, in any agreement with a neighbour on sharing the water of a common river, India can show generosity by making a disproportionate sacrifice of its claims in order to reach a settlement; but while doing so, it cannot be oblivious of its obligation to ensure that its long-term interest of continuing to obtain the maximum possible supply of water for meeting its far greater need is not sacrificed.

In dealing with Nepal, India, while extending, as it presently does, almost unlimited access to Nepali workers into its labour market, might agree to the reciprocal entry of Indian labour into Nepal being subjected to some restrictions. But once Indian workers are granted entry into Nepal, the Indian public opinion will not permit the government to put up with official discriminations against them, particularly when India is treating Nepali immigrants as its own citizens for all practical purposes. Similarly, it will be politically, and otherwise, impossible for India to accept the claim of a section of Bangladeshi policymakers, intellectuals and think tanks that Bangladeshis have the right to migrate to India. It will also not be possible for India to ignore its genuine security interest as perceived by it, in dealing with its neighbours. For example, India cannot be expected to countenance any of its neighbours permitting terrorists the use of their territory to carry out subversive activities or mount terrorist attacks against India. These set out some of the *Lakshman Rekha*s (absolute limits) that India would not expect its neighbours to cross.

Factoring Neighbours' Interests into Broader Policymaking

Our neighbours feel threatened by some of the policies we adopt for serving our global interests and safeguarding security interests going beyond the region. In response, they take actions that introduce further complications in our bilateral relations with them. India should take initiatives to explain to its neighbours the real intentions behind such policies and factor their interests into such policymaking. It could even devise structured consultations for this purpose. However, in the ultimate analysis, India cannot downsize itself or neglect its broader security interests only in order to remove the misperceptions of its neighbours regarding the policies it adopts in these realms.

Who is Pro-India or Anti-India

There is a tendency among Indian officials dealing with neighbouring countries as well as the media and the intellectual community to brand political groups or individuals in these countries as pro-India or anti-India. For example, in Bangladesh, pro-liberation elements are regarded as pro-India and anti-liberation elements as anti-India. On this basis, the Awami League is regarded as pro-India and the BNP as anti-India.

In Nepal, the Communist Party of Nepal (CPN) (Maoist) and the Royalists were regarded as anti-India and the Nepali Congress as pro-India. There is no doubt a historical background to these categorizations. In Bangladesh, India supported the cause of liberation and the Indian armed forces fought along with those who waged the war for the liberation of their motherland. These freedom fighters were inspired by the values of democracy, secularism and pluralism which we cherish in India, and when they won the war, they put in place a state structure broadly based on these values. The Awami League was in the vanguard of this movement. It is, therefore, natural that it is regarded as pro-India.

The Nepali Congress was the first political party in Nepal that carried out a prolonged struggle for, and ultimately succeeded in ushering in democracy in Nepal. In its struggle, the party was inspired by the values cherished by the Indian National Congress. Some of the stalwarts of this party had fought side-by-side with Indian leaders for India's independence. On the other hand, the Royalists, in their bid to preserve the autocratic monarchical regime, were arrayed against the Nepali Congress. The CPN (Maoist) was, until the Jan Andolan of 2006, perceived by India as undemocratic and perpetrators of violence and destruction.

In spite of these historical reasons, the categorization of people in our neighbourhood as pro-India and anti-India is an oversimplification. History is important and ought to be kept in mind while formulating foreign policy or for that matter, any policy, but it cannot be the only guiding factor. To decide on a course of action, we have to go by the current reality on the ground. An individual or a group may, over time, undergo radical transformation in its attitude and approach. Yesterday's anti-India elements may become staunchly pro-India today. The character and ideology of a political party may undergo transformation with a change in circumstances or leadership. For example, in Bangladesh, since its liberation in 1971, secularism has been compromised to a substantial extent, with the tacit approval of all political parties, including the Awami League. Though after the return to power in January 2009 by a thumping majority of the Awami League-led coalition, there is an expectation that Bangladesh will go back to the original stipulation on secularism in its Constitution, it is unlikely that under the present circumstances, Prime Minister Sheikh Hasina will be in a hurry to take the risk of initiating a move to expunge from the Bangladesh Constitution all the anti-secular clauses that have been inserted since the 1975 coup d'état.

The Nepali Congress, when in power, did not see it in its perceived national interest to always toe the Indian line. After the Jan Andolan, the

CPN (Maoist) gave up guerrilla warfare and joined the political mainstream under a democratic framework. India played an important role in this transition. Besides, since India is itself seeking to forge a friendly relationship with China, the hobnobbing of CPN (Maoist) with China should not by itself make them anti-Indian. Moreover, the CPN (Maoist), as much as other major political parties in Nepal, know that in dealing with India they can ignore the cultural, religious, ethnic and historical commonalities they share with India only at their own peril. They are also expected to be aware of Nepal's economic dependence on India.

India looms so large in the calculations and policymaking process of any political party in power in a neighbouring country that it regards its ability to manage relations with India as a litmus test of its success. Therefore, unless driven by desperation, either by domestic compulsion or India's indifference, every party in power will try to develop a relationship with India that is conducive to serving mutual interest. It is, therefore, incumbent on India to meet all these parties and the governments led by them halfway instead of treating them as anti-India, and hence, untouchable.

In almost all major parties dominant in the politics of the neighbouring countries, there are both pro- and anti-India elements. For example, though the leadership of the BNP has relied on anti-liberation forces to come to and remain in power, there are many pro-liberation elements in it. Ziaur Rahman, who founded and first led the BNP, was himself a prominent freedom fighter. The Awami League, on the other hand, has been infiltrated by anti-liberation elements masquerading as the supporters of the liberation ethos. The Jamaat, no doubt, has many religious fundamentalists in its ranks. But all religious fundamentalists are not communalists. And all communalists are not necessarily anti-India. Thus, no political party in the neighbouring countries should be regarded as implacably anti-India or decisively pro-India.

In dealing with its neighbours India should proceed on the assumption that every party and individual in the policymaking loop will be fiercely nationalistic. They will first and foremost seek to serve their national interests. In several cases, these interests may be in conflict with those of India. For example, in Bangladesh, there is virtually a national consensus on the Farakka issue. Most people believe that the Farakka barrage should never have been built and the best course would be to dismantle it. In Pakistan, similarly, there is a consensus that Kashmir should rightfully belong to Pakistan. In Nepal, a large section of the people is against taking up the construction of large dams on common rivers, which

India considers to be extremely important to its national interest. We should not expect groups in these countries to easily depart from these national positions and take a view that is not in consonance with their perception of national interest. These groups should not, therefore, be regarded as anti-India, but as favouring the interests of their own nations. It will be counterproductive to brand as anti-India any group that champions its national cause which may happen to be in conflict with that of India. At this rate, we would end up branding the entire world as anti-India. This will amount to a self-inflicted paralysis of Indian diplomacy.

Notes

1. Calculated from data accessed from the International Monetary Fund, Direction of Trade Statistics database, http://elibrary-data.imf.org/ (accessed on 4 January 2015).
2. Nisha Taneja, 'Informal Trade in South Asia: How to Channelise to a Formal Route?' (Briefing Paper of Consumer Unity & Trust Society [CUTS] International, Jaipur, 2005).
3. Calculated from data accessed from the International Monetary Fund, Direction of Trade Statistics database, http://elibrary-data-imf.org/ (accessed on 4 January, 2015).
4. Nisha Taneja puts it at $2 billion in her article 'Informal Trade in the SAARC Region: Implications for FTAs', *Economic and Political Weekly*, Vol. 39, No. 51 (18 December 2004).
5. This figure of $10 billion is an estimate made by the author. Nisha Taneja and Pallavi Kalita have estimated the bilateral trade potential between India and Pakistan to be $25.2 billion in 2010, 10 times larger than the current $2.5 billion trade. See Nisha Taneja and Pallavi Kalita, 'Most Favoured Nation: New Trade Opportunities for India and Pakistan', *Economic and Political Weekly*, Vol. 46, No. 49 (3 December 2011).

Appendix

Address by His Excellency Mr Muchkund Dubey, the High Commissioner of India to Bangladesh, at the Rotary Club of Dacca, on 15 January 1980*

I am most grateful to the President of the Rotary Club of Dacca for inviting me to address this weekly meeting of the Rotary Club. I regard it a great privilege to have this opportunity to meet you all and exchange views on a subject which is legitimately our common concern. I am aware that it is not an easy task for an envoy of India to speak in Bangladesh on such a sensitive subject as Indo-Bangladesh relations. In the beginning, I showed a preference for speaking on certain aspects of multilateral development cooperation in which I have acquired some expertise. However, I took the gentle hint of the organizers that they would prefer me to speak on Indo-Bangladesh relations and therefore, decided to abide by their wishes. I am not sure whether I would be able to cut any new ground in dealing with the subject; but I can assure you that I shall do my utmost to avoid the common pitfall of being platitudinous or propagandist while expressing my views.

The current relationship between India and Bangladesh can be characterized as reasonably satisfactory. India would like the relations to be closer, warmer and more cordial. Our desire to have closer relations is not guided by any ulterior motive as is so readily presumed in certain quarters here. In fact, a desire for friendship and closer relations need not always be motivated by specific political, strategic or economic purpose. Such a desire is an aspect of human gregariousness which imparts greater meaning and purpose to our collective life. It is an innate urge and a reward by itself.

But beyond this, it has its advantages. Very often, it suits nations just as it suits individuals to do things together than doing them alone. On the other hand, equally often there is an opportunity cost for doing things alone rather than together. The more closely the two countries are situated, the greater the geographical compulsions and the complementarities in their economies, the greater will be the gain by cooperating and hence the greater will be the opportunity cost in foregoing cooperation. Seen in the light of these criteria, no two countries are better placed than are India and Bangladesh. In many instances, the two countries have inherited the same system of physical and institutional infrastructure such as in the fields of railways, other modes of transport, water resources management etc. It is much more convenient and fruitful to forge links of cooperation through this system than look for assistance from third countries which are situated far

* This address is included almost without any change because, though confined to Indo-Bangladesh relations, it brings out challenges that are typical of those India faces in dealing with other neighbours.

off and which are operating entirely different systems in these areas. Because of proximity, there is an obvious freight advantage in exchanging goods and for the same reason such exchanges can take place with greater speed than with other countries.

Due to the broad similarity of socio-economic conditions prevailing in the two countries, the technology evolved by them is more appropriate for the needs of each other. If something goes wrong in the process of industrial or technological operation, it is much more convenient and expeditious to call for experts and consultants from across the border and get it rectified. Finally, cooperation with a country which has gone through a similar development experience and faces similar development problems can be much more conducive to developing self-reliance in the long run than with those which have a different development experience and which generally provide technology developed in an entirely different socio-economic and cultural milieu. An important factor making for complementarities between the two countries is the diversified and sophisticated industrial and technological base which India has been able to build since independence. Many other developing countries such as Libya, Tanzania and Iraq have recently made a decisive shift from economic and technical collaboration with more advanced countries and have started procuring their supplies of machinery, equipment, technology and consultancy services increasingly from India.

While saying all this, I would like to make it clear that in spite of the geographical necessity and other forms of complementarities, it is not indispensable for Bangladesh to have economic cooperation with India. In this age of highly advanced science and technology, geographical disadvantages are not difficult to transcend. If there is the willingness to pay the price, everything that Bangladesh can expect to get through cooperation with India can be substituted by supplies from other countries. However, though it is not indispensable for Bangladesh to cooperate with India, it can be certainly profitable for Bangladesh in many areas to forge links of cooperation with India. If Bangladesh shows cost or profit consciousness and wants to cooperate, we will heartily reciprocate. If, on the other hand, for some reasons Bangladesh decides to dispense with cooperation with us and substitutes it with cooperation with other countries, we will fully respect its prerogative to do so. It will be appreciated that by paying some price, India can also afford to go without such cooperation because substitutability is available as much to India as to Bangladesh.

We are bound to reach a stalemate and our relations will stagnate if we make cooperation between our two countries in the economic and other fields conditional upon the solution of particular problems, howsoever important they may be. Problems are bound to arise between close neighbours like India and Bangladesh. What is important is to ensure that these problems do not come in the way of the long-term objective of the two countries marching forward together on the path of development. By all means, all efforts should be made to solve such problems expeditiously so that they do not become a festering sore and affect our relations in the long run. But we must avoid distorting, exaggerating and using such problems for sectarian purposes. This is a very tall order in the light of our past and current experience. There is no doubt that the government has a very important role to play here, even where the press is not fully under its control. The government can do a great deal by way of presenting a balanced picture and bridging the information gap which often becomes the main factor accounting for distortion or exaggeration.

To a very great extent, our problems are psychological. This psychology is derived from our common past. At times, it is also due to what one can call the small-neighbour-big-neighbour syndrome. Many of us in India tend to take Bangladesh for granted. Either we are too attached to Bangladesh or we become unrealistic enough to try to forget all about it. Either we expect too much from Bangladesh or we give it up altogether. We have in our minds a presumed and set pattern of behavioural expectations from Bangladesh. If, for an entirely valid and legitimate reason, Bangladesh does not conform to this set pattern of expectations, we tend to overreact and sometimes go to the extent of characterizing this as ingratitude or anti-Indian.

Now, this sentimental basis for a relationship is as unhealthy and undesirable between nations as between individuals. To the extent that it is present, we need to impart to our relation a perspective of detachment and objectivity. We have to show greater respect for each other. We have to judge Bangladesh's attitude towards us and its stance in a particular situation affecting us entirely on its merit. We must not see it through the prism of a predetermined pattern of expectations from Bangladesh.

On the side of Bangladesh, the psychological factor operates in the sense of every move towards improving relations with it being viewed with suspicion. Whatever step is taken is regarded either as a deliberate, pre-planned and conscious effort by India to dominate or as having the potential of assuming a form of domination. This kind of psychological complex which I have earlier described as the big-neighbour-small-neighbour syndrome is understandable because of the unique situation of Bangladesh vis-à-vis India. But it will be appreciated that this is not a healthy trait of a nation's personality and certainly it is not the basis for forging a normal relationship between two close neighbours. It is important for India to understand this psychological complex, make allowance for it in its dealings with Bangladesh and ignore it or not feel touchy about it. But it is equally important on the part of Bangladesh to judge issues or schemes and proposals for cooperation on their merits and cooperate in all those cases where it is in the mutual interest of the two countries to do so.

Part of the reason why a move or a proposal for establishing closer relations with India is not taken at its face value is historical, in the sense that for more than two decades when Bangladesh was a part of Pakistan, a conscious and sustained effort was made to treat India as an enemy. There is evidence to demonstrate that the people of then East Pakistan did not share this point of view. The emergence of Bangladesh as a sovereign state should normally have been a final act of disapproval by the people of Bangladesh of this bogey of seeing India as an enemy.

We fully recognize and respect Bangladesh's distinctive national personality. It is not at all necessary for us to seek to define it in terms of whether it is Bengali or Bangladeshi. We take it for granted, because in the ultimate analysis it is an essential attribute of sovereignty.

I would, however, humbly urge that it is not necessary for Bangladesh to deny its cultural heritage, particularly that which we have the privilege of sharing with it, in order to maintain its distinctive national personality. France, the UK and the USA do not deny Mozart because he was born in Austria, or Beethoven and Bach because they were born in Germany. Switzerland claims Voltaire and Rousseau as its own even though they were born French. Similarly, Switzerland never thought of giving up speaking French, German or Italian for fear of its national identity being lost. All European countries take great pride in their common cultural heritage, irrespective of the languages, nationalities and ideologies dividing them. It is thus possible to share a common cultural heritage without being subservient to each other. In this context one cannot but view with a sense of dismay the current restrictions on cultural contacts between India and Bangladesh. There is a cultural agreement between the two countries as a broad framework for cooperation, but for the last four years it has not been possible to finalize any annual programme for cultural cooperation within the framework of the cultural agreement.

There are also certain internationally agreed criteria which must govern the relationship between India and Bangladesh. As developing and non-aligned countries, India and Bangladesh are committed under the terms of various resolutions adopted in the forums of the non-aligned, the Group of 77 and the UN to cooperate with each other both bilaterally and with other developing countries. Moreover, as a country which is at a relatively higher stage of development, India must assume special obligations towards Bangladesh which is among the least developed among developing countries. For example, Bangladesh can expect tariff concessions from India without being obliged to grant reciprocal treatment. Similarly, in matters of extension of credit and supply of essential commodities, Bangladesh can expect to be accorded special treatment. These so-called concessions or special treatment by India should not be regarded as a favour for Bangladesh but as a moral obligation on the part of India. Even otherwise, as the closest neighbour more favourably placed in certain respects, it is the moral duty of India to meet the urgent needs of Bangladesh without expecting reciprocity and even when it involves some sacrifice. For in the ultimate analysis, the prosperity and stability of Bangladesh is bound to redound to the benefit of India. For example, if there is a short supply of an essential commodity in Bangladesh which can be made good most speedily by India, it is the moral responsibility of India to respond positively to Bangladesh's request for the supply of such a commodity. In certain situations, I shall be in favour of India supplying such commodities even if there is a shortage of it in India itself. This should be the case where the total requirement of Bangladesh is a small part of the supplies available in India, where non-availability of the commodity in Bangladesh will cause immense human suffering and where India is the only source from where supplies can arrive on time.

However, in any bilateral relationship the interests of both sides are involved. There are a number of issues in India's relations with Bangladesh in which India's vital interests are at stake. It will be unrealistic to expect that any government or leadership in India will be able to sacrifice these interests unless the sacrifice is shared and is in mutual interest. It is not possible to build a lasting relationship between two nations by systematically ignoring the interest of one of them, howsoever fortunately placed it may be. For no country can be placed fortunately enough in all respects, and a developing country even less so. Bangladesh must have a perception of our vital interests in order to ensure that our relations are based on really firm foundations. A relationship based on a systematic belittling of the interest of the other side is bound to receive a setback sooner or later, rather sooner than later. The issues which are of vital interest to India are those which affect our territorial integrity, security or sovereignty, which have a bearing on the future of the coming generations, which affect the well being of the millions of our poorer masses. In all these matters, no party can be expected to reach an agreement unless it is in its interest too. It cannot be expected to take the next step without ensuring that the measures already agreed to are being faithfully implemented by the other party.

To conclude, India should wait until Bangladesh makes up its mind regarding the extent and nature of cooperation with India. We should not feel hurt when we are deliberately ignored or sidetracked. But so long as we have normal relations with Bangladesh, we shall certainly protest if we are discriminated against. India should neither impose itself on Bangladesh nor should it isolate itself from Bangladesh out of any feeling of hurt. India should wait till our mutual relations are seen in the correct perspective from both sides. We should never burn our boats. We should do our utmost to keep intact the sinews of our relationship even if for the moment they are deprived of vital circulation. We should seek to preserve the institutional infrastructure of our relation even if for the time being we are unable to raise on its foundation a superstructure of active cooperation. We should be extremely sensitive to those feelings in Bangladesh which arise out of its being the relatively smaller neighbour vis-à-vis India. We should continue to make sacrifices and concessions on a non-reciprocal basis not as a gesture of generosity but as a moral responsibility whenever it can alleviate human suffering in Bangladesh or meet a critical need in the process of its development.

But I shall be less than frank if I do not say that beyond a point India cannot afford to remain aloof from Bangladesh. For what happens in Bangladesh may crucially affect India's stability and security, and vice versa. Moreover, such is the nature of our relationship that it cannot remain stagnant for long without getting worse. However desperately we try to avoid or ignore each other we will not be able to dispense with each other. So would it, therefore, not be appropriate to give up this pretension of our mutual expendability and embark on the path of positive cooperation right from the beginning?

THREE Democracy and Governance in Bangladesh

Historical Background

The Bangladeshis have for decades demonstrated their penchant for democracy. They have resolutely opposed every form of tutelage, exploitation and denial of human rights. They have also repeatedly and strongly asserted their cultural identity—both religious and linguistic. In fact, they have made one of the most heroic sacrifices anywhere in the world in pursuit of these objectives and values.

The language movement in Bangladesh started on 21 February 1952, when four Bangladeshi students[1] became martyrs for opposing the imposition of Urdu and demanding the rightful status and place for the Bengali language. Since then, *Ekushe* (The Twenty-First) has become the symbol of the celebration of the Bengali language. One has to be present in Bangladesh on 21 February to understand what the mother tongue means to the Bangladeshis. One of the most popular songs sung in every home during the Liberation War (1970–71) was:

Amar bhaiyer rokte rangano,
Ekushe February
Ami ki bhulite pari?

The twenty-first February,
Besmeared with the blood of my brothers,
Can I ever forget it?[2]

In the political realm, whenever the Bangladeshis got an opportunity to participate in a fair and free election, they returned to power with a resounding majority, the party, or the coalition thereof, representing their cultural aspirations and identity. The last time it happened before the liberation of Bangladesh, was in the 1969 Pakistan general elections when Sheikh Mujibur Rahman got an absolute majority to head not only the government in the then East Pakistan, but that of the whole of Pakistan.

Thousands of Bangladeshis made the ultimate sacrifice of their lives and millions suffered unprecedented suppression and humiliation for the same cause during the Liberation War. The strength of the Liberation Movement should not be judged merely by the military clout of those who participated in it or in terms of whether they could have won the independence of Bangladesh on their own, without the help of the Indian Army. What is really important is the fact that the movement released a force that was irresistible until independence was won. Without the intervention of the Indian Armed Forces, it would have taken a somewhat longer time before the goal was achieved; but ultimately, victory was inevitable. Moreover, the spirit of the liberation movement permeated all aspects of life—political, economic, social and cultural. It was powerfully articulated in the poems, songs and plays composed, written and staged during that period. The liberation, for Bangladeshis, meant according rightful status to their language, exercising their fundamental human rights and fulfilling basic economic needs. In his famous poem, *Swadhinata Tumi* (O Liberation), Shamsur Rahman, the greatest poet of the Liberation War and one of the greatest poets of Bangladesh in the subcontinent's post-independence period, stated,

Swadhinata tumi,
Chaitra mase kalboisakhir matta jhapta
Shrabane, akool Meghnar book
Swadhinata tumi,
Khokar gaye rangeen kurta.

O Liberation,
You are the wild assault of the cyclone in the month of Chaitra
You are the heart of the river Meghna which has breached its banks
In the month of Shravan.
O Liberation,
You are the red shirt on my child's body.[3]

Another equally famous poet of the Liberation War, Nirmalendu Goon, wrote:

Amar dharmo niye kono din proshno koro na, jodi chao,
Ekti phooler naame, doyel pakhir naame,
Padma, Meghna, Jamuna, Kansha, Gorai, Madhumati, Sheetalakshya,

Matamuhuri o Brahmaputrer naame,
Bangabandhur naame,
Garo paharer udyam buno batasher naame,
Rabindranather naame,
Rajdanda hatey nibo.

Never raise a question regarding my religion, if you want,
In the name of a flower, in the name of the national bird, Maina,
In the name of the rivers, Padma, Meghna, Jamuna, Kansha, Gorai,
Madhumati, Sheetalakshya,
Matamuhuri and the Brahmaputra,
In the name of Bangabandhu,
In the name of the enthusiastic wild wind of the Garo Hills,
In the name of Rabindranath,
I shall take the sceptre in my hand.[4]

A Nation Divided

However, even during the Liberation War, a section of Bangladeshis opposed liberation and acted as the collaborators (commonly referred to as 'Razakars') of the oppressive Pakistani regime. Some Bangladeshis did not really collaborate, but were indifferent to the Liberation War and would have preferred not to be separated from Pakistan. At the time of the war, the tide of public opinion turned overwhelmingly towards those who were fighting for liberation while the anti-liberation elements and those not very enthusiastic about it were reduced to a thin minority. However, the latter never disappeared from the political scene.

Within a couple of years after the liberation of Bangladesh, these elements started resurfacing in the country. Some of those who were deprived of their citizenship for actively working against liberation started reclaiming it. Others took advantage of the democratic privileges available to all citizens after liberation to join different political parties and groups or form groups of their own. Several religious groups and parties lying dormant during the Liberation War also got revived during this process, with the help of sizeable amounts of aid from foreign countries. Thus, within a few years after liberation, Bangladesh found itself divided sharply into two groups—pro-liberation and anti-liberation. This division exists even today and a bridge across this divide is yet to be built.

Almost coinciding with the division between pro-liberation and anti-liberation forces, another interesting divide appeared in Bangladesh—the one between Bengali and Bangladeshi nationalism. Bengali nationalism gives salience to the linguistic feature and as such is regarded as being closer to West Bengal and India, whereas in Bangladeshi nationalism, the religious aspect is accorded greater salience. However, the divide between these two forms of nationalism is somewhat artificial. For, the overwhelming number of those who believe in Bangladeshi nationalism are the ones who are steeped in Bengali culture and almost all those who believe in Bengali nationalism are never forgetful about their Islamic identity.

Another interesting development in the context of the evolution of the democratic process in Bangladesh has been the emergence, a few years after liberation, of a sharply bipolar political spectrum. Two political parties have dominated the scene: the Awami League, ostensibly representing pro-liberation and Bengali identity, and the BNP, supposed to represent Bangladeshi identity. However, this division, though convenient for understanding the political system in Bangladesh, is grossly oversimplified. A very large number of BNP followers are staunchly pro-liberation and very proud of their Bengali heritage. The BNP has also persistently emphasized the contribution of its leaders, particularly that of its founder, Ziaur Rehman, to the Liberation War. On the other hand, there is no dearth of obscurantists and religious fundamentalists in the ranks of the Awami League. Besides, its leadership has constantly felt the need, for the sake of winning votes and remaining in power, to placate and pander to religious elements, including the extremists.

However, the fact remains that Bangladeshi society has remained divided since 1975. No reconciliation has been achieved between the pro-liberation and anti-liberation forces. There is no consensus that both the ruling and the Opposition parties are part of the same system of governance as established under the Constitution. In spite of the state functioning under a nationally adopted Constitution, there is no agreement on the rules of the game for conducting the parliamentary process. The party in power generally remains hostile to the Opposition and a deliberate effort is made not to give the latter its dues. As a result, the Opposition suffers from a sense of alienation from governance as well as the parliamentary process and therefore, resorts to unconstitutional and unparliamentary means to make its presence felt. No doubt, transfer of power has taken place after each general election, but immediately after a duly elected government has come to power, the Opposition has resorted to illegal and undemocratic means, such as continuous boycott of Parliament and frequent *hartal*s (work stoppages), to topple the government in power. This has come in the way of the functioning of the democratic system, eroded democratic institutions and inflicted untold harm on the economy of the country. On the other hand, not very different from the conditions prevailing in India, the party in power has resorted to all possible means, legal or illegal, to perpetuate itself in power. These have included misappropriating public funds to amass personal wealth and funds for the party. This has resulted in a large-scale criminalization of politics and the development of a nexus between criminals, politicians and civil servants. This has also included rigging elections and undermining key democratic institutions like the Parliament, the judiciary and the Election Commission. Moreover, as in the case of India, in Bangladesh too, the major political parties have no internal democracy and have been characterized by dynastic succession of leadership, diktats from the supreme leader and cronyism. The institution of the Election Commission was so thoroughly compromised at one point that the country had to resort to the device of a caretaker government coming into being after the completion of the term of the previous government, mainly to hold parliamentary elections, on the basis of which a new government could be formed. This device became a part of the Constitution through the 13th Amendment.

Setback to Democracy and Military Rule

It is worth recalling that in spite of the fact that Bangladesh, after liberation, adopted a fully democratic constitution based on a multi-party system, periodic elections, the guarantee of fundamental rights, and providing for such key democratic institutions as the Parliament, judiciary and the Election Commission, the country does not have a tradition of uninterrupted democracy. Three years after the Constitution came into force, the first Prime Minister of Bangladesh, Sheikh Mujibur Rahman, amended the Constitution to introduce a single-party government by a party called the Bangladesh Krishak Shramik Awami League (BAKSAL). Sheikh Mujib established BAKSAL by amalgamating other pro-liberation parties with the Awami League. The suspension of the other parties under the BAKSAL regime was one of the reasons behind the frustration that led to the violent coup against Sheikh Mujib in August 1975, in which he and almost his entire progeny were killed. After a couple of coups and counter coups, General Ziaur Rahman came to power in November 1975. Even though he tried to impart democratic legitimacy to his government by giving up his position in the Army, setting up his own political party, namely the BNP, and getting elected as President on behalf of the party, he basically ran an autocratic government with the help of the Armed Forces. At the time it was brought into being, the BNP had no grassroots support or structure and consisted of elements drawn from anti-Awami League groups and political parties, particularly the religious ones, some nouveau riche businessmen, industrialists and a handful of ex-army officers. After Ziaur Rahman's assassination in 1980 by one of the seniormost Bangladeshi army generals and his one-time close confidante, Vice President Justice Sattar subsequently got elected as President, on a BNP ticket, though it was believed to be a 'managed election'. During the brief spell of Sattar's Presidency, it was the Army that exercised the greatest influence on the government from behind the scene. This, however, changed when the Army took direct control of the government after its Chief, General Ershad, staged a coup in 1982. Ershad also ruled the country with the help of the Army and was as autocratic, if not more, as Ziaur Rehman. In trying to legitimize himself in power, he followed exactly the same path as charted out by Ziaur Rehman. He formed a party of his own called the Jatiyo Dal (Nationalist Party), aligned with religious parties and got elected as the President.

Both Ziaur Rehman and Ershad remained in power with the tacit support of Western countries. The support came in the name of good governance and their so-called commitment to development. The façade of democratic legitimacy acquired by these military rulers was regarded as sufficient by the Western powers to salvage their democratic conscience. Towards the end of the 1980s, when nepotism, corruption and misgovernance under Ershad reached the nadir, a movement launched jointly by the two major political parties of Bangladesh and joined by a number of minor political parties, ultimately led to his overthrow and the ushering in of a democratically elected government in 1991. This form of government has continued since then, but with the flaws and aberrations described earlier.

One can derive the following conclusions from this brief history of military, camouflaged as democratic governance in Bangladesh:

- Bangladeshis cannot take their democracy for granted. To borrow a phrase from John Stuart Mill, and substituting the word 'freedom' used by him by the word 'democracy': 'Democracy does not descend upon people; it comes to those who deserve it'.
- The military is always lurking in the background in Bangladesh to take over the reins of power when things go terribly wrong in popular perception. It takes over ostensibly to set things right but in reality, it does so to wield autocratic power to safeguard its own collective and individual interests and those of its allies.

- Each time a military coup takes place and during the period when a military dictatorship is in power, democratic traditions suffer a shock and democratic institutions get severely eroded. The vestiges left by military regimes in Bangladesh have been very aptly summarized by Rounaq Jahan, an eminent political scientist:

  During the tenure of cantonment rule, we witnessed monopoly control of State power by the executive; State sponsored party building; emergence of intelligence agencies as political players; 'managed' elections; revival of political use of Islam to mobilize regime support; removal of secularism and socialism as fundamental principles of State from the Constitution; institutionalization of corruption'.[5]

- Whenever the military has an upper hand, it seeks to acquire a permanent role for itself in governance so that it can continue to advance its interests even after there is a transfer of power to a democratically elected government.
- There is an inevitable ascendancy of religious forces during a military regime, dilution of the pro-liberation spirit and undermining of pro-liberation forces. This is because if major political parties, particularly the Awami League, have to be kept out of power in a façade of democracy based on rigged elections, the military has to fall back upon the support of religious political parties and other religious groups. Besides, over the last few decades, there has been a considerable accentuation of religious overtones in the training of the Bangladesh Armed Forces. It is also believed in some quarters that Pakistan's external intelligence agency, the Inter-Services Intelligence (ISI) has till recently exercised considerable influence on the Bangladesh Army through the country's main military intelligence agency, the Directorate General of Forces Intelligence. This association with ISI resulted in the accentuation of religious overtones in the orientation of the Armed Forces of Bangladesh and the military government adopting a softer attitude towards religious forces.
- In this era of rising democratic consciousness, the army generals do not find it convenient to rule directly, but prefer to do so under the façade of democracy. This is more so in Bangladesh mainly because of the tremendous influence that the major world economic powers, particularly the US and the EU, exercise on the government in power in Bangladesh. These countries provide the main market for Bangladesh's principal export—that is, readymade garments—and extend financial and technical assistance to it.

Above all, they also determine the extent of Bangladesh's involvement in UN peacekeeping operations which has emerged as a major source of foreign exchange earnings and which brings economic benefits directly to the members of the armed forces. Since curbing corruption figures very high on the agenda of the aid programmes of major aid-giving countries, one of the first moves of a military government that comes to power is to crack down on corruption.

These anomalies and distortions in the Bangladesh political system appeared and became accentuated over a period of time after the liberation of the country, but they assumed most grotesque proportions by the end of Begum Khaleda Zia's second term as the Prime Minister of Bangladesh in 2006. Her elder son Tareq Zia became the main centre of corruption in the country. He assumed extra-legal powers and several branches of the government became subservient to him.

The domestic politics of Bangladesh was poised in a delicate situation at the beginning of 2007. The country was heading towards a general election which was doomed to be a farce. The caretaker government which came to power after the expiry of the five-year term of Begum Khaleda Zia, had been reconstituted by President Iajuddin Ahmed, following the resignation of a number of members in protest against the arbitrary arrests of people in the name of curbing corruption and preventing lawlessness, in wanton violation of human rights. The reconstituted caretaker government was heavily tilted in favour of the BNP and the Bangladesh Jamaat-e-Islami combine. Subsequently, this was also dismissed and the President, who had been handpicked for the post by Begum Khaleda Zia, and whose allegiance to the BNP was widely known, took over the direct control of the government. He declared his intention to go ahead with the general elections as scheduled on 22 January 2007 in spite of the prolonged agitation of the Awami League and its allies for the replacement of the Election Commissioner whose links with the BNP were well known, and for a drastic revision of the electoral roll which had been heavily rigged, mainly by the removal of millions of pro-Awami League voters. This left the Awami League and its allies with no alternative but to announce a boycott of the elections.

Military-Backed Caretaker Government

The country was thus heading towards a disaster of monumental proportions. If the predictably rigged elections had taken place, there would have been large-scale and widespread disturbances and violence, verging on civil war. The situation was so serious that even the UN was compelled to issue a statement in which it urged 'the non-party Caretaker Government and the Election Commission to create a level playing field and to ensure that parties can have confidence in the electoral process'. It warned that 'Bangladesh's democratic advances and international standing will be negatively affected if the current crisis continues'.[6]

It was at this point that the Bangladesh military intervened through the backdoor and assumed control of the government. On 11 January, an emergency was declared, the general elections were suspended and a new caretaker government was sworn in. The nation heaved a sigh of relief, particularly as the Head of the caretaker government, Fakhruddin Ahmed, was generally regarded as a person of integrity, probity and quiet efficiency.

The new administration immediately launched a campaign to cleanse Bangladeshi society of corruption with a view to creating conditions conducive to holding a free and fair election. This evoked widespread support because of the all-pervasive resentment against corruption prevailing in the country. Senior officials, prominent businessmen and politicians were arrested on charges of corruption and fraud. As they came from the entire range of the political spectrum in the country, this went towards confirming the impartiality and objectivity of the new government. Some of the big ticket arrests, like that of Tareq Zia and the execution of religious extremists who were found guilty of setting off a series of bomb blasts in the country, proved to be popular and gladdened the heart of the liberal forces in the country.

The second important move made by the new administration was to seek to weaken and sidetrack the two mainstream political parties of the country, the Awami League and the BNP. This was in response to a general feeling that these parties, which had ruled the country alternately for 15 years, were the fountainheads of corruption and mainly responsible for bringing the country to its present state of chaos. The caretaker government wanted to turn a new leaf altogether in the political history of Bangladesh by paving the way for an honourable and respectable leader with a brand new party of his own to ascend to power. It was in this context that Professor Muhammad Yunus, the noted Bangladeshi economist who was awarded the Nobel Peace Prize in 2006, announced his intention to float a party of his own for contesting the election. It was universally seen as a step taken under the sponsorship of the caretaker government. Some intellectuals and leaders of civil society organizations enthusiastically welcomed Yunus's initiative and announced their intention to work for him. It was extraordinarily naïve on the part of the leaders of the caretaker government and their advisors as well as Yunus to believe that he would be able to win a free and fair election when pitted against the leaders of established parties like the Awami League and the BNP. The reality dawned upon Yunus after a few months when he found that the response to his call for supporting his party was, at best, lukewarm. The leaders of the established parties were the only ones who judged the situation correctly. They did not even express their concern at Yunus's decision because they knew that in the absence of grassroots support and party infrastructure, his initiative was doomed to fizzle out.

After realizing, though belatedly, that it would not be possible to dispense with the mainstream political parties, the military-backed government fell back on what it considered to be the next best course of action, which was to encourage internal reforms within these parties in order to remove the ills that afflict them. The agenda of reforms comprised the exclusion of the possibility of any leader holding the post of chairperson of a party for more than two terms, eliminating dynastic transfer of leadership and introducing internal democracy in the election of leaders or members of the executive bodies of political parties. One of the purposes of these reforms was to remove Sheikh Hasina and Begum Zia from the chairpersonship of the Awami League and the BNP respectively. In fact, reforms somewhat along these lines had already started in the parties and the process had moved forward to an extent. But the intervention of the military-backed government to give it a push had a negative effect on the reform process.

The government simultaneously decided to take direct action to remove the top leaders of the Awami League and the BNP. The first step was to get a conviction against Tareq Zia and his younger brother. Negotiations started for an agreement on a package whereby the sentences against the two sons would not be carried out in return for Begum Zia agreeing to go out with them to a foreign country, that is, Saudi Arabia, and stay there for a few years. Newspaper reports indicated that such a package was more or less agreed upon, but in the meantime Sheikh Hasina threw a spanner in the works by insisting on returning to Bangladesh from her brief foreign sojourn. All attempts to persuade her to remain voluntarily exiled for a few years in Europe or the US failed. Then, desperate attempts were made to prevail upon the airline concerned not to bring her on its flight. Defying all pressure, Sheikh Hasina landed in Bangladesh and declared her intention to wage a struggle for the restoration of democracy. This turned out to be the main reason behind Begum Zia going back on the tentative agreement with the government and deciding to stay on in Bangladesh.

The next move of the caretaker government in its bid to implement the formula of the two mainstream political parties 'minus two' was to clamp charges of extortion and corruption against the two leaders and take them into custody even before their cases were investigated and charges framed against them. There was no compelling need, according to the law of the land, to arrest these leaders. They were neither likely to become fugitives from the law nor had the courage to tamper with the evidence being collected against them with the full backing of the Army. In spite of this, the bail petition of Hasina was summarily rejected before she was taken into custody. Subsequently, even after the High Court ordered her release, the government kept her in custody by appealing against the judgment to a superior court and getting a verdict in its favour. The argument given by the superior court for staying her release was that she had been arrested and held in custody under emergency laws.

It was clear that the arrests of the two leaders were designed to humiliate and harass them and tarnish their image before the people. There was no doubt that of late, both Sheikh Hasina and Begum Khaleda Zia had become highly unpopular in the country except among their loyalists, because they were seen as a symbol of dynastic rule and because of their sordid record of holding the Bangladesh economy and democracy to ransom through frequent *hartal*s and prolonged boycotts of the Parliament. It was reported in the newspapers that the major outside powers exercising influence over the Bangladesh government were also in favour of these leaders being eased out of the country for the same reasons, particularly their being the fountain-head of corruption which accounted for the leakage of a substantial part of the aid being provided by them to Bangladesh.

Even more than a year after its takeover, the military-backed government did not succeed in bringing to the final stage any of the initiatives it took. This was clearly not feasible in the circumstances prevailing in Bangladesh. It should have been clear to them right from the beginning that corruption cannot be eliminated by military measures like mass-scale arrests, punishment through trials in kangaroo courts and removal from politics of the leaders of major political parties. Corruption is basically a social and political phenomenon and the only means of curbing it is by the adoption of measures of social transformation and widespread popular campaign against it at the grassroots level. Besides, history shows that the military breeds its own brand of corruption, at times more pernicious and ubiquitous than the civilian one.

Moreover, the caretaker government should have realized that corruption in the two mainstream parties and in the country as a whole was not going to be eliminated by removing the leaders of these parties from their positions. For, the evils that these leaders had come to symbolize were too deep-rooted in the society and polity to be amenable to solution by the quick-fix and simplistic approach of removing these two leaders from the scene. The fact was that the next rung of politicians in these parties, who were expected to assume leadership after the exit of Sheikh Hasina and Begum Zia, were dyed in the same wool. They themselves might not have inherited leadership on the qualification of dynasty as Sheikh Hasina and Begum Zia did, but as the Indian politics also shows, dynastic political inheritance and the cronyism that inevitably goes with it, prevails pervasively at all rungs of political leadership in most South Asian countries. Besides, most of the leaders spearheading internal reforms in the Awami League and the BNP were not known to be free from corruption.

The caretaker government did not succeed in its initial move to build democracy in Bangladesh on the debris of the two mainstream parties. It also did not get very far in implementing its formula of 'minus two'. The BNP was no doubt split and Abdul Mannan Bhuiyan, the Secretary General of the party at that time, appropriated the party and appointed new office bearers, including the President of the BNP in the person of Saifur Rehman, the long-serving finance minister in the cabinets of Khaleda Zia. This appeared for a while to have sidetracked Begum Zia from the mainstream of BNP. But the Begum retaliated quickly and appointed a new Secretary General and other office bearers of her own choice. Very soon, those who had split from the party were marginalized. The majority of the leaders and workers rallied round Begum Zia. On the other hand, the arrest of Sheikh Hasina and the superior court's repeated staying, based on the application of emergency rule, of bails granted to her by lower courts, evoked widespread sympathy for her in Bangladesh and abroad. The Awami League leaders closed ranks and decided to suspend all reform initiatives until Hasina was released. This not only lowered the caretaker government's prestige domestically but also tarnished Bangladesh's image abroad.

There were also complaints from some quarters in Bangladesh that the caretaker government, after taking decisive action in the beginning against religious extremist elements, had started going slow in taking further actions against them. Some of the leaders of religious groups, against whom various legal cases were pending, were carrying out their activities with impunity. One of the reasons for less stringency with regard to dealing with these elements could be that they were relatively less corrupt than leaders belonging to the mainstream parties. It is also possible that in Bangladeshi society as a whole, there is greater tolerance for religious extremism than for corruption. The caretaker government's relative inaction against these extremist religions elements could have been only a reflection of this sentiment. However, it should be realized that religious fanatics, though relatively less corrupt, can be more dangerous in that they are the purveyors of much of the violence that takes place in society and because of their links with global terrorists groups. They thus pose a greater long-term threat to social cohesion, peace and progress than corrupt politicians.

By the middle of 2008, most of the initiatives of the caretaker government had reached a dead-end. Moreover, the government found itself embroiled in several other difficulties. There was a steady deterioration in the economic condition of the country. The inflationary pressure became stronger and prices of most essential food items increased significantly in 2007. This became the major factor behind workers' unrest, mainly in the garment industry. There were signs of slowdown in the growth of exports, reduced flow of foreign investments and a sharp decline in domestic investment. These were mainly attributed to the demoralization prevailing among the business community on account of what was perceived as arbitrary arrests of business leaders, supposedly for their dubious links with political leaders. The decline in foreign direct investment was also at least partly due to the demoralization of the local partners of potential foreign investors. The government also failed to handle effectively the devastation caused by the Cyclone Sidr, which had an adverse effect on the growth of the economy.

In spite of these developments, there was no sign of a popular uprising against the caretaker regime. But arbitrary actions taken by the government against students and teachers of universities in Bangladesh, who have traditionally been in the vanguard of resistance movements, triggered widespread resentment and protests. These, in turn, angered the caretaker government which arrested and put in prison thousands of students and also some senior teachers of the University of Dhaka and the University of Rajshahi, who command considerable respect in society. For fear of the situation in the universities getting worse, the government hurriedly arranged a pardon by the President for the teachers who had been sentenced to various terms of imprisonment. This pardon was granted without the teachers having gone on appeal. The resentment in the universities continued even after the release of the teachers because they still carried the stigma of conviction, which was likely to come in the way of their career prospects.

The government was also facing a major test in deciding how to treat those who were collaborators at the time of the Liberation War, but who subsequently found themselves in respectable positions in different walks of life. There was a rising demand for the trial and speedy sentencing of those who were involved in the killing of Sheikh Mujib and for action against some of the Razakars who collaborated in the killing of intellectuals and innocent citizens during the Liberation War. An upsurge of the pro-liberation sentiment in the country was witnessed on a large scale when the remains of the freedom fighter Hamidur Rehman were brought from India to be buried at his native place in Bangladesh. The anti-liberation elements, on the other hand, were of the view that the Liberation War had been a kind of a civil war and it so happened that they belonged to the losing side. There was, therefore, no reason why they should be brought to trial or punished. The caretaker government was finding it extremely difficult to handle this delicate issue.

In the second half of 2007, there were talks in Bangladesh of an exit strategy for the caretaker government.[7] One plank of the strategy was to send the leaders of the two mainstream parties out of the country and hold elections as promised, towards the end of 2008. This strategy apparently did not succeed. In any case, it was illegal, immoral and high-handed, apart from being undemocratic.

Another plank of the exit strategy talked about at that time, was that before going for elections and handing over power after the elections to the majority party, the caretaker government should try to preserve the gains of the actions taken by it. These related to the reconstitution of the Election Commission, energizing the Anti Corruption Commission, reform of the judiciary by separating it from the executive at the lower levels and purging the universities of politics. There was a talk that the government would hold negotiations with the major political parties with a view to reaching an understanding on retaining these gains. This move was misconceived and self-serving. First, the claims about some of the gains were not valid. Second, what was achieved by force and military means in the short run was bound to be short-lived and could not be sustained without structural changes in the political institutions and society. Third, some of the so-called gains like the separation of the judiciary from the executive were long pending and decisions on them would have in any case come sooner or later. Lastly, it was impractical for an interim military-supported government to impose changes on political parties that, in a democratic system, are free to take decisions on their own after they come to power. Thus, what could have been agreed upon before the elections, between the caretaker government and the mainstream parties would have been easily reversed or annulled by the actions taken by a duly elected government.

Though there were talks about preserving the so-called gains of the caretaker regime through dialogue with the mainstream political parties, the government did not permit even indoor political activities by the parties until a few weeks before the elections were held. Without this, the parties would have been ill prepared to hold any serious dialogue with the government. The delay in permitting political activities also cast doubts on the genuineness of the promise of the caretaker government to hold elections and transfer power by the end of 2008.

Almost until the last quarter of 2008, there were doubts on the prospects of democracy in Bangladesh. There was, in fact, widespread complacency in the country regarding the threat posed to democracy after the installation of the military-backed caretaker government. The intelligentsia as well as the people in general came to believe that the general elections would be held and power transferred to an elected government, as promised, by the end of 2008. Therefore, they would not have to bestir themselves. A section of Bangladeshis went on extending their support to the anti-corruption drive continuing under the regime and did not mind getting rid of the leaders of the two parties. The government also had the support, though somewhat qualified, of a section of the media, particularly of the *Prothom Alo*, the largest circulating Bengali daily. The regime continued to enjoy the support of the governments of the major aid-giving countries. These countries took at face value the assurance of the caretaker government that democracy would be restored by the end of 2008. In any case, they did not seem to be in a hurry to put pressure on the government to expedite the process of restoring democracy.

Close to the end of 2008, four possible scenarios were projected by observers of the political scene in Bangladesh. The first scenario was going for elections before the end of the year with both the main parties in and with their chosen leaders, that is, Sheikh Hasina and Begum Khaleda Zia, at the helm. It was envisaged under this scenario that the caretaker government would hand over power to the party which would win the elections. It would be left to the parties to decide which of the reforms carried out by the caretaker government they would preserve and what other structural changes they would introduce in the political institutions of the country, including in the political parties. This was the only scenario consistent with the principle of democracy and the only feasible way of restoring democracy in Bangladesh.

According to the second scenario, there was a possibility of the elections being postponed and the continuation of the caretaker government beyond 2008. This sceario was warranted by the fact that the government was still busy striking a deal with the leaders of the Awami League and the BNP, whereby they would voluntarily go into exile from Bangladesh. Its anti-corruption drive under the emergency law was still going on. As a result, it was not known who was eligible to take part in political activities. Though only a few months were left before the expiry of the deadline for holding the elections, the emergency continued to be in force and the parties had not been allowed to start even indoor political activities. Cleansing Bangladesh's politics of corrupt elements in order to pave the way for holding free and fair elections was an open-ended goal, the fulfilment of which could take years. This or any other convenient excuse could be used for further extending the life of the caretaker government.

A third scenario was that the elections would be held, but would be effectively managed and manipulated by the Armed Forces. This would ensure that the new government that came to power would remain under their influence and control. Only, the present set of 'caretakers' would be replaced by a new set of 'caretakers' belonging to a sanitized Awami League or BNP, or a combination thereof. Given the historically demonstrated penchant of Bangladeshis for democracy, the military could rule from behind the scenes under a façade of democracy rather than by taking over power directly. This kind of sham democracy could continue for several years until it was brought down by a popular resistance and mass movement. But this would be an uphill task, because it is difficult to build resistance against a power which rules from behind the curtain. It would not be possible unless the enemy could be clearly identified. That was one of the reasons why the resistance against the military-based regime had been feeble or non-existent.

The fourth and the most grim scenario being talked about was that before the end of the year, there would be a coup in Bangladesh, engineered by middle and lower level officers of the Armed Forces who have links with extremist religious groups in the country and the ISI of Pakistan. Though this scenario had very few supporters among observers of Bangladesh's political scene, it was not ruled out altogether.

Restoration of Democracy

As it happened, it was the first scenario that came to pass before the year came to an end. The elections to the ninth *Jatiyo Sangsad* (Parliament) were held on 29 December 2008. Observers, both from Bangladesh and abroad, generally agreed that the elections were peaceful and orderly. Some called it the country's most credible and transparent election ever. The voter turnout was as high as 87 per cent, a rare phenomenon in any democracy except for elections under an authoritarian rule, paraded as democratic. The painstaking efforts of the military-backed government to prepare a new computerized voters' list with photographs, from which some 21.2 million bogus voters were eliminated, along with a more rational delimitation of constituencies, went a long way towards ensuring the fairness and impartiality of the elections as well as the high turnout.

The Awami League secured a landslide victory in the elections. The grand alliance led by it secured 260 of the 299 seats for which elections were held. The League alone won 230 seats. The percentage of votes polled by it went up from 40.21 in the previous elections to 49.02, whereas the percentage of those who voted for the BNP came down from 40.86 to 32.94. Thus, it was not an electoral arithmetic but a real shift of public opinion in favour of the Awami League, which was reflected in the results of the elections. Though the percentage of votes polled by the religious party Bangladesh Jamaat-e-Islami increased marginally from 4.29 per cent in the previous election to a 4.5 per cent in the last one, the seats won by it went down sharply from 17 to two. Within a week after the election, there was a smooth handover of power from the military-backed government to one led by the Awami League.

There were several reasons for the League's unprecedented election victory. First, its leadership was able to better maintain the party's unity when it came under threat from the military-backed government, than the BNP leadership could do. The BNP, therefore, had to cope with the phenomenon of defection and rebel candidates on a much larger scale than the League. Second, with the revision of the voters' list, a large number of new and young voters were added, a big majority of whom voted for the Awami League. Third, as corruption became a major issue in the election, the League suffered less on this account than the BNP. This was because of Sheikh Hasina's rejection of many of the leaders known to be corrupt and her nomination as candidates, of young leaders free from the stain of corruption. It was also due to the fact that a party in power is seen more as a fountainhead of corruption than a party outside power. Fourth, the Awami League was able to take advantage of the nationwide campaign against war criminals. On the other hand, the BNP's alliance with the communal parties became a big negative factor in this context. Lastly, the Awami League's manifesto also played an important role in winning votes. It was a notable departure from the traditional wish lists included in the manifestos of earlier elections and made tangible and daring suggestions for bringing about a *din bodol* or a change from the past. In its manifesto, the League promised to control terrorism and religious extremism; the trial of the war criminals of 1971; the prohibition of the use of religion and communalism in politics; better security for and safeguarding of the rights of the minorities; independence of the judiciary and the Election Commission; effective functioning of the Parliament, depoliticization of administration and the police; decentralization of the administration through the strengthening of local government; and effective action against corruption. For what it was worth, the manifesto also promised to inculcate courtesy and tolerance in the political sector and take initiatives to formulate a consensual charter of political behaviour.

A moot question is why the military sprung to the nation the surprise of the first scenario. The main reason was that during the two years that it controlled the government, it failed in all its efforts to manipulate Bangladeshi politics to serve its avowed purpose. As Rounaq Jahan has stated, '[u]nlike in the 1970s and the 1980s when the military leaders could aspire to cannibalize established political parties', this time around the military could not recruit credible political leaders to float an alternative party which could pose a credible electoral challenge to the two dominant parties.[8] Moreover, beginning from the 1990s, the Bangladesh military has increasingly been drawn into UN peacekeeping operations which has persuaded it of the advantages of keeping out of domestic politics in order to maintain its international credentials as a professional force suitable for recruitment into the UN Peacekeeping Force. This corporate interest also played an important role in the military adhering to the promised time limit of holding the elections. Finally, Bangladesh's two-party political system, combined with the strength of its civil institutions, also served as a deterrent to the military going back on its promise of holding the elections and sticking to power.[9]

Steps towards Strengthening Democracy

During the period it has been in power, the Awami League government has undertaken a number of steps to redeem the pledges made in its election manifesto and respond to the demands made by the people during the elections. It has acted firmly against the growing menace of religious extremism and militancy which, over the past few years, were threatening to undermine the liberal democratic system in Bangladesh. A large number of the cadre of militant organizations like the Jamaat-ul-Mujahideen, Bangladesh and the Harkat-ul-Jihad were taken into custody. As a result of this and other measures adopted, Bangladesh was no longer perceived as a country harbouring terrorists reared in the creed of religious extremism and out to perpetrate it by violent means. Moreover, to demonstrate that the law must prevail, soon after coming to power, the new government promptly sent the convicted killers of Sheikh Mujib to the gallows.

A major issue in the general elections was the trial of the Liberation War criminals. An overwhelming majority of the people, particularly those belonging to the younger generation, unequivocally indicated their support for this demand. The trial was supposed to bring to justice those who sided with the Pakistan Army in carrying out brutal suppression and murders during the war. The trial, which had been an unfulfilled national demand since the liberation of Bangladesh, was also expected to make the moral point that the rule of law and justice cannot be flouted with impurity and must prevail in the country. It was also expected to put straight the record of the history of independence and exorcize the ghosts of the past so that the nation could move on with confidence and a clear conscience. Moreover, it was seen as an opportunity to commemorate the supreme sacrifice made by those who fought in the war.

In July 1973, the Bangladesh Parliament had passed the International Crimes (Tribunal) Act to allow the prosecution of the war criminals. Arrests in thousands were made, of whom 700 were convicted. However, after the political turmoil of December 1975, all convicts and under-trials were released by the military rulers which also subsequently annulled the legislation.

The new government took a decisive step towards dispensing the long-pending justice by announcing on 25 March 2010 the formation of a tribunal, an investigating agency and a prosecution team under the law enacted in 1973. It also took steps to arrest some of the accused leaders. This included Salahuddin Qader Choudhury who, in spite of being widely perceived as a complicit in the war crimes, was fully rehabilitated politically.

Another major issue on which the government took action to expose criminality at high places and let the law take its course, was the reopening of the trial of the 2004 Chittagong arms smuggling case in which the Bangladesh Armed Forces and Military Intelligence Agency, Pakistani intelligence agencies and highly placed government officials, both at the local and central levels, were allegedly involved in smuggling arms for an insurgent group in north-eastern India.

The government also adroitly and firmly handled the situation created by the Bangladesh Rifles (BDR) mutiny at its headquarters in Dhaka in February 2010, in which 57 army officers were murdered in cold blood. Many observers of the Bangladesh scene saw in this mutiny a conspiracy to discredit the government and destabilize it by creating a rift with the Army. They thought that the mutiny was engineered by religious extremist elements, with links to political forces, which had managed to infiltrate the BDR. In the beginning, the government showed a great deal of sensitivity and flexibility in responding to the grievances aired by the mutineers. But when the situation was getting out of control, it ordered the Army to crush the mutiny. In spite of the loss suffered by the Army and the resultant anger, it fully stood behind the government. The ringleaders of the mutiny were identified and arrested, tribunals were established to try them and those found guilty were punished, including death sentences and removal from the force. Subsequently, the BDR was restructured, reorganized and rechristened as the Border Guard Bangladesh.

All these actions of the government, that is, the hanging of Sheikh Mujib's killers, arresting leaders and cadre of militant organizations, re-activation of the process for the war crime trial, reopening the Chittagong arms smuggling trial and the trial and punishment of those involved in the BDR mutiny, were extremely divisive for the nation and carried the risk of retaliatory action by extremist forces. This could lead to selective killings, violence and sabotage, with the potential of throwing the whole country into chaos and disorder. Despite this, the government took this risk for the sake of dispensing justice, establishing the supremacy of the rule of law and redeeming the pledges made to the people.

In a multi-religious society, secularism is of great importance for sustaining democracy. The term 'secularism' is referred to in the Preamble and Articles 8(1) and 12 of the original 1972 Bangladesh Constitution. Article 12 includes secularism as one of the principles on which the Bangladesh Republic is based. It also provides for the removal of abuses of religion for political purposes. This is an essential condition for the prevalence of secularism. The Article stipulates the elimination of communalism in all forms, of granting of political status in favour of any religion by the State and of discrimination against or prosecution of persons practising a particular religion. A day after assuming the reins of the government, General Ziaur Rahman, by a Martial Law Ordinance, amended the Constitution, by which the words 'Bismillah ir-Rahman ir-Rahim' were added before the Preamble, and secularism was dropped as a fundamental principle of State policy and substituted by the words 'absolute trust and faith in the Almighty Allah'. This subsequently became the 5th Amendment of the Constitution. In May 1977, another Martial Law Ordinance revoked Article 38 of the Constitution, which stated:

> [N]o person shall have the right to form, or be a member or otherwise take part in the activities of any communal or other association or union which in the name or on the basis of any religion has for its object or pursues a political purpose.

This paved the way for the return of religion-based parties to politics. Finally, in 1988, President Ershad through the 8th Amendment of the Constitution gave Islam the status of state religion.

A very important development after the new government came to power was the annulment of the 5th Amendment of the Constitution by the Supreme Court of Bangladesh in February 2010. Following this, all the changes made in the Constitution during General Ziaur Rahman's regime became redundant and invalid. The Court also declared illegal the 8th Amendment made during the Ershad regime. With this, it became incumbent for the Constitution to revert in an unqualified manner to the core values of democracy, nationalism, socialism and secularism enshrined in the original 1972 version. This would have been a very good augury for pluralism and democracy in Bangladesh.

The government set up a Parliamentary Committee to review the Court's verdict and recommend follow-up action. After a year-long exercise, the Committee recommended reverting to the original Constitution in a somewhat modified form. It suggested the retention of the clause 'Islam as the State religion' and the phrase *Bismillah ir-Rahman ir-Rahim* at the beginning of the Constitution before the Preamble. The Committee's recommendations were adopted by the Parliament on 30 June 2011 in the form of the 15th Constitutional Amendments. To declare Islam as a State religion and at the same time to restore secularism as a fundamental principle of the Constitution is self-contradictory. The ruling Awami League took this rather cautious but inconsistent position presumably in order to avoid the implicit risk of hurting the sentiments of the overwhelming Muslim majority of the country's population.

The new government took two other steps which make valuable additions to democratic institutions. It reactivated the National Human Rights Commission (NHRC) and enacted a Right to Information (RTI) legislation. The NHRC was reinstated by the Parliament on 9 July 2009. The Information Rights Bill was passed on 18 March 2009. It came into effect from 1 July 2009. Subsequently, the Bangladesh government constituted, through a gazette notification issued on 1 July 2009, an Information Commission as an independent statutory body to give effect to the RTI Act.

Bangladesh's Democratic Dividends

The remarkable cultural homogeneity of Bangladesh society, particularly its language, can be regarded as a very important democratic dividend, though it also carries the danger of the marginalization of the minority communities in the country. On the whole, the minority factor has played a less important role in the democratic functioning of Bangladesh than it has in Sri Lanka, Pakistan and even India. The signing of the Chittagong Hill Tracts (CHT) Peace Agreement between the then Awami League government and the tribal leaders on 2 December 1997 was an important step towards ending insurgency and restoring peace in the CHT and dealing with the grievances of one of the most important ethnic minorities of Bangladesh, the Chakmas. Over the years, several problems have arisen in the process of the implementation of this accord, particularly when the BNP government was in power. However, it is remarkable that the accord has been in place all these years, and after the accession of the Awami League government to power, one can expect that it would be implemented in its true spirit.

Another important advantage for democracy in Bangladesh is the emergence of a two-party system. In spite of the prevailing anomalies and distortions both in the structure and functioning of the two major parties, there is no doubt that this imparts a measure of stability to the political system.

A vibrant civil society can play a very important role in the process of democratization and the deepening of democracy in a state. Bangladesh is placed in a uniquely advantageous position in this respect, as it is home to a large number of, and some of the largest, civil society organizations in the world. The total number of registered NGOs in Bangladesh was estimated at 2,383 in April 2009.[10] These include the Bangladesh Rural Advancement Committee (BRAC), the largest NGO in the world. BRAC and other NGOs have rendered invaluable service to the nation by way of mitigating poverty, reducing gender disparity in the social sector and contributing to the development of human resources. BRAC, through its non-formal primary schools and oral rehydration programmes, has made a significant contribution to raising the literacy rate and reducing the infant mortality rate in Bangladesh. The Grameen Bank has through its microcredit programme, helped in alleviating poverty on a very large scale in the country. Some of the NGOs have been carrying on nation-wide campaigns for arousing citizens' interest in the election process and have been very successful in attracting female voters to polling booths in very large numbers. There is no doubt that the civil society organizations in Bangladesh will continue to function as a bulwark against the weakening or interruption of the democratic process.

The introduction of the institution of the caretaker government through the 13th Amendment to the Constitution, carried out in 1996, was yet another measure designed to strengthen democracy in Bangladesh, by providing credibility to the Parliamentary election process. This institution worked well during the first two elections held under it. However, it came to a severe strain at the time of the third election, which was supposed to be held in 2007, at the end of the term of the then BNP government. There are also some serious questions about the long-term implications of such a system. First, it amounts to a constitutional admission that politicians are not to be trusted in the matter of holding impartial elections. Second, it puts under test the integrity of the institution of the Chief Justice, as the interim caretaker government is supposed to be headed by the last retired Chief Justice.[11] In spite of these inherent limitations, the system, by and large, served the country well. However, in May 2011, the Supreme Court of Bangladesh ruled against the provision of a caretaker government in the Constitution, declaring it unconstitutional. Accordingly, the Parliament, through the 15th Constitutional Amendment, abolished the system by scrapping the 13th Amendment. This enraged the Opposition parties led by the BNP and gave rise to resentment among wider sections of society. The BNP threatened to boycott the next general elections if the system was not restored.

The two main political parties could not come to an agreement on the modalities of a poll-time government overseeing the conduct of the elections. The agitation in favour of a caretaker government mounted by the BNP and its Jamaat-e-Islami ally unleashed large-scale violence which continued for several months prior to, during, and after the elections. It inflicted a heavy price on the nation in terms of loss of life, property and sense of security. In the city of Dhaka, hundreds of thousands of followers of the religious group Hefazat-e-Islam entered the city and created mayhem in retaliation to the law and order measures taken by the government against the supporters of Jamaat-e-Islami, the main agenda of which was to thwart the trials of the 1971 war crimes.

The Awami League-led government went ahead and held one-sided and somewhat truncated parliamentary elections in January 2014. The BNP led alliance did not participate in the elections, leaving it to the Awami League and its allies to divide the 300 seats of the Parliament among themselves. Even before the elections were held, as many as 153 Members of Parliament were declared elected uncontested. Having assured itself of the majority in the Parliament, the government organized elections for the remaining 147 seats for which the main contestants were the Awami League and its own allies, including the Jatiyo Party, which later joined the Cabinet.

The Awami League justified the elections on the ground that it had no option but to organize them in order to meet the constitutional requirement of having a new Parliament within its five-year term limit. They also took credit for having organized the elections in spite of the violence unleashed by the Opposition. The BNP-led alliance, on the other hand, alleged lack of credibility of the elections and expressed doubts in the legitimacy of the government formed on the basis of its results. Though the turnout of voters at 40 per cent of the electorate was less than half of what it was in the 2008 elections, the Awami League claimed it to be a respectable figure, given the circumstances in which the elections were held. An important section of public opinion in Bangladesh and outside observers and public figures, mainly from key Western countries, questioned the legitimacy of the elections and gave a call for a dialogue between the two main political parties to pave the ground for holding a free and fair election. The US Senate passed a resolution stressing the 'critical need for political dialogue'. The UN also sought to promote a dialogue between the two main political parties of the country. These voices have by now subsided because of the people of Bangladesh getting reconciled to the outcome of the elections mainly on account of the restoration of relative freedom from disorder, violence and political stability, for which there was a natural longing among them.

A section of opinion in Bangladesh believes that the fear of vote-rigging in the polls held under the Awami League government was not the real reason for the boycott of elections by BNP and its allies. If that was the case, the BNP would not have participated in so many other elections under the same government not so long ago in which their candidates won handsomely in many cases. According to this section of public opinion, the most important reason for the BNP's decision was on the one hand their problem to support the demand of their ally Jamaat-e-Islami (JI) to end the war crime trials and restore the immunity being enjoyed by them and for the continuation of the unbridled use of religion in politics, and on the other, their compulsion to bank upon JI's capacity and propensity to generate violence for serving their political purpose.

In this context, the BNP was aware of the Shahbag movement which arose as an expression of outrage by the youth of the country against a lenient punishment meted out by the War Crime Tribunal to one of the accused. The movement continues to remain an important force and voice in the country and can come into play to tilt the political balance whenever there is a serious threat to its followers' demand for justice.

From this perspective, there is a logic in the view of some observers of the political scene in Bangladesh that 'it will be a grave mistake to see the present political crisis in the country from the perspective of elections only'.[12] The issue, thus, is not holding a free and fair election but evolving a consensus on the identity of Bangladesh and the basic principle of its nationhood. The issue is whether Bangladesh can continue to limp along the path of democracy with its conflicting and mutually exclusive concept of nationhood or whether the time has come, as evident from the nation-wide demand for justice against the 1971 war crimes, and the Shahbag movement, to resolve this conflict once for all.

In country after country in the developing world, the stability of democracy has come to depend heavily on the ability of the democratic system to deliver the social and economic goods to the common citizens, to meet their basic needs, to reduce income disparity and to bring the marginalized sections into the mainstream of the economy. In addition to facing these challenges, Bangladesh remains vulnerable to natural disasters, like floods, cyclones and drought conditions in parts of the country, which have, from time to time, made the democratic functioning of the State extremely difficult.

For more than two decades now, the overall economic performance of the country has been quite impressive. This trend has continued during the six years of the tenure of the present government. In spite of the global recession the economy of Bangladesh registered a growth rate of 5.5 per cent during the fiscal year 2009–10. The agricultural growth during this period was an impressive 4.7 per cent, that is, more than 1 per cent above the historical growth of 3.6 per cent. The negative effect of the global recession on growth in exports and remittances were either marginal or non-existent. For example, remittances increased marginally from $10.77 billion in 2009 to $11.28 billion in 2010. The GDP growth rates registered a further increase in the following three years, that is, 2011–13 when they averaged 6.16 per cent. The increase in remittances was highly impressive, from a little over $11 billion in 2010 to an estimated figure of over $15 billion in 2014. In the social sectors, Bangladesh has succeeded, more than other countries in the South Asian region, including India, in significantly reducing infant and maternal mortality rates and gender disparity, in increasing life expectancy and in the general provisioning of education and health services.

Challenges to Democracy

In spite of these positive factors, the country faces a host of economic and social problems that have the potential to bring about political instability. These include widespread poverty, inadequate provisions for basic social services and their poor quality, poor connectivity in the rural areas, rising prices and acute energy shortage. The stability of democracy in Bangladesh will greatly depend upon how effectively and speedily these challenges in the economic and social fields are met.

There are some important areas where, in spite of being in office for more than six years now, the government has not fulfilled the promises made in its election manifesto. These include running the national Parliament in the true bipartisan spirit, reforming and revitalizing political parties, establishing the rule of law at the grassroots level and controlling corruption.

The ruling parties in Bangladesh have adopted a negative attitude towards allowing the Opposition to play its proper role in governance, particularly in the functioning of the Parliament. In reaction to it, and also in an attempt to return to power prematurely by destabilizing the government in power, the Opposition parties have been boycotting the Parliament and in the process, severely undermining its functioning. As a result, the Parliament has ceased to be a centre of democratic politics and the major forum of accountability in governance. The present government has done very little towards fulfilling its electoral promise of correcting these anomalies. Nor has it done much to restore democracy within political parties, to make their leadership accountable to the people and to promote inter-party dialogue. To quote Imtiaz Ahmed, 'The nurturing of democratic tradition within and between political parties remains vital in any strategy of keeping the military at bay'.[13] There should be a regular dialogue between the political parties.

There has not been much improvement in the law and order front during these six years. The situation has been graphically depicted by Rehman Sobhan,

> The partisan approach to law enforcement extends from the top to the bottom of the political system and applies to the behaviour of both the parties when in office. It is this selective and maleficent approach to law enforcement which has, more than anything else, underwritten the emergence of the mastaan or muscleman as a major factor in political and social life, thereby undermining the credibility of the law enforcement process.[14]

Sobhan adds, 'Bangladesh's increasingly dysfunctional political system is not only subverting the development potential of the country but also posing a threat to the sustainability of democratic politics'.[15] It is important for the government to develop and implement a well-thought-out strategy, preferably based on consultations with political parties and civil society institutions, to bring about a change in this situation. A similar initiative is called for on the anti-corruption front also where there has been little amelioration.

A healthy, corruption-free and effective local self-government is of crucial importance for the functioning of democracy in any country in that it ensures people's participation in governance and the political process and helps in inculcating democratic values at the grassroots level. Local self-government is the nursery of democracy and perhaps the most effective channel for the delivery of public goods. It can play a very important role in breaking the stranglehold of bureaucracy and thereby reducing corruption and injecting urgency and a sense of purpose in the development process.

The 1972 Constitution made a decentralized government system mandatory for the governance of the country. Successive governments since then, both military/authoritarian and democratic, have reiterated their commitment to a viable local self-government. Despite this, the establishment of a truly decentralized local government system remains a distant dream more than 42 years after the adoption of the original Constitution. The local governments have been poorly managed, institutionally and financially weak and without social and political credibility. The main reason for this is the failure of democracy to strike deep roots in Bangladesh. Successive governments, backed by their political parties, have been deeply divided over issues relating to local self-government, such as its structure, finances, functions and extent of devolution. Positions on all these aspects have been circumscribed by the same conflictive politics as have characterized the political parties' approach to national issues. These parties and the governments led by them have over the past few decades seen the local government system primarily as a means to strengthen their control over local politics and to consolidate their local power base. They have, therefore, only tinkered with some aspects of the system, depending on their political convenience. In the prevailing political environment, decentralization and devolution are regarded as alien values. Unless there is a change in the situation, both local governance and democracy will remain in peril in Bangladesh.[16]

Notes

1. The four students were: Rafiquddin Ahmed, Abdul Barakat, Abdul Jabbar and Abdus Salam.
2. Abdul Gaffar Choudhury, 'Ekushe February', *Gopon Eshtihar*, 22 February 1952. All translations are by the author of this book unless mentioned otherwise.
3. Shamsur Rahman, 'Swadhinata Tumi', *Shamsur Rahmaner Shreshtha Kobita* (Dhaka: Jatiyo Shahitya Prakashani, 1989). Originally published in the collection of poems entitled *Bondi Shibir Theke* (1972).
4. Nirmalendu Goon, 'Rajdondo', *Banglar Maati, Banglar Jol* (Dhaka: Samakal Private Limited, 1978).
5. Rounaq Jahan, 'Democratic Renewal in Bangladesh: Breaking Away from Path Dependence' (lecture, Centre for the Study of Developing Societies, New Delhi, 2010).

6. Statement issued by the spokesman of the Secretary-General of the United Nations (New York, 10 January 2007).
7. Rehman Sobhan, 'Exit Strategies: Some Lessons from History', *Forum* (Dhaka), July 2007.
8. Jahan, 'Democratic Renewal in Bangladesh'.
9. Ibid.
10. Imtiaz Ahmed, 'State, Society and Democratic Futures: Challenges for Bangladesh', in *Democracy, Sustainable Development and Peace: New Perspectives on South Asia*, ed. Akmal Hussain and Muchkund Dubey (New Delhi: Oxford University Press, 2014) 67–94.
11. These points are made in Nihad Kabir's paper, 'National Governance—New Challenges and Opportunities' (presented at the workshop 'Democracy, Development and Participation: Issues and Experience in Bangladesh and India', organized jointly by the Society for Peace, Security and Development Studies, Allahabad; and Konrad Adenaur Foundation, New Delhi at Gangtok, 12–13 October 2003).
12. Shamsul Bari, 'Free and Fair Elections Alone Cannot Solve the Political Crisis in Bangladesh: Views of a Concerned Citizen of Bangladesh' (paper in circulation, Dhaka, January 2014).
13. Ahmed, 'State, Society and Democratic Futures', 79.
14. Rehman Sobhan, 'Moving from Confrontational Politics towards Sustainable Democracy', anniversary issue, *Weekly Holiday*, 2 December 2002.
15. Ibid.
16. Shamsul Bari, 'Decentralization, Devolution and People's Empowerment: The Bangladesh Experience' (paper presented at the workshop 'Democracy, Development and Participation: Issues and Experience in Bangladesh and India', organized jointly by the Society for Peace, Security and Development Studies, Allahabad; and Konrad Adenaur Foundation, New Delhi at Gangtok, 12–13 October 2003).

FOUR Indo-Bangladesh Economic Relations

The economic relations between India and Bangladesh constitute a very significant aspect of the overall relations between the two countries. They are of an extensive nature, including trade relations, credit arrangements, joint ventures, transit and transport. They benefit both countries and have an overall stabilizing effect on the political relations between them. They have implications also for their linkages beyond their borders, with other countries of South Asia, South-East Asia and East Asia.

Bangladesh is one of the most important markets for India's exports. For the past several decades, it has been the largest export market for India in the SAARC region. During 1985–90, the growth rate of Bangladesh's trade with India was higher than that with the world and SAARC countries, the respective figures being 20.3 per cent, 7.94 per cent and 16.68 per cent. This growth rate increased sharply during 1990–95. Whereas the growth rates of Bangladesh's trade with the world and the SAARC countries were 16.7 per cent and 57.85 per cent respectively during this period, that with India was 87.29 per cent. India's trade with SAARC countries is dominated by its trade with Bangladesh. In 2003, Bangladesh's contribution to India's total trade with SAARC countries was 49.64 per cent.[1] In 2013–14, there was a decrease in this share, but it was still 33.02.[2]

During the period from 1988–89 to 1992–93, whereas India's global export increased by 164 per cent, the increase of exports to Bangladesh was 293 per cent.[3] In 1995, India jumped to the first position among the major exporters to Bangladesh, with China being a distant second. The other major exporters were Singapore, Japan and Kuwait. India maintained the first rank among the exporters to Bangladesh until 2005–06, after which it was overtaken by China. China has remained in that position until now. In 2013–14 India's total legal exports to Bangladesh amounted to nearly $5.25 billion.[4] To these should be added the substantial amount of illegal exports which, according to some estimates, are as high as legal exports and the sizeable amount of trade in services for which estimates are not available. Thus, India's total earnings from trade with Bangladesh may very well be in the range of $12–15 billion. This makes Bangladesh one of the most important export markets for India in the world.

Bangladesh's exports to India, on the other hand, have been a very small percentage of its imports from India. This percentage continuously declined from 14.4 per cent in 1980 to 12.9 per cent in 1990, to 5.3 per cent in 2000 and 3.6 per cent in 2003.[5] There is a recent trend of a sizeable increase in these exports. Bangladesh's exports to India increased fourfold between 2003–04 and 2007–08—from $89.3 million to $358.1 million.[6] They exceeded $500 million both in the years 2010–11 and 2011–12, after which they declined to $472.98 million in 2012–13. In spite of this increase, as a percentage of Bangladesh's imports from India, these exports still remain at a low level. For example, the percentages in 2012–13 and 2013–14 were 11.05 and 9.02 respectively.[7]

In spite of the impressive performance on the trade front, the full potential of economic cooperation between India and Bangladesh remains to be realized. Except during the first four years after the liberation of Bangladesh, there has been a lamentable lack of planned and concerted efforts on the part of the two governments to nurture their economic relations and impart dynamism to them. These relations have, by and large, grown on their own, dictated by the logic of the market forces, geographical proximity and other objective factors.

The minimum necessary legal and institutional infrastructure for underpinning economic cooperation between the two countries has long been in place. These include a Bilateral Trade Agreement, periodic trade review exercises, Joint Inland Water Transit and Trade Agreement, Joint Rivers Commission and Joint Economic Commission. The first one-year trade agreement between the two countries was signed on 28 March 1972, under the umbrella of the Treaty of Friendship, Cooperation and Peace signed on 19 March 1972. In this agreement, export and import items from the two countries were identified, trade was limited to the government level and the payment was to be made in rupees. The agreement also provided for border trade between Bangladesh and the neighbouring Indian states. Within 16 km of the borders of both countries, free trade was allowed up to a specified limit and in selected commodities produced and consumed in the border region. In view of the large volume of illegal trade that started taking place soon after the agreement was signed, the border trade provision in the agreement was scrapped in October 1972 by mutual consent. Rupee trade was abolished from 1 January 1975, after which the trade started being conducted in free foreign exchange. The trade agreement, which also provided for periodic reviews, has been extended from time to time after the expiry of the first agreement and has remained in force till date. The last time the Agreement was renewed was in 2012.

A Joint Economic Commission (JEC) at the ministerial level was established soon after the liberation of Bangladesh. This commission established four committees dealing respectively with economic matters, trade and transport issues, science and technology and agriculture. There is also an Inland Water Transit and Trade Agreement, which has been extended periodically and continues to remain operational till date. Besides, there are several memoranda of understanding covering cooperation in specific areas.

However, these institutions have suffered from the neglect of the two governments. For example, the JEC, after remaining active for a couple of years, went into a period of hibernation when it became almost dormant. As a result, a new joint economic commission had to be set up in 1982. But this commission also met only infrequently. For example, between 1982 and 1993, it met only thrice—in 1986, 1990 and December 1993. The periodicity of the trade review talks has also been subjected to the vicissitudes of the domestic political conditions in the two countries and their bilateral political relations.

In spite of Bangladesh being a fairly large market for India's exports, Indian businessmen and entrepreneurs do not bestow upon it the care and attention it deserves. They are not as eager to come to Bangladesh for selling their wares and rendering post-sales services as they are in rushing to the markets of developed countries. Thus, what is in reality a principal market is, in practice, treated as a residual market. One hears frequent complaints from Bangladeshi businessmen and industrialists that their Indian partners do not respond to their calls on time and regard the Bangladesh market as a dumping ground for their inferior products, keeping the superior varieties of the same product lines for the more prosperous markets in developed countries. Though there is an element of exaggeration in these complaints, they are at least partly true and constitute a major constraint to the expansion of economic relations between the two countries.

The credit packages extended by India to Bangladesh over the years have played an important role in Indo-Bangladesh economic relations.

They would have played a much greater role if there would not have been undue delays in their utilization and long hiatuses in offering them. Though India is a natural source of supply of essential commodities and services required by Bangladesh for meeting emergency needs, it has often been unduly tardy in responding to requests from Bangladesh for such assistance and in delivering supplies after making commitments.

Economic relations between any two countries are influenced by the climate and state of their political relations. This is all the more so between India and Bangladesh because of their being immediate neighbours with asymmetrical size and strength. As an eminent Bangladeshi economist, Nurul Islam, the first deputy chairman of the Bangladesh Planning Commission, put it, 'Indo-Bangladesh economic relations are, therefore, likely to hold out greater prospects if they are anchored within the broader framework of political and strategic relationship'.[8]

The economic reforms introduced by Bangladesh in 1982 and by India in 1991 have inevitably brought about changes in the nature and forms of economic transactions and interaction between the two countries. For one thing, the State is now playing a far diminished role in economic cooperation, which now rests more and more with private enterprises. Less inward-looking economic policies, reductions in import barriers and enhanced incentives to investors in both the countries should have led to an increasing interaction and collaboration between the private sectors of the two countries. But this has not happened to the extent it was expected. The private enterprises in the two countries, on account of the burden of past attitudes and the lure of the markets in developed countries, have not responded adequately to the opportunities opened up by the process of liberalization. As a result, potentialities of economic cooperation still remain unrealized, particularly in the absence of the compensating role of the State. Moreover, since the liberalization in both the countries has been on an MFN basis, the stronger economic partner, that is, India, has gained more from it than the weaker one, Bangladesh. Besides, India has enjoyed relatively greater access to the Bangladesh market on account of the latter's greater depth and longer duration of liberalization than that of India. This makes a strong case for India granting unilateral, non-reciprocal trade concessions to Bangladesh.

Trade Relations

Table 4.1 shows a statistical view of Indo-Bangladesh trade during the last 32 years.

Table 4.1 Evolution of Trade between India and Bangladesh (values in US$ million)*

Year	*Bangladesh's Exports to India*	*Bangladesh's Imports from India*	*Total Trade*
1982–83	20.29	43.33	63.62
1983–84	6.92	37.89	44.81
1984–85	28.29	60.09	88.38
1985–86	29.60	64.89	94.89
1986–87	7.72	57.22	64.94
1987–88	11.04	74.40	85.44
1988–89	8.69	90.02	98.71
1989–90	10.69	120.73	131.42
1990–91	21.68	170.27	191.95
1991–92	22.80	189.49	212.29
1992–93	4.22	283.86	288.08
1993–94	12.52	380.20	392.72
1994–95	24.31	466.61	490.91
1995–96	35.77	994.08	1,029.86
1996–97	21.01	1,018.32	1,039.33
1997–98	37.22	795.62	832.83
1998–99	55.02	1,178.83	1,233.85
1999–2000	49.51	1,023.77	1,073.28
2000–01	50.13	945.45	995.58
2001–02	60.80	1,195.49	1,256.29
2002–03	39.33	1,145.83	1,185.16
2003–04	55.34	1,494.22	1,549.56
2004–05	66.15	1,745.06	1,811.21
2005–06	118.88	1,951.24	2,070.12
2006–07	168.11	2,061.71	2,229.82
2007–08	232.93	2,646.58	2,879.51
2008–09	318.82	3,498.15	3,816.97
2009–10	268.23	2,748.59	3,016.82
2010–11	320.90	3,859.82	4,180.72
2011–12	523.02	4,870.25	5,393.27
2012–13	519.97	4,704.23	5,224.20
2013–14	472.98	5,246.12	5,719.10

Source: Adapted from data sourced from International Monetary Fund, Directorate of Trade Statistics online database, http://elibrary-data.imf.org/ (accessed on 15 January 2015).

Note: * Data available for calendar year but presented in terms of fiscal. The year 1982–83 has been selected as the starting point because this was the year when Bangladesh started liberalizing its economy in a full-fledged manner.

The figures shown in Table 4.1 reveal that during the first decade after Bangladesh embraced liberalization, that is, between 1982–83 and 1992–93, India's exports to Bangladesh increased by six and a half times, that is, at the rate of 65 per cent per annum. They reached close to the billion dollar mark ($994.08 million) in 1995–96. They were sustained around the figure of $1 billion during the next seven years from 1995–96 to 2002–03 when they started increasing at a very fast pace. In 2006–07, the figure exceeded the $2 billion mark. The increases during the next two years were 28.37 per cent and 32.18 per cent respectively. In 2008–09, the Indian exports reached the figure of nearly $3.5 billion. The growth rate between 2003–04 and 2008–09 was 134.11 per cent or 26.82 per cent per annum. After a decline in 2009–10, it increased to $4.87 billion in 2011–12 and peaked at $5.246 billion in 2013–14. The average per annum growth rate during the last four years was 18.7 per cent.

India was a major trading partner of Bangladesh during the initial years after its liberation. During this period, India's exports to Bangladesh depended very much upon its aid, including credits. Indian exports started stagnating and even declined as Bangladesh started receiving aid from international financial institutions and third countries, as bilateral aid from these countries was dominantly tied to supplies from them. India's exports to Bangladesh continued to stagnate or decline till 1983–84, after which they started rising again. The spurt in the Indian exports to Bangladesh after this period has been without any crutches and driven mainly by the liberalization policy adopted by the Bangladesh government in 1982 and by the assertion of India's competitive advantage over third countries due to geographical proximity and other factors.

Throughout this period, Indo-Bangladesh trade remained lopsided, dominated by Indian exports, while imports from Bangladesh remained at very low levels. Till 1997–98, Bangladesh's exports to India remained below $30 million except in 1995–96, when they were at the level of $35.77 million. The exports started increasing from 1997–98 and reached the level of $118.88 million in 2005–06. Since then Bangladesh's exports to India have been steadily rising, though it is still low in relation to its imports from India. The rates of increase during the next three years were 41.41 per cent, 38.56 per cent and 37 per cent respectively. Bangladesh's exports to India peaked to the figure of more than half a billion US dollars in 2011–12 and then registered marginal declines during each of the next two years. During the four-year period of 2010–11 to 2013–14, the average annual rate of growth was 14 per cent.

Bangladesh's exports to India have fluctuated considerably during the period from 1982–83 to 1997–98. After rising to $29.6 million in 1985–86, the exports sank to a low of $4.22 million in 1992–93. The exports were also very low in 1986–87 ($7.72 million) and 1988–89 ($8.69 million). The main reason for this fluctuation was the uncertainty about the supply of the few items that Bangladesh was in a position to export in reasonable quantities and India was prepared to lift. For example, newsprint used to be one of the very important export items from Bangladesh, but exports to India would dwindle to insignificant levels whenever the country could not spare supplies for India due to either production shortfalls or the need to husband other export markets, or when India managed to procure from other sources supplies of a better quality and at cheaper prices. This factor acquired a greater salience after the policy of liberalization initiated by India in 1991, when with the entry of private operators there was a greater diversification of the sources of supplies. Subsequently, with Bangladesh finding comparative advantage in the export of readymade garments, which became its principal export item, newsprint became a sunset industry in Bangladesh and virtually disappeared from its export basket for India.

From time to time, India used to import sizeable quantities of fertilizers from Bangladesh, but the export of this item to India also fluctuated sharply. In the first half of the 1990s, it figured prominently among Bangladesh's exports to India, partly because of a memorandum of understanding (MoU) signed between the Mineral and Metal Trading Corporation (MMTC) of India and its Bangladesh counterpart for the supply of specified quantities of fertilizers from Bangladesh. In 1992–93, fertilizer was Bangladesh's single largest item of export to India, accounting for as much as 50 per cent of its total exports. It still figured among Bangladesh's exports to India till three years back, but ranked much lower than other items. Since 2001–02, textiles, including woven fabrics, have emerged as the single largest export of Bangladesh to India. This is followed, not exactly in that order, by edible fruits, nuts, etc.; mineral, fuels, oils, etc.; salt, sulphur, earth, stone, etc.; fish and other aquatic products; and copper and articles thereof. Over the past decade or so, there has been a noticeable change in the structure of Bangladesh's exports to India with the share of the traditional items like jute and jute manufactures coming down sharply and new items entering the export basket. Moreover, Bangladesh is currently claiming very small proportions of India's total imports of several of the items exported by it to India.[9] This would indicate that there is sufficient scope for Bangladesh to expand the exports of both traditional and non-traditional items to India.

The main Indian exports to Bangladesh during the last decade have been cotton yarn, textiles, cereals, vegetables and edible roots and tubers, and sugar and sugar confectionery, vehicles other than railway rolling stock, iron and steel, other minerals, fuels and oil, organic chemicals, electrical machinery and equipment.

Informal Trade

A sizeable amount of clandestine trade takes place between India and Bangladesh, mostly across the borders. Since it is illegal, such trade is characterized as smuggling. The estimates of the extent of the illegal trade vary widely. But there is no doubt that it is fairly large and according to most estimates, could very well be as large, if not larger, as the legal trade between the two countries.

The whole phenomenon of informal trade is politicized by sections of Bangladesh media and political parties, with the insinuation that Bangladesh is being drained of its precious resources because of their being smuggled out to India. This is cited as yet another example of India's rapacity against Bangladesh. However, the reality on the ground would seem to point in just the opposite direction. The economic factors which account for the kind of imbalance that prevails in the legal trade are likely to produce the same results in the illegal trade. The well-known Bangladeshi economist, Mosharraf Hossain, pointed out in an article he wrote for the periodical *Weekly Holiday*: 'The prices of agricultural commodities across the border are substantially lower than those in Bangladesh. At the current rate of exchange, the rice price in India is half of that in Bangladesh. This is true of almost every commodity'.[10] This would indicate that the flow of illegal trade between the two countries is largely a one-sided affair, that is, from India to Bangladesh.

The optimum solution to the problems created by illegal trade is to totally liberalize the trade between the two countries. An FTA between them can help in expediting the process. There are many advantages in legalizing the informal trade. Some of these are:

- With liberalized trade regimes in both the countries, restriction on the border trade cannot be justified except on security grounds which are largely irrelevant and generally exaggerated.
- Legalization of the informal trade will eliminate one of the major arguments, that is, the drain of Bangladesh's resources, being used

by motivated quarters for creating tensions in the bilateral relations between the two countries.

- It will prevent the harassment of the poor and ordinary people from both sides of the border who, for economic compulsions, are obliged to resort to such trade.
- It will reveal new complementarities in the economies of the two countries.
- It will generate new economic activities along the border based on the assured supply of commodities. Small industries of various kinds are likely to spring up on both sides of the border. This will provide employment to a large number of Indians and Bangladeshis residing in the border areas.
- It will push the legal trade transactions between the two countries to new heights, posing new challenges and opening up new opportunities.

A regime of free trade between the two countries would automatically legalize the informal trade. But as a first step, all barriers to trade across the border in goods and services produced in the border areas on both sides should be removed. A modest step in this direction was taken during Prime Minister Sheikh Hasina's visit to India in 2010 when 'it was agreed that border haats (markets) shall be established on a pilot basis at selected areas ... to allow trade in specified produces and products'.[11] As of now, two border haats are in operation, two are under construction and four more have been agreed upon along Bangladesh–Tripura border. Construction of border haats along the Bangladesh–Mizoram border is also being discussed.

Trade Imbalance

Bangladesh's trade balance with India has always been in the negative by huge margins. The deficit, which was $47.6 million in 1980, increased to $148 million in 1990 and to $895 million in 2000. Soon thereafter, it crossed the billion dollar mark and reached the level of $1,435.9 million in 2003.[12] During the last few years, growth rates of exports of both countries to each other have been very impressive. But since Bangladesh's exports have grown from a very low base as compared to India's, the gaps in absolute terms have further increased and the lopsidedness of Indo-Bangladesh trade has become starker. The trade deficit increased from nearly $1.5 billion in 2003–04 to over $3 billion in 2008–09. In 2013–14, the deficit was as high as $ 4.7 billion. It will be significantly higher if the informal trade between the two countries is taken into account.[13]

However, the massive trade imbalance in favour of India should be viewed in proper perspective. An attempt by any country to balance its trade separately with each of its trading partners would amount to the negation of the very concept of free trade and the principle of comparative advantage. Because of the operation of these factors, India has for decades had a persistent imbalance in its trade with almost all major developed countries. Bangladesh also runs adverse balance of trade with China and several developed countries. In fact, for the last several years, Bangladesh's largest trade deficit has been with China. In 2013, it was above $6.5 billion as against the deficit of $4.7 billion with India.[14] And yet, protests against the trade deficit with China can be heard only in murmurs, whereas those against the deficit with India are loud and shrill. This can be explained only by political factors.

It is the overall balance of trade of a country, and not the balance with individual countries, that has macroeconomic implications. Even an overall deficit in trade need not be of much concern if it can be financed by capital inflows and other forms of transfers from abroad. Moreover, trade benefits both partners, even if unbalanced. For, imports can be as important for an economy as exports. They can help export efforts and the general growth of the economy and act as an anti-inflationary force that benefits consumers and assists producers in remaining competitive both in the domestic and foreign markets. In the case of Bangladesh, a high percentage of its import from India is in the nature of inputs, that is, cotton yarn and textiles, meant for the production of its main item of export—readymade garments. Moreover, imports from India are market-driven as they are cheaper and of higher quality than from other sources.

In spite of the soundness of these arguments, Bangladesh's persistent and massive imbalance of trade with India does have important adverse implications. As psychological and political factors play an important role in the relations between the two countries, the large trade imbalance with India readily becomes susceptible to exploitation for political purposes, which can adversely affect future trade flows between the two countries. Moreover, India has, in the medium and long term, a stake in the growth and prosperity of Bangladesh. To the extent that exports contribute to growth and prosperity, it is in India's interest that there is a steady growth in Bangladesh's exports. India can make an important contribution in this regard by substantially increasing its off-take of Bangladesh's products.

There are various reasons for the trade imbalance between the two countries. These include faster trade liberalization by Bangladesh as compared to that by India and the declining rate of the exchange value of the Rupee as compared to that of the Bangladeshi currency, Taka.[15] However, the main reason lies in the structural asymmetry of the economies of the two countries. Whereas the Indian economy is diversified and technologically advanced, the economy of Bangladesh suffers from a backward industry and inadequate infrastructure, low productivity and a limited export base.

Impact of Regional Economic Groupings

Regional groupings like the North American Free Trade Agreement (NAFTA), the EU, and the ASEAN Free Trade Agreement (AFTA) are bound to have, at least in the short and medium term, an adverse effect on the trade of countries outside these groupings, including India and Bangladesh. The immediate effect of these groupings is trade diversion from countries outside these arrangements to member countries. However, in the long run, such groupings may have a trade-creating effect via an increase in the growth of the Gross National Product (GNP) of the member countries that is likely to be brought about by production for a larger market.

The only way countries like India and Bangladesh can avoid marginalization in the world trading system as a result of the mushrooming of such groupings is either to join one or more of these groups or to form a free trade area or customs union of their own along with the other countries of South Asia. The first alternative is not easily available as it depends upon a variety of economic, political and geo-strategic considerations. For a least developed country like Bangladesh, it is even more difficult to be welcomed as a member of economic groupings outside South Asia.

Free Trade in South Asia

The first tentative step in the direction of free trade in South Asia was taken in 1991, with the signing under SAARC of the South Asian Preferential Trading Arrangement (SAPTA). But the selective commodity-by-commodity negotiations for progressive tariff reductions provided for under SAPTA turned out to be a slow and long drawn out process. This was not unexpected in the light of the experience of other regional economic groupings like the Latin American Free Trade Association (LAFTA) and ASEAN which, in the initial phase of their evolution, had followed the same path. These groupings, therefore, subsequently moved to the higher trajectory of free trade areas within a time-bound framework. The experience of another preferential trading arrangement based on commodity-by-commodity negotiations—the Bangkok Agreement—to which both India and Bangladesh are parties, had also demonstrated the limitation of such an approach. In the Bangkok Agreement, some tariff preferences had been exchanged. As a least developed country, Bangladesh received non-reciprocal concessions from India on tariffs on newsprint, urea, fish, mechanized wood pulp, raw jute and viscose filament yarn. But the reductions offered constituted only a 10 percentage-point margin of preferences. Moreover, the number of products on which tariff concessions were given by participating countries was highly limited. And virtually no progress was made in the removal of quantitative restrictions and other non-tariff barriers. Besides, the time frame for the implementation of the agreed measures was not adhered to. SAPTA encountered the same problems and suffered from the same limitations.

That is why in the second half of the 1990s, when three rounds of negotiations under SAPTA had been completed and the results achieved were still meagre, alternatives to the SAPTA process were explored by the governments of the SAARC member countries as well as at the non-governmental level. The SAARC countries, at their summit meeting in 1996, declared their intention to move from SAPTA to a South Asian Free Trade Area (SAFTA) arrangement. They set up a Group of Eminent Persons (GEP) with the mandate to suggest how such a transition could be made. The GEP, in its report submitted in 1997, projected a vision of South Asia moving within the next 20 years to an economic union via a free trade arrangement and a customs union. The datelines for achieving these landmark objectives were fixed and a roadmap was drawn up for moving from one stage of integration to the higher stage, culminating in the establishment of the economic union. The GEP also recommended that the member countries would be required to enter into a separate treaty or agreement for establishing a free trade arrangement and moving beyond that. According to the recommendations of the GEP, the process of drafting and reaching an agreement on a free trade arrangement was to be completed before the end of 1999 and the journey towards an economic union was to begin from the year 2000.

For want of political will, the SAARC member governments did not accept either the vision, the goal posts or the roadmap projected and prepared by the GEP. It was only at the Islamabad SAARC Summit in

January 2004 that the members signed a Framework Agreement for the SAFTA. This agreement, which came into force in January 2006, suffers from a large number of basic deficiencies and fundamental flaws. This is not the place to go into these deficiencies.

Trade Concessions by India

Bangladesh has, for a long time, contended that high Indian tariffs on products of export interest to it have served as a major constraint to its efforts to expand its exports to India. It is true that even after liberalization Indian tariffs on an average are higher than those of Bangladesh. Besides, Bangladesh has reduced tariffs at a faster rate and has maintained a lower tariff regime over a longer period than India. That is why Bangladesh has for some time been demanding duty-free entry for its exports into the Indian market. At a meeting of the Joint Economic Commission held in 1995, Bangladesh submitted a list of 21 items for the grant of duty-free entry by India. These included tea, jute carpets, other jute goods, garments, electronic goods, video cassettes, electrical goods, leather goods, ceramic tableware, cables, computer software, insulation, books and periodicals, dried fish and printed paper. In response, the Government of India stated that Bangladesh should identify from this list items for which it is the only supplier to India and that India would consider reduction or removal of duties only on these items. The other items in the list could be covered only under the special preferential arrangement which would come into force after the completion of the negotiations then underway for SAPTA. Given the time-consuming nature of the SAPTA negotiations, this virtually amounted to an indefinite postponement of any worthwhile tariff concessions on these items.

In bilateral dialogues between India and Bangladesh at the non-governmental level, several participants have made suggestions regarding the extension by India of unilateral free trade treatment to Bangladesh. This suggestion has been predicated on the assumption that the growth and prosperity of Bangladesh would redound to the benefit of India and would also be a major factor in bringing stability to the region as a whole. Unilateral free trade would push the trade exchanges between the two countries to a much higher level, and substantially reduce the trade gap and pave the way for the integration of the two economies. This, in turn, would have a beneficial spillover effect on the political climate of the relations between the two countries, which would improve the prospects of cooperation in other areas.

It is very unlikely that if India establishes a unilateral free trade regime for Bangladeshi products, there would be a flooding of exports from Bangladesh to India and thereby a disruption of the domestic industry in India. That this is unlikely to happen was demonstrated in the case of the export of *jamdani* saris from Bangladesh to India. In the beginning, only a small preferential margin was created by India for the entry of this product. When exports of the *jamdani* did not pick up, a regime of duty-free quota was established. Even then, exports did not exceed Rs 5 lakh (Rs 0.5 million) against a quota of Rs 50 lakh (Rs 5 million). This made it clear that the quota restriction was not at all necessary. In 1992, India agreed to remove the quotas and allow the product to be imported duty-free without any quantitative restriction. This did not cause any flooding of the Indian market by *jamdani* saris. This was mainly because of the numerous problems that Bangladesh faced in mobilizing supplies, mounting an effective export promotion campaign and overcoming transport and other infrastructural bottlenecks.

A second list of products was prepared in 1996 by the Metropolitan Chamber of Commerce and Industry of Dhaka and submitted to the Ministry of Commerce of the Government of Bangladesh for negotiating their duty-free entry into India. A third list of 36 items on which duty-free entry should be given was included in the report commissioned jointly by the Confederation of Indian Industry (CII) and the Metropolitan Chamber of Commerce and submitted in January 1997.

India adopted an incremental approach in responding to Bangladesh's request for duty-free entry of its goods into the Indian market. It did extend tariff concessions to Bangladesh from time to time but it was always too little and too late. During his visit to Bangladesh in June 1999, the then Prime Minister of India agreed, in principle, to Bangladesh's request for duty-free entry of products of its export interest. Soon thereafter, in August 1999, Bangladesh submitted a list of 25 product groups consisting of 121 items at the four-digit level for the grant of duty-free entry by India. India took almost three years to respond to this request and offered, at the Commerce Secretary-level talks in Dhaka in April 2002, duty-free access to 40 out of 121 items on Bangladesh's request list. This was notified in August 2002. Bangladesh did not find it satisfactory and added 70 more items to its list. Later, India agreed to allow duty-free entry for 39 more items. Bangladesh still did not find it of much consequence as it did not include most of the items of export interest in which it enjoyed competitive advantage, like jute and jute goods, footwear, readymade garments, knitwear and ceramic products. Thus, on the whole, the manner in which the concessions were extended by India only generated frustration and mistrust among the Bangladeshi negotiators.

The Government of India, on the other hand, also got frustrated because it felt that there was no appreciation of the concessions given by it in the face of what it considered to be formidable domestic opposition. Therefore, in the meeting of the Commerce Secretaries held in New Delhi in late March 2003, India indicated to Bangladesh that further liberalization would be possible only within the framework of a bilateral FTA, of which India subsequently submitted a draft. This draft has since then been under consideration by the Bangladesh government. Bangladesh had in the beginning said that it needed more time to consider the proposal. The reason given was that it was not equipped with the expertise to examine the proposal quickly from different angles. Besides, it wanted to wait longer to observe the functioning of the Indo-Sri Lanka Free Trade Agreement.

While Bangladesh's response to India's offer of an FTA was still pending, at the 14th SAARC Summit held in New Delhi in 2007, India announced its decision to grant duty-free access to all imports from Bangladesh that are not in the negative list of India under SAFTA. In addition, India offered to open its market for 8 million pieces of readymade garments from Bangladesh, out of which access would be given to 3 million, on the condition that Bangladesh would source from India the fabric required for producing these garments. Finally, India announced the application in its bilateral trade with Bangladesh, the SAFTA Rules of Origin of 30 per cent domestic value content. Initially, in 2006, India's negative list for imports from Bangladesh under SAFTA, consisted of 763 items. In 2007, it was reduced to 744 and in 2008, to 480. Since then, there have been further reductions, the latest two being of 47 items at the time of Sheikh Hasina's visit to India in January 2010 and of 46 textile items during Prime Minister Manmohan Singh's visit to Dhaka in September 2011.

By removing all the 46 textile items that are of export interest to Bangladesh from India's negative list for the least developed countries, under the provisions of SAFTA, the Government of India has taken a major step forward towards meeting Bangladesh's concerns regarding the widening trade gap between the two countries. Now these items will get duty-free and quota-free entry into the Indian market. Recently, Bangladeshi exporters have demonstrated their ability to capture a larger share of the Indian market for textiles. After the Government of India increased the tariff quota for certain textile items from 8 million tonnes to 10 million tonnes, Bangladeshi exporters utilized 7.5 million tonnes of the quota during the first seven months of the year 2010, indicating that the full quota of 10 million tonnes would have been utilized by the end of the year. Now, with the duty-free and quota-free entry into the Indian market of the 46 textile items, there is a prospect for a sizeable increase in the exports of textile products from Bangladesh to India. This was already reflected in the trade data for 2011–12 when the value of the export of all textile items increased to $203.3 million as compared to $128 million in 2010–11.[16]

India's reluctance till recently to further reduce the negative list arose out of its apprehension that the free import of textile items from Bangladesh could cause disruption to the Indian industry because of the competitive edge that Bangladesh has acquired in the export of these items. Now that the Government of India has removed the items which are the cause of real concern from its negative list, there seems to be little rationale for maintaining the list at all. The Prime Minister of India would have been well advised to declare during his visit that there would be no negative list for Bangladesh and that henceforward, Bangladeshi exporters should treat the entire Indian market as an extension of their domestic market. This would not only have enhanced the prospect of Bangladesh narrowing the trade gap with India, but more importantly, would have provided incentives to Bangladeshi manufacturers and their Indian and other foreign collaborators to invest in industrial development in Bangladesh with an eye on the vast Indian market. Fortunately, the necessary amends were made soon after the Indian Prime Minister's visit when in November 2011, the Government of India announced the grant of duty-free and quota-free access to all items of exports from Bangladesh except 25 tariff lines prohibited on security and health grounds.

Compulsions for an FTA

Bangladesh's lukewarm attitude towards India's offer of an FTA could be partly because of its expectation that under international pressure and in its own enlightened self-interest, India would, in any case, extend duty-free access to imports from Bangladesh without the latter being required to extend similar treatment to imports from India. This has actually come to materialize to a considerable extent through India's successive reductions in its SAFTA sensitive list which is of interest only to Bangladesh, as other least developed countries of South Asia already enjoy duty-free access to the Indian market. Second, Bangladesh might be entertaining a genuine fear of some of its industries being swamped by imports from

India in the event of the grant of duty-free access to Indian products under an FTA. Finally, its apprehension on the political ground of compromising its sovereignty if it linked its economy too closely with that of India might have also come into play.

An FTA is no panacea for dealing with trade problems, including that of trade imbalances. Besides, designing an FTA between two countries placed in a highly asymmetric economic position, as India and Bangladesh are, is by no means going to be an easy task. At the same time, there are obvious advantages in an FTA which cannot be ignored and which the extension of unilateral tariff concessions alone cannot ensure.

Whereas unilateral trade concessions are voluntary and discretionary and can be withdrawn, the concessions under an FTA are within a contractual framework and hence more stable.

Some of the conspicuous advantages to Bangladesh of an FTA with India are:

- A unilateral tariff concession may not provide for the elimination of non-tariff barriers, but an FTA, to be true to its nomenclature, must provide for the elimination of such barriers within a time-bound framework.
- An FTA is likely to substantially reduce illegal imports from India by diminishing their profitability vis-à-vis legal imports. This would eliminate several anomalies that have surfaced in the current trade relations between the two countries.
- An assured access to the large Indian market within a long-term contractual framework will be an incentive for Bangladesh to create export capacity for even those products in which it has potential competitive advantage, but which currently do not figure in its export basket.
- An FTA with India will enable Bangladesh to avoid discrimination against its exports in the Indian market vis-à-vis similar exports from countries with which India has signed FTAs recently, like Sri Lanka, Singapore, Thailand, Indonesia, Malaysia, Japan and Korea.
- Because of geographical proximity, and commonalties of language and consumption patterns, Bangladesh has a competitive advantage over the rest of India in exporting to the north-eastern part of India. With the implementation of an FTA with India, this advantage will come fully into play, assuming that other barriers to trade like cumbersome customs formalities and transport bottlenecks are also removed.

- An assured access to the Indian market would result in an enlarged flow of foreign private capital, including that from India, for investment for building export capacity and infrastructure in Bangladesh.
- An FTA will open up opportunities for specialization and division of labour between the two countries and thereby, the generation of intra-industry trade opportunities.
- An FTA is likely to improve the overall competitiveness of the Bangladesh economy through access to the marketing network, skill and technology of Indian manufacturers and trading partners.
- Finally, an FTA can contain measures for deeper integration of the economies of two countries, including trade facilitation measures; mutual recognition, certification and harmonization of standards; transport; liberalization of investment flows and trade in services; joint development of infrastructure; monetary and financial cooperation; and coordination of macroeconomic policies.

Bangladesh, as a less developed country, is likely to gain more than India by the linking of the two economies through an FTA. This has been demonstrated in the way the Indo-Sri Lanka Free Trade Agreement, which came into force in 2000, has so far worked. After the FTA came into force, the trade imbalance between the two countries markedly narrowed in favour of Sri Lanka. In 1998, Sri Lanka's import–export ratio with respect to India was 14.3:1; in 2005, this ratio got narrowed down to 2.8:1. In the five years following the agreement, Sri Lanka's exports grew ten-fold, while imports from India grew less than four-fold. Moreover, taking advantage of the agreement, Sri Lanka was able to export a number of non-traditional items to India and thereby diversify its export basket. The number of products exported from Sri Lanka to India increased from 505 in 1999 to 1,062 in 2005. And above all, free trade provided Indian investors an incentive to invest in Sri Lanka. Consequently, there was a sharp increase in the inflow of Indian private capital into Sri Lanka. Cumulative Indian investment as of 1998 was a mere Rs 165 million; it increased to Rs 19.7 billion in 2005,when India became the fifth largest investor in Sri Lanka.[17]

In the Indo-Sri Lanka Free Trade Agreement, the question of asymmetry has been addressed by allowing Sri Lanka to have a longer negative list and a longer time period (eight years as against India's three years) to reach the zero-tariff level. Since Bangladesh is a least developed country these provisions can be better calibrated in its favour.

However, benefits to Bangladesh will depend largely on how the FTA with India is designed. In order to enable Bangladesh to derive maximum benefits from an FTA with India and make it really worthwhile, the following features should be introduced in it:

- The speed of liberalization should be much faster by India than by Bangladesh in order to provide a level playing field to the latter. In this respect, the Indo-Bangladesh FTA should be Indo-Sri Lanka FTA plus.
- Free trade must provide for the elimination within a time-bound framework of all non-tariff barriers, including administrative regulations and taxes, inclusive of those levied by Indian states, which discriminate against trade. A suitable mechanism should be created to identify such barriers and monitor their elimination.
- The negative list should be confined to a few commodities justified exclusively on security and health grounds and not on protectionist or revenue grounds. (This was done in November 2011.)
- If tariff quotas are resorted to for the import of sensitive items like readymade garments, there should be a provision for phasing them out within a time-bound framework and allowing all imports duty-free.
- If there is a provision in the FTA for special safeguards, Bangladesh should be given greater flexibility with regard to sector coverage, duration of safeguards, establishment of injury, etc.
- The FTA should include measures for deeper integration, particularly trade facilitation and investment promotion measures.
- It should provide for a regular dialogue between the Finance Ministers of India and Bangladesh for a better understanding of the changes in the two countries, in macroeconomic policies in the areas of tariffs, exchange rates, interest rates, administered prices and subsidies.
- India should establish within the framework of the FTA, a sizeable fund for investment in Bangladesh in order to improve and strengthen its infrastructure, and for capacity-building for export production and human resources development.

In negotiations for an FTA, Bangladesh will be in a stronger bargaining position, both because of its status as a least developed country and its trade regime being more liberal than that of India. Moreover, there will be lesser difficulty and lower costs for it in moving to a free trade regime because there is a virtual FTA in place in respect to a large number of commodities, which are in any case imported duty-free through the clandestine route.

Comprehensive Economic Partnership Agreement (CEPA)

An FTA between India and Bangladesh should provide for or be a part of a wider arrangement for cooperation in other related areas such as liberalization of investment flows and of trade in services, management of water resources, joint development of infrastructure, science and technology, energy and environment. To this end, the two countries should enter into a Comprehensive Economic Partnership Agreement (CEPA), of which the FTA could be the kingpin and cooperation in areas outside trade, the other key components.

In the paper on Indo-Bangladesh trade, published in 2011 in the *South Asia Economic Journal*, Mustafizur Rahman et al. have also made a similar suggestion:

> Indeed, a broad-based, two-track Common Economic Partnership Agreement that includes trade in goods, services, connectivity and investment-related aspects, along with scope for sectoral cooperation, in a phased manner, could be considered with a view to exploring the opportunities of multi-dimensional cooperation between the two countries.[18]

The suggestion for concluding a CEPA between the two countries was informally made by this writer on the occasion of the recent high-level exchange of visits by leaders of the two countries. However, neither the Government of India nor the Government of Bangladesh showed the preparedness to embrace it. Perhaps, the political consideration of not appearing to be coming too close to India too soon after coming to power, weighed with the Bangladesh government. Again for political reasons, India wanted the initiative in this matter to be taken by Bangladesh. However, a hint that the two countries might be moving in that direction was given in the following paragraph of the Joint Communiqué signed on the occasion of Sheikh Hasina's visit to India in January 2010.

> The two Prime Ministers agreed to put in place a comprehensive framework of cooperation for development between the two countries, encapsulating their mutually shared vision for the future, which would include cooperation in water resources, power, transportation and connectivity, tourism and education.[19]

If and when a CEPA is negotiated between the two countries, it must include cooperation for optimal utilization of the waters of the common rivers, including more effective functioning of the Joint River Commission (JRC). Among other things, it should be made mandatory for the JRC to meet at the political level at pre-fixed regular intervals, to analyze on a continuing basis the flows of the waters of important common rivers and to develop models for the optimum utilization of the waters of these rivers in the interest of both countries. An agreed provision on arbitration should also be included in the JRC's statute. The CEPA should further include mandatory provisions for the two countries to come to each other's assistance, in situations of natural disasters, sudden shortage of essential supplies and economic and financial crisis.

A very significant development towards putting in place an institutional framework for exploring new avenues and approaches to mutual economic cooperation was the signing, during the Indian Prime Minister's visit to Dhaka in September 2011, of a Framework Agreement on Cooperation for Development. Under this agreement, the two countries can, if and when they muster the necessary political will, negotiate an FTA or a CEPA, which, apart from providing for free trade, can include measures for deeper integration of the economies of the two countries. An important provision under the agreement is the establishment of a Joint Consultative Commission for its effective and smooth implementation. The Commission will function under the leadership of the foreign ministers of the two countries. It is encouraging that the Commission has been meeting regularly since its establishment at the level of foreign ministers.

The Framework Agreement on Development Cooperation also provided for sub-regional cooperation. A trilateral working group meeting on sub-regional cooperation between India, Bangladesh and Bhutan in the power and water sectors and in connectivity was held in April 2013. Since cooperation under SAFTA is faltering and, in any case, there is no effective provision in the Agreement for deeper integration, sub-regional cooperation between India and its north-eastern neighbours hold out the best promise for economic integration in South Asia. But, for this to succeed, India will have to take the major initiative by way of making financial resources and technology available for building infrastructure in the sub-region.

Credit Arrangement

India has extended credits to Bangladesh since the liberation of the country, with brief interregnums without credit from time to time. Credits granted to Bangladesh soon after its liberation were designed to ensure the supply of essential commodities and to meet the need for relief and rehabilitation. They were extended under exceptionally soft terms and conditions and a good part of them was in the nature of grants. As they were geared to meet specific urgent needs, they were quickly disbursed.

Subsequently, Indian credits to Bangladesh increasingly assumed the form of export credit. As Bangladesh needed the commodities and equipment supplied under these credits for rehabilitating some of the industries devastated by the Liberation War and for meeting the requirements of its damaged and depleted infrastructure, these credits were also quickly utilized. Further, they generated a demand for Indian goods, met through the normal trade channels.

In retrospect, it would appear that it would have been to the benefit of both the countries if these credits were forthcoming in larger magnitudes and under more liberal terms and conditions. Bureaucratic delays in processing requests, particularly from the Indian side, and insistence by the Indian Ministry of Finance on meeting avoidable technical requirements often led to delays in their utilization and hence extensions of the period of utilization.

In the third phase, the terms and conditions of Indian credits became stiffer. The Export-Import (EXIM) Bank of India (earlier IDBI) credits were granted on commercial terms. But the average rate of interest was softened by including in the package government credit at a subsidized rate of interest. During this phase, as a least developed country, Bangladesh became the recipient of aid under highly soft terms and conditions from almost all major donors and international financial institutions. Most of the bilateral export credits extended to Bangladesh by third countries were also under better terms and conditions than those extended by India. Thus, Indian credits became increasingly less attractive to Bangladesh. This situation was aggravated by the conditionalities imposed by India on the utilization of the credits. Bangladesh, on its part, became choosier about accepting Indian credits. The combined effect of these factors was increasingly longer delays in utilizing Indian credits. To give an example, a credit of Rs 30 crore (Rs 300 million) extended by India in 1990 was to expire in 1991. This was extended to July 1993. As the progress in utilization was still not satisfactory, it was further extended to July 1995.

Both because of the terms of Indian credit and the conditionalities attached to their utilization, Bangladesh, for the past several years, has evinced less and less interest in Indian credits. However, if restrictions on utilization are relaxed and the terms further softened, Bangladesh can still use Indian credits with profit because it is in need of resources for investment and it is easier and faster to get supplies from India than against the credits extended by other countries. Besides, some of the supplies available from India are uniquely suited to meet the requirements of Bangladesh. In this context, India's announcement during the Bangladesh Prime Minister's visit to India in January 2010, of the extension of credit of $1 billion to Bangladesh represented a significant move forward in bolstering the economic relations between the two countries. It was the single largest amount of credit extended by India to any country. It was to be utilized mainly for expanding and upgrading the transport infrastructure of Bangladesh. This has an important bearing on Indo-Bangladesh trade. The credit was granted under very soft terms and conditions, with 1.7 per cent rate of interest, 20 years of maturity and a five-year grace period. An agreement for the utilization of this credit was signed on 7 August 2010 between the EXIM Bank of India and the Government of Bangladesh. An agreement was also reached at that time on a number of projects for which the Indian credit would be utilized. These included projects for the development of railway infrastructure, construction of roads and bridges and purchase of buses.

In the Joint Statement issued at the end of the Indian Prime Minister's visit to Dhaka in September 2011, both sides expressed their satisfaction with the progress in the implementation of the $1 billion line of credit. However, in his speech at the University of Dhaka, the Prime Minister of India stated that the two sides had mutually agreed on projects worth over $750 million. This implies that during the period of one year and eight months after the announcement of the extension of the credit, hardly any project under it had been implemented. This demonstrates India's incapacity for speedy and timely delivery of projects in foreign countries. It is true that a part of the blame for the tardy implementation of projects under Indian credit lies with the recipient country, but by all accounts, the main responsibility for non-delivery or excessively delayed delivery rests with the Government of India. This is where China decisively scores over India.

India has converted into grant $200 million out of the $1 billion credit. It has also reduced the rate of interest on the $800 million credit to 1 per cent. By November 2014, $175 million of the grant portion had been reimbursed which, as indicated by the Bangladesh Government, would be used for the construction of the Padma Bridge. Out of the loan portion, nearly $752 million for 15 projects had been committed. Out of these seven had been completed, four more were under execution and the remaining four were being tendered. The completed projects were mostly for the delivery of buses, wagons and locomotives. Projects under execution included construction of bridges, strengthening of the Bangladesh Standards and Testing Institution, construction of the Khulna–Mongla Port rail line and other sections of railway tracks.

If the facilities for connectivity granted by Bangladesh during Sheikh Hasina's visit to India in 2010 are operationalized, India would develop a large stake in the railways, roadways and riverine infrastructure of Bangladesh. Given this stake, the renovation and expansion of this infrastructure would be equivalent to the renovation, modernization and expansion of India's own infrastructure. As indicated by the then Indian Prime Minister on more than one occasion, India at that time was planning to invest $500 billion for the development of infrastructure within its territory during the next three years. In that context, an amount of $1 billion, earmarked for the development of infrastructure in Bangladesh, was too meagre. Now that most of the projects under the $1 billion credit are nearing implementation, India should commit several times larger resources, say in the range of $10–15 billion, mostly in the form of grants, for the development of infrastructure in Bangladesh.

Joint Ventures

Diversification of the export production capacity of Bangladesh is essential for bringing about a substantial reduction in its trade imbalance with India. Both joint ventures and direct investment can play an important role here. These can also contribute to the process of the industrialization of the country and the acceleration of the growth of its economy.

A number of joint venture projects, including buy-back arrangements, have been under consideration ever since the commencement of the economic relations between India and Bangladesh. However, very few of them have materialized so far. The Joint Economic Commission had identified three joint ventures—sponge iron, fertilizers and cement—to be undertaken by the two countries. Sponge iron production was supposed to be based on the utilization of the natural gas of Bangladesh and iron ore from India. The output of sponge iron in excess of Bangladesh's domestic needs was to be exported to India. Fertilizer production was also to be based on Bangladesh's gas and the final product was to be exported exclusively to India. Cement production was to be based on limestone of Meghalaya in India and was meant for meeting the domestic needs of Bangladesh.

The negotiations between the two countries on these joint ventures had reached a fairly advanced stage by the year 1974–75. But political upheavals in Bangladesh towards the end of 1975 brought them to an abrupt halt. They were subsequently resumed but at a lacklustre pace, partly because of political reasons and partly because the underlying assumptions behind these projects had undergone drastic changes with the passage of time.

The most frustrating story was that of the proposed joint venture for sponge iron production. It appeared several times, including during the regime of President Ziaur Rahman, that an agreement on the project was at hand. But every time, some technical hitch would crop up at the last moment bringing the negotiations to a halt, to be resumed all over again at a later propitious time. At one stage, the Birlas took over the negotiations from the public sector enterprise MECON, but before they could reach an agreement with the Bangladesh Engineering Corporation, the latter indicated that it was no longer interested in the project being set up in the public sector and that the Birlas should, therefore, find a partner from the private sector in Bangladesh. Thereafter, the project was virtually abandoned until it got included in a different form in the Tatas' ambitious proposal for investment in Bangladesh.

One reason why none of the negotiations on these joint venture projects could be finalized before the political changes in 1975 was that India was unable or unwilling to provide the entire resources for the project and was looking for alternative or supplementary sources of finance. And when alternative sources were found, the entire focus of the project got changed at the behest of the third-party sources of financing. This resulted in a loss of interest on the part of India and the consequent loss of momentum in the negotiations. On the other hand, the Chinese government gave a better account of itself by taking up a few major projects, particularly in the power sector, entirely on its own and delivering them on time.

The character of joint-venture negotiations between the two countries changed drastically after the introduction of economic reforms in

Bangladesh and subsequently in India. The state ceased to be the key player in bringing about the ventures though it still retained a catalytic role. Private firms in India started showing interest in setting up joint ventures in Bangladesh, including some with buy-back arrangements. Joint venture projects to be taken up by the private sectors of the two countries were identified several times. These included composite textile mills, pharmaceuticals, chemicals, machine tools, mini steel plants, assembly plants for automobiles, electronic goods, cement, food processing and leather goods. Recently, joint ventures in the services sector, particularly health, education and tourism, have been added to the list.

Harnessing Complementarities

The Bangladeshi and Indian economies have many complementarities that can be harnessed to mutual advantage. Their inability so far to have done so has carried immense costs for both of them which, over a period, have become cumulative. In the meanwhile, the situation on the ground has altered inexorably, which has virtually closed the options for cooperation which were available earlier. For example, before the Partition of the Indian subcontinent, the part of the greater province of Bengal which constitutes the present state of West Bengal, did not produce any significant quantity of raw jute, as the part lying in the then East Bengal had comparative advantage in producing this commodity. If the trade flows between India and the then East Pakistan had remained uninterrupted, the latter would have continued to supply raw jute for the jute mills in West Bengal, which would have continued to remain a marginal producer of raw jute. But since the trade was interrupted after the 1965 Indo-Pakistan War, West Bengal was obliged to produce its own raw jute in order to feed its jute mills and soon emerged as a major producer, competing with the then East Pakistan (now Bangladesh), for a share of the foreign markets. Now, even if in the changed political context, the two governments want to reverse the process, it will not be possible for them to do so. India will not find it politically feasible to make the Indian farmers of raw jute to shift to the production of other commodities. And Bangladeshi farmers are unlikely to have an interest in expanding their production of raw jute due to the diversification of land to more beneficial crops, especially with jute manufacturing fast becoming a sunset industry in both India and Bangladesh. It is problematic whether it would be possible to revive the fortunes of this industry by taking advantage of the eco-friendly nature of its products.

However, there is scope for joint collaboration between the two countries in order to improve the export prices of raw jute and to increase their share in the global market for jute and jute manufactures as well as to meet the threat from synthetics and substitutes. This form of collaboration was actively explored by the Joint Economic Commission during the early 1970s, but could not be taken to its logical conclusion because of the intervening political turmoil in 1975.

Another example of complementarity that prevailed until a few years ago, was in the production of newsprint and paper. It would have made tremendous economic sense for India to have invested in upgrading the quality and expanding the capacity of the Khulna mills for producing newsprint and paper and reaching a long-term agreement with Bangladesh to buy back a substantial part of the production to meet its requirement. But India did not put forward any proposal for such a collaboration, partly because it wanted to keep its options open for getting supplies from other sources, and also because Bangladesh was not prepared to undertake any long-term commitment for supply to India.

We have already referred to the complementarities existing in the production of fertilizers, sponge iron and cement in Bangladesh. The first two projects, based on gas supply from Bangladesh, have been abandoned after the position taken by the Bangladesh government that the gas supplies available in the country are not adequate even for meeting its minimum domestic requirement. Only the project for the production of cement in Bangladesh, based on limestone supplies from Meghalaya, materialized because of the investment made by the private foreign company, Lafarge. However, the Lafarge plant has run into difficulty because of the agitation mounted against it at the local level on environmental grounds.

The other areas in which private-sector joint venture projects have materialized are garments and assembly plants for trucks and three-wheelers. These, however, are not accompanied by buy-back arrangements. There is distinct complementarity in the field of tourism. The two countries can cooperate to their mutual advantage by way of joint marketing and publicity for tourism as well as joint upgradation and development of infrastructure for tourism.

Investment

India can be a very important source of Foreign Direct Investment (FDI) for Bangladesh, thereby contributing to the expansion of its export capacity as well as to the growth of its economy. The Bangladesh government claims that it maintains one of the most liberal regimes in the developing world for foreign investment. In spite of this, the overall amount of FDI in Bangladesh has not amounted to any substantial sum and hardly any major project with FDI has materialized so far. This is mainly because foreign investors feel a sense of insecurity in investing in Bangladesh. Indian investors are particularly apprehensive on this account.

In 2005, the Tatas put forward a proposal for the investment of close to $3 billion in Bangladesh for setting up a steel plant, fertilizer factories and power units, mainly based on the local supply of gas. It was the largest investment proposal made by any foreign investor to Bangladesh. This led to other Indian companies like Reliance, Mittal and the Birlas also showing interest in similar and other projects for investment in Bangladesh. If the Tatas' proposal had materialized, many of these other investors would have followed suit. But after keeping the proposal under consideration for about three years, the Bangladesh government rejected it on the grounds that because of the limited gas reserves in Bangladesh, it could not guarantee the supply of gas needed for operating these projects.

In spite of the sad fate of these major project proposals, FDIs from India have constituted a significant proportion of the total amount of foreign investment flows into Bangladesh. According to an estimate in 2010, Bangladesh attracted investment amounting to nearly $2 billion in the previous two years, out of which investment from India was around $400 million, or 20 per cent of the total.[20] Among some of the important investment ventures that had materialized were the Apollo Group's collaboration in opening a state-of-the-art hospital in Dhaka, and involvement of several Indian companies in the pharmaceuticals, information technology (IT) and readymade garment sectors in Bangladesh. Moreover, Indian companies had a share in the ownership and operation of some of the major trading houses in Bangladesh. A significant development in Indo-Bangladesh economic relations was the signing in 2009 of the bilateral Investment Promotion and Protection Agreement. Following that, a large number of Indian firms from both the public and private sectors have been working on various turnkey projects in Bangladesh in sectors such as power, telecom, textiles, chemicals, pharmaceuticals and engineering. Total investment in Bangladesh from India in the year 2011 amounted to $210 million. This was not an impressive figure.

The real breakthrough in Indian investment in Bangladesh will come only if there is a significant improvement in the political relations between the two countries. These relations have no doubt improved after the Awami League government under Sheikh Hasina came to power following the Parliamentary elections in December 2008. But there is still a long way to go as Indian investors would like to be sure about the stability of the law and order situation in Bangladesh and the durability of the improved climate of relations. Besides, in view of the operation of the big-neighbour-small-neighbour syndrome between the two countries, even the present government is unlikely to go very far, at least in the short and medium run, in welcoming Indian investments.

Gas Supply to India and Cooperation in the Energy Sector

A proposal for piping out a part of the gas reserves of Bangladesh to India had been under consideration for a long time after the liberation of the country. During the regime of President Ziaur Rahman, a tentative understanding had been reached on the approximate volume of gas to be supplied to India; foreign sources to be tapped for financing the pipeline to transport the natural gas; India's contribution to the construction of the pipeline; and alternative approaches to reach an agreement on the price at which the gas would be supplied. But before the remaining issues could be sorted out and the deal finalized, political parties and forces in Bangladesh raised, mainly on political grounds, a hue and cry against the supply of gas to India. Thereafter, the whole issue became highly controversial and the governments that came to power subsequently decided to leave the proposal alone. From 1995 onwards, the Bangladesh side started taking the view that as the proven gas reserves of Bangladesh were not adequate to meet even its own need in the foreseeable future, until more wells were dug and new discoveries made, the question of making gas available to India either for direct commercial purposes or for setting up gas-based industries in Bangladesh did not arise. For all one knows, the political factor and not statistical reality might have played a role in the formulation of this position.

Currently, Bangladesh suffers from an acute energy shortage. Its power production is estimated to be 25 to 50 per cent less than its total demand. It was in this context that during Sheikh Hasina's visit to India in January 2010, India offered to supply 250 megawatts of electricity to Bangladesh from its grid and also agreed to expedite inter-grid connectivity between the two countries. This offer was subsequently enhanced to 500 megawatts. An additional 100 megawatts was promised from the Paltana power plant then under construction in Tripura. In addition, a joint venture agreement between the National Thermal Power Corporation (NTPC) of India and Bangladesh Power Development Board was signed in January 2012 involving an investment of $1.5 billion for setting up a coal-based power plant in Khulna for generating 1,320 megawatt of electricity. The work on it is in progress and the plant is likely to be commissioned by 2016. The supply of 500 megawatt of electricity was completed in March 2014. Grid connection to facilitate the flow of electricity from India to Bangladesh was jointly inaugurated by the prime ministers of the two countries through video conferencing on 5 October 2013. India has also agreed to share information with Bangladesh on hydro-power projects coming up in the North-Eastern region and invited it to consider the prospect of participating in them through possible import or joint venture collaboration

Transit of Indian Goods through Bangladesh Territory

The transit arrangement to transport Indian goods to the country's north-eastern part through what has now become the Bangladesh territory was operational till 1965. This arrangement was brought to an end by the Indo-Pakistan War of 1965 and has not been restored since. Some of the infrastructure through which the goods in transit were carried have decayed or been disrupted because of sheer negligence and prolonged disuse. After the liberation of Bangladesh, India took up the question of restoring these transit facilities with the Bangladesh government. But Bangladesh has until now continued to deny them to India. When this issue was raised with the then prime minister of Bangladesh by the then Indian commerce minister during the latter's visit to Dhaka in December 1993, as the leader of the Indian delegation to the meeting of the Joint Economic Commission, the former made Bangladesh's acceptance of this proposal conditional upon India reaching an agreement with Bangladesh on the permanent sharing of the waters of the Ganga at Farakka. The Indian side was apparently not in a position to accept such a condition. As a result, during most of the period since 1993, the issue was never officially or publicly raised by the Indian side.

While Bangladesh has been denying the grant of transit facilities through its territory for the passage of Indian goods, it has, at the same time, been putting pressure on India by various means to grant transit facilities through Indian territory, for the passage of Nepalese and Bhutanese goods to Bangladesh and to overseas markets through the Bangladesh ports of Mongla and Chittagong. It has also been demanding transit through the Indian territory for its goods destined for Nepal and Bhutan. The extension of each of these transit facilities will bring distinct and irrefutable economic and political advantages to the parties concerned. Their denial is the most glaring example of short-sighted political consideration coming in the way of economic cooperation even in areas where such cooperation is a positive sum game. Therefore, purely from the economic point of view, linking the extension of such facilities to other political and economic goals does not make much sense. Such linkages generally lead to a race to the bottom in economic cooperation and can even have the effect of freezing such cooperation for a long time to come. All the four countries would have gained immensely if these transit facilities had been in operation. The following are some of the obvious benefits of the two countries opening up their territories for transit:

- India would be able to send goods to its north-eastern region at a cost much lower than that being incurred presently.
- It would help in attracting investment to the north-eastern region—both foreign and Indian—which is currently not taking place due to, among other reasons, high transportation costs, in the absence of a direct transit route through the Bangladeshi territory. This would remove one of the reasons for the continued backwardness of the north-east and link the states in the region more closely with the mainstream of the Indian economy. This would have a salutary political effect.
- It would facilitate large-scale investment by India for the expansion and upgrading of transport infrastructure in Bangladesh.
- It would have also led to large-scale investment for the development of the Chittagong and Mongla ports in order to handle the additional volume of Indian, Nepalese and later, Bhutanese cargo. According to a statement made by Sheikh Hasina during her visit to India in January 2010, only 40 per cent of the capacity of the Chittagong port and 10 per cent of that of Mongla were being utilized at that time.
- The reactivation of the transit routes for carrying Indian goods through Bangladeshi territory would trigger the development of throbbing service centres like banks, insurance, hotels, rest houses and petrol pumps along the routes in Bangladesh.
- There would be direct economic gain to Bangladesh by way of transit fees which, according to the most conservative estimates, would amount to at least $1 billion per annum.

- With the acceleration of growth in the north-eastern states of India, Bangladesh's exports to these states would increase substantially.
- Bangladesh's earnings from its exports to Nepal, due to the availability of transit facilities through India, would also increase sizeably.
- Due to the same reason, Nepal's export earnings from Bangladesh and from destinations beyond Bangladesh would also increase.
- With India's grant of transit facilities for trade between Bhutan and Bangladesh there would be an increase in the two-way trade between these two countries.

Till recently, Bangladesh was giving mainly three reasons in justification for denying transit facilities to India through its territory. There is little validity in any of these reasons. The argument that figured most prominently in the Bangladeshi media and the statements of political leaders was that India would take advantage of the facilities to transport troops and weapons, which would pose a threat to Bangladesh's sovereignty. This is patently a false argument because an agreement for granting transit facilities can easily include provisions prohibiting the transport of armed personnel and weapons. Besides, sending such cargo is the farthest from India's intentions. Finally, transit facilities granted by various countries to each other for the passage of goods through their territories have not posed any such problem. Thus, this argument is only a false alarm raised by Bangladesh. The real reason may lie somewhere else.

The second argument is that the transit of Indian goods through its territory will overburden and even 'destroy' Bangladesh's transport infrastructure, that is, railways, waterways, roads and highways. While addressing a seminar in Dhaka, the then Finance Minister of Bangladesh, Saifur Rahman said that the country's entire road system would collapse if transit facilities were given to India.[21] This argument is exaggerated because the transport infrastructure must be seen in the dynamic context of their being constantly updated, improved and expanded in response to the growing demand for their use. The grant of transit facilities for Indian goods will, in fact, accelerate the process of upgradation and improvement by attracting investment from the Government of India and Indian companies as well as from foreign companies.

The third argument, which is not advanced officially or publicly but mentioned informally, is that with the acceleration of the development of the north-eastern states of India, assisted by the grant of transit facilities by Bangladesh, their dependence on Bangladesh for imports would decrease and that, in fact, they might start selling their own products to Bangladesh. But the fact is that even now, the dependence of these states on imports from Bangladesh is very limited. Moreover, it would be short-sighted on the part of Bangladesh to seek to keep the north-eastern states of India permanently backward in order to preserve it as a captive market for its products. Neither the Government of India nor the north-eastern states would ever accept such a position. These states would exert all their efforts and for this purpose, put maximum pressure on the Government of India, to march in tandem with the rest of the country on the path of development. Bangladesh should, therefore, take the more enlightened view of seeing the benefits of its economic links with the north-eastern states in the dynamic context of their accelerated growth. It should, in fact, make its own contribution towards it.

India continues to enjoy transit facilities through Bangladeshi territory by means of inland water transport. This is covered under the Inland Water Transit and Trade (IWTT) Agreement between the two countries. The Protocol under this agreement has been extended from time to time and amended through the exchange of letters, mainly to provide for enhanced fees for the grant of transit facilities. The latest renewal was in 2012 for a period of two years. The amount of goods carried by this means of transport to the north-eastern part of India is very limited. Political considerations on the part of Bangladesh and indifference on the part of the Indian side have combined to keep these facilities to a minimum and at an utterly inadequate level. If Bangladesh would have agreed to it, and India would have made adequate investment, this transit facility would have been considerably improved and expanded to the mutual benefit of the two countries.

There are many obstacles to the movement of goods along the Indo-Bangladesh border. No thorough passage of vehicles or trains carrying goods is allowed across the borders of the two countries. Goods have to be trans-shipped, that is, unloaded and loaded again for onward movement. There is prolonged delay in the clearance and trans-shipment of goods because of cumbersome procedures, outdated methods and inadequacy of facilities such as warehousing and parking yards.

A rail link from the Indian border to the northern part of Bangladesh, which had existed before but had been lying in disuse and in a damaged condition, was opened some years ago. In the beginning, it was mainly used for carrying boulders from India for the construction of the Jamuna Bridge. The economic viability of the bridge can be enhanced immensely if it is used as a transit route for Indian goods and services destined for the north-eastern part of India.

In the ultimate analysis, the restoration and revival of the transport infrastructure between the two countries will be viable only if there is a steady expansion of trade between them. On the other hand, adequate transport infrastructure is a precondition for supporting expanded trade transactions. Thus, there is a vicious circle between limited trade transactions and lack or under-utilization of transport infrastructure. This circle can be broken only by a political determination to expand cooperation simultaneously in both the areas, that is, in trade as well as transport.

During Sheikh Hasina's visit to India in January 2010, a number of far-reaching measures were announced by Bangladesh to provide transit facilities through its territory to India. India in its turn announced that it would assist Bangladesh in the upgradation and expansion of its transport infrastructure. During the Bangladesh Foreign Minister Dipu Moni's visit to India in September 2009, Bangladesh had already agreed to the movement through its territory by road and rail, of containerized cargo from India. During Sheikh Hasina's visit, by far the most important decision taken was Bangladesh's agreement to 'allow use of Mongla and Chittagong ports for movement of goods to and from India through road and rail'.[22] At the same time, Bangladesh declared its intention to give Nepal and Bhutan access to Mongla and Chittagong ports. Another important move in the direction of providing transit facilities was Bangladesh's agreement to the construction of the proposed Akhaura–Agartala railway link, to be financed by a grant by India. When the construction of the railway link is completed, at least passenger travel between Kolkata and Agartala through Bangladesh would become possible.

Yet another important decision taken at the end of Sheikh Hasina's visit was facilitating greater use of the traditional waterways between the two countries for carrying cargo. It was decided that Ashugang on the Bangladesh side and Silghat on the Indian side would be declared 'ports of call' and the IWTT Protocol would be amended accordingly through exchange of letters. This would facilitate the transport through the riverine route, of very heavy dimension cargo to the Palatana power plant in Tripura. India agreed to provide dredgers to Bangladesh on an urgent basis for facilitating the movement of cargo along this waterway. It also agreed to make the necessary investment for the assessment of the improvement of infrastructure and the cost of transportation for enhanced use of the waterways.

India announced simultaneously to provide transit for the transport of Bangladesh's goods to Nepal and Bhutan. It further agreed that the Rohanpur–Singabad broad gauge railway link would be available for the transit of Nepali goods to Bangladesh and to the Mongla and Chittagong ports for export to third countries. India also agreed to consider providing facilities for transit to and from Bhutan. Bhutan has already started using a newly agreed trade route through India's north-eastern region to export its products to Bangladesh. Bhutanese trucks are entering Sylhet after crossing the Dawki–Tamabil Land Custom station.

The $1 billion line of credit India agreed to extend was to be devoted to a range of projects, mostly for the improvement of transport infrastructure, including the railway infrastructure, supply of locomotives and passenger coaches, rehabilitation of the Saidpur workshop, procurement of buses and dredging projects. India also agreed to consider Bangladesh's request for assistance to construct road infrastructure in Dhaka, including flyovers. India agreed to provide dredgers to Bangladesh on an urgent basis.

The implementation of these decisions would have constituted a decisive step towards facilitating the transit of Indian goods through Bangladesh territory and of Bangladeshi goods to Nepal and Bhutan and vice versa, and for upgrading and expanding transport infrastructure in Bangladesh. It would have opened a new chapter in Indo-Bangladesh economic relations.

Another important decision taken by the Government of India and announced before the visit of the Indian Prime Minister to Bangladesh, in early September 2011, was to develop seven Integrated Check Posts to facilitate trade between the two countries. In an Integrated Check Post, all services like customs, immigration, parking, cold storage, quarantine facilities, etc., are made available as part of a single integrated facility. Such an Integrated Check Post has been in operation in Agartala since November 2013. The conversion of several other land customs stations along the border, into Integrated Check Posts is under consideration.

By the time the Prime Minister visited Bangladesh, very few projects for upgrading and building transport infrastructure had taken off the ground. The only projects that seemed to have materialized were the operationalization of Ashuganj and Silghat as additional ports of call; the passage of over-dimensional cargo for the Palatana project; and the additional rail route provided by India for the transit of Nepalese goods to Bangladesh.

It was expected that during the Indian Prime Minister's visit, some major steps would be taken in the areas of transit and transport infrastructure. However, the withdrawal at the last minute, of the agreement reached between the two countries on the sharing of the waters of the

Teesta River turned out to be a big setback. The immediate response of the Bangladesh Government was to postpone the signing of MoUs for the operationalization of some of the crucial transit facilities offered by Bangladesh. These included the port facilities at Chittagong and Mongla. Since then, India's inability to deliver on the land boundary agreement and that on the Teesta River has been the principal obstacle to India availing itself of the transit facilities.

It is hoped that the BJP-led new government at the centre, which has a majority in the lower House of the Indian Parliament, would be able to push through the Parliament the constitutional amendment to give effect to the Protocol on the Land Boundary Agreement and develop a national consensus on the draft Agreement on the Distribution of the Water of the Teesta River. With regard to the latter, much hope is pinned on the forthcoming visit to Dhaka of the West Bengal Chief Minister Mamata Banerjee whose negative attitude has so far come in the way of the signing of this Agreement.

River Water Issues

The sharing of the waters of the common rivers between India and Bangladesh has been a bone of contention and a major source of tension in the relations between the two countries. Given the sensitivity of the issue and the importance of rivers for the economic, social and cultural life of the peoples of the two countries, particularly of Bangladesh, this problem will persist in varying intensity in the coming years as well. However, during the last few years, the two countries have made commendable progress in finding solutions to some of the major river water issues and forging mutual cooperation in dealing with the problem. There is in operation a treaty on the sharing of one of the largest rivers traversing the territories of the two countries, that is, the Ganga. This treaty has been in force for over 17 years now, and both the countries appear to be satisfied with the way it has been working. An indication of it is that neither has so far invoked its optional clause for demanding a review in order to meet any grievance. Joint monitoring is carried out at Farakka in India and the Harding Bridge in Bangladesh to observe and record water flows during the lean season every year.

In appreciation of the desire of Bangladesh as a lower riparian to claim its shares of the river waters as a legal right derived from bilateral agreements, India agreed in 1997 to set up a Joint Committee of Experts which took up seven rivers for negotiating water-sharing agreements, that is,

Teesta, Manu, Khowai, Gumti, Muhuri, Jaldhaka and Torsa. The river Feni was added to this list in September 2005. The Agreement on the Sharing of the Teesta Water was thrashed out before the visit to Bangladesh of the then Prime Minister of India in September 2011. However, due to a last-minute problem of a domestic political nature in India, the agreement could not be signed during the visit. India has since been trying to develop an internal political consensus on this issue. Meanwhile the Teesta water continues to flow to Bangladesh as before. At the technical level, for the first time in 2012, both sides exchanged data on the flow of the river at Galazdoba in India and Dalia in Bangladesh.

Bangladesh has expressed concern about India's Tipaimukh project on the Barak River in the state of Manipur. The main purpose of the project is to generate hydro power, control floods and stabilize the flow of the river. There is no component in it for diverting water for irrigation. Stabilization of the flow and flood control would be of benefit to Bangladesh too. As a move towards winning Bangladesh's confidence, a sub-group on the Tipaimukh project has been set up under the Joint River Commission. In the first meeting of the sub-group held in August 2012, the detailed project report was made available to the Bangladesh side. Apart from its repeated assurance that no action will be taken that will adversely affect Bangladesh's interest, India has offered to Bangladesh a stake in the project.

While appreciating Bangladesh's desire to claim its shares of the waters of the common rivers on the basis of legal agreements, it should be realized that to arrive at such an agreement for 54 trans-boundary rivers between the two countries would be highly time-consuming and not even feasible for several of these rivers. Moreover, in view of the looming scarcity of water in the two countries, the issue of the augmentation of the flows of the common rivers and collaborative management of water resources should be accorded equal, if not higher, priority. In this context, it is important to take into account the impact of climate change which can influence floods, droughts, sea level, rainfall and salinity. Moreover, any effort for sustainable management of water resources of the trans-boundary rivers would be meaningful only if there is also an efficient utilization and quality control of the water resources within each of the two countries. It is also extremely important for the two countries to explore how the water resources can be utilized as an instrument of broader economic cooperation in the areas of connectivity, energy, tourism and other commercial activities. Finally, a collaborative, integrated and sustainable management of the water resources of the common rivers of the two countries will call for robust institutions that can withstand short-term political shocks. In this connection, the need for restructuring the Indo-Bangladesh Joint River Commission in order to revitalize and empower it should be a matter of high priority.[23]

Notes

1. The figures are taken from Mohammad Mafizur Rahman's article, 'Bangladesh-India Bilateral Trade: Causes of Imbalance and Measures for Improvement', *Journal of Applied Business and Economics*, Volume 8, No. 1 (2008). The original source of the data used in this article is the IMF.
2. Calculated from data accessed from International Monetary Fund, Direction of Trade Statistics database, http://elibrary-data.imf.org/ (accessed on 15 January 2015).
3. Mafizur Rahman, 'Bangladesh-India Bilateral Trade'.
4. Calculated from data accessed from International Monetary Fund, Direction of Trade Statistics database, http://elibrary-data.imf.org/ (accessed on 15 January 2015).
5. Mafizur Rahman, 'Bangladesh-India Bilateral Trade'.
6. Mustafizur Rahman, Towfiqul Islam Khan, Ashiqun Nabi and Tapas Kumar Paul, 'Bangladesh's Export Opportunities in the Indian Market: Addressing Barriers and Strategies for Future', *South Asia Economic Journal*, Volume 12, No. 1 (March 2011) 117–41.
7. Calculated from data accessed from International Monetary Fund, Direction of Trade Statistics database, http://elibrary-data.imf.org/ (accessed on 15 January 2015).
8. Nurul Islam, 'Indo-Bangladesh Economic Relations: Some Thoughts', *Economic and Political Weekly*, Volume 39, No. 36 (2004) 4069–75.
9. Mustafizur Rahman et al., 'Bangladesh's Export Opportunities in the Indian Market'.
10. Mosharraf Hossain, *Weekly Holiday*, 11 June 1993.
11. Government of India, 'India-Bangladesh Joint Statement, January 2010: Joint Communiqué Issued on the Occasion of the Visit to India of Her Excellency Sheikh Hasina, Prime Minister of Bangladesh' (Ministry of External Affairs, New Delhi, 12 January 2010), http://www.satp.org/satporgtp/countries/bangladesh/document/papers/indiabangjoint2010.htm (accessed on 22 April 2015).
12. From Table 9, in Mafizur Rahman, 'Bangladesh-India Bilateral Trade'.
13. Calculated from data accessed from International Monetary Fund, Direction of Trade Statistics database, http://elibrary-data.imf.org/ (accessed on 15 January 2015).
14. Ibid.

15. Mustafizur Rahman et al.,'Bangladesh's Export Opportunities in the Indian Market'.
16. Calculated from data accessed from http://www.comtrade.un.org (accessed on 15 January 2015).
17. Deshel del Mel, 'Indo-Sri Lanka Free Trade Agreement: Sri Lankan Perspective', *Trade Insight*, Volume 4, No. 4 (2008).
18. Mustafizur Rahman et al., 'Bangladesh's Export Opportunities in the Indian Market'.
19. Government of India, 'India-Bangladesh Joint Statement'.
20. Figures taken from *Asia Pulse* (Dhaka), 23 August 2010.
21. *The Hindu*, 'Bangladesh Rejects Transit Facility for India', 12 December 2002.
22. Government of India, 'India-Bangladesh Joint Statement, January 2010'.
23. Several ideas in this paragraph are taken from the press release issued after the Indo-Bangladesh Roundtable organized by the Strategic Foresight Group in Mumbai on 2 July 2013. The author of this book participated in the Roundtable. The text of the press release is included as annexure to Strategic Foresight Group, *Rivers of Peace: Restructuring Indo-Bangladesh Relations* (Mumbai: Strategic Foresight Group, 2013).

FIVE Pakistan and Indo-Pak Relations

Pakistan: Polity, Society and Economy

Pakistan's State Ideology and Prospect for Democracy

Pakistan has variously been called a failed state, one of the most dangerous places in the world and an epicentre of terrorism. Indian scholars, strategic thinkers, and other commentators have been particularly prone to presenting a grim picture of Pakistan's economy, society and system of governance. Much of it is in the nature of wishful thinking. There is, however, a strong element of truth in the observation of Hussain Haqqani, the well-known Pakistani journalist, scholar and former Pakistani Ambassador to Washington, that today Pakistan is the world's only nuclear-armed military country that has been described as sliding towards state failure for the last at least two decades.[1] But in spite of being on the brink over the past several decades, Pakistan's polity and society has so far held together. This in itself is significant as it carries hope for the future of Pakistan and for the India–Pakistan relationship.

The prevailing state of affairs in Pakistan derives mainly from the ethos or the organizing principle of the state that Pakistan decided to embrace after the Partition. The root of this ethos lies in the two-nation theory on the basis of which Pakistan came to be established. It was implicit in this theory that Pakistan would opt for a national identity based on religion, that is, Islam. India's rejection of the two-nation theory and its adoption of secularism as one of the organizing principles of the state posed a standing threat to Pakistan's *raison d'étre* as an Islamic state. That led to Pakistan going out of the way to reject commonalities with India, regard India as an arch enemy and mount a relentless assault on its secularist credentials. It was, of course, open to Pakistan's rulers and their collaborators from the elite class, who were responsible for defining Pakistan identity in this fashion, to have opted for a softer and moderate version of Islam characteristic of the Indian subcontinent. They could also have incorporated in their definition of Pakistan's identity the Quranic precepts of brotherhood, equality, piety and peace and the universally recognized modern values of fundamental freedoms, human rights, equality, non-discrimination, social justice and tolerance. Some of these values indeed find place in Pakistan's Constitution adopted in 1973 after prolonged toil and bitter debate. But what came to be established and practised was neither these Quranic precepts nor the values of the Constitution nor the humanistic version of Islam of the Sufis, but the exclusive, rigid Wahabi version that preached hatred towards other religions, including other sects of Islam, like the Shias and the Ahmedis, and sanctified jihad against them. This school of thought has always been present in the Islamic tradition of the Indian subcontinent. But a distinct tilt towards and preference for it by the Pakistani rulers and their associates brought about far-reaching changes in the new state of Pakistan, in the language, and social and cultural norms and practices. It also steered Pakistan away from close cooperation and collaboration with India, to the detriment of the interest of the peoples of the two countries.

Owing to a combination of indoctrination and coercion, practised over decades, practically all sections of society in Pakistan now share this ideology defining the ethos of the State. It began as a commonly shared belief of the elites from the Army, civil services, top political leaders who mostly came from a feudal background, and professionals occupying high positions in society. But today it pervades the entire social and political spectrum. The middle class in Pakistan has shown an increasing tendency towards religious extremism. A British Council survey found that a majority of the youth prefers Islamic laws and military rule. In fact, it constituted the youth brigade of Imran Khan's party, Tehreek-e-Insaf. Many among the generation of Pakistanis educated, especially in *madrasa*s since the Zia period, believe in extremism and religious intolerance as is evident in the widespread support for the blasphemy law which targets non-Muslims on the basis of generally false allegations of their defiling the Quran and Prophet Mohammed. Besides, the recruits of the Tehrik-i-Taliban Pakistan (TTP) come not only from the madrasas but also from vernacular schools, as has been revealed in the findings of studies done on the background of captured Talibans.[2]

Sixty-eight years after its independence and 42 years after the adoption of its Constitution which provides for a democratic form of government, democracy is yet to take root in Pakistan. This is in contrast to most other South Asian countries that have witnessed the overthrow of autocratic rule and the restoration of democracy from time to time spearheaded by popular movements. In Pakistan, even during the periods when democratically elected governments have come to power, they have functioned under the shadow of the Army that has run a virtually parallel system of governance and has had a decisive say in the formulation and conduct of the most important dimensions of Pakistan's domestic, foreign and security policies, particularly those having a bearing on Pakistan's relationship with India, the US and Afghanistan. The political parties that have come to power through elections have been able to do so with the tacit approval, if not the connivance, of the Army. The Army has either bolstered an existing political party, or floated its own political party mostly with pronounced Islamic fundamentalist orientation, like the Pakistan Muslim League by Zia-ul-Haq and Pakistan Muslim League (Qaed-e-Azam) by Pervez Musharraf, in order to exercise or influence political power. By virtue of an amendment introduced in the Pakistan Constitution first in 1985,[3] empowering the President to remove a prime minister on the ground of corruption and incompetence, the Army has managed to get rid of inconvenient prime ministers and governments from time to time. This is how Benazir Bhutto and Nawaz Sharif were removed from their positions as prime ministers in the 1990s.

During the rule of the Pakistan Peoples Party (PPP) (2008–13), the political parties in the National Assembly united to annul the amendment to the Constitution authorizing the President to remove Prime Ministers. Nawaz Sharif is the first elected prime minister since General Zia's rule who is no longer held hostage to this notorious Constitutional amendment. In spite of this, he seems to have limited manoeuvrability on account of the pressure exercised on him by the Army. Imran Khan and Tahirul Qadri would not have been able to launch their agitation seeking Nawaz Sharif's ouster from power, thereby creating a first class law and order problem in the country, without the tacit support of the Army. This was confirmed by the indication given by Imran Khan that he expected Nawaz Sharif to be forced out of power by the 'third empire'.[4] Apparently, the Army does not find it convenient, at least for the present, to take over power and start ruling directly. It is, therefore, trying to strengthen its leverage over the present government by undermining its stability by letting Imran Khan and Qadri throw it out of gear. It does not seem to matter what happens to Pakistan in the process.

In the matter of pursuit of strategic policies, there is little to choose between the Army and political parties of Pakistan. The political leaders who have come to power have basically continued, and some of them have even intensified, Pakistan's efforts for acquisition of nuclear weapons, assistance to Kashmiri militants and interference in the internal affairs of Afghanistan. When Nawaz Sharif was replaced by Benazir Bhutto as prime minister at the beginning of 1993, Pakistan's clandestine support for Kashmiri militants was intensified and Pakistan assisted the Talibans to usurp power in Afghanistan.

The general elections in Pakistan appear fair and impartial. There is no coercion or rigging in the process of casting and counting votes. Despite this the elections are rigged and unfair. This is because of the institutional framework within which they are held. The rigging takes a variety of forms, including declaring candidatures invalid by the arbitrary application of laws relating to disqualification, clandestine use of funds, holding out of intimidation and threat to the life of candidates and encouragement given and assistance provided to new parties to fight the elections. The Accountability Commission could disqualify any candidate from fighting elections. Similarly, the President could debar a political party or an individual for overriding state reasons from participating in an election. In Balochistan and Federally Administered Tribal Areas (FATA), local male tribal leaders prevented their womenfolk from going out to the polling booths to cast votes.[5] In the elections held in 1990, ISI funnelled funds to the candidates of Nawaz Sharif's party. With this help, Sharif was elected as prime minister with a thumping majority. Years later, the ISI Director admitted the role of the ISI in that election before the Supreme Court of Pakistan.[6] Some democratic deficiencies are unique to Pakistan, like the sway of radical Islam which is fundamentally undemocratic, and the looming and ever-deepening shadow of terrorism. Others it shares with other South Asian countries, including in some cases, India, like absence of internal democracy in political parties, rampant election-related corruption and fundamental weakness of the democratic institutions established under the constitution.

The relative freedom that the media has recently enjoyed in Pakistan has been cited as an example of the growing strength of its democracy. There is no doubt that recent rulers of Pakistan, starting from Pervez Musharraf, have provided a lot of leeway to Pakistani media which has relished and fully exercised the privileges given to it. This is indeed commendable. But the Pakistan government, particularly the ISI on behalf of the Army, continues to adopt draconian measures, including physical liquidation, to silence voices and opinions found inconvenient or jarring to its strategic goals. A more recent example was the attack in Karachi on 9 April 2014 on Hamid Mir, the award-winning Pakistani journalist and anchor for the Pakistani television station, GEO-TV. That was not an isolated event but one of the series of attacks carried out against journalists in Pakistan. According to the 2014 Human Rights Watch Report, from 1992 to January 2014, 78 journalists or media workers had been killed in Pakistan. In the World Press Freedom Index, Pakistan ranks 158 out of 180 countries, and scores just above Somalia, Rwanda and Egypt. Under the Pakistan Electronic Media Regulatory Authority, no programme shall be aired that contains aspersions against the judiciary and the integrity of the Pakistani Armed Forces.[7]

The Military in Pakistan

The Military has been the key factor in the power structure of Pakistan. Since it assumed power under General Ayub in 1958, it has either been ruling the country directly or exercising decisive power from behind the scene in matters of strategic importance to the nation. The Military has played a key role in shaping and maintaining Pakistan's identity in terms of a bastion of Islam. It has mobilized Islamic forces and used Islamic-oriented political parties and groups for usurping and remaining in power and exercising its influence in the governance of the country. It has been the leading protagonist of perpetual hostility towards India and looking at Pakistan's relationship with India in adversarial terms and as a zero-sum game. Primarily in order to maintain its pre-eminent position in the power structure and ensure diversion of resources on a large scale for military purposes, it has raised the spectre of threat from India to Pakistan's security to the highest pedestal and maintained military parity with India. This has resulted in Pakistan becoming a 'garrison state' in which the military ethos is deeply engrained and where war or preparation for war is regarded as a normal and desirable part of social activity. Moreover, Pakistan civilian life is deeply penetrated by the military.[8]

The Military in Pakistan enjoys prestige and respectability in society, not found in any other South Asian country or in any of the normal democracies in the world. This is because it is seen as the only bulwark against the deliberately propagated national perception of threat posed by India to Pakistan's existence as a sovereign nation state. It is also regarded as the only institution which has held the country together and provided it a modicum of stability.

The Military has shown no inclination to remove the structural deficiencies and to bring about sustainable and inclusive development of Pakistan's economy. Taking advantage of its unique position in society, the Military in Pakistan has been able to sequester a major part of the economy for serving its institutional interest or that of its personnel. In an attempt to perpetuate the myth created by it and maintain its dominant position in society, it runs a large number of institutions for doling out charity, providing public goods like education and health and conducting research in and advocacy of its proclaimed mission and purpose. In the entire history of Pakistan since the Military first came to power, there has hardly been any effective effort on the part of the civilian government or the public, to reduce the Military's role or dominance. During the rule of the PPP from 2008 to 2013, the PPP leadership vaguely expressed its intention to subject the ISI to accountability to the Parliament and Prime Minister Gillani declared in the Parliament on 22 December 2011 that the Military's continuing role in politics was unacceptable. However, there was no serious follow-up of this intention or declaration.

Terrorism

Terrorism is a policy of choice of successive Pakistani governments vis-à-vis India and Afghanistan. Pakistan sees terrorism directed against India as a sub-conventional deterrent against India's overwhelming advantage in conventional military capability. In order to use terrorist groups as an asset for pursuing their strategic objectives in India and Afghanistan, successive Pakistani governments have devoted considerable resources and energy to organizing and training them, providing facilities to them and arming and equipping them. The fact that the ISI, and hence the Pakistani Army as well as the government, has played an important role in spawning, nurturing and using terrorist groups has been corroborated from several impeccable sources. The linkages between ISI and jihadi groups have been very well documented by researchers on the subject and in the eye-witness accounts given by reporters. Bruce Riedel has mentioned that a secret network study leaked in 2012, based on the interrogation of 4,000 captured Talibans, Al-Qaeda and other fighters, concluded that 'ISI support was critical to the survival of the Talibans after 2001. It provides sanctuary, training camps, expertise and helps with fund raising ... the ISI is thoroughly aware of Taliban activities and the whereabouts of all senior Taliban personnel'[9] The former US Secretary of State Hillary Clinton, in her meeting with the then Pakistani Foreign Minister, Hina Rabbani Khar, told her that the US Intelligence had ample evidence of ISI support for the Haqqani network[10] President Obama told General Kayani, the then Army Chief of Pakistan in October 2010, that he cannot accept that Pakistan's strategic concerns should include support for murderous groups.[11]

The Pakistani government's complicity with terrorist forces has reached a point where the state itself is in the danger of being devoured by these forces. The terrorist groups have captured swaths of territory in the FATA and other parts of Pakistan. They have attacked at their will army convoys, military installations, civic centres and religious places, particularly Shia mosques, and caused death and destruction. Their activities are no longer confined to inaccessible areas in FATA and contiguous areas of Pakistan and Afghanistan, but now extend to all parts of the country, including the Punjab. They are embedded in armed forces, civil services and political parties. A large proportion of the madrasas in Pakistan are under their control.

I. A. Rehman, the president of Pakistan Human Rights Commission (an NGO), has stated that they are now fighting to capture Pakistan. They believe that both dictatorship and democracy have failed and now it is their turn.[12] Whether they will succeed in this objective depends very much upon the people of Pakistan. But the very fact that they have come far enough to project such a vision is a tragic commentary on the state ideology of Pakistan and the policies towards India and Afghanistan followed under it by successive governments.

Pakistan's decision to join the war on terror in Afghanistan did not make any difference to its operation in India through the jihadi groups. Its announcement to participate in the war on terror was followed by an attack on the Indian Parliament in December 2001. In Afghanistan, Talibans resurfaced in 2005 with the active clandestine support of Pakistan.

After the brutal killing of school students in Peshawar on 16 December 2014, Pakistan announced the launching of a full-fledged military campaign against the terrorist groups under the code name 'Zarb-e-Azb'. But this campaign turned out to be highly selective, directed mainly against the Uzbek and Uighur fighters. According to the military, 150 Uzbek fighters were killed in the operation.[13] This was done mainly to placate China which had been putting pressure on Pakistan to act against this group because of its alleged involvement in the terrorist attacks carried out in China. Among the local tribals, only those were attacked who were harbouring Arab and Central Asian terrorists. Zarb-e-Azb was never meant to nor did it touch Kashmir-oriented jihadi groups.

Sporadic attempts made by the Pakistani government to eliminate terrorist groups have never been meant seriously and have been undertaken mainly to placate Pakistan's main benefactors, that is, the US, and now China. While, on the one hand, the Pakistani Army has taken credit for action against terrorist forces, on the other hand, it has kept intact the terrorist groups nurtured by it as an asset to be used against India and Afghanistan.

Pakistan's Economy and its Growth Process and Trajectory

The growth of the Pakistan economy in the post-Partition period until 2010 was, on an average, 5 per cent per annum.[14] This was an impressive rate of growth when compared with those registered by other countries of South Asia, including India. But this growth conveys only a superficial notion of prosperity and welfare. For, behind this growth were hidden a number of anomalies and structural problems. First, the growth was in spurts, the higher rates of growth occurring only when military governments were in power. Each time the military rule was followed by a democratic form of government in the formal sense of the term, the growth rate came down appreciably. It so happened that each military dictator took the right strategic decision to be able to prevail upon the US to provide huge amounts of economic and military aid to Pakistan. This no doubt boosted economic growth. But it created its own problems of a structural nature. The economy remained constrained by such problems and could not generate a self-sustaining growth.

The real GDP growth rate at the market prices during the period 1960–73, more or less coinciding with Ayub's rule (1958 to 1968), was 6.26 per cent. During the period 1973 to 1978, coinciding with Z. A. Bhutto's prime ministership (1972 to 1977), it came down to 4.49 per cent.[15] The growth rate went up again and averaged 6.6 per cent during the decade 1978–88, coinciding with General Zia's rule (1977 to 1989). It went down to 4.92 per cent during 1988–93 when Benazir Bhutto was in power, and to 3.14 between 1993 and 1998 when Nawaz Sharif was at the helm as prime minister. The growth rate went up again to an average of 5.28 per cent per annum during the period 1998 to 2007, coinciding with General Musharraf's rule (1999–2007).[16]

Since then the growth rate has been on an average half the historical trend rate of 5.5 per cent. It plummeted to 1.2 per cent in 2008–09 from the peak of 6.8 per cent in 2006–07.[17] It rose to 3.51 per cent in 2012 and further to 4.41 per cent in 2013.[18]

The structural deficiencies of the Pakistani economy are mainly low rates of saving and capital formation; narrow industrial and export base; poor export competitiveness; inadequate infrastructure development, particularly the acute shortage of electricity; insufficiency of trained manpower on account of low literacy and poor quality of education; and on-going war against terrorism. These deficiencies, in the periods of decline in foreign aid inflows, are reflected in fiscal imbalance, balance-of-payment problems and inflation. Another manifestation of the structural problem of the Pakistani economy is continuing increase in indebtedness. Pakistan's external debt and liabilities increased from $35.7 billion in 2005–06 to $50.8 billion in 2008–09. It was estimated to be $57 billion in 2009–10.[19] Pakistan's total government debt as a proportion of GDP was between 55 per cent and 60 per cent during the period 2006–07 to 2008–09.[20]

Inflation rate was 14 per cent in 2010. This was in spite of high interest rates and sharp reduction in development expenditure. The food inflation rate that year was 18 per cent. This further intensified the pressure on the poor. With GDP growth at a historic low and food inflation rate at a historic high, it is not surprising that as many as 40 per cent of the population was estimated to be living below the poverty line in 2010 and 46 per cent of them were food insecure.[21] The majority of the population is deprived of access to safe drinking water, sanitation, quality healthcare and education. Only 30 per cent of the population has access to safe drinking water and 45 per cent to sanitation. Consequently 45 per cent of the poorest section of the society is suffering from diseases.[22] Gender bias in access to education is indicated by the fact that school enrolment rate for girls was 49 per cent as compared to 61 per cent for boys (in 2010). In higher educational institutions, women formed only 28.9 per cent of the student body in public sector universities. Further, 47 per cent of girls children were fully immunized as compared to 52 per cent of boys.[23] Adult female literacy rate in Pakistan at 40 per cent was lower than that in most other South Asian countries. It was 50 in India, 52 in Bangladesh, 48 in Nepal and 90 in Sri Lanka.[24] Infant mortality rate (per 1,000 live births) at 59 and maternal mortality ratio (per 100,000 live births) at 260 were also much higher in Pakistan than in any of the previously mentioned South Asian countries.[25]

The Pakistani society and polity has come under heavy strain due to the intensification of inter-personal and inter-regional economic disparity. During the period of Ayub, the government adopted an urban industrialization policy based on import substitution and heavy protection which led to large-scale transfer of resources from the rural to the urban areas. At the end of the 1990s, a small group of families with interlocking directorates dominated industry, banking and insurance in Pakistan. As much as 46 per cent of the value added in the large-scale manufacturing sector was generated in firms controlled by only 43 families.[26] The process of concentration of income in the hands of the urban elites was re-enforced by rapid enrichment of the traditional rural elites as a result of the green revolution on the one hand and the government policy of subsiding agriculture inputs on the other. In 1992, as much as 30 per cent of the total farm area was owned by farmers with holdings of 150 acres and above.[27] When cultivation became profitable after the green revolution, rich farmers took back the rented-out land for self-cultivation which led to the polarization of the rural society, driving rural self-employed persons to the position of being landless labourers.[28] During the period 2001–08, the average income growth for the top-income quintile of the population was 2.36 times greater than for the lowest quintile. This was rooted in highly unequal distribution of productive assets, accentuated by the differential impact of high food inflation on the rich and the poor.[29]

Regional inequality, particularly between East and West Pakistan, was accentuated in the Ayub period. Soon thereafter, it assumed a dimension that turned out to be the most important factor leading to Bangladesh splitting from Pakistan and becoming an independent sovereign entity. Since then, inter-regional disparity has been between the better-off provinces like Punjab and Sindh and the backward ones of Balochistan and former North-West Frontier Province (NWFP), now renamed Khyber-Pakhtunkhwa. To cite some statistical evidence of this disparity, the growth in employment in Punjab and Sindh at 2.7 and 2.2 per cent, respectively over the period 2001–02 to 2009–10 was over twice as high as in Balochistan and former NWFP, at 1.1 and 1.2 per cent, respectively. The percentage of food insecure population was much higher in the latter provinces during the same period (61.2 and 56.2 per cent, respectively) than in the more developed states of Punjab (38.5 per cent) and Sindh (48.3 per cent).[30]

Pakistan has been getting a regular supply of a very large amount of foreign aid from the US. In large part at the latter's behest, it has been one of the most important beneficiaries of assistance by international financial institutions, particularly the IMF and the World Bank. In recent years, the Chinese government has also been pumping billion of dollars of resources into the Pakistan economy. Military assistance received by Pakistan from both the US and China provides an extremely important cushion for pursuing its economic development. The Gulf countries, particularly Saudi Arabia, have also been very generous in granting sizeable amounts of resources to Pakistan, both for development and military purposes. Moreover, for the past several years, Pakistan has been receiving large amounts of personal remittances sent by its nationals working abroad. In 2010, the remittances reached the level of a little over $14 billion which was 6.24 per cent of Pakistan's GDP. The remittances received by Pakistan as a percentage of GDP compare very favourably with those received by India which in 2012 was 3.70 per cent of the GDP. But for these remittances, Pakistan would have been obliged to dig deeper into foreign grants and loans received by it for acquiring military hardware.

The question arises as to why Pakistan's economy has stayed weak and vulnerable in spite of such a massive infusion of foreign capital. The main reason is that the disposal of aid resources is largely determined by the Pakistan Army. Most of the economic aid money and even the remittances are diverted for the purchase of arms and keeping the armed forces in battle readiness. A portion is funnelled to the segment of the economy that is owned and operated by the Army. This includes land, key business interests, foundations and charitable and other institutions. The size of this segment has been variously calculated. One figure quoted is $21 billion.[31]

Moreover, there is a negative correlation between high military expenditure and GDP growth. According to one calculation, if defence spending in Pakistan, which in late 1980s reached 7 per cent of the GDP, had been half of that level, if the resources thus released were allotted to social and economic development, and if the potential economic gains from regional cooperation had been available, Pakistan's economic growth rate over the period 1970–2010 would have been at least 2 per cent higher than it actually was. That would have meant an economic size double of what it currently is.[32]

The second reason is that foreign aid flows to Pakistan have not been accompanied by domestic or foreign investment on the desired scale. Domestic investors have generally been shy of making large-sized fresh investments mainly because of the widespread corruption prevailing in the country which enables them to make their money without taking risk. The general insecurity prevailing in the country on account of the activities of terrorist groups that have expanded manifold in recent years has become a major constraint for both domestic and foreign investors.

One of the results of the unsatisfactory rate of domestic investment has been the narrowing industrial base of Pakistan, dominated mainly by low-end textile products.

Pakistan has a relatively low rate of domestic savings and fixed capital formation as a proportion of GDP. In 2011, these rates for Pakistan were 8 and 11 per cent respectively, which was the lowest among South Asian countries like India, Bangladesh, Nepal and Sri Lanka.[33]

On the surface, Pakistan has a very liberal foreign investment regime. It ranks second among the SAARC countries in the ease of doing business, though its overall position globally is 107. It provides several incentives to investors with respect to tax and regulation on repatriation of capital and profit. In its special economic zones, it offers liberal incentives, infrastructure and investors' facilitation services. However, these policies are more or less cancelled by the unstable political situation in the country. According to World Bank indicators, political insecurity index for the year 2009–10 was the worst for Pakistan, along with Afghanistan, among the South Asian countries.

In recent years, the highest FDI flow into Pakistan was $5.6 billion in 2007. Since then, the figure has been declining, reaching a rock bottom of $0.8 billion in 2012.[34] It was $3.7 billion in 2008–09, $2.1 billion in 2009–10, $1.6 billion in 2011–12, $820 million in 2012–13 and $1.4 billion in 2013–14.[35]

Although Pakistan defined its self-identity in religious terms soon after the Partition, a thoroughgoing effort to make Islamic fundamentalism a national creed was commenced by General Zia-ul-Haq. It was during his regime that for the first time in Pakistan, government funds were provided for establishing madrasas in small towns and rural areas devoted to indoctrinating children. As General Zia engaged in a proxy war both in Afghanistan and India, some of the militant religious groups together with their associated madrasas were provided with official funds, combat training and weapons to conduct guerrilla operations. It was also at that time that the Al-Qaeda and Taliban groups nurtured by the state turned against it.[36]

The violence and destruction perpetrated by the militant religious extremists is a major constraint to investment, both domestic and foreign. It also harms the economy in several other ways. Poverty and inequality are feeding on terrorism. To quote Akmal Hussain: 'They [young people] don suicide jackets to escape a heartless world in pursuit of paradise'.[37] At the same time fear and insecurity engendered by terrorists perpetuates poverty.

Pakistan's National Crisis Management Cell estimated that between 2002 and April 2010, there were 8,141 incidents of terrorism in Pakistan resulting in 8,875 deaths of both civilians and law enforcement personnel and injuries to another 20,675 people. In the Pakistan Economic Survey, 2009–10, the estimated total cost of terrorism to the economy from 2005 to 2010 was calculated to be $43 billion.[38]

If we look at it in the historical perspective and in the context of the conditions generally prevailing in South Asia, including India, Pakistan's socio-economic situation on the whole has not been as dismal as it is made out to be by most of the scholars and commentators in India. At least in terms of economic performance and resilience, Pakistan can by no means be described as a failed state or one on the verge of failure.

The rate of growth of 5 per cent per annum during the period 1947–2010 is no mean achievement. During this period, so far as the rate of growth is concerned, there was not much to choose between India and Pakistan. During most of the period between 1961 and 1992, Pakistan's rate of growth was higher than that of India. Only since 1993 has India maintained year after year, with the exception of the year 2000, a higher rate of growth than Pakistan. Even in the recent years when the Indian economy has been quite buoyant, Pakistan registered more than 6 per cent average rate of growth during the five-year period between 2003 and 2007, and it is projected at more than 4 per cent for 2015. Considering the continuing recession in most parts of the world, these are rates not to be scoffed at.

The average annual growth rate of per capita GDP was higher in Pakistan than India during the decades of the 1960s and the 1970s and it was almost equal (3.3 per cent and 3.2 per cent, respectively for India and Pakistan), in the decades of the 1980s.[39] Since the 1990s, India has been maintaining a higher per capita GDP growth than Pakistan. This is because of both the relatively high performance of the Indian economy during the 1990s, as well as the higher rate of population growth in Pakistan. The total fertility rate in Pakistan in 2011 was 3.4 per cent as compared to 2.6 per cent in India.[40] An area in which Pakistan has historically done better than India is the rate of growth in exports. The average annual growth rate of the value of exports from Pakistan during the 30-year period between 1961 and 1990 was 6.8 per cent, higher than the 6.1 per cent rate of growth in Indian exports. Even during the next 20 years, that is, 1990 to 2011, Pakistan export continued to grow at 6 per cent per annum though India surpassed it decisively by achieving a growth rate of 13.6 per cent per annum.[41]

In the social field, there are important areas in which Pakistan has done better than India. Perhaps the most important among them is the sex ratio. The female–male ratio in the population in the year 2011 was 968 in Pakistan as compared to 937 in India.[42] In the field of education, the estimated mean years of schooling for the population above the age of 25 was 4.9 per cent in Pakistan as compared to 4.4 per cent in India. Pupil–teacher ratio at the primary level was only slightly higher in Pakistan at 41 than in India at 40. In 2010, the estimated proportion of population below the international poverty line of $2 per day was higher in India at 68.7 per cent than in Pakistan at 60.2 per cent.[43] Life expectancy at birth in both the countries was the same at 65 in the year 2010.

In recent years, the areas in which India has really forged ahead of Pakistan, and Pakistan has to work hard to catch up, are savings rates, investment rates, FDI inflows, IMR and Maternal Mortality Rate (MMR). In 2011, the gross domestic savings as a proportion of GDP in India was 31 against only 8 in Pakistan.[44] In 2013, the gross capital formation as a part of GDP in India was 31.43 per cent as against only 14.57 per cent in Pakistan.[45] In 2011, India had an IMR of 47 and an MMR of 200 as compared to 59 and 260, respectively, in Pakistan.[46] The recent data do not show much of a change in these figures. FDI in India as a proportion of GDP in 2010 was 1.7 per cent as compared to 0.6 per cent in Pakistan.[47]

There are several areas of social development and governance in which India has no reasons to be complacent. There is rampant corruption and misgovernance in both India and Pakistan. As against the terrorist menace in Pakistan, India is infested with Naxalite violence, which affects 125 out of 640 administrative districts. Recently, there have also been several assaults on minority worshipping places and acts of intimidation against the minorities. The rise of majoritarianism is threatening the security and constitutional rights of ordinary citizens, particularly those belonging to the minority communities. There is endemic problem of unemployment, denial of the payment of minimum wages and large-scale prevalence of child labour. The country also faces food shortage and is inhabited by one of the largest number of malnutritioned children in the world. These issues are at the root of the prevailing violence and poor law and order situation.

Foreign Policy of a Rentier State

Pakistan has been described as a rentier state which has lived off massive flows of foreign aid from time to time. According to one source, between

1960 and 2012, Pakistan received some $73.1 billion (2001 prices) from bilateral and multilateral sources.[48] According to another source, Pakistan has received aid amounting to some $20 billion since 2001.[49] In order to receive foreign aid, both economic and military, on such a large scale, Pakistan has made foreign policy choices of great strategic significance from time to time. The main thrust of its foreign policy has been to be on the right side of its benefactors at critical turning points in the post-Second World War history. Pakistan's geo-strategic position, its well-trained and one of the largest standing armies in the world, and its carefully nurtured Islamic credentials have gone a long way towards enabling it to make these choices and taking full advantage of the opportunities available to it.

During the Cold War, Pakistan sided with the West against the Soviet bloc. It joined most of the military alliances formed to contain communism. It became a member of the Southeast Asia Treaty Organization (SEATO) after its creation in 1954. It joined the Baghdad Pact, later renamed as the Central Treaty Organization (CENTO), at the end of 1955. Under these arrangements, it made available to the US locations and facilities for carrying out intelligence activities against the Soviet Union. When the US started its operation against the Soviet presence in Afghanistan, it promptly climbed the US bandwagon and took the risk of harbouring millions of Afghan refugees in its territory. It assembled, armed and trained Mujahideens, both from Pakistan and Afghanistan as well as from the neighbouring West Asian and Central Asian countries, to fuel jihad in Afghanistan against the Soviet presence there. This eventually resulted in the flow of illicit arms and spread of terrorism inside Pakistan culminating in the creation of TTP which has for the past several years turned against the state and is posing it an existential threat. After the Al-Qaeda attack on the Pentagon and World Trade Centre Towers in New York on 11 September 2001, Pakistan joined the global war against terrorism declared by President George W. Bush. It joined the US to fight Al-Qaeda and the Afghan Talibans in spite of the fact that it had helped the latter to assume power in Kabul in 1996.

Pakistan started opening up to China from the early 1960s, but the turning point came after the arms embargo imposed by the US following the India–Pakistan War in 1965. Its objective of replacing Western arms by the supply of Chinese arms coincided with China's objective of keeping India bogged down in South Asia, in order to prevent it from rising as a rival Asian power. Till the end of the 1960s, Pakistan clandestinely procured arms from China while continuing its military relationship with the West, but from the early 1970s, when Henry Kissinger used Pakistan as the intermediary for opening up to China, it started and maintained an open and full-fledged bilateral military relationship with China. Subsequently, it took the crucial decision to allow its territory, including that of the State of Jammu and Kashmir under its occupation, to be used as a corridor for linking up through the shortest possible route, the western part of China with South Asia, West Asia and Africa.

Pakistan was not moved by any shared objective with the Western countries, in taking its decision to join the alliances formed by them and supporting their other initiatives. It joined them in pursuit of its objective of ensuring continued flow of sophisticated and advanced weapons in order to maintain military parity with India, of keeping its economy afloat through regular inflows of foreign economic aid and maintaining the position of the Army as the supreme authority in the country. These objectives were not shared by Pakistan's Western allies. In fact, they were alien to their objectives and declared policy. In spite of this, they continued to provide resources on a large scale to Pakistan because it did the minimum required to keep them happy. It gave them base to carry out air surveillance in the Soviet territory. It mounted periodic campaigns against terrorist forces associated or affiliated with Al-Qaeda and located in its territory adjacent to Afghanistan. And it effectively prevented the terrorist groups in Afghanistan from inflicting severe damages to the military contingents of the US and its allies during their operation in Afghanistan and later during their withdrawal from there. However, it never gave up the asset of the terrorist groups that it has created, trained and nurtured to be used for perpetrating terrorism against India, particularly in Jammu and Kashmir, and for re-establishing its dominance in Afghanistan after the US withdrawal.

The unfolding of events in the last few years has demonstrated that this brand of foreign policy has not done much good to Pakistan. Apart from the terrorist forces turning against the Pakistani state, infusion of massive foreign aid from time to time has created and accentuated the structural problems in the Pakistan economy. Donor funding has acted as a substitute for revenue generation and has come in the way of the government taking the hard decisions necessary to set the economy right. Many scholars, including distinguished Pakistanis, who have analyzed the developments in the Pakistan economy, have come to the conclusion that it is this policy that has brought Pakistan to the brink of being a failed state.

India–Pakistan Relations

Indo-Pak Trade Relations

India and Pakistan before the Partition constituted, in a sense, a single market. It was, therefore, not surprising that immediately after the Partition, a major part of their trade flowed to each other. At that time, India's exports to Pakistan amounted to 50 per cent of its total global exports and its imports from Pakistan were 25 per cent of its total imports. This pattern continued, though on a diminishing scale, until the 1965 India–Pakistan War. Before 1965, 11 routes were open for trade between the two countries; six Indian banks were operating in Pakistan while the Habib Bank of Pakistan had a branch in Mumbai. The trade between the two countries came to a standstill for almost nine years after the 1965 War until a protocol on resuming trade relations was signed in 1974 and lists of items to be mutually traded were agreed upon.

In 1996, India extended MFN treatment to Pakistan, but the latter continued to import from India only a limited number of items announced by it from time to time. Pakistan linked the granting of MFN treatment to India to the resolution of the Kashmir issue. Trade relations between the two countries, even on this limited basis, remained vulnerable to political developments from time to time. For example, the attack on the Indian Parliament by terrorists having links with Pakistan, in December 2001, led India to ban trade via the air and land routes between 2001 and 2004. As recently as in 2013, cross-border trade was completely halted after incidents of ceasefire violations between the two countries.

Between 1998–99 and 2003–04, India's export to Pakistan increased from $100 million to $286 million and imports from Pakistan increased from $45 million to $200 million.[50] This was followed by a kind of mini boom in trade relations between 2003–04 and 2007–08 when India's export increased to $1.9 billion. India's exports came down to $1.3 billion in 2008–09 when imports from Pakistan amounted to $370 million. It was a big improvement over the figure of only $45 million in 1998–99.[51] During the last four years, India's exports reached a high peak in 2010–11 at $2.25 billion. It came down to $1.67 billion and $1.74 billion in 2011–12 and 2012–13, respectively. The next year, that is, in 2013–14, it approximated the peak reached in 2010–11, at $2.24 billion.[52]

In spite of the recent impressive growth in trade transactions, in 2010, India's exports to Pakistan were 0.8 per cent of its total exports, and its imports 0.1 per cent of the total. In 2013, Pakistan's trade with India was 3.49 per cent of its global trade.[53]

Mainly on account of the imposition of artificial constraints on trade, particularly non-extension of MFN treatment to India by Pakistan and its permitting trade only in a limited number of items, there is a flourishing informal trade between the two countries. Over the last couple of decades, various estimates have been made of the magnitude of this informal trade. A very recent study conducted by Nisha Taneja and Samridhi Bimal, presented at a seminar in New Delhi on 2 February 2015, estimates tentatively that India's exports to Pakistan through the informal channel amounted to $4.24 billion and its imports from Pakistan to $700 million during the year of the survey. The study is based on a survey method covering respondents in India and Dubai, comprising traders and persons knowledgeable in trade between the two countries. The list of exports from India, according to the survey, was led by jewellery followed by textiles, machinery and electronic appliances. The import list from Pakistan was headed by textiles followed by dry fruits and spices. The three top Indian items exported through the legal trade in 2011 were chemicals, textiles and vegetable products and the three top Indian import items from Pakistan were mineral products, vegetable products and textiles. The three categories with the largest import potential are textiles, jewellery, precious stones and base metals. India has a huge export potential for mineral fuels consisting of petroleum products.[54]

Various estimates have been made of the potentiality of the trade between the two countries. Given the size of the two economies, the relatively high growth rate of the Indian economy and a growth rate of 2 to 3 per cent of the Pakistan economy, it will not be far off the mark to surmise that if the trade between the two countries is normalized, if all WTO-inconsistent non-tariff barriers are removed and if the SAFTA free trade range duty of 0 to 5 per cent is applied, the two-way trade between the two countries would move up sharply to at least $10 billion per annum. Applying the Potential Trade Approach method, Nisha Taneja and Pallavi Kalita calculated the bilateral trade potential of India and Pakistan to be $25.2 billion in 2010 which was 10 times larger than the trade volume of $2.5 billion that year.[55]

In recent years, India has been consistently running favourable balance in its trade with Pakistan. Trade balance as a proportion of total trade increased from 55 per cent in 2000 to 68 per cent in 2011.[56] For the year 2012–13, Pakistan's trade deficit with India was $1.34 billion.[57] Trade imbalance is not an unusual feature of trade relations between two countries. It is in fact very unusual for a country to have balance or surplus in its trade with all the countries of the world. Historically, developing countries have had adverse balance of trade with practically every developed country. In 2012–13, Pakistan ran trade deficits much larger than that with India with Saudi Arabia ($3.45 billion), the US ($2.86 billion) and China ($2.02 billion).[58]

It is not only the mercantile trade balance but the overall balance of payment in which investment flows and balance-in-services trade also come into play, which has important macroeconomic implications. Moreover, an adverse balance of trade can bring significant welfare gains by making consumption goods available to the common man at cheaper prices. It can also have a positive impact on growth by way of reducing the capital–output ratio. Most of the Pakistani imports from India are essential for meeting consumer demands and as inputs for development and for exports. Cheaper imports can make export more competitive. Finally, there have been several years in the past when Pakistan enjoyed favourable balance of trade with India. There is no reason why this should not come to pass again in a situation of normal trade relations.

A major constraint to trade expansion between the two countries has been on the transport side. The Maritime Protocol signed between India and Pakistan in 1975 allowed only Indian and Pakistani flag vessels to carry cargo between the two countries. It did not permit them to carry consignments to a third country from the ports of either. Another transport bottleneck till recently was that there was only one rail route for cargo movement between the two countries and road transport was not allowed to be used for trade. Both these problems were addressed in 2005 when the Maritime Protocol was revised bringing the sea trade between the two countries under global maritime arrangement and it was also decided to open the road route for trade. From October 2008, the two governments started permitting trade and travel across the line of control in the state of Jammu and Kashmir. The opening up of the road route after 58 years was a major event. Recognising its importance, India opened an integrated check post at Attari in April 2012. The importance of the road route is brought out by the fact that when the route was closed in 1995–96, trade by rail accounted for 63 per cent and that by sea 33 per cent of the total, but by 2011–12 the share of rail fell to 15 per cent and of road increased from 0 to 17 per cent.[59]

Both countries deny transit of the goods of each other through their territory to third countries. Granting of such transit facilities is considered so sensitive politically that the subject does not even figure in the agenda for discussion of trade and transport between the two countries. In July 2010, Afghanistan and Pakistan signed a revised trade agreement called the Afghanistan–Pakistan Transit and Trade Agreement which provides for a larger number of transport routes and of trucks to move from Afghanistan to Pakistan. However, Pakistan does not allow India's export goods to reach Afghanistan through its territory. Even for the Afghan goods destined for India, Afghan trucks are allowed to come only up to the Wagah border post on the Pakistan side and not up to Attari on the Indian side. The Afghan goods have to be carried from Wagah to Attari, a distance of one kilometre, in Pakistani trucks. This increases their transport cost.

For several years, Pakistan has been arguing that its export products face non-tariff barriers in accessing the Indian market. In the discussion on the subject that the two sides have carried out during the past several years. India has sought to demonstrate that it does not maintain any WTO-inconsistent non-tariff barriers, nor are any of its trade restrictions Pakistan-specific. A study conducted in 2008 for an inter-governmental task force on non-tariff barriers found that while measures adopted by India were not discriminatory, the procedure relating to clearance of goods for entry into India were cumbersome and lacked transparency. There were also problems relating to the recognition of standards. Some of the reported barriers included overvaluation of goods, tedious packaging and labelling requirements, access to a limited number of ports and inadequate infrastructure.[60] In a move to tackle some of these problems, the two countries signed three agreements in September 2012: a Customs Cooperation Agreement to avoid arbitrary stoppage of goods at ports, a Bilateral Cooperation Agreement on Mutual Recognition and an Agreement on Redressal of Trade Grievances.

Pakistan started liberalizing its economy under an IMF/World Bank programme from 1982–83. Most of the reforms measures agreed to with these institutions were implemented by the mid-1980s. The process, however, continued during the latter part of the 1980s and the beginning of the 1990s, when Pakistan made significant moves towards integrating its economy with that of global economy through linkages of trade and investment.

Both India and Pakistan signed the South Asia Free Trade Agreement (SAFTA) in 2004. After all the ratifications were in, the Agreement came into force from the beginning of 2006. But Pakistan did not accord MFN status to India and trade between the two countries was confined to 137 items permitted by Pakistan at that time. In the absence of normal trade flow between India and Pakistan, SAFTA retained very little significance as a platform for launching free trade in South Asia and as a move towards regional economic integration.

The extension of MFN treatment to India by Pakistan was the principal item on the agenda of trade dialogue that started between the two countries in 2004 and continued till recently. Four rounds of this dialogue were held until the entire process of the composite dialogue came to a standstill after the Mumbai attack in November 2008. Trade talks resumed when the fifth round was held in April 2011. In a Joint Statement issued in April 2011, agreement was reached on the sequence and timelines for the full phasing in of an MFN regime between the two countries. In the first phase, Pakistan would move from the then prevailing positive list to a small negative list; and in the second phase the negative list would be phased out, marking the entry into force of MFN status. In March 2012, Pakistan did make a transition from the positive list approach to a negative list of 1,209 items, the same number as included by Pakistan in its negative list under the SAFTA. In the Joint Statement issued after the seventh round of the talks held in September 2012, India offered several concessions in exchange of the anticipated move by Pakistan towards MFN basis of trade. It announced that simultaneously with the phasing out of the negative list and moving towards MFN status by Pakistan, India would bring down its negative lists under SAFTA to only 100 tariff lines and reduce its duties on Pakistan's exports to India to 5 per cent according to the norm of free trade laid down in SAFTA. As it happened, the two countries never reached that long expected stage of the MFN status of trade. With the elections around the corner, the Government of Pakistan announced on 25 February 2013 that the decision to grant MFN status to India would be left to the next government. The Nawaz Sharif government that came to power after the elections publicly linked granting of MFN status to India to the solution of the Kashmir problem. So the process slid back to status quo ex ante.

The real decision makers in Pakistan, that is, the Army and political leaders generally working in sync with the former, have left no scope for ambiguity about their intention to link the issue of extending MFN treatment to India with the Kashmir dispute or with the broader political issue of the Pakistani rulers seeing their vested interest in perpetuating hostility towards India. In this context, it is pathetic to hear Pakistani scholars, particularly economists, commentators and decision-makers, advancing economic, legal and technical arguments against the grant of MFN treatment to India. None of these so-called substantive arguments stand the scrutiny of fact or logic.

An argument frequently advanced is that Pakistan can extend MFN treatment to India only if there is a level playing field between India and Pakistan in the trade sphere. This argument is *prima facie* invalid. For, extension of MFN treatment in WTO by one member country to another is absolutely unconditional.

Leaving the MFN issue aside, is there any factual basis to Pakistan's complaint that India does not provide a level playing field to Pakistan for trade? From the Pakistani side, several arguments have been advanced in support of this contention. One of them is that India's tariff rates are on the whole higher than that of Pakistan. This may have been the case in the past. But in recent years, particularly from the beginning of this century, India's tariff rates have come down sharply. They are now almost on par with those prevailing in South-East Asian countries which have gone very far towards trade liberalization. Moreover, India's tariff rates should now be seen as what they will be after the full implementation of SAFTA following the trade normalization between India and Pakistan. And that will be in the range of 0 to 5 per cent with the exception of duties on products put on the negative lists of the two countries. India has promised to reduce its negative list to 100. Moreover, what is important is not the level of duties but the fact that the same rates of duties will be applicable to all WTO member countries. Leaving aside competition from domestic products, even if the Indian duties are on the higher side, but as long as they are applied to all trading partners of India, Pakistan would have comparative cost advantage over other exporters to the Indian market on account of geographical proximity and various commonalities that it shares with India.

The second argument that Pakistan advances for justifying that it does not enjoy a level playing field in trading with India is the alleged maintenance by India of non-tariff barriers. Let us first set aside the point that even if this is factually correct, it does not justify the non-extension of MFN treatment which is unconditional. But is it correct that India's non-tariff barriers amount to denial of a level playing field to Pakistan? Almost all the countries of the world apply non-tariff barriers on health, security and other grounds. The issue basically is whether these barriers are WTO-consistent. In various rounds of trade dialogue held recently between India and Pakistan, Pakistan's grievance on non-tariff barriers imposed by India was seriously addressed. India tried to demonstrate that most of the non-tariff barriers maintained by it are WTO-consistent. India also adopted measures to facilitate trade with Pakistan, like setting up a modernized border post and putting in place an instrumentality for harmonization of standards. If Pakistan is still not satisfied, it can raise dispute in the Disputes Settlement Mechanism of WTO. In any case, it cannot use this grievance as an argument for denying MFN treatment to India.

A third argument advanced by sections of the business community in Pakistan and others is that if trade is normalized between the two countries, Pakistani industry will be swamped by competitive Indian products and its growth will be adversely impacted. This argument is mainly speculative; no empirical evidence has been cited to justify it. Besides, the very logic of free trade implies that more competitive low-cost imports from outside countries will replace high-cost domestic products leading to economic restructuring which will enhance the efficiency and competitiveness of the economy as a whole, including the export sector. This may have some adverse effect on employment and production in the short run, but in the long run such restructuring is the basis for innovation and sustainable development. Finally, if competitive imports from India are really going to adversely affect Pakistan's industry, then there is a provision in the GATT, Article XIX to apply import-restrictive safeguard measures. However, they would have to be temporary and non-discriminatory. It will also be necessary to prove, based on facts and figures, that additional imports from India have in fact caused injury to a particular industry in Pakistan.

Pakistan has also been wrongly propagating that extension of MFN treatment will be a concession to India. This is far from the truth. The fact is that both the countries stand to lose, Pakistan, perhaps, more than India, because of the present artificial restriction on trade, and if MFN becomes the rule in force, then both of them will gain hugely. Extension of MFN treatment to India by Pakistan will be a quintessential example of positive sum bargain between the two countries in matters of trade.

In reality, the Pakistani rulers are on record having said that they are denying themselves the benefits of trading with India on a normal basis for political reasons. They have frequently linked the MFN issue with that of Kashmir. But is even Kashmir the real issue? Pakistani rulers cannot demonstrate that they have advanced even an inch towards getting the Kashmir issue resolved in their favour by denying the extension of MFN treatment to India. Nor can it be said that this has helped in keeping the Kashmir issue alive. Kashmir and all other disputes between the two countries are alive because of the kind of overall relationship that Pakistan has decided to maintain with India. Pakistani rulers have right from the very beginning decided to maintain a relationship of perpetual hostility towards India, and for that purpose, to invoke any dispute that comes in handy. Until now, it has been the Kashmir dispute. Soon it will be the Indus Water issue. There is no dearth of sensitive issues in a complex and difficult relationship between two countries like India and Pakistan, which can be exploited for serving political purpose.

The truth is that the current stalemate in the trade relations between the two countries suits the vested interest of Pakistan's Army, that of a section of business community which is thriving on imports from countries other than India and on the development of industries insulated and protected from India's competition, religious extremists whose very *raison de'etre* is jihad against India, and politicians who rely on these elements or their sympathizers in the society to come to and stay in power. Thus, the MFN treatment is related to the very ethos of Pakistan as defined by the ruling class.

Military Parity with India

Pakistan has sought and succeeded in maintaining military parity with India. This has, in fact, been the central component of its security policy towards India. Maintaining parity with India in security matters is a logical consequence of Pakistan's definition of self-identity in terms of perpetual hostility towards India. Pakistani rulers believe that they can preserve such an identity only by remaining fully prepared to meet any threat to Pakistan's security emanating from India. Inevitability to maintain military parity also provides a readymade rationale for the Pakistan Army to keep on amassing huge quantities of arms and ammunition, always be in battle readiness vis-à-vis India, and, for this purpose, to be accepted as the supreme authority in the country.

One of the arguments given in justification of maintaining parity is that Pakistan's existence is under constant threat from India because the latter never got reconciled to the reality of the Partition and that given an opportunity, it would like to undo it. Pakistan can prevent this from happening and preserve its status as a sovereign state only by foiling this effort by equal or superior military might.

Though there have been some diehards among the believers in Hindutva in India who, from time to time, have given vent to their desire to unite Pakistan with India, they have been very few in number and in no position to execute their design. Some elements in various socialist political formations in India have also talked about unity between India and Pakistan. But theirs has been a more enlightened vision of binding the two countries together through a web of economic, social and cultural cooperation where with the exception of the maintenance of separate sovereign status, other differences disappear and the two countries join in a confederation. This is by no means another version of *Akhand Bharat*, or undivided India, but closer to what happened in Europe in the post-war economic union and the creation of a regional structure unique in modern history. One of the most famous socialist leaders of India, Dr Ram Manohar Lohia, believed in the objective of bringing the two countries together in this mode, and many of his followers cherish this dream even today.

In the early phase of the debate on Partition, some of the leaders of India's independence movement, including Jawaharlal Nehru, believed that the Partition would be short-lived as objective factors would undo it and restore the unity of the country. But after the Partition, these leaders got fully reconciled to Pakistan's existence as a separate State. In a speech delivered in March 1948, Jawaharlal Nehru stated that 'there is no going back in history' and that India has no desire to 'strangle or crush Pakistan and force it into a reunion with India'.[61]

There is no evidence since the Partition, of India having tried to obliterate Pakistan's existence as a sovereign nation state, annex it or otherwise make it a part of India. Some of the wars that were fought between the two countries were followed by territorial adjustments in order to restore the status quo prevailing before the war. It is for history to judge who—Bangladeshis themselves, Pakistan or India—was responsible for the splitting of East Pakistan from the parent state and the formation of the sovereign state of Bangladesh. But this landmark event in the history of the Indian subcontinent cannot by any stretch of imagination be attributed to India's design to reunite Pakistan with it. Today, barring a handful of rightwing Hindu extremists, nobody in India talks about *Akhand Bharat* any more. Most Indians recognize that it is an outmoded concept and is neither feasible nor desirable. Moreover, since the early 1990s, India as a major economic power has started looking for opportunities of economic integration going beyond its neighbourhood. Coveting a part of Pakistan's territory figures nowhere in India's objective and its plan to play its due role in the transformed global and regional scenario in the 21st century.

An important part of the reason for Pakistan's aspiration to achieve military parity with India derives from its perception of its own role in the region and in the world. Pakistani rulers have regarded themselves as the inheritors of the Mughal kings who ruled India and were dominant in the region for over two centuries. By virtue of its size, strategic location and military might, Pakistan casts itself in the role of a leader in the Islamic world. This self-perception does not admit the acceptance of a position inferior or subordinate to India, hence the urge for maintaining military parity with India.

Finally, it cannot be altogether denied that in the context of its perceived security threat from India, Pakistan has tried to catch up with India each time the latter has acquired arms of superior quality or in large quantities. This has been a major factor fuelling an arms race between the two countries. Even though India's acquisitions might have been to meet a possible threat to its security from China or designed to play a role in the Asian and Indian Ocean region befitting its size and interest, it has invariably given rise to apprehensions in Pakistan regarding its own security. Whether it would have been possible to prevent this arms race through discussion between the two countries each time a new acquisition was contemplated is a debatable point, made complicated because of the intrusion of the Chinese factor.

In spite of the asymmetry in the size or capabilities of the two countries, Pakistan has succeeded in achieving military parity with India partly by diverting for military purposes, a disproportionate part of its GDP and total budget expenditure and partly with the help of outside powers, mainly the US and China, but not excluding Saudi Arabia and other Gulf countries. Pakistan's successful ploy of raising, nurturing and deploying terrorist groups against India has also contributed in no insignificant measure to the maintenance of parity. Pakistan's task in this regard has been rendered easier also because of India's compulsion to deploy a major portion of its conventional weapons, armed forces and strategic assets to meet the threat to its security posed by China.

Since the second half of the 1950s, the US has been persisting with large-scale military supplies to Pakistan. The Eisenhower Presidency underwrote a very significant modernization of Pakistan's armed forces. In spite of the US ban on arms supply to India and Pakistan following the 1965 War, the Nixon–Kissinger duo found means of keeping arms aid to Pakistan trickling and clandestinely enabling Pakistan to acquire F-16 aircrafts through third countries. The Reagan Administration made a long-term commitment for providing billion of dollars of mili-tary aid to Pakistan. From the early 1980s, successive US Presidents sanctioned military aid to Pakistan in spite of their being in possession of solid intelligence reports testifying rapid progress in the development and subsequent acquisition of nuclear weapons by Pakistan. This they did on the basis of the patently false assurances given by Pakistan authorities that it did not have a nuclear weapon programme. Even as recently as in February 2015, President Obama announced a fresh military aid package of $1 billion for Pakistan. This includes some highly sophisticated weapons like AH-12 Viper Helicopters, Hell Fire Missiles and communication equipment that US was using in its war in Afghanistan and which on its withdrawal it decided to transfer directly to Pakistan. There is little doubt that these will not be used only to fight Islamic terrorism.

The US has maintained its military assistance to Pakistan over decades in spite of its knowledge that contrary to the agreement between the two countries, the US arms were not used for the purpose for which they were supplied, but to build military parity with India. Moreover, the US military assistance was provided in spite of the fact that Pakistan did not genuinely share the objectives of the alliances or the campaign, under the US, which Pakistan joined in order to get military supplies. Surely, Pakistan was never motivated, as were most other members of the alliances, to roll back communism. Nor did Pakistan join the alliance under the US to drive out the Soviet Union from Afghanistan in order to make this country secure for the Western style of democracy. As a matter of fact, Pakistan, like Saudi Arabia and other Gulf countries, is more interested in keeping Afghanistan in the middle ages and as a fertile ground for the operation of religious extremist groups having close links with the Al-Qaeda against whom the US launched its war against terrorism that Pakistan joined. US provided military and economic assistance to Pakistan for combating terrorist groups notwithstanding the fact that Pakistan created and has been nurturing some of these groups to be used as an asset against India and in Afghanistan. And the US aid is continuing in spite of the vast majority of the Pakistanis having turned against the US and in spite of the complaint lodged by the then Secretary of State Hillary Clinton with her Pakistani counterpart that there was an effort in Pakistan to paint everything the US did for it negatively and that 'this effort is led by the ISI'.[62]

The US has been giving military aid to Pakistan apparently because it is satisfied with the cooperation it has elicited from Pakistan as an alliance partner. This has included provision of base and other facilities for conducting intelligence over the Soviet Union, intermediation for opening to China and protection of its men and material engaged in fighting in Afghanistan. Today the US counts on Pakistan's help in bringing about reconciliation in Afghanistan. Moreover, the US reckons

Pakistan to be of strategic importance to it in the future as well because of its unique relationship with China with which US is trying to seek a modus vivendi.

China has played a crucial role in helping Pakistan to maintain military parity with India. Next to the US, China has been the most important supplier of arms to Pakistan. China has a direct interest in enabling Pakistan to maintain parity with India because of its strategy not to have a rival military power in Asia, which India alone is capable of becoming. There is no ideological consideration like sharing of common values bearing on China's military relations with Pakistan. In fostering and maintaining these relations, both sides are engaged in pure real politics. China has supplied and built capacity in Pakistan to manufacture various categories of weapons including jet fighters, tanks and medium- and short-range missiles. It has provided to Pakistan nuclear reactors proven nuclear weapon design, enriched uranium and ring magnets used for enriching uranium. Recently Pakistan announced its decision to acquire eight Chinese submarines worth $5 billion. This is going to be the single biggest military deal for both China and Pakistan and will significantly augment the existing submarine fleet of the latter. A colossal aid package of $46 billion was officially unveiled when the Chinese President during his visit to Pakistan on 20 April 2015, launched the China–Pakistan Economic Corridor under which China's western city of Kashgar will be linked by road, rail and pipeline with Pakistan's port of Gwador in the development of which the Chinese have already invested billions of dollars and the management of which was handed over to a Chinese company in 2013. This will provide an opening by the shortest route, for China to South Asia, Arabian Sea and the African countries on the eastern coast of the Indian Ocean. If implemented with speed and efficiency, this will provide a tremendous boost to the sluggish Pakistani economy. It will also have far-reaching military implications.

Pakistan has suffered grievously from its pursuit of military parity with India and both India and Pakistan have suffered self-inflicted injuries by getting involved in a large-scale and prolonged arms race. Pakistan has paid a heavy cost in terms of deferred development and the accumulation of structural problems in the economy. It has also been the main reason for the perpetuation of authoritarian military rule in Pakistan either directly or indirectly, and the fragile state of democracy in the country. In the process, Pakistan's social fabric has undergone a drastic change for the worse. It is the impact of the pursuit of this policy on Pakistan society that has brought Pakistan to the brink of a failed state and not so much the way it has damaged the economy. It is also relevant to recall here that the ideology underlying the policy of military parity with India was a major factor accounting for the loss of more than half of Pakistan's population and a huge chunk of its territory in the form of East Pakistan.

India has also borne the brunt of this policy because of the loss of life and property involved in the four wars fought by the two countries and in the proxy war that India is continuing to fight with its neighbour. More frightening is the spectre of a nuclear war looming over the region. The way the development of the nuclear weapon programme is proceeding in Pakistan has created a highly unstable and volatile security situation in the region. Unlike India, Pakistan has not accepted a no-first-use of its nuclear weapons. This means that Pakistan's nuclear weapons will be kept in readiness to unleash a nuclear war against India in the event of apprehension of an attack by the much superior conventional forces of India. Pakistan's first strike policy has also led to a very fast rate of growth of tactical weapons by Pakistan, the only purpose of which is to be used on the battlefield in a war against India. In a bid to maintain parity, Pakistan is augmenting its nuclear arsenals at a much faster pace than India. Pakistan today is reported to have an arsenal of as many as 120 nuclear warheads and is expected to triple that number in a decade.[63] Pakistan has tested missiles that can carry nuclear warheads to any part of India.

Prospects for a Turnaround in Indo-Pak Relations

The decisive factor determining Indo-Pak relations is Pakistan's definition of its self-identity as a diehard Islamic state and in terms of perpetual hostility towards India. A turnaround in the relations between the two countries is possible only if there is a change in this definition of Pakistan's identity. According to the prominent American historian, Walter Russell Mead, Pakistan can become an economically powerful country if it transforms its military competition with India to a development competition.[64] For this to happen, Pakistan will have to give up its hostility towards India and forge with it normal trade and economic relations without giving up its claim on any of the disputed issues, including Kashmir, between the two countries. Such a paradigm shift will require Pakistan to give up the paraphernalia of extremist Islamic traits inherited from one of the mainstream Islamic traditions of the Indian subcontinent and reinforced by its decision to borrow from the Wahabi mainstream of Arab countries.

A logical consequence of this shift will be to turn against the Islamic terrorist groups originating from West Asia and now operating in Pakistan and Afghanistan as well. The next step will be internal reforms starting with the full restoration of, and putting into practice, its broadly democratic Constitution and a determined effort to build the institutions provided in and essential for upholding it. A drastic reform of other institutions, particularly of the madrasas; scrapping of the blasphemy law; showing respect for and ensuring minority rights; and adopting a zero tolerance policy towards attacks on religious places of the minorities, including those of the Shias and Ahmedias, would be important milestones in the process of this paradigm shift. Beyond this, while maintaining its good relations with West Asian countries, Pakistan should return to its South Asian roots. It should take a leading part, along with India, in bringing about South Asian economic integration and, eventually, South Asian economic union. It will then be able to march along with other South Asian countries towards integrating with wider regional groupings like RCEP which are taking shape in the Asia-Pacific region. From this perspective, it does not make much sense for Pakistan to remain stuck with West Asia where nothing of consequence is happening except internecine wars, made more complex and intractable by the operation of various terrorist groups and the intervention of outside powers.

It is for the people of Pakistan to recognize that the policy that their rulers have followed has, instead of yielding any benefits, brought the country to the brink of a failed state and that one clear option they have to reverse the current drift and put their country on the path of peace and prosperity is to forge normal relations with India. Akmal Hussain believes that 'normalizing economic relations [with India] is necessary for economic growth which would provide the material basis of maintaining the integrity of the nation and strengthening the state'.[65] But in the ultimate analysis, it is for the people of Pakistan to redefine their national identity and state ideology. India can contribute very little to bringing this about. Nevertheless, India must play a positive role in the process of this transition.

Unfortunately the chances of the Pakistani people bringing about such a change appear slender. This is mainly because none of the forces that have shaped, and swear by, the prevailing ideology can be relied upon to transform it. The most important among them, of course, is the Army which will be strongly in favour of maintaining the status quo from which it has everything to gain and nothing to lose. It is true that today the Army is beleaguered and threatened by the extreme religious groups created and nurtured by it. But by now these groups have become so strong and penetrated so deep in Pakistani society that even if the Army wants to rein them in, let alone eliminate them, it is hardly in a position to do so. In the beginning, there was a modus vivendi between the Army and these groups. These groups wanted to preach their fundamentalist ideology and remain satraps in the areas of their influence but they had no design on the state itself. But today they are strong enough to embark upon this ambition. The situation has become vastly more complicated by the intrusion of foreign terrorist groups whose aim is not only to take over Pakistan but also to carve out in that region a radical Islamic State of their own. Much of the anti-Americanism raging in Pakistan today is pan-Islamic in character, fanned by extreme religious forces of all hues now deeply entrenched in Pakistan and Afghanistan.

The political parties in Pakistan are neither inclined towards, nor capable of, bringing about a paradigm shift. They have always acted in concert with the Army in pursuing a policy of hostility towards India. As a matter of fact, in some cases they have proved to be more radical than the Army because of their reliance on popular votes influenced by the extremists, to remain in power. For example, during General Pervez Musharraf's rule, an outline of a solution of the Kashmir problem essentially based on the elimination, and not the redrawal, of the line of control had emerged. This was, however, relegated to the background, if not jettisoned, by the PPP and subsequently the Nawaz Sharif governments. Moreover, whereas General Musharraf had set aside, may be only for tactical purposes, the UN resolutions as the basis for solving the problem, the Nawaz Sharif government has publicly gone back to these.

Political parties in Pakistan rely on the extremist elements not only to seek votes but also for other kinds of assistance. Imran Khan's Tehreek-e-Insaf derived its strength mainly from these elements. At the time of the last elections, it was reported that important leaders who contested the elections under the banner of the Pakistan Muslim League (Nawaz Sharif) (PML[NS]) also received support from extremist elements, who even provided bodyguards to the candidates. The extremist religious groups are internalized in most of the mainstream political parties of Pakistan. That is why the Islam-pasand parties publicly participating in the elections do not fair very well in them. It was a measure of the reliance of the PML(NS) on religious extremist elements that after winning the elections, Nawaz Sharif, contrary to the advice of the Army, decided to negotiate with the TTP. It is a different matter that it did not work, mainly because of the excesses committed by the TTP culminating in the attack on a military school in Peshawar, killing 132 students. The Army then, with the approval of the government in power, launched a campaign against the terrorist groups under the code name Zarb-e-Azb. Though this campaign achieved some notable results, in the very nature of things it could not be taken to its logical conclusion. While the campaign was still going on, lawyers were out in the street voicing support for Tahirul Qadri. In early February 2015, a large number of Shia worshippers at an *Imambara* at Shikarpur were killed in a bomb blast. As Nadir Hassan, a Pakistani journalist has pointed out: 'We are not about to launch operations against every militant group in the country for the simple reason that we can't. Doing so would require sending the Army into every city of Pakistan, to aerially bombard every major urban area. It should go without saying that this is something no one wants . . .'.[66] Hassan has further stated that there is no denying now that the militant groups are allowed to operate freely because 'the state is seen by some as having a vested interest in their doing so, whether it wants to keep them around to fight future wars in India and Afghanistan or out of the fear of the monster it created'.[67]

The third agent which can bring about a shift in the state ideology of Pakistan could be civil society organizations and peoples' movements. Among major South Asian countries, Pakistan provides the narrowest space to such organizations and movements. This is mainly because of the prolonged sway of authoritarian regimes in Pakistan and the dominance of elite and feudal groups in the governance system who regard such organizations and movements as inimical to their interest. Since most of the public space is occupied by the Army and these elitist and feudal groups, there is hardly any left for civil society organizations. Moreover, even those who come out on the street—as lawyers of Lahore did in support of the dismissed Chief Justice of the Supreme Court, Iftikhar Muhammad Chaudhry—do not have a liberal attitude when it comes to religion. The same group also came out in support of the assassin of the Punjab Governor, Salman Taseer, who was killed for his opposition to the country's blasphemy law.

If domestic political and military forces cannot be relied upon to bring about a paradigm shift in Pakistan either because they have a vested interest in the status quo or they are incapable of doing so, can one turn to foreign powers for this purpose? Here the two major powers that readily come to mind are the US and China. Both India and Pakistan have been trying to leverage the influence of the US for bringing about changes in each other's policies on contentious issues. After the Mumbai attack masterminded by terrorist groups located in Pakistan and having links with the Pakistan government, India has been putting pressure on the US to persuade Pakistan, through sanctions if necessary, to bring the culprits of the attack to book, to give up sheltering and supporting the terrorist groups and to close down their infrastructure in Pakistan. Since Atal Bihari Vajpeyee's tenure as prime minister, every political leader has succumbed to the temptation of falling back on the US to achieve results in this front. But this has not yielded any concrete results so far, leaving Pakistan free to pursue with impunity its policy of using terrorism as an instrument of policy against India. In view of the importance that it attaches to maintaining good relations with Pakistan for serving its broader interest in the region, the US is unlikely to go beyond advising Pakistan to deal more effectively with terrorism. In any event, there is no chance of its applying sanctions against Pakistan to achieve the outcome desired by India. The US undoubtedly acts when the terrorist activities affect its own interest, as in Afghanistan. Here it by and large succeeded in eliciting Pakistan's cooperation in preventing the terrorist groups under its control there from hurting vital US interests. Moreover, we should not forget that each time we approach the US for putting pressure on Pakistan we make ourselves vulnerable to US pressure in turn to change our policy to suit its interest, including those related to Indo-Pak issues.

As a superpower with interests all over the world, the US has been concerned about the tensions between India and Pakistan escalating into a full-fledged conflagration with the possibility of its sliding into a nuclear war. The US therefore has consistently advised both the countries to maintain their dialogue and has dispatched special missions—for example, the Gates mission in May 1990—whenever it has apprehended a crisis situation enveloping the region. President Clinton's intervention for facilitating Pakistan's withdrawal from Kargil should be seen in this light. So should be his admonition in his televised address to the people of Pakistan in 2000 that in the modern times an attempt to solve bilateral problems through resort to violence cannot be viewed with equanimity.

The US has equally resisted pressure from Pakistan to intervene with India for finding a solution to the Kashmir problem. This has been mainly due to the strong position taken by India against mediation or intervention by outside powers for solving the Kashmir issue or any other issue figuring in the Indo-Pak bilateral relationship. It is, therefore, unlikely that the US will take any initiative to put pressure on Pakistan to bring about a change in its basically anti-Indian self-perception or in the fundamentalist orientation of its state ideology. The nearest that the US came to it was when it exercised its influence on General Pervez Musharraf who in an address to the nation on 12 January 2002 announced far-reaching changes in the government structure and public institutions in Pakistan, including the madrasas education system. In that address, he projected the vision of a 'progressive, forward-looking and tolerant' Pakistan based on the teachings of Iqbal and Jinnah. He castigated theocratic tendencies and even talked about the separation of the state from religion. He criticized those fighting against the presumed enemies of Islam and told them to stop interfering in the affairs of others. He significantly declared: 'We are Pakistanis first'. However, this fleeting chance for change remained unrealized because General Musharraf himself did not believe in them but announced them mainly as an expedient to buy peace at home and secure large military and economic assistance from the US.

China, the only other major power having influence over Pakistan, has absolutely no incentive to seek a change in Pakistan's state ideology or self-identification. China has throughout followed the policy of not allowing ideology to come in the way of pursuing bilateral relations which it sees in terms of pure real politics. The Chinese believe in dealing with any government in power that can serve their interest. China's main current interest in the region is to keep India embroiled in South Asia by fuelling rivalry with Pakistan through arms supply, successfully build the China–Pakistan Economic Corridor in order to be able to find an opening to the Indian Ocean countries through the shortest route, and find access to raw materials in Afghanistan. The status quo in the region ideally serves all these purposes. Any change in it is likely to introduce elements of uncertainty which China would like to avoid.

Strategy for Dealing with Pakistan

To be realistic, in developing its strategy for dealing with Pakistan, India cannot count on Pakistan changing either its self-identity based on the two-nation theory or its state ideology predicated on its leadership of the Islamic world and perpetual hostility towards India. This, however, does not warrant India turning away from Pakistan or its adopting a hostile attitude towards it. The consequence of such a negative and defeatist policy will be the perpetuation of the tension between the two countries, which has inflicted immense costs on their peoples, and its dangerous drift to a full-fledged war with catastrophic consequences.

It is, therefore, indispensable for India to have a constructive and positive approach towards dealing with Pakistan. India should give up the factually incorrect and wishful thinking prevalent in responsible quarters here that Pakistan is a failed state and will wither away. India should be under no illusion that in the coming years and decades, there is no escape from dealing with Pakistan as it is and has been for the past several decades. Developments in Pakistan are going to affect India in a major way. Therefore, India has a major stake in Pakistan's security and prosperity. We should, therefore, as a matter of conscious policy conduct our relationship with Pakistan in such a manner as to promote peace, security and prosperity in both the nations.

Pakistan is a major Third World country with a population of about 200 million and with hard-working and talented people representing one of the richest and greatest civilizations on earth. It is an attractive market for goods, services and investment from foreign countries. It is located in the vicinity of, and on the route to, the supply of the richest oil reserves in the world. It has traditionally exercised considerable influence in the Islamic world and has acquired a leadership position there. It has one of the world's largest and best trained standing armies and it is now a nuclear weapon power. It is because of these strategic, political and economic considerations that the US and its democratic allies have been engaging and doing business with successive military governments of Pakistan in spite of their trampling of democracy in their country. Precisely for these reasons and others of even greater importance in the subcontinental context, it is necessary for India to remain engaged with Pakistan.

Resumption of Dialogue

We should resume our dialogue with Pakistan without attaching precondition to it and maintain it by and large uninterrupted, without allowing any long hiatus to emerge in the process. It is recognized that events may occur like the Mumbai terrorist attack, which may make it politically difficult to continue the dialogue. However, when we are obliged to interrupt the dialogue under extreme political pressure, we should not publicly announce conditions for its resumption nor should we lapse into a long spell without dialogue.

There is a very strong common sense case for remaining engaged with Pakistan more or less on a continuing basis. Given the military parity between the two countries and the fact that both of them are nuclear weapon powers, there is very little scope for unilateral action or limited retaliatory measures by either side. Nor can India, for valid reasons, accept third party mediation or intervention on controversial issues between the two countries. In the circumstances, the only alternative left to defuse tension and avoid an involuntary drift to disaster is through bilateral dialogue. Moreover, in the absence of dialogue, there are bound to be unwarranted speculations regarding each other's intentions. This can result in avoidable pre-emptive actions having the potential to trigger conflicts. This can be best avoided by maintaining continuing dialogue.

India has made the resumption of dialogue with Pakistan conditional on the latter taking punitive action against Pakistan-based terrorists who are plotting or engaged in perpetrating violence and destruction in India. It is putting particular emphasis on bringing to justice those who were involved in the Mumbai attack. But this pre-condition has not yielded the desired result. Besides, the interruption of dialogue has served the interest of the terrorists whose objective is to widen the chasm separating the two countries by preventing them from coming together. Thus, by not resuming dialogue, we are allowing terrorists to use us as an instrument for the execution of their design in the subcontinent.

Solving Outstanding Problems

Through dialogue, India should seek to solve outstanding bilateral issues between the two countries. India should play with Pakistan all the possible positive-sum games, that is, those which bring benefits to both the countries. There are huge opportunity costs involved in keeping these issues unresolved, as calculated by scholars and think tanks from both the countries. Taking the Siachen issue as an example, we know that it has involved, on a regular basis, the loss of precious lives of the soldiers of the two countries, has affected their morale because of being obliged to operate in an inhospitable climate, and has been a drain on the budgets of the two countries.

All the outstanding issues between the two countries—the principal ones being Kashmir, Siachen, Sir Creek and the Tulbul Navigation Project—have been under negotiation for several decades and at one stage or the other, the two countries had come very close to a final settlement on each of these issues. However, each time, the advance made was frittered away because of the pressure exerted by detractors from both sides to link the issue under negotiation with other bilateral problems between the two countries. In the case of Pakistan, the final agreement on every issue was invariably linked to the Kashmir problem, whereas from the Indian side, convenient excuses were discovered to stall progress. Time has come to get out of this syndrome and clinch a settlement on an issue when the moment is propitious and before frequent postponements result in a hardening of attitudes on it on both sides. This is precisely what has happened with the Siachen problem. The Indian Armed Forces are now opposed to the tentative agreement reached earlier that both sides should withdraw troops from the Siachen heights subject to the delineation on a map and its authentication, of the positions occupied at present and each side putting in place a mechanism for surveillance on the movement of troops on the other side.

Even on the Kashmir issue, the two governments through the special envoys of the Prime Minister of India and the President of Pakistan, had at one stage worked out a blueprint for solving the problem. This was predicated on the principle of making the boundary irrelevant rather than redrawing it, ensuring free flow of commerce, communication and contact among the Kashmiri people on both sides, and the establishment of institutions for undertaking joint development projects.[68]

Importance of India–Pakistan Economic Relations

Pakistan has nothing to lose and a great deal to gain by establishing a relationship of full-fledged economic cooperation with India. The history of international relations during the post-Second World War period testifies that nations can have flourishing economic relations without detriment either to their state ideology, their socio-economic system or their positions on contentious issues with their partners. The prime example in this regard is the economic relationship between Europe and the Soviet Union/Russia at the peak of the Cold War and during the post-Cold War period. Other examples are Sino-US relations after the opening up of China to the US and Sino-Indian relations. During the best part of the post-Second World War period, Europe remained the principal destination for the export of gas and other energy resources from the Soviet Union/Russia. Even while challenging the very existence of the Republic of Formosa (Taiwan) as a sovereign state and claiming it to be a part of the Chinese mainland, one of the most significant economic relations of China has been with Taiwan. In spite of India's border dispute with China and other contentious issues between the two countries, China has emerged as the largest trading partner of India in the last 12–15 years. The value of two-way trade between the two countries went up from $2.21 billion in 2002 to $73.9 billion in 2011. It was, therefore, not surprising that in his address to the Pakistan Parliament in December 1996, the then Chinese President Jiang Zemin advised: 'We should look at the differences or disputes (with neighbours) from a long perspective. If certain issues cannot be resolved for the time being, they may be shelved temporarily so that they may not affect the normal state-to-state relations'.[69]

The immediate benefit of economic cooperation between India and Pakistan will be releasing the Pakistan economy from its present structural constraints of low rate of savings, uncompetitive and inefficient export sector and constant pressure on its balance-of-payment and fiscal position.[70] Linking Pakistan's economy with that of India through normal flows of trade and investment is one of the best opportunities available to Pakistan to return to the trajectory of earlier higher rates of growth, while at the same time liberating it from the structural problems that have come in the way of its sustainability. For India too, this will be an important positive factor for accelerating and sustaining the relatively higher growth of its economy.

The normalization of trade between the two countries is likely to result in a dramatic increase in the trade volume mainly because of their being natural trading partners. Pakistan will gain as much as, if not more than, India from this trade expansion. Pakistan will have competitive advantage vis-à-vis third countries in the Indian market. Pakistan will have the opportunity of tapping one of the largest markets in the world, backed up by the purchasing power of the people in an economy growing at 6 to 8 per cent per annum. By trading with India, Pakistan will be able to replace in a significant measure its higher cost domestic inputs and imports from third countries with lower cost imports from India. This will enhance the competitiveness of its export sector and of the economy as a whole and ensure better utilization of its foreign exchange resources. A State Bank of Pakistan study has revealed that a large number of items outside Pakistan's negative list under SAFTA but not allowed to be imported from India can be imported from the latter at a lower cost than the current cost of imports from the rest of the world. The Bank has calculated that allowing these items to be imported from India will give Pakistan an average annual saving of $400–900 million.[71]

Pakistan will also gain considerably in terms of accrual of additional revenue to its exchequer because of the formalization of the current illegal trade, which according to some estimates is larger than the legal trade. This is apart from the alleviation of the suffering of traders, particularly small traders, who resort to informal trading on account of the constraint imposed by the present trade regime between the two countries.

It is widely recognized that the normalization of trade between India and Pakistan is the *sine qua non* for achieving economic integration in South Asia. An economically integrated South Asia will be in a better position to link with the new generation of economic groupings, particularly the RCEP, that are being negotiated in the Asia-Pacific region. Individually, it will not be possible for South Asian countries—with the exception, perhaps, of India—to be a part of the big game of economic integration that is on in the Asia-Pacific region and which will determine the character of economic relations among the countries of this region in the years to come. Clearly, South Asia can play its rightful role in this wider game only if it is itself economically integrated.

Gains from the normalization of trade between India and Pakistan cannot be estimated only from the assumption of the benefits of free trade between the two economies, but also that of the deeper integration of the two economies, which would include, apart from trade normalization and liberalization, trade facilitation, transport, liberalization of services and capital flows, cooperation in the field of energy and technology and for ensuring food security to the people, and coordination of macroeconomic policies. The benefits of trade normalization and liberalization will be multiplied several times if conceived in the dynamic framework of such deeper integration.

Akmal Hussain has argued that trade normalization between the two countries will have a positive impact on the GDP growth and towards removing some of the structural problems of the Pakistani economy. Imports of cheaper capital and intermediate goods will reduce capital–output ratio in Pakistan, thereby leading to higher growth in GDP for the given amount of investment. Cheaper imports from India will also reduce income inequality because food imports from India during the period of seasonal shortages will reduce food inflation which adversely affects mainly the economically disadvantaged people.[72]

If there is a liberalization of capital movement between the two countries, the likelihood is that of larger capital inflows from India to Pakistan than the other way round. This is because of India's higher investment capability, both domestically and outward bound, as reflected in the sharp increase until 2008 in outward movement of capital from India and its reasonably large foreign exchange reserves. India's total outflow of capital had reached a peak of $21.1 billion in 2008.[73] In the short term, enhanced inflow of FDI from India will have the effect of improving Pakistan's balance-of-payment position and reducing its capital account deficit. Indian investment in Pakistan will also enable the latter to tap the pool of Indian skilled workers and technology, improve international competitiveness of its firms and thereby accelerate its economic growth. In the long run, efficiency seeking movement of capital from India to Pakistan could lead to a restructuring of important sectors of Pakistan economy that will make it more efficient and sustainable. It could also have the effect of broadening the narrow industrial base of Pakistan.

Trade normalization and liberalization will have a limited impact if it is not accompanied by the removal of transport bottlenecks to trade and granting by both countries of transit rights to each other. If the two countries allow free transit of goods of each other to third countries, through their territories, it will remove a major obstacle to the actualization of major projects such as the Iran–Pakistan–India gas pipeline. Implementation of projects for the joint development of infrastructure and mutual grant of transit facilities will also enable the two countries to participate meaningfully in the international production network covering the entire Asia-Pacific region.

Services now contribute the largest value addition to the GDP of the two countries. In 2011–12, this sector accounted for 59 per cent of India's and 54 per cent of Pakistan's GDP.[74] It is, therefore, logical that normalization and liberalization of trade between the two countries should cover in its sweep services like tourism, health, education, IT (Business Process Outsourcing [BPO]), the retail trade sector and telecommunication. Enhanced flow of services would increase employment elasticities and improve income distribution.

It will, no doubt, be difficult because of the persistence of old stereotyped thinking, to adopt measures for deeper integration of the economies of the two countries, particularly in the field of transport, transit, services and even investment. An enlightened view, however, will be that a great deal of cooperation in these areas can also take place within the existing paradigm of the relationship between the two countries. However, such other benefits of mutual cooperation as holding their pluralistic societies together, imparting resilience to their democracy, protection from the onslaught of terrorist groups, and reaping the benefits of disarmament dividend cannot be realized without the abandonment of Pakistan's officially defined and maintained national ethos and without its consequent outcome of a sea change in Pakistan's attitude towards India.

A Phased Programme of Indo-Pak Economic Cooperation

This sub-section contains suggestions for a phased programme for the normalization and liberalization of trade and enhancement of economic cooperation between the two countries.

(*a*) Pakistan should take the lead in keeping its promise of eliminating the negative list that it still maintains for trading with India, and start trading on an MFN or non-discriminatory basis.

(*b*) Simultaneously with the restoration of MFN status of trade between the two countries, India should, in pursuance of the announcement made by it towards the end of 2012, reduce its negative list under SAFTA to 100, justified exclusively on security and health grounds. It should also, as promised, move to reduce its duties on imports from Pakistan to the range of 0–5 per cent as provided in SAFTA. This would amount to granting unilateral free trade treatment to Pakistan.

(*c*) In the third stage, Pakistan should also reduce its current negative list of 1,209 items under SAFTA to the minimum necessary on health and security grounds, and start granting to India free trade treatment as provided under SAFTA.

(*d*) At the next stage, India and Pakistan should undertake negotiations for liberalizing trade in services and movement of capital between the two countries.

(*e*) The ideal situation would be to undertake such negotiation along with other South Asian countries, within the framework of a revamped and strengthened SAFTA with a view to achieving South Asian economic integration within a specified time limit. It is, however, recognized that the process of such negotiation under SAFTA may be very complicated and time-consuming. In that event, India and Pakistan should launch negotiation for concluding a bilateral CEPA. This could become the platform for the integration of the other South Asian countries.

(*f*) Trade facilitation measures should constitute an indispensable and integral part of Indo-Pak CEPA. Under this component of the Agreement, the two countries should try and implement a comprehensive and integrated land transport policy in order to provide rail and road services connecting the two countries and linking the sea ports through land borders to ensure connectivity with the rest of the world. This should include the expansion and strengthening of facilities and capabilities both at the ports and at the border crossing points in India and Pakistan, as well as removal of procedural difficulties at the border points and harmonization of standards.[75]

(*g*) CEPA should include projects for joint development of infrastructure, particularly in the transport and energy fields.

(*h*) Both India and Pakistan face the problem of power deficit and hence low per capita commercial energy consumption as well as poor quality of energy infrastructure. This indicates the potential for cooperation in the energy sector. A way forward would be to initiate limited power purchase between India and Pakistan. In addition, the two countries should develop grid connectivity to facilitate power exchange. Cooperation in the power sector could either be included in the CEPA or a separate memorandum, or an agreement can be signed to cover it.

(*i*) Finally, the CEPA should include commitment of the two countries to rush goods and services to each other's centres of population in the event of unexpected shortfall of supply or emergency situations.

The Pre-Conditions

India can effectively deal with Pakistan and can contribute to bringing about changes in its state ideology only by remaining strong militarily and economically, and faithful to its own national ethos of secularism and respect for diversity.

Remaining Militarily Strong

In the military field, India should maintain and keep updated its deterrent in the form of its second strike capability. There is no need for this purpose to enter into an arms race with Pakistan to match each addition to Pakistan's nuclear warheads, fighter aircrafts, or nuclear submarines. On the contrary, every opportunity should be sought to make a reduction in the existing strength of conventional forces and stockpiles of nuclear arms. This was successfully achieved by the major powers, the US and the Soviet Union/Russia during the last phase of the Cold War and the post-Cold War period. The peace dividend that the two countries reaped as a result ran into hundreds of billions of dollars. We should certainly take a leaf out of their page.

However, an agreement on any substantial reductions in the conventional forces or the nuclear deterrent capability of India and Pakistan is not possible without China joining the process of negotiation. This is because a large part of India's conventional forces are deployed in India's

North and North-Eastern region to meet possible threats to security from China. India's nuclear deterrent is also designed to deter a possible nuclear threat from China. But China is unlikely to join a regional disarmament process between itself, India and Pakistan, because it is expanding its armed forces and nuclear capability mainly to meet a possible threat to its security from the US. In view of the current asymmetry in the nuclear capability of China and the US, China has refused to join any global arms control or disarmament talks until the US reduces its nuclear arsenals to a level close to that of China. In these circumstances, any disarmament dialogue between India and Pakistan does not seem to be feasible unless it is a part of a global disarmament process which China can join.

India and Pakistan should expand the range of confidence-building measures they have already adopted and implement more such measures to avoid conflict by accident. India should also maintain its no-first-use rule even though Pakistan has ruled out the adoption of such a policy. This would imply that India should not emulate Pakistan and go in for the production and deployment of tactical weapons. India has no alternative but to continue to rely on its second strike capability for dealing with Pakistan's first strike threat. For, we would not be more secure by developing a first strike capability. Moreover, if both India and Pakistan switch over to a first strike mode, the security situation in the region will become extremely unstable and volatile, putting it beyond the capacity of either of these countries to manage it. India should proceed on the assumption that in the present era of globalization, it will not be possible for any country to resort to first strike. And if Pakistan does so, our second strike capacity should be sufficient to deal with it.

Resumption and Maintenance of High Economic Growth

Very few factors will be more conducive to Pakistan accepting the logic of cooperation with India and giving up its policy of hostility towards it than the resumption and maintenance of high economic growth of the Indian economy. India's goal should be to maintain a growth rate of 7 per cent or above during the next two decades, further increase its current savings and investment rates of around 30 per cent of the national income, add substantially to its current foreign exchange reserves of close to $300 billion, keep its debt burden and inflation under reasonable control, restructure the education and health sectors, make massive investments for the development of infrastructure and achieve inclusive growth by enabling the poorest and marginalized sections of society to derive equitable benefits from, and participate in, the process of development. This will enable India to make its growth process self-sustaining, attract additional foreign investment and play a leading role in the restructuring of the international monetary and financial architecture. In such a scenario, Pakistan may very well see its interest best served in marching together with India for solving its domestic economic problems and playing its own rightful role in the Asia-Pacific region and the world.

Preserving the Ethos of the Indian State

To be able to deal effectively with Pakistan to the mutual benefit of the two countries and place itself in a position to exercise even a modest influence on the restructuring of Pakistan's social dynamics, it is absolutely necessary for India to uphold the basic principles of its national ethos of secularism and respect for pluralism, as enshrined in its Constitution. There have recently been far too many cases of aberration from these values. If we are not able to adhere to and practise the values that set us apart from Pakistan, we shall scarcely be able to stand on the moral high ground to cast an aspersion, let alone seek to bring about a change, in the national ethos of Pakistan, which is the single most important inhibiting factor in the normalization of relations between the two countries.

Notes

1. Husain Haqqani, 'Re-Imagining Pakistan' (Second Khan Abdul Ghaffar Khan Memorial Lecture delivered in Jamia Millia Islamia, New Delhi, 11 August 2014).
2. T. V. Paul, *The Warrior State: Pakistan in the Contemporary World* (Gurgaon: Random House, India, 2014).
3. This amendment was later annulled, then reintroduced and finally expunged from the Constitution in April 2010.
4. Husain Haqqani, 'Pakistan's Perennial Crisis', *The Hindu*, 6 September 2014.
5. This author was an Observer of two general elections in Pakistan in the early 1990s.
6. Husain Haqqani, *Magnificent Delusions: Pakistan, the United States and an Epic History of Misunderstanding* (New York: PublicAffairs, 2013) 281.
7. Sanchita Bhattacharya, 'Is the Sword Mightier than the Pen in Pakistan?' (East Asia Forum, 16 May 2014), http://www.eastasiaforum.org/2014/05/16/is-the-sword-mightier-than-the-pen-in-pakistan/ (accessed on 20 July 2015).
8. Paul, *The Warrior State*.

9. Bruce Riedel, *Deadly Embrace: Pakistan, America and the Future of the Global Jihad* (Washington Brookings Institution Press, 2011).
10. Haqqani, *Magnificent Delusions*, 281.
11. Ibid.
12. Rajiv Dogra, *Where Borders Bleed: An Insider's Account of Indo-Pak Relations* (Delhi: Rupa Publications, 2015).
13. Shahid Javed Burki, 'Pakistani Militants Strike Back' (Insight No.256, Institute of South Asian Studies [ISAS], Singapore, 20 June 2014), http://www.isn.ethz.ch/Digital-Library/Publications/Detail/?lng=en&id=185394 (accessed on 20 July 2015).
14. Table 1 in Akmal Hussain, 'Pakistan Economic Crisis: Structure and Growth in Historical Perspective' (paper presented at the Institute of South Asian Studies [ISAS] Workshop on Political and Economic Challenges in Pakistan, National University of Singapore, 28 April 2011).
15. Ibid.
16. Ibid.
17. Ibid.
18. World Bank, World Development Indicators.
19. Hussain, 'Pakistan Economic Crisis'.
20. Ibid.
21. Ibid.
22. Ibid.
23. Ibid.
24. Jean Drèze and Amartya Sen, *An Uncertain Glory: India and its Contradictions* (New Delhi: Penguin Books, 2013).
25. Ibid.
26. Hussain, 'Pakistan Economic Crisis'.
27. Ibid.
28. Ibid.
29. Ibid.
30. Ibid.
31. Dogra, *Where Borders Bleed.*
32. Parvez Hasan, *My Life My Country: Memoirs of a Pakistani Economist* (Lahore: Ferozsons, 2011).
33. Drèze and Sen, *An Uncertain Glory.*
34. Cited in Palakh Jain and Samridhi Bimal; 'Enhancing India-Pakistan Economic Relations: Perspective for Indian Investment in Pakistan' (Working Paper no. 274, Indian Council for Research on International Economic Relations [ICRIER], May 2014).
35. United Nations Conference on Trade and Development (UNCTAD), World Investment Report (WIR), various years, http://www.unctad.org (accessed on 20 July 2015).
36. Hussain, 'Pakistan Economic Crisis'.

37. Ibid.
38. Government of Pakistan, 'Pakistan Economic Survey 2009–10' (Ministry of Finance, Islamabad, 2010) 7.
39. Drèze and Sen, *An Uncertain Glory*.
40. Ibid.
41. Ibid.
42. Ibid.
43. Ibid.
44. Ibid.
45. World Bank, World Development Indicators.
46. Drèze and Sen, *An Uncertain Glory*.
47. Ibid.
48. Paul, *The Warrior State*.
49. Dogra, *Where Borders Bleed*.
50. The trade figures from the year 2000 onwards cited here are calculated from data taken from International Monetary Fund, Direction of Trade Statistics database, http://elibrary-data.imf.org/ (accessed on 28 April 2015).
51. Ibid.
52. Ibid.
53. Calculated from data taken from International Monetary Fund, Direction of Trade Statistics database, http://elibrary-data.imf.org/ (accessed on 28 April 2015).
54. Nisha Taneja, Sanjib Pohit and Radhika Saini, 'India-Pakistan Trade Relations: An Introduction', in *India-Pakistan Trade: Strengthening Economic Relations*, eds Nisha Taneja, Sanjib Pohit and Radhika Saini (New Delhi: Springer, 2015).
55. Nisha Taneja and Pallavi Kalita, 'Most Favoured Nation: New Trade Opportunity for India and Pakistan', *Economic and Political Weekly*, Volume 46, No. 49 (3 December 2011).
56. Taneja et al., 'India-Pakistan Trade Relations'.
57. Economic Data, State Bank of Pakistan, quoted in Shahid Javed Burki, 'Pakistan's New Choices in Economic Diplomacy' (Working Paper No. 188, Institute of South Asian Studies [ISAS], Singapore, 15 May 2014), http://www.isn.ethz.ch/Digital-Library/Publications/Detail/?lang=en&id=180378 (accessed on 20 July 2015).
58. Ibid.
59. Taneja et al., 'India-Pakistan Trade Relations'.
60. Ibid.
61. Quoted in Haqqani, *Magnificent Delusions*, 31.
62. Ibid, 321.
63. *New York Times*, 'Nuclear Fears in South Asia', 6 April 2015.
64. Paul, *The Warrior State*.
65. Akmal Hussain, 'A Perspective on Pakistan-India Relations: Power Dynamics, Democracy and Development', in *India's Economic Growth: Opportunities and*

Challenges for the Region, eds Mallika Joseph and Happymon Jacob (Colombo: Regional Centre for Strategic Studies, 2014).

66. Nadir Hassan, 'Let's Get Real', *News,* Karachi, 5 February 2015.
67. Ibid.
68. This blueprint has never been made public. The details given here are derived from a statement made by Ambassador Satish K. Lamba, Special Envoy of the Prime Minister of India, in a seminar held in Srinagar on 13 May 2013, in which he participated in his personal capacity.
69. Haqqani, *Magnificent Delusions*, 324.
70. Hussain, 'A Perspective on Pakistan-India Relations'.
71. Shuja Nawaz and Mohan Guruswamy, *India and Pakistan: The Opportunity Cost of Conflict* (Washington DC: South Asia Centre of the Atlantic Council, 2014).
72. Hussain, 'A Perspective on Pakistan-India Relations'.
73. Jain and Bimal, 'Enhancing India-Pakistan Economic Relations'.
74. Cited in Taneja et al., 'India-Pakistan Trade Relations'.
75. Ibid.

SIX Indo-US Relations

The US has always been and remains one of the most important factors in India's foreign policy calculations. Despite the recent decline in its economic power and the resurgence of China, it remains the world's pre-eminent military and economic power. This status is unlikely to change in the foreseeable future. The US is India's second largest trading partner, coming after China, and the most important source of foreign investment and technology. Due to its major involvement with the countries and regions in India's neighbourhood, the US exercises considerable influence on India's security environment. Moreover, India's future role in the international arena, particularly in the shaping of the world order, depends critically on how it manages its relations with the US.

In spite of the phenomenal increase during the last decade in India's two-way trade with China, the US remains its most valuable trading partner. The two-way trade between the two countries, after reaching the level of $39.74 billion in 2008 came down to $34.92 billion in 2009 mainly due to the global recession. But after that it recovered and has been growing at a very fast pace, reaching $62.19 billion in 2013.[1] Unlike in the case of trade with China, India has enjoyed a trade surplus with the US every year during the decade between 2000 and 2009. This surplus varied from $5.2 billion to $7.6 billion between 2000 and 2006. In 2007, it came down to $1.5 billion. In 2009, it was $1.6 billion, and reached the level of a little over $11 billion in 2012 and over $15 billion in 2013.[2] Moreover, India's exports to the US are much more diversified than those to China. In 2005, its exports to the US were 16.78 per cent of its total exports. This share has been declining since, but it was still 11 per cent of the total in 2009. The US's share in FDI in India between August 1991 and 2002 averaged 13.4 per cent of the total FDI in India during this period.[3] In 2004–05, its share reached 17.8 per cent of the total. It has been declining since then and was at the level of 3.32 per cent of the total FDI in India in 2013–14.[4] Through licensing and joint-venture arrangements, the US currently ranks as the largest source of foreign commercial technology for the Indian industry.

Relations During the Cold War

The US and India share several common values and interests. They are the two largest democracies in the world—the US the oldest and India the biggest. Both are pluralistic societies committed to basic human rights, freedom, rule of law and secularism. They have a common interest in containing transnational problems like terrorism, environmental degradation and climate change, drug trafficking and pandemics. Both countries share dependence in varying degrees on the supply of oil from West Asia and have, therefore, a common interest in the maintenance of peace and stability in that region and in keeping open the sea lanes and other routes to it.

The US has regarded India as an important partner ever since the latter's independence. It has viewed India not as yet another country, but as a continent, a region and a civilization. Even before the beginning of the ongoing process of globalization, the US was aware of the huge commercial and investment opportunities available in India. It has also been aware of the strategic significance of its relations with India. Earlier, the emphasis was on tapping India's leverage with developing countries individually as well as a group, in the form of G-77 and NAM. Later, the US came to recognize the significance of cooperation with India in dealing with international trade, monetary and financial issues, with strategically important regions of the world and with transnational issues.

Most of the mainstream analysts of the Indo-US relationship have taken a dim view of it, until it is supposed to have started looking up after the conclusion of the Indo-US nuclear deal in 2008. The relationship has been described by them as being estranged, unstable, troubled, bedevilled and, at best, far from being harmonious, warm and cordial. These analysts have attributed the far from satisfactory state of the relationship between the two countries, to what they call India's pro-Soviet policy in the garb of non-alignment and its consistent anti-US postures, reflected, among others, in its voting pattern in the UN and other multinational fora.

The problem with these analysts seems to be their belief that good relations between two countries with asymmetrical power is possible only if the less powerful partner becomes either an ally or a client state of the more powerful one. In such a scenario, there is little scope for honest difference of opinion and democratic contestations of views on regional and global issues. The policy prescription of these analysts is for the weaker power to go along with the US in all its initiatives and actions for which the former's cooperation is sought and give up all its principled positions on regional and global issues, which the US finds irksome.

In their deliberate bid to peddle their negative view of the Indo-US relationship till recently, these analysts conveniently ignore the fact that there have been many positive sides to this relationship even during the Cold War. Throughout this period, successive Indian prime ministers took initiatives, which included their visits to the US, to impart new momentum to India's relationship with the US. This was reciprocated in good measure by US presidents. It is, therefore, not surprising that till the early 1970s, for over a decade and a half, India was the largest recipient of US economic aid. During this period, year after year, US aid to India was close to $400 million.[5] This was irrespective of whether a Republican or a Democratic president was in power. The aid reached its highest level—of $1.65 billion—during the Republican administration of President Eisenhower. It again exceeded $1 billion during Lyndon B. Johnson's presidency. The aid amount was at the level of $556 million and $444 million in 1962 and 1963, respectively, when John F. Kennedy was the President.[6] After 1971, US aid to India started tapering off and from the mid-1980s, it has been insignificant. In spite of the criticisms, some of them no doubt valid, levelled against it, the US PL-480 Programme for Food Aid to India came as a great relief to the country during periods of food shortage, particularly during famine conditions. It prevented a huge number of starvation deaths. It was also largely because of the green signal given by the US government that India, for several years, was the highest recipient of assistance from the International Development Association (IDA), the soft lending window of the World Bank, and from other UN aid agencies. The importance that the US attached to its relations with India was also reflected in the appointment of some of its most distinguished public servants and intellectuals as ambassadors to India, for example, Chester Bowles, John Kenneth Galbraith and Daniel P. Moynihan, to name only a few.

These positive factors do not detract from the fact that the Cold War did have a debilitating effect on Indo-US relations. This was mainly because some of the original authors of the Cold War, particularly John Foster Dulles, openly declared that the countries that were not with the US in its alliance against the rival power bloc were, in fact, against it. India was labelled by these political leaders as anti-US, simply because it remained with the NAM, which did not favour its members joining any military alliances conceived in the Cold-War context. Moreover, from India's point of view, one of the most insidious consequences of the Cold War was the US's bilateral security agreement with Pakistan and its military aid to that country, because of its being a member of US-dominated military alliances. This military assistance was provided on such a scale and for such a long duration that it became a major factor in enabling Pakistan to very nearly achieve military parity with India. This was also mainly responsible for triggering an arms race between the two countries, thereby impeding their development. This also came in the way of India occupying its rightful position of supremacy in the South Asian region. Later, it was again this alliance relationship that prompted the US to turn a blind eye to Pakistan emerging as a de facto nuclear weapon power. But for this, India's nuclear deterrence might have remained 'recessed' even today.

During the 1980s, India again took initiatives to add new dimensions to Indo-US relations. Some important measures for the liberalization of the Indian economy were adopted, which also served US interests in India. Prime Minister Indira Gandhi visited Washington in July 1982. One of the important goals pursued by India at that time was to obtain advanced US technologies for both civilian and military applications. This was the purpose behind the Indira Gandhi-Reagan Science and Technology Initiative of 1982. Prime Minister Rajiv Gandhi paid special attention to maintaining and further improving India's relationship with the US and established a reasonably good personal equation with President Reagan. Obtaining cutting-edge US technology was an important goal during the period of Rajiv Gandhi's prime ministership as well.

Post-Cold War Adjustments by India

After the end of the Cold War, the US emerged as the only superpower or 'hyper power', a term first used by Hubert Vedrine, the then French foreign minister. The US saw this as a unique opportunity to refashion the world according to its desire and interests. India took a series of initiatives to adjust to the new situation in the global power structure. The most important among these was to fine-tune its foreign policy in order to free the Indo-US relationship from the prejudices and stereotypes of the past. To this end, a number of concrete gestures were made by India towards the US. For example, India supported the US-led UN Security Council embargo on Iraq in 1990 and implemented it more faithfully than even some of the US allies. India refrained from criticizing the deployment of US forces in the Gulf. It permitted over-flights and refuelling facilities for US transport aircrafts flying from their base in East Asia to the Gulf. This was, however, done on the basis of an understanding that the aircrafts involved would be carrying non-lethal supplies and civilian personnel for humanitarian assistance in the event of a conflict. It was also made clear from the Indian side that these facilities would not be available in the event of a war breaking out in the Gulf region. India supported most of the Security Council resolutions sponsored by the US and its allies relating to the Gulf crisis. In 1991, India also voted in favour of repealing the UN General Assembly resolution condemning Zionism as a form of racism. It was also the time when India established full diplomatic relationship with Israel. And finally, India agreed to the US proposal for putting in place a mechanism in the form of a Steering Committee, for military cooperation and strategic dialogue on a regular basis. This was superseded in 1995 by Defence Policy Group ultimately leading to the Defence Framework Agreement of 2005 and the launch of the Defence Trade and Technology Initiative in 2013.

In its attempt to be on the right side of the US, in the 1993 session of the UN General Assembly, the then government of India co-sponsored with the US, resolutions on the CTBT and Freeze on the Production of Fissile Material, without the inclusion of the usual disarmament clause. This was a departure from the erstwhile NAM position on these resolutions.

The US, in its turn, extended to India various kinds of support to help it cope with the foreign exchange reserve crisis it faced following the Gulf War. It supported all Indian applications for loans and assistance from the International Monetary Fund (IMF), World Bank and Asian Development Bank and persuaded other industrialized countries to do the same.

These changes were not due to the rediscovery by the two countries of each other after the end of the Cold War. Quite a few of these policy shifts by India would have taken place in any case due to autonomous reasons. For example, India had its own reasons, arising out of the compulsion of regional politics, to vote for the Security Council resolutions relating to the Gulf crisis. India's establishment of full diplomatic relations with Israel in 1992 was a necessary corrective to foreign policy long overdue. India was only looking for a proper time to do so and this opportunity was provided by the end of the Gulf War.

A Decade of US Confrontationist Posturing

In its zeal to pursue some of its global strategic objectives, the Democratic administration under President Clinton displayed scant appreciation of the far-reaching changes that India tried to bring about in its foreign policy towards the US. The new US administration mounted relentless pressure on India to oblige it to change its policy in areas where its national interests were directly and vitally at stake. For example, given the threats to its security from Pakistan and China, no government in power in India could have afforded to give up the nuclear option. In spite of this, the new US administration made it clear that its objective was nothing short of capping, rolling back and ultimately eliminating India's nuclear capability. It insisted on India's signing not only the newly negotiated CTBT, but also the discriminatory NPT. It may be recalled that soon after the end of the first Gulf War, the then US Republican administration had threatened and tried to prepare the ground for applying sanctions in order to compel non-signatories to accede to the NPT.[7]

The New York Times, which on matters like these, not too infrequently reflects the position of the US administration, had significantly suggested in its editorial of 28 April 1992 under the title, 'Stop the Subcontinent's Bomb', that the vulnerability created by India's opening up to the global market forces should be utilized as 'a source of potential leverage for all countries with an interest in a nuclear-free India'.[8] As a step towards preventing India from acquiring nuclear weapon capability, the US successfully persuaded Russia in 1992–93 to renege on its agreement to transfer to India cryogenic engines and the technology to manufacture them. On the trade side, the US took retaliatory action against India under Section 301 of its Trade and Competitiveness Act and withdrew tariff concessions under its Generalized System of Preferences (GSP) on pharmaceutical and chemical exports from India. It threatened to take further unilateral measures in the field of trade until all its demands for opening up the Indian market for US goods and services and for the protection of US patents in India were conceded. The US also started pointing an accusing finger at India at the highest political levels, including by the President and the Secretary of State, with regard to its record on human rights, particularly that in the state of Jammu and Kashmir.

The Indo-US relationship remained confrontationist through the best part of the Clinton administration, which coincided with most of the 1990s. The confrontation reached a crescendo after the nuclear explosions by India in Pokhran in May 1998. Short of military coercion, the

Clinton administration did its worst in its attempt to stop India on the track of becoming a nuclear weapon power.

For this purpose, it worked in concert with its Western allies, China and Russia, and used all relevant international fora, particularly summit-level meetings of the G-8, the forum of the five Permanent Members of the UN Security Council, the EU and the Disarmament Conference. It got resolutions adopted and statements and declarations issued at these fora, which condemned the nuclear explosions conducted by India, regarded them as a threat to international peace and security and called upon India to cap, roll back and liquidate its nuclear weapons programmes, sign the CTBT and accede to the NPT. These resolutions contained provisions for monitoring compliance with the demands made on India, keeping the issue under continuing review and taking further action, if necessary. In the Joint Statement issued after President Clinton's visit to China, soon after the nuclear explosions in the subcontinent, China was asked to share the responsibility of ensuring the maintenance of peace and security in South Asia. This irked India to no end because it sees China as a part of the problem rather than its solution. In the context of China's armed attack against India in 1962, its occupation of a part of the territory of the state of Jammu and Kashmir, its occupation by force of a large part of what India claims to be its territory across the Indo-Chinese border and its military assistance to Pakistan, India could scarcely have been expected to accept China as a peacemaker in the subcontinent.

On the economic side, the US and its Western allies applied comprehensive sanctions against India. They prevailed upon the World Bank and the IMF to freeze their economic assistance to India. Bilaterally, the US put restrictions on the extension of credit to India by government financial institutions, including its EXIM Bank. Restrictions were also imposed on all cooperation in the military field. As a result, Indo-US relations descended to the lowest level it had reached in past decades.

The extreme measures taken by the US against India were mainly due to the threat it perceived from the nuclear explosions by India, to the world order over which it was presiding as the only superpower and which it was trying to reshape after the image of its interests. As stated by President George H. W. Bush soon after the end of the Gulf War (1990–91), the preservation of this order was essential for maintaining the prosperity and lifestyle of the US. The US and its allies were also concerned because they saw a threat to the non-proliferation regime maintained by them coming not only from India and Pakistan but also from other countries which could feel encouraged to follow their example.

After a few long months of tension, the two countries decided to enter into a dialogue to see if a mutual understanding could be reached that could take into account the interests of both parties. This led to eight rounds of talks between Strobe Talbott, the then US deputy secretary of State and Jaswant Singh, the then external affairs minister of India. This was the longest period of intensive bilateral talks at such a high political level ever conducted by the two countries. The process of the dialogue helped in mitigating India's international isolation. India had thought that an understanding reached with the US would help in reaching a similar understanding with the other major powers, particularly the Western countries and Japan. However, the dialogue did not produce any spectacular result or lead to any significant change in the positions of the two countries on the nuclear issue. Among the demands made by the US, the one asking for restraint by India on the export of material, technology and substances which could be used for manufacturing weapons of mass destruction by other countries, did not create much of a problem because of India's impeccable record in this area. India did not accept the US demand for putting a moratorium on the production of weapon-grade fissile material. However, it had no problem in giving a commitment to join the US and other countries in negotiating a Fissile Material Cut-off Treaty. In this regard, the US position that such a treaty should not cover existing stocks coincided with that of India. At the end of the talk, Talbott recognized the futility of trying to force a policy to cap, roll back and eliminate India's nuclear weapons programme. Short of this, he had reason to claim some success in persuading India to apply strategic restraint. India postponed its planned tests of Agni-I and its first test of Agni-II during the pendency of the talk and also agreed to build a national consensus on signing the CTBT. It requested the US to facilitate this task by removing some of the sanctions imposed against it.

The Strobe Talbott–Jaswant Singh talks played a positive role in preparing the ground for President Clinton's visit to India in March 2000, which proved very fruitful in turning the Indo-US relations in a positive direction. A major factor responsible for a significant shift in US policy towards India at that time was the dynamism displayed by the remarkable momentum of growth picked up by the Indian economy and the opportunities that the US saw for itself in the coming years in India. The role played by young non-resident Indian (NRI) entrepreneurs in bringing about the IT revolution in the US which gave it a new competitive edge in the world market over its rivals also made a significant contribution towards its perception of India's importance in the world. This was reflected in the remark made by President Clinton at the meeting organized by the Federation of Indian Chambers of Commerce and Industry (FICCI) in Mumbai, that 'it will be difficult to imagine the world that I would like to leave for my children without a deeper and better partnership with India'.

President Clinton left the Indian audience in no illusion that the basic US positions on subjects of concern to India, particularly on the nuclear, the WTO and Kashmir issues, remained unchanged. On the nuclear issue, in his address to the Indian Parliament, Clinton asked his audience to ponder whether India was not less secure after the Pokhran-II tests. He asserted that India was moving in the opposite direction of the global trend of foreswearing nuclear weapons. On the WTO issues, he reiterated the familiar US demand at that time for 'a dialogue about the connection between labour, the environment and trade and development'. He clearly insisted on establishing a link between trade on the one hand and labour and environmental standards on the other. He said that 'trade should not be a race to the bottom in environmental and labour standards', further clarifying that 'those who believe that trade should contribute not just to wealth but also to fairness [in] societies' were speaking 'for a large part of humanity'.[9]

Positive Turn after 2000

There were, however, clear indications during President Clinton's visit of a shift in the US position in a positive direction, in understanding India's position on the Kashmir issue. While reiterating the basic US position that Kashmir remained a dispute which needed to be resolved, and in any such endeavour the Kashmiri people must be consulted, Clinton warned Pakistan against any attempt to change the status quo by force. In his press conference in New Delhi on 21 March 2000, he stated, 'You cannot expect a dialogue to go forward until there is absence of violence and respect for the line of control'. In his address to the Pakistani people, he warned that 'this era does not reward people who struggle in vain to redraw borders with blood'. On the invocation of the 1948 UN resolutions on Kashmir, he said that 'there [has] been a lot of changes since 1948, including what happened in 1971'.[10] This shift was brought about by the US perception that any attempt to alter the boundary by use of force could lead to an all-out war between India and Pakistan, which could slide into a nuclear war. As the only superpower with a deep interest in the region, the US deemed it a duty to prevent such a drift towards disaster in South Asia. On the question of US mediation on the Kashmir issue, India has made it clear from time to time that it would not brook interference from the US or any other outside power over this issue, but is prepared to discuss it bilaterally with Pakistan within the framework of the Shimla Agreement. The US agreed that the negotiations between the two countries, as envisaged in the Shimla Agreement, provided the best means of resolving the Kashmir dispute. However, it did not rule out extending a helping hand in the matter, as it did during the 1999 Kargil crisis.

The most significant outcome of President Clinton's visit was the decision of the two countries to institutionalize a whole series of high-level multifaceted consultations and cooperation between them, covering a wide range of issues, including security, international economic issues, trade, finance, science and technology, energy and environment. During the Republican administration under President Bush, these institutions were further strengthened and diversified, so much so that today they constitute the most promising and extensive infrastructure ever built for conducting Indo-US relations.

A major step during the Bush administration was the conclusion of the Indo-US nuclear deal, which came closest to the US getting reconciled to the strategic component of India's nuclear programme while still trying, as during the Clinton regime, to minimize the size of India's nuclear deterrent, and facilitated India's passage to energy security by flinging open the nuclear energy route to this goal.[11]

There is a bipartisan support in the US Congress for escalating the level of relationship with India. This was reflected in the strong bipartisan support for the Indo-US nuclear deal. The doubts expressed in several quarters in India that the new Democratic administration under President Barack Obama would push India lower down in its foreign policy priorities and revert to the typical Democratic stance on issues of concern to India were soon laid to rest by subsequent events. In this process, President Obama's visit to India from 6–9 November 2010 was of great significance. Nothing could have been more reassuring about the future of Indo-US relations than his resounding declaration in his address to the Indian Parliament on 8 November: 'It is my firm belief that the relationship between the United States and India . . . will be one of the defining partnerships of the twenty-first century'.[12] In their Joint Statement, the two leaders 'welcomed the completion of steps by the two governments for implementation of the India-US Civil Nuclear Agreement'.[13] This dispelled all doubts regarding the new US administration's commitment to the implementation of the nuclear deal. In this context, the US also indicated that it intended to support India's full membership of the four multilateral regimes for the control of dual-purpose technologies and materials, that is, the Nuclear Suppliers Group, the Missile Technology Control Regime, the Australia Group and the Wassenaar Arrangement. This would bind India more comprehensively with the global non-proliferation system and at the same time make it easier for it to have access to dual-purpose material and technologies. On the nuclear disarmament issue, in his address to the Indian Parliament, President Obama said, 'And together we can pursue a vision that Indian leaders have espoused since independence—a world without nuclear weapons'.[14] Though there is no evidence until now of the two countries pursuing this vision, President Obama's statement did mark a convergence in the views of the two countries on a highly significant strategic objective after long years of divergence and contentions. During the visit, further additions were made to the areas of functional cooperation and new issues were agreed to be taken up for regular consultations. The former included civil space, joint research and development in clean energy resources and working together in agriculture to spark a second 'Evergreen Revolution'.

Since President Obama's visit to India in November 2010, the frequency of high-level visits between the two countries has further increased. The foreign minister of India and the secretary of State of the US have been meeting every year to have Indo-US Strategic Dialogue under the rubric of Bilateral Strategic and Global Partnership. Secretary of State John F. Kerry visited India in June 2013 for the fourth Indo-US Strategic Dialogue. The fifth Dialogue was held in Washington in July 2014 and the sixth one is scheduled in 2015. Prime Minister Narendra Modi went to Washington on an official visit in September 2014 and as an unprecedented gesture, President Obama accepted to be the Chief Guest on the Republic Day of India in January 2015. He is the only US President who has made official visits to India twice during his presidency. The two countries have created mechanisms of cooperation on an expanding number of critical and strategic issues. These include ministerial-level Trade Policy Forum, High-Technology Cooperation Group, Joint Science and Technology Committee, Joint Clean Energy Research and Development Centre, and Joint Working Group on Climate Change and Dialogue on Peacekeeping, which has now been converted into a broader Dialogue on UN issues. During Prime Minister Modi's visit to the US, two new institutions—that is, an Indo-US

Investment Initiative and an Infrastructure Collaboration Platform —were set up. Subjects covered under bilateral cooperation now include health, education, science and technology, space, peaceful uses of nuclear energy, and consultations on global and regional issues, including Afghanistan which is of great importance for India. In a press conference in New Delhi on 24 January 2013, Secretary of State John Kerry had mentioned that in 2012 as many as 112 senior officials and high-level visits had taken place between the two countries.

Unrealistic Expectations

One of the pronouncements made by President Obama in his address to the Indian Parliament, which generated a great deal of interest verging on elation in India, was the US's support for India's Permanent Membership of the UN Security Council. In his address, Obama said, 'I can say today, in the years ahead I look forward to a reformed UN Security Council that includes India as a Permanent Member'.[15] This formulation was repeated in the Joint Statements issued at the end of Prime Minister Modi's visit to the US and President Obama's recent visit to India. This implies neither a support for nor a rejection of the Indian candidature. All it says is that the US would be happy to work with India if it becomes a permanent member of the Security Council during the coming years. There are a number of problems yet to be resolved before the UN comes to taking a decision on the expansion of the membership of the Security Council. The size of the expanded Security Council is yet to be agreed upon. The US is in favour of a modest expansion, which is unlikely to accommodate even the minimum aspirations of the developing regions of the world. There is also no agreement on the procedure for electing the additional permanent members. It is still disputed as to whether the aspirants should be nominated by regional groups or elected directly by the General Assembly through a process of uninterrupted voting until the final slate is approved. The issue as to whether the new permanent members should have the power to veto still remains unresolved. The US has not thought it necessary at this stage to spell out its position on these issues. Even if it changes its position on all these issues to bring them in conformity with that of India's, the stand taken by countries like China, Pakistan and Italy will continue to come in the way of a consensus. It is, therefore, neither desirable nor necessary for India to test US's friendship and goodwill for India on the touchstone of its support for or opposition to India's candidature for the permanent membership of the Security Council.

One of the major flaws in our foreign policy has been the excessive reliance we have placed on the US for solving some of the problems we face in our neighbourhood, particularly with Pakistan on the issue of terrorism and Kashmir. We have unsuccessfully tried to seek the support of the US to get Pakistan declared as a State sponsoring terrorism. We have also entertained the hope that the US would one day turn against Pakistan and take pre-emptive action, including sanctions, to pressurize the Pakistani authorities to close down terrorist camps within its territory from where operations against India are carried out, and to hand over to India the terrorists whose names it has made available to Pakistan from time to time.

The US is aware that acts of terrorism mounted against India, both from across the border as well those perpetrated inside the Indian territory, have the support of the Pakistan government, mainly of the ISI. The US, in particular, has sufficient evidence of the ISI's complicity in the terrorist attacks in Mumbai on 26 November 2008. It can also be expected to be aware that Pakistani authorities have strong links with international terrorist elements like al-Qaeda and the Taliban, and that while pretending to or actually taking sporadic action against them to impress the US, Pakistan is complicit in their activities and continues to provide to some of the terrorist groups safe havens in its territory or in the adjoining areas across the border in Afghanistan. The US has reasons to be worried about the recent pronounced lurch of the Pakistani polity and society towards religious extremism. There are reasons to believe that the US was a major factor behind the announcement on 12 January 2002 by the then President General Pervez Musharraf, of a whole set of measures to deal with religious extremism in Pakistan. This had given rise to the hope, including in some quarters in India, that Pakistan would be able to bring under control the extremist religious elements which, by their activities, were posing a threat to the state and to the rule of law in that country. This could not but have had a positive impact on the efforts to normalize relations between India and Pakistan. However, the measures announced by President Musharraf remained on paper, partly because it was already too late to implement them and also because they were never seriously intended to be implemented. The main purpose of the announcement seemed to be to impress the US in order to continue getting its economic and military support.

Today, the situation in Pakistan appears to be almost beyond redemption. The whole country is now practically Talibanized and the government in power does not seem to have either the will or the capacity to bring under control the extremist forces that have infiltrated into every branch of the government. This includes the country's Armed Forces. The government has been regularly making concessions on major issues of domestic policy to the extremist forces. Every major political party is held hostage to the extremist elements embedded in it.

It is unrealistic to expect that the US, in spite of its might as a global power and in spite of Pakistan's heavy dependence on it for economic and military aid, would be able to bring about a change in the situation. In fact, recent events have demonstrated that the US is incapable of pressurizing the Pakistan government to take action even where its own interests are directly at stake. This is because of the decline of the US as a world power, the rise of China on which Pakistan is becoming increasingly dependent and the ubiquitous unpopularity of the US in the Muslim world, including Pakistan. On the other hand, the US cannot abandon Pakistan as a failed state or question the legitimacy of the Pakistani regime. This is because of its dependence on Pakistan for a variety of purposes. US wanted and succeeded in getting Pakistan on its side for carrying out its operation against the Taliban in Afghanistan and al-Qaeda in the Pak-Afghan region. When it decided to withdraw from Afghanistan, it needed Pakistan's assistance for preventing attacks on its withdrawing troops by the Afghan Taliban and other terrorist groups operating in the region mostly with the Pakistani Army's connivance. Moreover, Pakistan's size, its military clout and its geostrategic location places it in an important position to serve US interests in the region.

In South Asia, including Afghanistan, the US is engaged in operations against only those global terrorist groups that pose a threat to its security. In this, it is obliged to seek Pakistan's assistance. The US is, of course, sympathetic to India's plight as one of the worst victims of terrorism in the world. It expresses from time to time its solidarity with India in its fight against terrorism. Recently, it has extended a good deal of cooperation to India in the form of technology transfer, capacity building and information exchange for combating terrorism. For mutual cooperation for combating terrorism, the two countries have set up a Counter-Terrorism Joint Working Group and a ministerial-level Homeland Security Dialogue. In the Joint Statement issued during President Obama's recent visit to India, although Pakistan was never mentioned, the two leaders 'reaffirmed the need for joint and concerted efforts to disrupt entities such as Lashkar-e-

Toiba, Jaish-e-Mohammad, D Company and the Haqqani network', based in or actively supported by Pakistan.[16] However, assisting India to counter terrorism directed against it cannot be a foreign policy priority of the US. In any event, it is unrealistic to expect the US to turn against Pakistan in its effort to assist India in dealing with terrorism. It will be a very inept diplomacy to put pressure on the US to choose between India and Pakistan on the issue of terrorism, if for no other reason than for the fact that the US would never like to exercise such a choice.

Therefore, the ultimate responsibility for dealing with terrorist threats to India emanating from Pakistan and terrorist acts perpetrated by the Pakistani state and non-state agents inside the Indian territory rests squarely with India. This calls for not only streamlining the intelligence system and more effective border management but also efficiently dealing with broader issues of governance, like the maintenance of law and order and adoption of measures for preventing the alienation of the minorities and marginalized groups from the national mainstream. These are all options lying within India's competence and in the exercise of which the US or any other foreign country has no role to play.

One of the objectives of US policy towards India until almost the end of the 20th century was to prevent it from emerging as a major military power. The argument given by the US at that time—that the pursuit of military power would lead to the diversion of resources from development purposes—carried some plausibility. However, the main reason behind the US effort to contain India's military ambitions was that during the Cold War the US did not regard India as a reliable partner and, therefore, was apprehensive about any accretion in its military power.

Another reason was its perception of the threat that a militarily resurgent India could pose to the existing global power structure, which was dominated by the US and in the maintenance of which it had a vested interest.

Growing Convergence of Interests

There has recently been a change in the US perception of India's military power and in its attitude towards having closer military ties with India. The US is now reconciled to, and may even be comfortable with, India's enhanced military strength. This was reflected in the Indo-US nuclear deal which left India free to pursue its strategic objectives in a separate component of the deal. The US has not thought it necessary to register its usual protest against the development of new weapon systems by India, like the testing of its long-range ballistic missile—Agni-5—which has the potentiality of being developed into an Intercontinental Ballistic Missile (ICBM), and the induction into the Indian Navy of the nuclear submarine, Arihant. The fait accompli of India's emergence as a major economic and military power at the turn of the last century has been a major factor in bringing about this change. This is also because in the vastly improved climate of political relationship between the two countries, the US does not perceive a threat to its security emanating from India's enhanced military power. Moreover, in the context of China's rise, the US also sees it as a balance against China. But neither the US nor India would project it as such, because of the compelling reasons and supreme necessity for both of them to work constructively with China.

It was stated in a Carnegie Endowment Study Group Report[17] that, given the growing convergence of US and Indian geo-political interests, the growth of Indian military power could well prove advantageous to US interests in the context of an overall improvement in Indo-American relations. This prediction now seems to be coming true. India and the US now perceive a common interest in peace and stability in the regions adjacent to India, particularly Asia-Pacific, and in preserving the freedom of sea lanes to the Indian Ocean and to West Asia. If India acquires the necessary capability and takes the lead, the US may not be averse to relying on Indian military power in the region for serving common interest. This in fact would be welcome to the US because of its overstretched military capability and declining economic clout. The US is now also interested in conducting coordinated operations with the Indian Navy in situations of natural disasters like tsunamis and combating the menace of piracy. Moreover, it sees India as a major market for its military supplies, in which it still occupies the first position in the world. On the other hand, it is in India's interest to diversify the sources of its military supplies for which the US is apparently the first choice. Indo-US military cooperation has no doubt expanded after the end of the Cold War. It now includes institutionalized consultations on defence and strategic issues, joint military exercises, participation in training programmes and exchange of military personnel. In the Joint Statement issued during President Obama's visit to India, it was noted that the military cooperation in recent years between the two countries had strengthened mutual understanding on regional peace and stability and enhanced their capacities to meet humanitarian and other challenges. The two countries also agreed to promote trade and collaboration in defence equipment and technology. India has also shown preparedness to buy military hardware from the US in spite of the past experience of the latter not having been a reliable supplier of materials and spares. Recently, the US bagged some major contracts for supplying transport aircraft and military hardware to India. President Obama is on record having said in 2010 that the total amount of the contracts came to about $8 billion. Since then, this amount has gone up sizeably, as India has acquired more military hardware from the US. During the last decade, defence procurement contracts worth $10 billion have been signed and those worth at least $2.5 billion are in the offing.

However, there are several reasons why there is not much scope for going very far in this direction at least in the short and medium run. First, we cannot afford to antagonize Russia mainly because of the very fact of our overwhelming dependence on them for military supplies. Second, Russia has historically proved a very reliable partner and has been prepared to transfer technology and co-produce weapon systems, whereas the US is yet to be tested in these respects. Third, Russia has a competitive edge over the US with regard to most of the hardware we need for our armed forces. Fourth, we have far too many differences with the US on strategic issues, which will effectively come in the way of our getting very close militarily. And finally, our goal in the long run should be not just to diversify the sources of supplies, but be self-reliant, and the country which is of greater help in this regard, would be preferred.

During President Obama's visit this year, the two countries announced the renewal of their Defence Framework Agreement already in operation, for a period of 10 years. They also agreed that under the Defence Technology and Trade Initiative (DTTI), launched in 2012, four projects would be taken up for joint venture and production. These were: (*a*) next generation of Raven Mini-UAVs; (*b*) Roll-on and Roll-off intelligence for C-130; (*c*) mobile electric hybrid power source; and (*d*) Integrated Protection Ensemble Increment-II. These are not big ticket items though they can play an important role in the defence field. Greater hope is reposed on the agreement that a Working Group under the Initiative will explore the possibility of co-development and co-production of aircraft carrier technology and design and development of jet engine technology in India. One has to see what progress is made in these areas.

Perhaps, the most important strategic convergence of interests and positions of the two countries has been on what is currently happening in the Asia-Pacific region. This was reflected in the Joint Statements issued during Prime Minister Modi's visit to Washington in September 2014 and during President Obama's visit to India in January 2015. But this was spelt out very elaborately and explicitly in a separate document entitled 'U.S.-India Joint Strategic Vision for the Asia-Pacific and the Indian Ocean Region', issued on 25 January 2015 during President Obama's visit to India.[18]

The key sentence in this Vision Document is: 'Regional Prosperity Depends on Security'. The leaders then go on to 'affirm the importance of safeguarding maritime security and ensuring freedom of navigation and over flight throughout the region, especially in South China Sea'. As in the two Joint Statements, the Vision Document 'call[s] upon all parties to avoid the threat or use of force and pursue resolution of territorial and maritime disputes through all peaceful means, in accordance with universally recognized principles of international law, including the United Nations Convention on the Law of the Sea'.[19]

Another important feature of the Document is the resolve expressed by India and the US to undertake wide measures of cooperation in the regional context. The two countries declare: 'Over the next five years, we will strengthen our regional dialogue, invest in making trilateral consultations with third countries in the region more robust, deepen regional integration, strengthen regional forums, explore multilateral opportunities for engagement'.[20] An important implication of this statement is that it implicitly commits the US to move in tandem with India on the issue of regional integration, where there is deep difference of approach so far adopted by the two countries.

The Vision Document also underlines the importance of trilateral cooperation between India, US and Japan through 'identification of projects of common interest and their early implementation' and by deciding to explore the possibility of upgrading the dialogue among the three countries to the level of their foreign ministers.[21]

These provisions in the Vision Document may appear to be directed against China. No doubt it addresses the problems that have arisen in the Asia-Pacific region because of recent Chinese actions and activities there, particularly in and around the South China Sea. But it is clearly in India's national interest, and in keeping with the values underlying its foreign policy, to take a stand in defence of international law and in solidarity with the interests of the countries of the region whose sovereign rights are in danger of being infringed upon and with whom India has long-standing bilateral relations of considerable importance. It is also in India's interest to take a stand along with like-minded countries on keeping the air space and sea lanes in the area open for trade of all countries. Whether it will be possible for the US and India in collaboration with other countries of the region to enforce some of the key provision of this Document will very much depend upon the evolving situation in the Asia-Pacific region. But the very fact that the US and India have issued a joint Vision Document on this subject reflecting substantial agreement on main issues is of considerable strategic importance.

Recently there have been several other important forward movements in the relations between the two countries. These have no doubt added momentum to the relations, though they are yet to yield concrete results from the Indian perspective. By far the most important among them was the understanding reached on issues related to civil nuclear liability. This understanding, it is expected, will facilitate cooperation in the field of nuclear energy which Prime Minister Modi described as the 'cornerstone of a transformed relationship'.[22] As a result of negotiations between the two countries, India clarified during President Obama's visit in January 2015 that civil action for damage will not be permissible against suppliers. It was also agreed that India would create an insurance pool of Rs 1,500 crore (Rs 15 billion) in order to take care of suppliers' liability. In spite of the clarifications provided in the form of Q&A by the Government of India on some aspects of the understanding reached, there is still ambiguity regarding them. It is also not known as to how the US companies concerned, that is, General Electric and Westinghouse and their Japanese partners, would react to this understanding. Moreover, they will have to compete with the suppliers of nuclear reactors from Russia and France. After all, India cannot in the next 20 years or so go in for building more than 10 reactors because of the huge investment and the creation on a massive scale of technological capability they entail. As against these, Russia alone has offered to supply 20 reactors. In the meanwhile, the resurgence in nuclear energy witnessed in the early years of the current century has given place to scepticism and apprehension arising out of the Fukushima disaster. The US itself seems to have given up its earlier plan to build a few nuclear reactors. There is no movement in this direction in any of the European countries which had similar plans. In this context, it is doubtful whether India itself would pursue the very ambitious goal it had set in the wake of the Indo-US nuclear deal, for reliance on nuclear energy for meeting a part of its total energy requirement.

An agreement was announced by the two countries on 13 November 2014 on the food security and trade facilitation issues that had remained pending from the Bali Ministerial meeting of the WTO. According to this agreement, WTO members will not take food security programmes of a member country to the WTO Disputes Settlement Mechanism until a permanent solution regarding this issue is agreed and adopted. This is an improvement upon the Bali formulation of putting in place an interim mechanism of not raising disputes on public stockholding for public food security purposes. The agreement reached between the two countries also sets out elements of an intensified programme of work and negotiations to arrive at a permanent solution. The second important component of the agreement is that the Trade Facilitation Agreement reached in Bali would be implemented without conditions. The understanding between India and the US for the time being sets at rest a major controversy between the two countries, though it has an asymmetrical implication. Whereas the Trade Facilitation Agreement will irrevocably come into force, there is no indication that the demand of India and like-minded countries for legally permitting subsidies for food stockholding under the Agreement on Agriculture of the WTO, is going to be met any sooner.

During the last two years, the US and India have been able to manage their differences on the issue of climate change quite smoothly. In spite of the agreement reached in Beijing in November 2014, in which China, for the first time, agreed to a peak year after which it would start reducing emissions, the US has not put pressure on India to accept a similar commitment. India is clearly not in a position to do so consistent with its objective to retain sufficient space for further growth of its economy and the consideration of equity and the principle of differential responsibility. In the Joint Statements issued at the Summit level, in 2014 and 2015, the emphasis is on enhancing mutual cooperation on adaptation measures and on joint research and development and technology innovation, particularly in the area of clean energy, which will help India to achieve the goal of transiting to a climate-resilient and low-carbon economy. The real test will, however, come in the Paris Conference this year when a long-term and ambitious climate change agreement is expected to be given a final shape. China's breaking the line with other developing countries and accepting a peak year from which to start reduction in emission is likely to put India in considerable difficulty in the negotiations between now and the Paris Conference.

Continuing Divergence

In conducting relations with the US, it is important to bear in mind that there has traditionally been and still are serious divergences in the views of the two countries on world order issues. Following are some of the examples in this category:

- So far as the world economic order is concerned, the US has been a status quoist power, whereas India has been a part of the movement spearheaded under the aegis of G-77 and NAM, to change the status quo. Of late, on account of its embrace of the policy of globalization and liberalization, India has come to develop a stake in the existing world order and has, therefore, become a status quoist power itself. It would, nevertheless, still like to bring about changes in the world economic order which may not be to the liking of the US.
- Whereas India believes in a world order based on international law, the US has declared its intention to bend and has, in fact, even violated these laws in pursuit of its national interest.
- Whereas India has traditionally been wedded to supporting and strengthening multilateralism underpinned by the UN, the US has an à la carte approach to multilateralism under the UN, i.e., to use it only when it suits its purpose.
- Whereas India, according to the UN Charter, has regarded the Security Council as the ultimate arbiter on all matters relating to the use of force against a member country, the US has in recent years tended to resort to such use of force either unilaterally or in concert with the so-called coalition of the willing or under regional arrangement of its choice, like the NATO.
- In order to be consistent with its commitment to multilateralism under the UN, India should be expected to work for restoring to the UN its legitimate role in the economic field and bringing back to the UN agenda hardcore economic issues which have, at the behest of the US and its allies, by now been transferred to organizations controlled by them, i.e., the IMF, World Bank and WTO.
- On disarmament, whereas India has for decades worked for and continues to remain in favour of the complete elimination of nuclear weapons, the US—till President Obama's speech in Prague on 1 April 2009, pledging the US to work for the elimination of nuclear weapons—has persistently sought to justify the legitimacy of nuclear arms in the hands of a few countries. It has reiterated its determination to retain its nuclear arsenal as deterrence against rival powers and the so-called delinquent Third-World countries. Besides, the US has been engaged for the last several decades in developing a defensive weapon system in total disregard of the

concerns of other major powers, particularly Russia. In his attempt during the early years of his presidency to reset relations with Russia, President Obama decided to go slow on this, but did not agree to give it up. The latest position is that the US BMD system is back in place in Poland and the Czech Republic and now covers Japan as well. The BMD programme of the US has the potential to trigger an unprecedented nuclear arms race with horrendous implications for the security and stability of the world. India cannot afford to continue to remain neutral on this critical issue.

- There is also divergence in the interests of the two countries on several issues figuring on the agenda of the Doha Round of Trade Negotiations and that of the negotiations on climate change being held under the UN Framework Convention on Climate Change. Most of the recent US initiatives in the Doha Round have been insensitive to India's interest and seem to be specifically targeted against it and countries placed in a similar position.
- The United States has taken the initiative of launching a number of plurilateral trade negotiations outside WTO in which India is not participating mainly because it is not in a position to undertake the far-reaching commitments envisaged in these negotiations and in the areas coming under their scope. These include negotiations for concluding a Trade in Services Agreement (TISA), Trade in Environment Goods and a second round of negotiations for liberalizing the Information Technology Agreement (ITA-II). India is unable to accept the drastic commitments in these sectors sought by the United States and like-minded countries because these sectors are at an incipient stage of development in India and undertaking such commitments would impede the current and undermine the future growth of industries in these sectors. Moreover, these are plurilateral negotiations being conducted outside WTO. It is not clear how the outcome of these negotiations would be integrated into the WTO system without undermining it. Given India's stake in the multilateral trading system, it is concerned about these developments. Besides, once these negotiations are concluded, the US would pressurize India to join the regimes to be established as their outcomes. This would be clearly detrimental to India's interest.
- The US and India also have divergent approaches towards coping with the challenges of new regionalism, particularly in the Asia-Pacific region. The US has taken the initiative of launching the TPP

comprising most of the APEC member countries. India and China have not been invited to participate in the negotiations for TPP. However, China has recently indicated its desire to join if invited to do so. This leaves India, among important Asia-Pacific countries, outside these negotiations. In any case, India is not in a position to participate because its economy is not in a strong enough position for it to accept, at least during the next 15 to 20 years, the farreaching commitments envisaged under the TPP in the areas of agriculture, industry, services, investment and intellectual property rights. India is, therefore, concentrating on RCEP, in the on-going negotiations for which ASEAN+6 countries[23] are participating and where there is greater possibility of India's unique development needs to be taken into account. India is at the same time apprehensive that if the TPP negotiations succeed it will be brought under pressure by the US to bring its trade, investment and Intellectual Property Rights (IPR) policies in line with the agreement reached under TPP.

On bilateral issues, a major divergence between the positions of the two countries is on India's patent laws. India has developed a very coherent policy on IPR after years of debate in the public and parliament. Indian patent laws are generally regarded as being by far the most progressive in operation in the developing world. Two of its distinguishing features are the provision for granting compulsory licenses for local pro-duction in case the patent holder does not produce or otherwise supply life-saving drugs in sufficient quantities and at affordable prices; and the provision for additional efficiency requirement for patentability. The first mentioned provision has enabled India to produce and make life-saving drugs available to underprivileged people not only in India but also in many other developing countries. These provisions are also fully in keeping with India's obligations under the WTO Agreement on TRIPS.

However, these provisions are being strongly contested by drug multinationals, some of which have gone to the highest courts in India to challenges actions taken under them. The courts have upheld the decisions taken by the Indian authorities and pronounced that the provisions of the Indian Patent Act under which these actions have been taken are fully in compliance with the TRIPS Agreement.

In spite of this, the US has been putting tremendous pressure on India to revise its patent law in order to remove or dilute these key provisions. As a result, Prime Minister Modi, during his visit to US in September 2014, agreed 'to establish an annual high-level Intellectual Property Group with appropriate decision making . . . as part of the Trade Policy Forum'.[24] The Joint Statement issued during President Obama's visit to India in January 2015 stated that 'the leaders looked forward to enhancing engagement on Intellectual Property Rights (IPR) in 2015 under the High Level Working Group'. They also committed 'to stakeholders' consultations on policy matters concerning intellectual property protection'.[25] It will be extremely difficult for any government in power in India to agree to delete or modify the provision in the Indian Patent Act on compulsory licensing and stricter criteria for patentability. But the Intellectual Property Working Group will be a forum for continuous pressure on India to revise its patent law.

During the last decade and a half, the US has been putting relentless pressure on India to adopt measures of economic reforms. There are compelling reasons why India cannot go as far in this direction as the US would like it to. Economic reforms will, therefore, remain an issue of divergence between the two countries for quite some time to come.

Conducting Relations with the United States

True to the ethical foundations of its foreign policy and in the light of its national interest, India cannot afford to resile from its positions on the above mentioned world order and other issues. The best way not to allow these divergences to come in the way of the two countries pursuing a vigorous and dynamic bilateral relationship is to accept that they exist and maintain a continuous dialogue to narrow down the differences. India should explain to the US that by adopting the positions it has on global issues, it has no intention to hurt the latter's interest but only to safeguard its own perceived interests and that as democracies, the two countries should show tolerance and understanding of each other's views on issues where for the time being, there is no convergence. And for all one knows, in the medium and long run, the US itself may come to accept India's position as the best means of subserving its own interest and that of the international community as a whole. An example in this regard was President Obama's decision soon after he ascended to presidency to embrace and promote the goal of elimination of nuclear weapons, which India has pursued since its independence.

It is difficult for any nation to conduct bilateral relations with a stronger nation. It is all the more so with the US. This is not only because of the asymmetry of power, but also because of the manner in which the US conducts its foreign policy. It has neatly divided the world into two categories—those who are with it and those who are against it. There is no scope for an independent or middle position in this scheme of things. Besides, those who are with the US have to be so in all respects. This creates a huge problem in dealing with this country.

Another problem in dealing with the US is that it has created a category of the so-called rogue states whom it wants to isolate by adopting all possible measures, including sanctions. It expects countries friendly to it to join in its efforts to isolate these states. Iran is a conspicuous example of such a state. Washington should be persuaded to recognize that India cannot share all its prejudices and predilections, all its friends and foes. India cannot be expected to join the US in promoting, even at the cost of its own interest, all US ambitions in the international arena, including those which in India's view are not best calculated to promote regional and global peace and stability. For example, India cannot endorse the policies that the US has adopted towards Syria and Iran, and its current policy towards Russia.

President Obama, while broadly following the US's traditional rigid approaches to conducting foreign policy, has displayed remarkable flexibility in applying them in the interest of global peace and stability and in US's own long-term interest. He has engaged with Iran in negotiating a deal that could be a game changer in the politics of the Gulf, West Asia and the whole world. He resisted domestic pressure to take military action against President Bashar al-Assad of Syria, which could have had disastrous consequences, and as a quid pro quo for this made Syria destroy its entire stockpiles of chemical weapons. He recently took the very courageous initiative to normalize relations with Cuba which has been subjected by the US to more than half a century of political isolation and economic and military blockade. However, he is at the same time responsible, along with other NATO countries, for reviving in full blast the Cold War with Russia, which represents a great setback to the process of global disarmament and the prospects for international peace and cooperation.

India's interests best lie in maintaining independence of judgement and action in the conduct of its foreign policy, which has been the hallmark of the policy of non-alignment. It would be self-defeating and not befitting a country of India's geographical position, its historical association with different countries and regions of the world, and its stature as a major emerging power, to climb on the bandwagon or toe the line of another country, however powerful it may be. India should continue to test every issue on the touchstone of its national interest and of the values and principles in which its foreign policy is anchored and determine its position accordingly. Its ability to do so will very much depend upon the US's perception of its inner strength, resilience and will power.

It is not going to be an easy task to pursue such a policy in the changed circumstances in India and globally. The US lobby in India is stronger today than ever before. It consists of leading lights of business and industry, prominent media houses and personalities and a large section of the elite which is close to the highest centre of power in the country. This lobby has for some time mounted a veritable campaign to bring about a change in India's independent foreign policy. It is persistently and relentlessly promoting the view that India's non-aligned foreign policy is outdated and must be jettisoned, that India should give up all idealistic pursuits in world politics, that it should drastically lower its profile in the international arena in order not to be on the wrong side of the major powers led by the US and that it should align its foreign policy in all its major aspects with that of the US. It contends that if India brings about these adjustments in its foreign policy, then the US will help it to become a major power, as promised by former US Secretary of State Condoleezza Rice in March 2005.

Under the influence of this lobby, there has been a continuous erosion of the basic tenets of India's foreign policy in spite of the government's frequent protestations to the contrary. India is no longer working seriously for nuclear disarmament. During the term of the first NDA government, the Government of India officially extended its support to the plan launched by the Bush administration to develop and deploy a global BMD system. This policy was implicitly endorsed by the UPA government in the 'New Framework for the US-India Defence Relationship', signed on 28 June 2005, in which India agreed to 'expand collaboration relating to missile defence'. In the Defence Framework, India also agreed to collaborate with the US in 'multinational operations' and 'assist in building worldwide capacity to conduct peacekeeping operations';[26] but without clarifying that these must be done under the aegis of the UN and that it ultimately boils down to building the capacity of the UN in the peacekeeping arena. This lobby has become stronger after the Bharatiya Janata Party- (BJP-) led government has come to power at the Centre.

As already pointed out, the positive changes noticed in the US attitude towards India during the last 12 years have been brought about mainly by the strength acquired by the Indian economy and India's enhanced military clout by virtue of having become a de facto nuclear weapon power.[27] Therefore, developments in the Indian economy in the coming years and the speed with which India is able to put in place a credible nuclear deterrent will be crucial factors determining Indo-US relations in future.

The maintenance of the dynamism in the Indian economy will, to a considerable extent, depend on India's ability to continue to take advantage of the opportunities offered by the ongoing process of globalization. Here, linkages with the US economy and expanded access to its market will be of crucial importance. At the same time, in the latest phase of globalization, linkages with the Chinese and other emerging economies, particularly those of Asia, will be extremely important. The US would, no doubt, seek reciprocity from India for granting enhanced access to its market, technology and capital. It would, among others, continue to put pressure on India to further liberalize its economy. It would, in this connection, put particular emphasis on the so-called third-generation reforms, which include liberalization of foreign investment in the retail and insurance sectors, full capital account convertibility and labour market reforms and measures for facilitating acquisition of land by private companies. India, in any case, is moving forward in some of these areas as a part of its policy of the further liberalization of the economy.

Several such measures were adopted during the 10-year rule of the UPA government. The BJP-led government, which came to power about a year ago, has gone further in this direction. The reform measures adopted by it include raising the foreign investment ceilings in several sectors of the Indian economy, particularly defence, insurance, railways and e-commerce, and diluting to the point of virtual scuttling, of the Land Acquisition and Rehabilitation Act. The US government has, while appreciating these reform measures, been pressing for more. It has succeeded in persuading the Government of India to accept the creation of institutions for bilateral dialogue on further reforms on a continuing basis. These include enhanced engagement on IPR under a High-Level Working Group and continuing discussion in the Trade Policy Group. The US is also putting pressure on the Government of India to bring to finality the negotiations underway on a Bilateral Investment Treaty. However, given the obligation of the government under the Constitution to protect and promote the interest of the vast number of the underprivileged in the country and the implications of some of the reform measures for restricting the space for independent macroeconomic policymaking by the government, there is a limit beyond which such measures cannot be pushed. While moving further in the direction of globalization and liberation, India would obviously like to maintain social harmony and political stability. It will call for selective departure from the path of globalization and liberalization and adopting reform measures in a well-considered and calibrated manner.

Moreover, globalization is not an unmixed blessing, as has been claimed by its proponents. Its discontents and adverse consequences have now increasingly started coming to the fore. Among others, globalization imposes limits on foreign policy options. It does so by increasing vulnerability to global market forces and enhancing dependence on foreign markets, capital and technology for a country's development. This is frequently used as a leverage to influence foreign policy. Therefore, while taking the maximum advantage of the opportunity offered by globalization, it is necessary to take precautionary measures to avoid its pitfalls and deal with its discontents.

In the case of India, the domestic factors are bound to play a greater role in maintaining the dynamism of the Indian economy than external factors. The current high rate of growth of the Indian economy cannot be sustained without its being inclusive. This means dealing proactively and in a systemic manner with the problem of the marginalization of the vast number of the population of the country; dramatically improving the poor conditions of health and education; undertaking measures for reducing inequalities in the distribution of income and assets, particularly through land reforms; and pursuing an employment-oriented development strategy. Misgovernance has also emerged as yet another basic constraint to the sustenance of the high growth rate of the economy. It will, therefore, be necessary to bring about drastic improvements in the system and practice of governance in the country.

Notes

1. Calculated from data taken from International Monetary Fund, Direction of Trade Statistics database, http://elibrary-data.imf.org/ (accessed on 14 March 2015).
2. Ibid.
3. Data taken from Department of Industrial Policy and Promotion (Ministry of Commerce and Industry, Government of India), http://dipp.nic.in/fdi_statistics/india_fdi_index.htm (accessed on 4 May 2011).
4. Data taken from Department of Industrial Policy and Promotion, 'FDI Synopsis on Country U.S.A' (Ministry of Commerce and Industry, Government of India, 30 September 2014), http://dipp.nic.in/English/Investor/USA_Desk/fdi_Synopsis_USA.pdf (accessed on 18 March 2015).

5. United States Agency for International Development, 'US Economic Assistance to India (1951–1996): An Overview and Highlights of the USAID's Current Programs and Past Assistance' (August 1997).
6. Ibid.
7. Document 3/23500 (note by the President of the Security Council at the Conclusion of the Summit-Level Meeting of the Council, 31 January 1992). Also see statement made by P. V. Narasimha Rao, the then Prime Minister of India, in the Security Council.
8. *The New York Times*, 'Stop the Subcontinent's Bomb', 28 April 1992.
9. Government of India, 'President Clinton's Address to Indian Joint Session of Parliament', http://pib.nic.in/archieve/indous/indouspr8.html (accessed on 23 April 2015).
10. William J. Clinton, *Public Papers of the Presidents of the United States: William J. Clinton, 2000–2001* (Washington DC: Office of the Federal Register, National Archives and Records Administration, 2001), p. 510.
11. No attempt is made here to get into the details of the nuclear deal, which is dealt with in Chapter 6 (this volume), 'The Indo-US Civilian Nuclear Deal'.
12. White House Press Office, 'Remarks by the President to the Joint Session of the Indian Parliament in New Delhi, India' (Office of the Press Secretary, US Government, 8 November 2010), https://www.whitehouse.gov/the-press-office/2010/11/08/remarks-president-joint-session-indian-parliament-new-delhi-india (accessed on 23 April 2015).
13. Ministry of External Affairs, 'Joint Statement of Prime Minister Dr. Manmohan Singh and President Barack Obama' (Government of India, New Delhi, 8 November 2010.
14. White House Press Office, 'Remarks by the President to the Joint Session of the Indian Parliament'.
15. Ibid.
16. Ministry of External Affairs, 'Joint Statement During the Visit of President of USA to India—"Shared Effort; Progress for All"' (Government of India, New Delhi, 25 January 2015), http://mea.gov.in/bilateral-documents.htm?dtl/24726/Joint_Statement_during_the_visit_of_President_of_USA_to_India_Shared_Effort_Progress_for_All (accessed on 23 April 2015).
17. Selig S. Harrison and Geoffey Kemp, *India and America after the Cold War: Report of the Carnegie Endowment Study Group on U.S.-Indian Relations in a Changing International Environment* (Washington DC: Carnegie Endowment for International Peace, 1993).
18. White House Press Office, 'U.S.-India Joint Strategic Vision for the Asia-Pacific and Indian Ocean Region' (Office of the Press Secretary, US Government, 25 January 2015), https://www.whitehouse.gov/the-press-office/2015/01/25/us-india-joint-strategic-vision-asia-pacific-and-indian-ocean-region (accessed on 24 April 2015).
19. Ibid.
20. Ibid.

21. Ministry of External Affairs, 'Joint Statement During the Visit of President of USA to India'.
22. Cited in *Business Standard*, 'Room for Optimism in Indo-US Ties', 30 January 2015, http://www.business-standard.com/article/news-ani/room-for-optimism-in-indo-us-ties-115013000399_1.html (accessed on 24 April 2015).
23. ASEAN+6 countries include Indonesia, Malaysia, the Philippines, Singapore, Thailand, Brunei, Cambodia, Laos, Myanmar, Vietnam, China, Japan, South Korea, Australia, New Zealand and India.
24. Joint Statement Issued during the Visit of Prime Minister Modi to the United States, Washington DC, 30 September 2014.
25. Ministry of External Affairs, 'Joint Statement During the Visit of President of USA to India'.
26. Government of the United States of America and Government of the Republic of India, 'New Framework for the US-India Defence Relationship' (28 June 2005), http://library.rumsfeld.com/doclib/sp/3211/2005-06-28%20New%20Framework%20for%20the%20US-India%20Defense%20Relationship.pdf (accessed on 24 April 2005).
27. India was already growing by 6.5 per cent per annum during the 1990s. This rate of growth accelerated to 7–9 per cent per annum during the first decade of the new millennium.

SEVEN The Indo-US Civilian Nuclear Deal

India has developed its nuclear energy sector almost entirely by its own efforts. In the process, it has mastered the complete nuclear fuel cycle ranging from the mining and enrichment of uranium, fabrication of reactors, separation of plutonium from spent fuel, to the numerous practical applications of nuclear energy for peaceful purposes. Aware of the country's acute shortage of uranium, the pioneer of India's nuclear programme, Homi J. Bhabha, had envisaged a three-stage development of India's nuclear sector, that is., pressurized heavy water uranium-based reactors, plutonium-based fast breeder reactors and thorium-based reactors. It was envisaged that by the time India reached the third stage, it would start using its abundant supply of thorium in its fast breeder reactors to become completely self-reliant in the generation of nuclear energy. India today is the leading country in the world doing research in fast breeder technology. It has been actively pursuing fast breeder research and development over the last 30 years, which perhaps no other country has done. It has been working on a 40 MW Fast Breeder Test Reactor; 80 per cent of the work on its larger capacity 500 MW Prototype Fast Breeder Reactor under construction in Kalpakkam, Tamil Nadu, had been completed by November 2011.[1] The commissioning of this reactor has been delayed, and 2015 is now cited as the expected timeline.

Indian scientists have achieved all this in spite of the usually great secrecy surrounding the international trade in nuclear equipment, substances and technologies and in spite of its being shut out from this trade altogether after it exploded its first nuclear device in Pokhran in 1974. It is in this background that one should try to grasp the significance of the understanding reached in the Indo-US Joint Statement of 18 July 2005, that the US and India would resume full civilian nuclear energy cooperation. This apparently brought a great sense of relief to Indian scientists, policymakers and the industry. This was particularly so because India was beginning to face a serious shortage of natural uranium even to fuel its pressurized heavy water reactors currently in operation or under construction. The follow-up actions taken after July 2005 were: the separation by India in March 2006 of its nuclear facilities into those meant for civilian purposes and those for military purposes; the enactment by the US Congress in December 2006 of the Henry J. Hyde United States–India Peaceful Atomic Energy Cooperation Act (briefly known as the Hyde Act) enabling the President of the United States to waive the relevant restrictive clauses of the US Atomic Energy Act of 1954 in respect of exports to India; the conclusion on 1 August 2007 of the Agreement for Cooperation between the Government of India and the Government of the United States Concerning Peaceful Uses of Nuclear Energy, also known as the 123 Agreement; the conclusion by India of an India-specific Safeguards Agreement with the International Atomic Energy Agency (IAEA) in February 2009; the waiver for India granted by the 45-member Nuclear Suppliers Group (NSG) from the restrictions that its members impose on the export of nuclear material to non-members; and the approval by the US Congress of the 123 Agreement with India.

Thus, given its inherent complexity, the passage towards unshackling India's nuclear programme was remarkably rapid. However, in one or two important respects, things did not go strictly according to the script. For example, in his statement in the Parliament on 29 July 2005, the Prime Minister announced that India 'shall undertake the same responsibilities and obligations' and 'acquire the same benefits and advantages' as other states with advanced nuclear technology, including the US.[2] But whereas other states in this category have exercised complete discretion in selecting the civilian nuclear facility to be put under IAEA safeguards, which are generally perfunctory, India had to negotiate strenuously with the US in order to finalize its separation plan. As a matter of fact, in the majority of the nuclear weapon states, there is not even the pretence of civilian–military separation of nuclear assets. Besides, whereas other similarly placed countries have been freely transferring fissile material from the civilian to the military side, India has been strictly forbidden from doing so. Moreover, India's safeguards agreement with the IAEA is more rigorous and detailed than the latter's safeguard agreements with other countries with advanced nuclear technology.

In addition, the 18 July Understanding and the 29 July statement of the Prime Minister in the Parliament promised the resumption of 'full civilian energy cooperation and trade'. This is, however, belied in both the Hyde Act and the 123 Agreement, which exclude from the scope of cooperation, the supply of equipment, material and technology for enrichment and reprocessing, and for the production of heavy water and the transfer of all dual-purpose material or technologies related to any of these processes.

Three aspects of the nuclear deal deserve particular attention. These are:

- Its contribution to India's energy security
- Its strategic aspect, or its implications for the development of India's nuclear weapons programme
- Its implications for Indo-US bilateral relations.

Energy Security

By far the most important gain from the Indo-US nuclear deal is the contribution it will make to building India's energy security. With the operationalization of the deal, over three-decade-old embargo on export of nuclear reactor, fuel and related parts and technologies was legally lifted, placing India in a position to import these items freely from the cheapest source. This will gradually lead to a sizeable expansion in India's capacity to generate nuclear energy. Several observers have called it the end of India's nuclear apartheid. It is estimated that with this deal coming into operation, the contribution of nuclear energy to India's total energy supply would increase from the present level of less than 3 per cent to 15–16 per cent in the next 25 to 30 years. Although even after this, India will be required to tap other sources—both conventional and non-conventional—to meet the bulk of its energy demands, a 15–16 per cent contribution to its energy security by nuclear energy would be quite significant. In spite of the reservations frequently aired against reliance on nuclear energy, on the ground of the uncertainty regarding the safety of nuclear installations and the hazards in the disposal of the spent fuel, nuclear energy has come to be widely accepted as an environmentally clean option, compared to other sources like coal and petroleum. A number of countries, particularly France, Japan and Korea, came to rely heavily on it for meeting the much larger proportions of their energy demand. Therefore, in any scheme of building India's energy security, the country will have to rely on the nuclear option to meet the largest possible part of its future demand for energy, which is likely to grow exponentially, in order to sustain and accelerate the current relatively high growth rate of the economy.

The 2011 Fukushima nuclear disaster in Japan has no doubt put a question mark on the emerging nuclear energy renaissance. But this was more a result of the panic characteristically associated with nuclear disasters rather than an assessment based on a careful calculation of the costs and benefits of the nuclear energy option. In a scenario of burgeoning demand for energy and a looming global shortage of conventional energy resources, it will be illogical not to pursue the nuclear option as a major plank of the multi-pronged strategy for meeting the shortage. Moreover, if the feasibility of the thorium route is demonstrated, it may very well become indispensable for satisfying global energy hunger in the long run. Both the abundant supply of thorium and the associated technology makes the thorium route a logical candidate for being the major source of future energy supply. No doubt, important lessons will be learnt from the Fukushima disaster, as has been the case with past nuclear disasters. This will inevitably trigger changes in the design of reactors and in the pattern of their location, and lead to the adoption of additional measures and new devices for nuclear safety.

It must be ensured that easier access to nuclear reactors and fuel do not result in the slackening of the country's effort or shelving of plans to harness non-conventional energy resources or in slowing down the effort for larger-scale exploitation and better utilization of the country's abundant hydro and coal energy potential. In the beginning of 2005, the contribution of thermal power to India's total energy generation was 71.6 per cent, and that of hydroelectric power, 26.7 per cent.

The dramatic increase envisaged in the contribution of nuclear energy to total energy supply would encounter several other constraints even after the lifting of the embargo on the supply of nuclear reactors, fuel and related technologies. Huge investment running into billions of dollars would have to be made. This would not come free of cost. The terms and conditions for such investment would have to be negotiated. Among other things, it would impose an additional foreign debt burden on the country. Moreover, there would be technological and managerial problems, including those related to safety, in carrying out such an ambitious nuclear energy programme. Indian scientists and technologists are no doubt capable of implementing such a programme, but this would require the creation of capacity by way of education, training and research on an unprecedented scale.

In the nuclear field itself, the government in power must ensure that the easy access to uranium and uranium-based reactors and heavy reliance on the enriched uranium route do not adversely affect India's current fast breeder research programme, which has the potentiality of unlocking the door to plentiful nuclear energy supply through the thorium route. There is a real cause of anxiety on this score because there are people placed in high positions in the country who are inclined to dismiss, purely on ideological grounds, any idea of self-reliance or autonomy in any sector of national endeavour and who are also instinctively in favour of conceding space to private players in most sectors of economic activity. Once the private sector, particularly foreign multinationals, get a foothold in this field, they will go all out to promote and entrench the uranium-based option in which they have competitive advantage, and to ensure that other options are banished.

Some of the eminent scientists who have occupied very high positions in India's nuclear energy establishment and who until recently swore by the three-stage programme for developing nuclear energy, have already started arguing that the cost of the non-uranium options would be high and that there would be the problem of waste disposal with the spent fuel. They would, therefore, like the market to decide the choice between uranium and other options. Their argument runs along the following lines: What is the point in maintaining the white elephant of public sector institutions and plants for research and development of fast breeder technology, when uranium and uranium-based technology and reactors are available from the advanced countries at competitive prices? Therefore, there is a strong possibility that as uranium-based imported megareactors go into stream, the three-stage indigenous nuclear programme would be sacrificed. Among foreign experts, George Perkovich, who is very sceptical about India's three-stage nuclear energy strategy, which he regards as 'technologically and economically dubious', believes that providing Indian decision makers with alternatives to plutonium processing can persuade India to give up the three-stage plan. He asserts that 'the economic benefits of buying fuel rather than investing in a still highly speculative breeder programme would be unmistakable'.[3] It is therefore important to exercise a strict vigilance on such a possible policy shift in order to ensure that there is no reduction in or denial of funds for pursuing research in fast breeder and thorium technology, and that the government in power is not allowed in any circumstance to jettison the vision of Homi J. Bhabha for achieving self-reliance in nuclear energy through the thorium route.

Reprocessing to separate uranium from the spent fuel is a critical aspect of the plan to become self-reliant in nuclear energy supply. This is because we need to build a sizeable stock of plutonium for running the fast breeder reactors and eventually the thorium reactors. The 123 Agreement is reasonably satisfactory from this point of view. It grants consent to India 'to reprocess or otherwise alter in form or content nuclear material transferred pursuant to this Agreement'. To bring this right into effect, it has been provided in the agreement that 'India will establish a new national reprocessing facility dedicated to reprocessing safeguarded nuclear material under IAEA safeguards'.[4] No doubt, building a new facility and transporting to this facility spent fuel from reactors located in different parts of the country would be expensive and cumbersome. But given the understandable sensitivity of the other side and the supreme importance of reprocessing for India, this price was worth paying.

Strategic Implications

The Indo-US nuclear deal, no doubt, implies an informal recognition by the US of India's position as a nuclear weapon power. The 123 Agreement as well as the Hyde Act leave India free to pursue its weapon-related nuclear programme in the separate military segment. Article 2, Paragraph 4 of the 123 Agreement states that the purpose of the Agreement is 'not to affect the unsafeguarded nuclear activities of either Party'.[5] The facilities in the unsafeguarded sector will remain outside the purview of the IAEA. The only constraint will be that India will no longer be able to transfer fissile material from the civilian to the military side. But it can, on its own efforts, and without seeking outside assistance, add on to the capacity on the military side.

Thus, the US has at long last got reconciled to India's nuclear weapon status. This is the culmination of a long drawn out effort initiated by the Vajpayee government following the Pokhran-II tests in 1998, to seek recognition, formal or informal, for India's status as a nuclear weapon power.

Though the US has now got reconciled to India's nuclear weapon programme, there is no doubt that from the US side, a principal purpose of the Indo-US nuclear deal is to contain India's nuclear weapon capability. This is sought to be achieved by the following devices:

- Preventing transfer of raw or fissile material from the civilian to the military side

- Keeping reprocessing confined to only one facility, which will be under IAEA safeguards
- India is expected under the commitments undertaken in connection with the Indo-US nuclear deal to strictly abide by the provisions of the NSG and the Missile Technology Control Regime (MTCR), not to transfer dual-purpose material, substances and technology covered under these regimes to countries that do not possess them. However, since it is not a party to any of these regimes, it will continue to face difficulties in gaining access to similar material, substances and technology. This will serve as a constraint to the expansion of India's nuclear weapon programme. During both his visits to India, in 2010 and 2015, President Obama consistently maintained the US intention to facilitate India's membership of these regimes. At the NSG annual meeting in 2011, the US had also circulated an informal 'food for thought' paper on how India could be admitted to the NSG, for consideration by members. However, in recent years, the US has shown caution in pushing India's admission due to anticipated reactions of some of the members. Though Russia and Western powers like France have expressed themselves in favour of India's membership of these clubs, there is uncertainty about the attitude of other members in this regard. Among these, the most problematic is the attitude of China which will evidently be under pressure from Pakistan to prevent India's membership. It is also not clear at this stage as to the terms and conditions under which membership would be given to India, in case it comes about.
- Non-resumption of trade in material and technology for refining, reprocessing and for manufacturing heavy water will prove to be yet another constraint to the expansion of India's nuclear weapon capabilities. India, of course, has its own technologies in these areas. But these restrictions will not make things easier for India so far as the development of its nuclear weapon programme is concerned.

The 123 Agreement has no provision preventing India from conducting nuclear tests. The international treaty prohibiting nuclear tests is the CTBT, which has not been ratified by the US and which is yet to be operationalized. India has not even signed it. India is also not a member of the Non-Proliferation Treaty (NPT) which prevents non-nuclear weapon states from carrying out any activity, including tests, for acquiring nuclear weapons. Besides, today every officially recognized nuclear weapon state—as well as those not so recognized like India and Pakistan—is observing a voluntary moratorium on nuclear testing. Unless the international situation, particularly the relations between the major powers, sharply deteriorates, it is very unlikely that there would be any breach in this moratorium in the near future. A breach by a non-recognized nuclear weapon state like Pakistan, which may compel India to give up its voluntary moratorium, is even less likely, as they would remain under tremendous pressure from the international community to maintain the status quo. Thus, India retaining its freedom to test nuclear weapons is basically a theoretical proposition in the short and medium run.

What is the long-term compulsion for India to test nuclear weapons? There is a view which the present author shares, that India can build its avowed minimum nuclear deterrent without further testing. Our scientists claimed after the Pokhran-II tests—a claim that has been reiterated subsequently—that these tests have made available to India all the data required to design, through computer simulation, the types of nuclear weapons India needs for building its minimum deterrent. Besides, India is also free to do sub-critical tests, which it has mastered, and which can be used for testing new weapons designs. According to this view, India's minimum deterrent should be really the minimum. Its main purpose should be to deter a nuclear attack from Pakistan. India need not get involved in a nuclear arms race with China, nor should it expand and upgrade its nuclear arsenals in order to acquire and maintain a great power status. The more effective way for India to acquire such status is by maintaining the dynamism of its economy and building a genuinely inclusive society rather than by getting involved in a nuclear arms race with China or with any other major power. In fact, the latter course of action may impose such a heavy burden on the nation's resources as to render it economically weak and socially maimed. So far as China is concerned, it would suffice if India's nuclear arsenal contains weapons that can target major Chinese cities, population centres and strategic plants and installations.

Rightist political parties and like-minded strategic analysts see nuclear weapons not just as a minimum deterrent, but also as a currency of power. They believe that the size and sophistication of India's nuclear arsenal is a critical factor determining its standing in the world and its stature as a major global power. They are, therefore, in favour of India developing and deploying Intercontinental Ballistic Missiles (ICBMs) and also going in for sea-based nuclear force. Moreover, they are of the view that the size and composition of India's minimum deterrent cannot be determined in advance and once for all; it would depend very much on what the countries in our neighbourhood, particularly Pakistan and China, would do. People belonging to this school of thought, therefore, would like India fully to retain its option to test because it is essential for developing new weapon systems and ensuring the reliability of the existing arsenal.

The Left political parties and pacifist groups have traditionally been against the acquisition of nuclear weapons by India. And now that India has acquired these weapons, they would like these to be kept to a minimum. It is, therefore, ironical that the Left political parties have now joined the rightist parties and like-minded strategic thinkers in opposing the provisions in the Hyde Act and the 123 Agreement, which has the effect of discouraging India from nuclear testing. The argument given by the former that they are opposing these provisions because they cannot accept any form of restriction on the exercise of sovereignty by India, is not at all convincing. Practically every bilateral or multilateral agreement involves the surrender of a part of sovereignty in order to serve larger national and international interests. The real issue, therefore, is not whether sovereignty is being compromised, but the purpose for which it is being done. By taking a stand against any curb on testing, the Left parties are aligning themselves with the Rightists, who are in favour of an open-ended expansion of India's nuclear force and India entering into a nuclear arms race with China and even the US.

The 123 Agreement does not prohibit nuclear testing, but by virtue of its provision for the 'right to call for return',[6] can have the effect of deterring such tests by imposing a heavy price for doing so. According to this provision, the US has the right to demand the return of the nuclear reactors, fuel as well as related material and technology supplied by it in case India carries out a nuclear test or if the agreement is prematurely terminated for other reasons. The exercise of this right can severely disrupt India's nuclear industry and by chain reaction, the other sectors of its economy. This can, thus, be a deterrent to nuclear testing. However, the 123 Agreement includes a number of provisions to ensure the continued functioning of reactors supplied by the US, even in the event of the termination and cessation of cooperation under the agreement. The provisions contained in the agreement to ensure the continued supply of nuclear fuel in such an event include:

- General assurance that the US will create 'the necessary conditions for India to have assured and full access to fuel for its reactors'

- The US will support an Indian effort to develop a strategic reserve of nuclear fuel to guard against any disruption of supply over the lifetime of India's reactors
- The US will join India in seeking to negotiate an India-specific fuel supply agreement with the IAEA
- If, despite these arrangements, a disruption in supply occurs, 'the United States and India will jointly convene a group of friendly supplier countries, including countries such as Russia, France and the United Kingdom, to pursue such measures as would restore fuel supply to India'.[7]

India's compulsion to carry out nuclear tests in the event of a threat posed to its security by nuclear tests carried out by Pakistan and China is taken into account in the 123 Agreement by the inclusion of the provision in Article 14, paragraph 2. According to this provision, in the consultation that will be held pursuant to a decision to terminate the agreement, the parties will 'consider carefully the circumstances that may lead to termination' and will 'take into account whether the circumstances that may lead to termination or cessation resulted from a Party's serious concern about the changed security requirement or as a response to similar actions by other states which could impact national security'.[8] This implies that if the termination results from India carrying out nuclear tests in response to similar tests carried out by Pakistan or China, which has an impact on India's national security, then it may not really come into effect and consequently the 'right to call for return' may not be enforced. Whether the US would invoke this right will eventually depend upon India's bargaining position at that time, that is, its economic clout, the progress made in building its nuclear deterrent and the then prevailing international security situation and global power equation.

There are some apparent contradictions between the 123 Agreement and the Hyde Act. Two of them need to be highlighted. The 123 Agreement provides in Article 2, paragraph 4, that the purpose of the agreement is not to affect the unsafeguarded nuclear activities of India. This means that the US would not in any manner interfere with the nuclear weapon programme activities carried out by India. On the other hand, the Hyde Act in Section 103, paragraph 5, provides that one of the policies of the US will be to 'seek to halt the increase of nuclear arsenals in South Asia and to promote their reduction and eventual elimination'.[9] In paragraph 7 of the same section, it is further provided that pending the implementation of a multilateral moratorium on the production of fissile material, the US will 'encourage India not to increase its production of fissile material at unsafeguarded nuclear facilities'.[10] By these provisions, the Hyde Act lays down the policy for the US to interfere in the activities being carried out in India's unsafeguarded nuclear facilities. This is contrary to the provision of the 123 Agreement quoted previously.

Second, whereas the 123 Agreement has multiple provisions to ensure the continuity of the supply of nuclear fuel in the event of the termination or cessation of cooperation under the agreement, the Hyde Act in Section 103, paragraph 6, enjoins upon the US administration to 'seek to prevent the transfer to a country of nuclear equipment, materials, or technology from other participating governments in the NSG or from any other source if nuclear transfers to that country are suspended or terminated'.[11]

The question arises: which of the two legal instruments, that is, the Hyde Act or the 123 Agreement, will prevail in the event of a dispute? Political leaders in the Government of India and its senior officials have strongly asserted that India's commitments derive only from the 123 Agreement and that it is not bound by the Hyde Act. This argument is not fully convincing. It is true that India is not bound by the Hyde Act, but the US administration certainly is. Moreover, if an international agreement itself provides that its implementation will be in accordance with national laws, then certainly it will be the domestic law that will prevail in the event of a dispute. The 123 Agreement clearly provides in paragraph 1 of Article 2 that the agreement will be implemented 'in accordance with respective applicable treaties, national laws'.[12] Here, the Hyde Act is the applicable national law. Besides, it may also be pointed out that in adhering to some international agreements, including the dispute settlement mechanism of the WTO, the US has made sure that in a dispute between its obligations under the relevant international agreement and the provision of its domestic law, it is the latter that will prevail.

An important question that has arisen with regard to the Hyde Act is whether it is at all mandatory for the US administration to implement in letter and spirit those of its provisions that are in the nature of general statements of US policies and which are couched in best endeavour terms. US officials have argued that these provisions are only of a recommendatory nature and it is up to the President to decide the extent to which the administration would comply with them. This was confirmed in the statement issued by President Bush after signing the Hyde Act into law on 18 December 2006, in which he clarified that he construed these provisions of the act as 'advisory' and that he would abide by them in a manner that would be consistent with his constitutional authority to conduct the nation's foreign affairs.

There are several policymakers and analysts close to the highest centres of power both in the US and in India who regard the Indo-US nuclear deal as an attempt by the former to build India's strength as a balance against China. They argue that this has become necessary because of the rapidly rising military power of China and the threat it poses to the US and its allies. On the other hand, India, which shares common values of democracy, freedom and rule of law with the US, does not pose any threat to the latter. George Perkovich, in his article, takes it for granted that US authorities have based their new strategy towards India on the premise that partnership with the latter should be cultivated and the US should help in enhancing India's international power in order to balance China's power in Asia.[13] In India also, this view is widely prevalent.

It is doubtful whether the US administration and Congress actually share this view. The US can be expected to realize that China's cooperation is essential for dealing with global problems in the areas of money, finance, trade and environment, which critically affect US interests. China is very much a part of the international security system of which the US is the kingpin. It is in the interest of both China and the US to preserve the existing balance of power in the world. The US is, therefore, very unlikely to go about consciously building up India's strength in order to disturb the existing power balance. In fact, India's nuclear ambition, if pushed beyond a point, like deployment of ICBMs or a sea-based nuclear force, is likely to be seen by the US as a threat to its own security. That is why both the Hyde Act and the 123 Agreement have a number of clauses designed to keep India's nuclear power ambitions within limits. The US administration went for this deal because India, on its own merit, irrespective of the China factor, deserves to be an important strategic partner of the US. India's own strategic interest also lies not in projecting itself as a balancing force against China, but in continuing to improve its relations with it. The right strategy for India is to cultivate and benefit from good relations with both the US and China.

Implications for Indo-US Relations

The Indo-US nuclear deal, apart from elevating the strategic relationship between the two countries to a new height, was expected to open the gateway for an all-round acceleration in Indo-US relations. For one thing, the implementation of the 123 Agreement was seen as giving a big fillip to Indo-US military cooperation. There was also the likelihood of a sharp increase in US investment in India, particularly in the nuclear sector. Some experts projected investments in this sector alone to run into hundreds of billions of dollars. Beyond this, the deal held out the promise of making it easier for India to import from the US dual-purpose technologies across the board, not necessarily confined to the nuclear field. Besides, the enhanced mutual trust and understanding between US and India, engendered by the 123 Agreement, was likely to prove very useful for India to deal with its neighbours.

These general statements about the advantages of the deal for India were subject to certain qualifications. Some of the conditionalities that the US might insist upon for providing military supplies to India might not be acceptable to the latter. US investments in the nuclear energy sector would very much depend on its competitiveness vis-à-vis other suppliers, particularly Russia and France. Until now, these have been withheld mainly because of India's Nuclear Liability Act, which US companies find objectionable on several counts. Moreover, each transaction for the supply of dual-purpose technologies by the nuclear weapon states would involve tough bargaining, which may call for adjustments in India's foreign policy stance. And, due to its recently diminished economic clout, its being embroiled in conflicts in the north-western part of Pakistan and Afghanistan and the backlash against the US in the Islamic countries, the US's leverage for influencing Pakistan's policy towards India stands considerably diminished.

The Indo-US nuclear deal must be seen in the context of the wider US objective of giving new salience to its relations with India in the context of the changed global power equation and India's enhanced military and economic clout. By offering and concluding the nuclear deal, President George W. Bush signalled a major shift in the Indo-US relationship. The shift has continued during the current Democratic administration. President Obama has repeatedly described the relationship as a defining feature of the 21st century. The two meetings between the US President and Indian Prime Minister after the May 2014 general elections in India have contributed to reinvigorating this relationship qualitatively and substantively.

By forging a special relationship with India, the US wants it to be its partner in the pursuit of its foreign policy goals across the board—on Iran, UN, peacekeeping, human rights situations in the world, the Doha Round of Trade Negotiations, etc. The US also wants to take advantage of this relationship to have an edge over its competitors to ensure a greater presence of its multinational companies in India and greater access to the Indian market for its goods, services, capital and technology. A related objective is to emerge as the most important player in India's lucrative arms market, replacing Russia and taking over its present pre-eminent position. The US's competitiveness, even in the supply of nuclear reactors, should not be underestimated. Though the US gave up the nuclear energy path decades ago, its multinational companies have continued research and development activities in this area. That is why Westinghouse, along with its collaborators, was able to sell four mega-sized nuclear reactors to China in January 2006, and negotiations for the supply of more reactors are continuing. In the article 'Our Opportunity with India', published in *The Washington Post* in 2006, the then US Secretary of State, Condoleezza Rice, stated that India planned to import eight nuclear reactors by 2012. 'If US companies win just two of these reactor contracts, it will mean thousands of new jobs for American workers'.[14]

The US also wanted India to be a part of the global non-proliferation regime. It came to the conclusion that an India inside the tent served its cause of non-proliferation better than an India outside it. The US has publicly recognized India's impressive contribution to non-proliferation on the ground. By opening the door of the global non-proliferation regime for India through the waiver given by the NSG, the US wanted to bind India's voluntary contributions, in the form of treaty obligations. In her article in *The Washington Post*, Condoleeza Rice wrote, 'our agreement with India will make our future more secure, by expanding the reach of the international nonproliferation regime'.[15] In this connection, she quoted Mohamed ElBaradei, the then Director General of the IAEA, who called the Indo-US Nuclear Agreement, 'a milestone, timely for ongoing efforts to consolidate the non-proliferation regime'.[16]

Another major benefit that the US saw in the nuclear deal was the way diversifying India's energy sector would help to alleviate the competition between India on the one hand and the US and other rapidly expanding economies on the other, for scarce carbon-based energy resources, thereby lessening the pressure on global energy prices.[17] This would apparently be in India's interest as well.

Yet another major objective of the US in striking the civilian nuclear deal with India was to co-opt the latter on its side on the issue of global warming. The US can now argue that by weaning India away from an almost exclusive reliance on fossil fuel, it has made a significant contribution to reducing pressure for global warming. In her *Washington Post* article, Rice advanced the argument, 'A threefold increase in India's nuclear capacity by 2015 would reduce India's projected annual CO2 emissions by more than 170 million tons, about the current total emissions of the Netherlands'.[18]

In the climate change negotiations, the US's goal has been to fashion a consensus on an agreement which sidetracks the Kyoto Protocol, imposes no legally binding commitment on the US to cut greenhouse gas emissions and shifts a large part of the burden for this on the emerging economies like India and China. The Indo-US nuclear deal fitted into this scheme of things perfectly.

A long-term benefit that the US saw in cooperation with India in the nuclear sector was the advantage it would be able to take of India's advanced research and development in this field to bolster its competitive position in the global market. This was indicated by Rice in her *Washington Post* article. She said: 'We plan to expand our civilian nuclear partnership to research and development, drawing on India's technological expertise to promote a global renaissance in safe and clear nuclear power'[19]

The progress on the implementation of the nuclear deal was, however, stalled due to the Civil Liability for Nuclear Damage Act passed by the Parliament in India in 2010. This Act allowed for supplier liability in addition to the liability of the operator of the nuclear plant in the event of an accident. Such a liability for damage attributable to suppliers nearly froze the interests of potential US suppliers, particularly since this provision in the Indian Act was in marked variance from existing international legal instruments on liability for nuclear damage, such as the Paris Convention or the Vienna Convention or the Supplementary Convention of the IAEA—none of which prescribes extending liability beyond the state and the operator concerned, to the supplier.

During the visit of US President Obama in January 2015, this matter appears to have been resolved to the satisfaction of both the governments. This should go a long way towards dispelling the reservations among potential suppliers about any liability of the supplier to be claimed by the operator or the suppliers being dragged to the law court for damages under the general laws of the country. At the joint press conference by Prime Minister Modi and President Obama in Delhi, both the leaders affirmed that the understanding reached on the issue of liability had resolved the problem satisfactorily. The Ministry of External Affairs in India subsequently placed on its website a detailed exposition on the situation as it obtained after the Obama visit, by way of a note on Frequently Asked Questions (FAQ).[20] However, the left political parties and likeminded critics of the nuclear deal have remained unconvinced about the claims of a breakthrough on the liability question after the Obama visit and sought to pick holes in government's position including that explained in response to the FAQ.

The Left political parties in India launched a veritable campaign against the Indo-US nuclear deal and on this issue, withdrew their support to the UPA government at the Centre in 2008. Their main objection to the deal was and still is that it will bolster and impart new depth and dimension to the ongoing Indo-US strategic partnership. Left political parties take a very dim view of this partnership. They have not concealed their unhappiness over improvements in Indo-US bilateral relations and have, in particular, expressed their disquiet at the way India is going about forging close military ties with the US. These concerns seem to arise from the doctrinaire anti-American attitude of the Left parties and are not based on a careful calculation of where India's national interest lies. If one sees it in the light of national interest, then it is indispensable for India to forge close links with the US. Every other country of significance in the world, including Russia and China, has moved in this direction. Though there has recently been a setback to the Russian effort to be a part of the Western capitalist world, this does not detract from its continuing pursuit of this objective. Besides, India has entered into strategic partnerships with almost every important country in the world. It would have been incongruous, if not absurd, if India had not done so with the US, which is economically and militarily still the most powerful country in the world.

The Left political parties took particular exception to the Defence Framework Agreement signed between India and the US on 28 June 2005. They alleged that through this agreement, India sought to 'interlock our armed forces with that of the United States' which 'is mounting pressure on India for military contracts to purchase fighter planes, naval ships, radars and artillery'.[21] The Left parties also objected to the Logistical Support Agreement and the Maritime Cooperation Pact concluded and the joint military exercises envisaged under the Defence Framework Agreement.[22]

The Left parties may object in principle to any defence cooperation with the US, though it is very difficult to justify such an objection on rational grounds. But once defence cooperation takes place, it is inevitable that other things will follow, including the purchase of arms, undertaking military exercises, logistical support in the event of a natural disaster or other emergencies and maritime cooperation. These are the warp and woof of modern defence cooperation and are bound to figure in defence engagements with any country. Moreover, India is still dependent on Russia for the supply of more than two-thirds of military hardware for the Army, Navy and Air Force. For the last few decades, India has been trying to diversify its source of supply in order to buy hardware incorporating the most advanced technology and from the cheapest source. The end of the Cold War provided India an opportunity for such diversification. The conclusion of the nuclear deal with the US has further improved the prospects in this regard. It stands to reason that India should take advantage of this opportunity. Any other country placed in India's position would adopt the same course of action. India's recent purchase of military hardware from the US sets a trend that is likely to continue in the coming years.

The Left parties also take exception to India becoming a part of military exercises with the US and like-minded countries like Australia, Japan and Singapore. It is extremely difficult to understand this stance of theirs. In the present-day world, almost all significant countries have been taking initiatives to forge links of mutual cooperation with different groups of like-minded countries in order to minimize loss, maximize opportunities, build leverages and acquire a measure of flexibility and manoeuvrability in the conduct of foreign policy. The groupings that are being forged these days to serve these purposes are not in the nature of military alliances directed against outside countries. Nor are they based on a common ideology. Ideology as a basis for forging alliances was discarded by Mikhail Gorbachev in the late 1980s and has not since been actively pursued by any major power. Present-day alliances are functional, need-based and issue-oriented. In the context of this global trend, there is no reason why India also should not take initiatives to form or join as many groups of like-minded countries as possible for mutual cooperation. In doing so, India would only be reflecting the vision projected by our great poet Rabindranath Tagore in the poem *He mor chitto* ('O My Heart') written almost a century ago. He said:

Dibe aar nibe,
Milabe milibe,
Jaabe na phire.
Ei bharater mahamanaber sagarteere.

We shall give and take,
We shall bring nations together and mix with them,
We shall never turn our back on anyone
On the shore of this ocean of great humanity, that is India.[23]

In this connection, it may be recalled that Russia took the initiative of forming a grouping called the Collective Security Treaty Organization (CSTO) with the Central Asian countries which were the Republics of the Soviet Union before it disintegrated. More recently, China and Russia took the lead in launching the SCO, of which India is now a member. Members of the SCO, among others, conduct joint military exercises from time to time. In August 2007, they conducted a massive joint military exercise involving all the three wings of the Armed Forces of member countries. China is a part of ASEAN+3.[24] It took advantage of its position in this forum to successfully thwart the Indian attempt at the first East Asia Summit conference in Kuala Lumpur in December 2005 to launch a Pan-Asian regional integration movement, with India as one of the original members. In the light of this trend worldwide, it is very difficult to understand the objection of the Left parties to India seeking closer cooperation with the US, Japan and Australia under a quadrilateral umbrella.

It is even more difficult to understand their objection to India joining these important democratic countries in an attempt to help fledgling democracies build and strengthen democratic institutions in their countries. Joining these countries in such an endeavour does not necessarily mean India becoming a party to US design to bring about a 'regime change' under the pretext of restoring or fostering democracy. India can legitimately extend assistance for democracy to take firmer roots in other countries, strictly in response to requests received from these countries and within the four walls of the existing international law. In the Joint Statement of 18 July 2005, India agreed to join the US in supporting democratic institutions and capacity building only in those countries 'that seek such assistance'. As a matter of fact, the idea of rendering assistance for democratization to the member states of the UN was first put forward by the then UN Secretary-General, Boutros Boutros-Ghali, in his report, *An Agenda for Democratization* submitted to the UN General Assembly in 1996.[25] Since then, the UN has made some progress, though modest, in this direction and has created a fund under its aegis to help member countries in building democratic institutions and practices. India is a legitimate partner in this venture. In the Joint Statement issued at the time of President Obama's visit to India, both countries reiterated their commitment to the UN Democracy Fund.

All this does not mean that India does not have serious problems in conducting its bilateral relations with the US. The fact is that on several global issues, India has serious differences with the US. Besides, in the conduct of its foreign policy the US has tended to create a category of 'rogue' States with which it maintains minimal or no relations and expects countries friendly to it to follow the same policy. Iran, with which India has reasons to have strong strategic, political, economic and cultural relations, happens to be included in the US's current category of 'rogue' States. Because of the US factor, India lost a big deal for the supply of compressed gas by Iran, which was concluded a few years prior to the 2005 vote and in spite of the positive noises we hear from time to time from the Government of India that the India–Pakistan–Iran gas pipeline project is still alive, in reality India has moved far away from the project, which a few years ago was re-launched as an Iran–Pakistan venture. Thus, the help that the US would render to India under the 123 Agreement in bolstering India's energy security through an expansion of its civilian nuclear sector may adversely affect India building such security in cooperation with Iran, through the augmentation of other sources of energy supply like gas and petroleum. The US is also not expected to be too happy with any big investment by India in Iran to avail itself of the opportunity of participating in Iran's development. But a lot will depend on the fate of the on-going diplomatic efforts to reach a negotiated accord on Iran's nuclear programme between Iran and the P5 plus Germany.[26] If an accord is indeed reached, India can look forward to availing itself of some of the opportunities available in cooperating with Iran.

There is no doubt that the Indo-US nuclear deal will compound India's problems in formulating and conducting independent foreign policy and in abiding by the fundamental principles of its foreign policy. The annual certification clauses in the Hyde Act are designed to give Washington additional leverage in influencing India's foreign policy. The provisions relating to certifications mention 'congruence' of India's foreign policy with that of the US. This includes India joining the US effort in isolating and applying sanctions against Iran. This is clearly not in India's interest.

In spite of these problems, India has to have a constructive, expanding and strategically significant relationship with the US. The Indian diplomacy has enough resourcefulness, ingenuity and skill to be able to deal with the US in an effective manner consistent with the basic tenets of its foreign policy. What is needed is eternal vigilance, will power, the courage of conviction and steadfast adherence to the basic values and principles in which India's foreign policy is anchored.

Notes

1. *The Hindu*, '80% of Work on Fast Breeder Reactor at Kalpakkam Over', 27 November 2010.
2. White House Press Office, 'Joint Statement by President George W. Bush and Prime Minister Manmohan Singh' (Office of the Press Secretary, US Department of State, Washington DC, 18 July 2005), http://2001-2009.state.gov/p/sca/rls/pr/2005/49763.htm (accessed 24 April 2015).
3. George Perkovich, 'Faulty Promises: US-India Nuclear Deal' (Policy Outlook, Carnegie Endowment for International Peace, Washington DC, September 2005) 12–13.
4. Government of the United States of America and the Government of India, 'Agreement for Cooperation Between the Government of the United States of America and the Government of India Concerning Peaceful Uses of Nuclear Energy' (Treaties and Other International Acts Series 08-1206, 10 October 2008).
5. Ibid.
6. Ibid.
7. Ibid.
8. Ibid.
9. 'Henry J. Hyde United States-India Peaceful Atomic Energy Cooperation Act of 2006' (Public Law 109-401, 109th Congress of the United States of America, 2nd session, 18 December 2006).
10. Ibid.
11. Ibid.
12. US Department of State, 'U.S. and India Release Text of 123 Agreement' (Office of the Spokesman, US Department of State, Washington DC, 3 August 2007).
13. Perkovich, 'Faulty Promises'.
14. Condoleezza Rice, 'Our Opportunity with India', *The Washington Post*, 13 March 2006.
15. Ibid.
16. Quoted in ibid.
17. From the testimony by the then US Secretary of State Condoleezza Rice to the US Senate Foreign Relations Committee, 5 April 2006.
18. Rice, 'Our Opportunity with India'.
19. Ibid.

20. Ministry of External Affairs, 'Frequently Asked Questions and Answers on Civil Liability for Nuclear Damage Act 2010 and Related Issues', http://www.mea.gov.in/press-releases.htm?dtl/24766/Frequently_Asked_Questions_and_Answers_on_Civil_Liability_for_Nuclear_Damage_Act_2010_and_related_issues (accessed on 24 April 2015).
21. Prakash Karat, 'Why the CPI(M) and the Left Oppose the Nuclear Deal', *The Hindu*, 20 August 2007.
22. Ibid.
23. Rabindranath Tagore, 'He mor chitto', in *Gitanjali* (Calcutta: Visvabharati Granthalaya, 1954 [1910]). Author's own translation.
24. ASEAN+3 countries include Indonesia, Malaysia, the Philippines, Singapore, Thailand, Brunei, Cambodia, Laos, Myanmar, Vietnam, China, Japan, South Korea.
25. Boutros Boutros-Ghali, *An Agenda for Democratization* (New York: United Nations, 1996).
26. P5+1 includes China, France, Russia, the United Kingdom, and the United States, plus Germany.

EIGHT Indo-(Soviet) Russian Relations*

The Soviet Era

India's fascination with the Soviet Union as a spearhead of the socialist movement in the world, started even before India gained independence. The leaders of India's independence movement, particularly Jawaharlal Nehru, who received their education in England, were exposed to and highly impressed by the then prevailing ideology of Fabian socialism there. They came to believe that the socialist model was better suited than the capitalist one to the socio-economic conditions prevailing in countries like India. However, there was no significant movement in India's relations with the Soviet Union while Joseph Stalin was alive. After the Stalin period, particularly with Nikita Khrushchev at the helm towards the end of the 1950s, ideological prejudices against India started melting away. The new Soviet leadership recognized the importance of India as a great civilization, as one of the largest countries of Asia with great economic potential, as the leader of the Non-Aligned Movement and as a country with which the Soviet Union shared common views on global issues like nuclear disarmament, multilateralism under the UN, anti-colonialism, anti-apartheid, anti-racism and the right of Palestinians to their homeland. The Soviet Union found it in its interest to forge economic ties with India which, like the former, was pursuing a policy of the state controlling the commanding heights of the economy. The severing of relations with China during the Khrushchev era proved to be another reason of bringing the Soviet Union closer to India.

India, on its part, was obliged to turn to the Soviet Union partly because of the refusal of the Western countries to extend economic assistance to it for building a self-reliant economy, and also in order to meet its security requirements arising out of the Western military assistance to Pakistan under the post-War military alliances formed against the Soviet

Union. The Soviet Union readily stepped in to meet these requirements. As a result, there was a quantum jump in the level of military and economic cooperation between the two countries. The infrastructure of the heavy and basic industries that India was able to build during its successive Five-Year Plans owed a great deal to the assistance extended by the Soviet Union. During the 1980s, the Soviet Union emerged as the biggest trading partner of India in the world. During this period, India's dependence on the Soviet Union for military supplies reached a level as high as 70 to 80 per cent. Despite the partial success achieved by India recently in its attempt to diversify the sources of its military supplies, it is still dependent on Russia for a very large proportion of the total supply of spares and equipment for its armed forces. On an average, 75 per cent of the Indian armed forces are equipped with military hardware of Soviet/Russian origin.[1]

Apart from the major steel plants in Bhilai and Bokaro, India was able to build a large part of its energy infrastructure and most of the heavy and basic industries, crucial for its development, with the assistance of the Soviet Union. These included a number of thermal power stations, the Heavy Machine Building Plant in Ranchi, the Coal Mining Machinery Plant in Durgapur, the Bharat Heavy Electricals Limited (BHEL) Heavy Electrical Equipment Plant at Haridwar, the Korba Coal Mining Project, the Bharat Ophthalmic Glass Ltd in Durgapur, the Bharat Pumps and Compressors Ltd in Naini, the Indian Drugs and Pharmaceuticals Limited (IDPL) Antibiotics Plant in Rishikesh, the Synthetic Drug Project in Hyderabad and the Surgical Instruments Plant in Madras (now Chennai).

The Soviet Union also helped India in emerging as an important space power. It assisted in setting up the Thumba Equatorial Rocket Launching Station at Thiruvananthapuram and in launching the experimental satellites, Aryabhata, Bhaskara-I and Bhaskara-II. It provided the cryogenic engines to the Indian Space Research Organisation (ISRO), which made an important contribution to India's progress towards self-reliance in launching spacecrafts. During the Gorbachev period, the two countries had agreed upon and were working on the details for jointly setting up an international space agency with the mandate to make information collected through satellites on resources and climate available to other countries and monitor peaceful uses of the outer space. This project could not materialize because of the ensuing political turmoil in the Soviet Union.

Most of the projects for heavy and basic industries undertaken with Soviet assistance were financed out of credits extended by the Soviet Union, which was also the case with Soviet military supplies. The Soviet credits carried an interest rate of 2.5 per cent per annum and were repayable generally over a period of 12 years. Another distinguishing feature of Soviet economic assistance to India during that period was that they were generally given for the establishment of entire complexes rather than individual plants. This involved assistance for the development of ancillary industries, both horizontally and vertically. Moreover, economic cooperation agreements with the Soviet Union were in most cases package deals, involving assistance in the preparation of blueprints, supply of raw materials, components and machinery, supply of technical documentations and provision for training personnel. The implementation of these package deals facilitated the transfer of technology to India from the Soviet Union on a very large scale, mainly through the association of Indian engineers and technicians with the designing and construction of the plants and by the training of thousands of Indians in Soviet technical institutions and plants as well as in technical institutions set up for this purpose in India with Soviet assistance. The fact that the Soviet economic assistance was made available to India on the basis of a long-term commitment facilitated its harmonization with the development plans of India. Another important feature of the Soviet economic assistance was the provision for making payments for the credits by the export of goods from India. This provision was of considerable importance at a time when India used to run chronic balance-of-payment deficits with the rest of the world and its reserve position was generally not very comfortable.

The first bilateral trade agreement between the two countries was signed in 1953. After that, trade between the two countries increased exponentially. What lent special significance to the trade relations with the Soviet Union was the purposive manner in which the two countries utilized the instrument of bilateral trade for the economic development of India as well as for the benefit of the Union of Soviet Socialist Republics (USSR). Adaptations and sophistications were introduced in the trade agreements for forging new and dynamic economic relations to serve mutual interests. These agreements made a significant contribution to India's planned development by imparting an element of stability to flows of exports and imports, including those of strategic products and raw materials like petroleum, petroleum products, fertilizers and metals. They also made it possible for India to expand and set up export-oriented industries, the production of which was geared to meet the requirements of Soviet consumers.

There has been endless controversy as to whether India made the right choice in pursuing an import substitution and heavy-industry-based development strategy during the earlier phase of its economic development and whether the state should have played as important a role in the economy as it did during that period. There is no intention here to enter into this controversy. It needs only to be underlined that within the framework of the strategy adopted by India and the development policy pursued by it, the Soviet Union made a signal contribution to ensuring its success, particularly by building India's infrastructure and industrial base.

The Soviet Union emerged as the largest trading partner of India as well as the biggest destination of India's exports, surpassing the US in the years 1981–82, 1982–83 and 1984–85. In 1991–92 also, India's exports to the USSR at Rs 5,255 crore (Rs 52.55 billion) were marginally higher than those (at Rs 5,245 crore [Rs 52.45 million]) to the US.[2]

The Indo-Soviet Treaty of Peace, Friendship and Cooperation, signed in August 1971, reflected the high peak reached in Indo-Soviet relations. This treaty became an important safeguard for India's security, sovereignty and territorial integrity. Its most important security clause was Article 9 which provided that the contracting parties would enter into mutual consultations when either of the parties was subjected to an attack, so as to remove the threat and take appropriate measures to maintain the security of the region. It is generally believed that the Soviet material and diplomatic support as well as the confidence provided under this treaty enabled India to successfully undertake the operation during the 1971 war for the liberation of Bangladesh. According to some analysts, it effectively prevented China from intervening in the war on the side of Pakistan. The treaty was renewed in 1993 during Russian President Boris Yeltsin's visit to India, but without its security clauses and ideological underpinnings.

While maintaining close relations with Leftist groups in India on a party-to-party basis, the Government of the USSR put no pressure on India to bring about any change in its socio-economic and political system. In the international arena, the two countries shared a great deal of ideological affinity. But here too, India retained its independence of action and judgement on international issues and thus remained true to its non-aligned status. Even during the peak of the Indo-Soviet relationship, India maintained very meaningful relations with the West and did not hesitate from articulating its differences with the Soviet Union on critical international issues. For example, Indira Gandhi, the then Indian Premier, rejected the Brezhnev Doctrine on an Asian security arrangement under the Soviet leadership twice during the 1970s. While not joining the Western bandwagon against the Soviet intervention in Afghanistan in 1979, India lost no opportunity to warn the Soviet leadership at the highest level, of the grave consequences of the latter getting bogged down in the Afghan quagmire.

The first half of the 1980s, which coincided with the early part of the Gorbachev regime in the Soviet Union, can be regarded as the golden era of Indo-Soviet relations. That was the time when economic relations between the two countries reached their peak. The drastic transformations that President Gorbachev brought about in the foreign policy of the Soviet Union made it almost entirely convergent with that of India. President Gorbachev extricated the Soviet foreign policy from its ideological and imperialistic moorings and planted it firmly on the ethical ground in which India's foreign policy was entrenched from the very beginning since its independence. There emerged after this change, an almost total identity of views between the two countries on disarmament, multilateralism under the UN and other world order issues. This shift in Soviet foreign policy and its convergence with the principal tenets of India's foreign policy was reflected in the New Delhi Declaration and other statements issued and important decisions taken during President Gorbachev's visit to India in November 1986.

The two countries decided to work for establishing 'a new dynamic multilateralism' and constituted a group of eminent social scientists drawn from the two countries to review developments in the world economy and international economic relations on a continuing basis, with a view to suggesting strategies and policy measures on the basis of which the two countries could take initiatives for the establishment of a just and equitable world economic order. In the New Delhi Declaration,[3] President Gorbachev joined the Prime Minister of India in giving a call for moving towards 'a nuclear-weapon-free and non-violent world'.[4] This became the title of the Rajiv Gandhi Action Plan on nuclear disarmament submitted by India to the UN in 1988. The New Delhi Declaration also stated that 'an end to the arms race is an essential prerequisite for the establishment of a new world order'.[5] This reflected the view firmly held and frequently articulated by Jawaharlal Nehru, India's first prime minister. The declaration was also the first official document signed by the leader of the world's second largest nuclear weapon power that specified a dateline, that is, before the end of the 20th century, for the elimination of nuclear weapons. The Soviet Union also for the first time joined India in proposing that 'pending the elimination of nuclear weapons . . . an international convention barring the use or threat of the use of nuclear weapons should be concluded immediately'.[6] The most tragic part was that this golden era of Indo-Soviet relationships was far too short-lived. The Gorbachev regime collapsed in 1992 and with this came the end of the Soviet Union.

Indo-Russian Relations

With the disintegration of the Soviet Union, an entire epoch of contemporary history came to an end, as did the Indo-Soviet relationship, as it was shaped and had evolved during the Soviet era. The Soviet experiment in socialism had profoundly influenced the course of events in the rest of the world. The Soviet system provided the much sought after alternative to the capitalist system prevailing in major advanced countries and was widely seen as the harbinger of social justice and equality. The socialist system in the Soviet Union collapsed not because there was anything fundamentally wrong with the ideology, per se, but because of the way it was sought to be put into practice. The system crumbled under the weight of its rigidities, excesses and resistance to change required to adjust to the changing environment.

Indo-Soviet relations went through a phase of drift and disarray during the last phase of the Gorbachev regime and the first few years after the disintegration of the Soviet Union. Russia became the inheritor state on which devolved the responsibility of carrying out all the treaty obligations, agreements and contracts entered into by the Soviet Union with other countries, including India. In the early 1990s, the Russian economy and polity as well as its foreign policy went through drastic, even traumatic transformations. The main emphasis on the economic front was on dismantling state controls, introducing privatization in a system where no private sector existed and giving a greater role to market forces. In the realm of foreign policy, there was a pronounced lurch towards the West, particularly the US. Integration with Europe has been an enduring Russian aspiration coming down from the time of Peter the Great. Gorbachev talked about a Common European Home[7] stretching from the Urals to the Atlantic. But Yeltsin followed a very lopsided policy on this matter. Under him, Russia started seeing itself mainly as a European power and almost forgot that vast tracts of its territory lay in Asia. Its relationship with Asian countries, including India, was thus relegated to the background.

India lost almost all its trading and other special economic advantages in the inheritor state, Russia. There was an overnight switch to conducting trade between the two countries through payments in free foreign exchange. Trade was sustained at a modest level, mainly in the form of exports by India, in payment for the revalued and rescheduled debts incurred in the past. But here too there were delays on the part of the Russians in issuing licenses to importers, due to the virtual breakdown of governance. The value of trade declined to the rock bottom figure of $0.94 billion in 1993–94. Thereafter, the two-way trade remained stagnant between $1 billion and $2 billion till the end of the 1990s.[8] After the breakdown of the Soviet Union, military supplies to India were disrupted as many military establishments in the Soviet military-industrial conglomerate closed down and government authorities were unable to coordinate supplies from defence units spread all over the Soviet Union. Due to the chaotic supply conditions, prices were sometimes raised unrealistically. Things started looking up somewhat after President Yeltsin's visit to India from 27 to 29 January 1993.

This visit was partly intended to restore the balance in the Russian foreign policy, which had drifted too far away from Asia towards Europe. President Yeltsin visited China and India in quick succession as they were regarded as the most important targets in the attempt to restore the balance. The visit laid the foundation for a new relationship with India. During the visit, the problem of ensuring uninterrupted and assured supply of spare parts and equipment for the Armed Forces of India was seriously addressed and the commitment to keep up the flow of supplies was reiterated. But in India, there were still doubts if things would start improving any sooner after the visit, as Moscow was not fully in control of the autonomous regions within the country. President Yeltsin also laid to rest all doubts about Russia honouring its commitment to supply the cryogenic engines to India. The first cryogenic engine arrived in India in September 1998, and the remaining six came at intervals of six months each. The problem of revaluation of the huge debt incurred by India during the Soviet period was sorted out just prior to the visit, on the basis of a give-and-take policy. There was no reduction in the debt stock, but 35 per cent of the debt was agreed to be rescheduled for payment on easy terms. This, in effect, brought down India's debt servicing burden on debts to Russia by 30 per cent. Out of the principal outstanding debt of Rs 31,377 crore (Rs 313.77 billion), Rs 19,643 crore

(Rs 196.43 billion) was to be repaid over the next 12 years at an average rate of interest of 2.4 per cent. The remaining Rs 11,734 crore (Rs 117.34 billion) was rescheduled for repayment over 45 years without any interest burden. India's annual trade plan with Russia came to an end. Therefore, there was to be no oil purchase by India under a trade plan.

There was no question of going back to the old Indo-Soviet economic relationship. The basic parameters of that relationship changed irrevocably. There was going to be no rupee payment for imports from Russia. There was no question of Russia making credit available for India's industrialization to be paid back through exports. There was also going to be no military or other strategic supplies on credit to be paid through exports. All purchases in this regard had to be made in free foreign exchange. Russia agreed to upgrade its relationship with India to a strategic level but there was going to be no special relationship of the past, at least during the period of Yeltsin's presidency. The new relationship was devoid of the geo-political significance of the old Soviet era.

In 1998, Russia faced an economic disaster. In August that year, the rouble was drastically devalued and bankruptcy was declared. A 90-day moratorium on payment due to non-residents was imposed on banks and there was a freezing of the short-term state bond market. As compared to 1992, the total output was reduced to half. The decline in output was greater than that in the US during the Great Depression of 1929–31, when output declined by 35 per cent. The rouble was rendered useless as 85 per cent of the total transactions were taking place in dollars, which totally replaced the rouble in international transactions.

After 1992, Russia decided to embark upon the IMF-prescribed programme of economic development. As a result, the real sector of the economy was starved of liquidity. There was, therefore, a collapse of investment in plants and factories. As investment in research and development dried up, technologies became obsolescent. For the same reason, human capital in the areas of education, health, science and culture also suffered deterioration and degradation. Privatization in the absence of a private sector led to the capture of industries by the personnel of the state apparatus and other non-business entities. This led to asset stripping on a large scale and the consequent transfer of capital to foreign banks. On the social side, pensions and wages, even of military personnel, remained unpaid for years, resulting in all-round demoralization and untold suffering of the common people. One-third of the population fell below the poverty line. The average longevity of the Russians went down significantly. The middle class was virtually wiped out.

The policy prescribed by the IMF did not deliver capitalism as it was intended to do, but in the process, it destroyed the economy and substantially weakened democracy, which was evident from the degradation and rigging of the political institutions in the country. Towards the end of the 1990s, particularly during Yevgeny Primakov's premiership, the government in power agreed on an outline of a new economic policy, according to which the state was to restore order to the budget, and honour all its obligations for payments to its employees, defend property rights, enforce tax payments and clamp down on the shadow economy. It was also intended to lower tax rates, impose partial currency control and print limited amounts of money to pay off wage arrears. The Russian Duma approved this policy, but the IMF was still resisting. It withheld the release of a substantial part of the emergency support it had agreed to provide in July 1998. Governments of the Western countries saw in this eminently reasonable economic policy the beginning of a return to communism. The US government kept away from Russia throughout the period of the crisis and did not bestir itself to arrange a rescue package, and US companies made hardly any investment in the country.

There were, however, some silver linings in the situation. Ordinary Russian citizens displayed a tremendous ability to put up with the ordeal of economic distress. Even during the worst of times, Russian society did not succumb to large-scale violence. In spite of the depredation of the economy perpetrated by domestic vested interests, much of the human and natural resources remained intact. There was also a clarity in the country on not returning to a state-controlled and state-directed economy and on maintaining the basic structure of democracy.

There was an evidence of a turnaround in the Russian economy under President Vladimir Putin's regime during the early years of the 21st century when the rate of growth of the economy reached the impressive figure of 5 to 6 per cent per annum. The size of the economy increased from $200 billion in 1998 to $1.4 trillion in 2008. In 2007, foreign investment crossed $100 billion. During the decade before 2008, per capita income increased by 20 per cent and some 30 million persons were lifted out of poverty.[9] This became possible partly because of the rise in the global oil prices, but mainly due to a nationally designed development strategy. A major factor was the restoration by Putin of national self-esteem after the humiliation of the Yeltsin period.

A major weakness of the Russian economy is that more than 60 per cent of the federal budget revenue comes from oil and gas taxes, and extractive industries contribute two-thirds of the value of exports and a quarter of the GDP.[10] However, in spite of these structural weaknesses, under the leadership of President Putin, Russia was till 2008 making a steady progress towards regaining its mid-1990 position and moving beyond it to emerge as a major economic power, a prospect which, given the potentialities, was well within the realm of possibility.

Unfortunately, before this could be realized, Russia, like other developed countries of Europe, found itself engulfed by the global economic and financial recession of 2008–09. At the peak of the recession in 2009, the growth of its GDP turned negative by 7.82 per cent.[11] The Russian economy recovered the next year and registered a rate of growth of 4.50 per cent. Since then the growth rate, though positive, has been decelerating year after year and stood at 1.32 per cent in 2013.[12] In spite of this, in the post-recession period there was a progressive increase in the overall size of the GDP, crossing the $2 trillion mark (at current prices) in 2012, and a steady growth in the GDP per capita from $8,615.67 in 2009 to $14,611.70 in 2013. Russia was also able to maintain its poverty headcount ratio at around 10 per cent of the population.[13]

During the last year and a half, the Russian economy has come under severe strain under the double jeopardy of falling oil prices and the tightening of sanctions by Western countries. This has triggered capital flight leading to a substantial drop in Russia's net foreign exchange earnings and a decline in the value of the rouble. International financial institutions have predicted slowdown of the Russian economy and rise in inflation.

We should not, however, underestimate the ability of the Russians to get over the current crisis and put the economy back on the trajectory of high growth. Russia is a vast country with rich natural resources and highly trained and skilled manpower. Universal spread of its educational system guarantees constant accretion to this manpower pool. In spite of some degradation of its technology since the 1990s, Russia remains a powerhouse of high technologies and its fundamental science is still considered as one of the best in the world. Moreover, Russia remains the second largest military power in the world, a position it is likely to retain in the foreseeable future.

Relations with Russia are of vital importance to India. This relationship has been time-tested and is based on mutual trust and support of the peoples of the two countries. A large part of the goodwill and friendship of the Russian people, which was cultivated during the period of Indo-Soviet relationship, still survives, though in a dormant form, partly because of the lack of energetic effort by India to revive and draw upon it for nurturing cooperation between the two countries.

India has enjoyed a much higher esteem among the establishment and people of Russia than in the West. The Soviet Union, and later Russia, steadfastly stood by India at several critical junctures of its post-independence history. The Soviet Union always supported India's position on Kashmir, even though it encouraged India to settle the issue with Pakistan and offered its assistance, if requested, to facilitate the process. The perception in Pakistan and among its Western friends, that the Soviet Union could use its veto in the Security Council, came in the way of their reviving the issue in the UN. The Soviet Union stood by India during the Bangladesh crisis in 1971. In the early 1990s, in spite of the tremendous pressure exercised by the Clinton administration, Russia adhered to the core part of its agreement with India for the delivery of the cryogenic engines to ISRO as per the original schedule. Russia refused to participate in sanctions against India following the latter's nuclear explosion in 1998. In fact, the same year, it signed a 10-year agreement with India on military and technological cooperation. It also reiterated its decision, taken in 1988, to supply two nuclear reactors for the Kudankulam nuclear plant. It defended its decision to do so on the ground that the agreement reached with India pre-dated the establishment of the NSG, which bars the transfer of nuclear equipment and technology to non-members of the NPT that do not accept full-scope safeguards. It continued uninterrupted the supply of equipment and spare parts for India's Armed Forces even in the midst of chaos, disorder and disruption in the Soviet Union.

In this connection, it is also important to note that Russia has till recently been the only major country engaged in global arms trade, which, as a matter of policy, did not supply arms to Pakistan. This was a vivid demonstration of its sensitivity to India's security interests. Some of the recent developments, particularly the current strain on its economy and India's large-scale acquisition of military supplies from the US, have, however compelled Russia to look for other lucrative markets for arms supply. Among these, Pakistan offers one of the best prospects. Russia, therefore, decided in mid-2014 to sell its Mi-35 helicopters to Pakistan. It is difficult to predict at this stage whether it marks a beginning of a large scale military engagement between Russia and Pakistan. For the present, this seems to be unlikely because of the divergences of a fundamental nature in the positions of the two countries on major global and regional issues. But a lot will depend upon the future evolution of Indo-Russian relations.

With the exception of China to a limited extent, India is the only country with which the Soviet Union, and later Russia, has shared technologies in critical sectors. Technology on a fairly large scale was transferred for establishing heavy and basic industries in India during the Soviet period. Recently, Russia has transferred or agreed to transfer key strategic technologies in the defence sector, mainly through the joint development and co-production of weapon systems. In this connection, the example of the Brahmos missiles, which are already being produced and have been deployed, readily comes to mind. In the late 1980s, the Soviet Union had leased a nuclear-powered submarine to India, which helped in capacity building in India for designing and operating such submarines. Russia has collaborated with India in a very significant way in the building and launching of the nuclear-powered submarine, Arihant. There is also joint collaboration for licensed production in India of SU-30 aircraft and T-90 battle tanks. During President Medvedev's visit to India in December 2010, deals were concluded for the joint development of Fifth Generation Fighter Aircraft and Multi-Role Transport Aircraft. Both of these involve the transfer of advanced sensitive technologies to India. The agreements by Russia for the supply of nuclear reactors also provide for the transfer of technology and the progressive indigenization of the reactors.

Russia is today the most important and reliable defence partner of India. The Prime Minister of India stated during President Putin's recent visit to India that 'even as India's options have increased today, Russia will remain the most important defence partner'.[14] During this visit, Russia, among others, offered to fully manufacture in India one of its most advanced helicopters with the possibility of India exporting the product to third countries. For the Navy, India took the delivery of Russian built frigate, Trikand, in 2013. Another significant event was the handing over to India of the new aircraft carrier INS Vikramaditya. In his press briefing on 11 December 2014, the Indian Prime Minister, while releasing the Joint Statement signed between the two leaders, declared that INS Vikramaditya 'sails over seas as a great symbol of our defence cooperation' with Russia.[15]

India and Russia elevated their bilateral relationship to the level of Strategic Partnership in the Declaration issued during President Putin's visit to India in October 2000, and decided to hold Annual Summit meetings to provide guidelines and perspective for the development of this Partnership. The relationship was upgraded to Special and Privileged Strategic Partnership during President Dmitry Medvedev's visit to India in December 2010. There is on the ground a comprehensive institutional framework for conducting the bilateral relationship between the two countries. Their Heads of State/Government have been meeting at annual summits for the last 15 years. In addition, they have the occasion of meeting and exchanging views on strategic and other bilateral issues on the sidelines of the gatherings of Heads of State/Government of the SCO, BRICS, and G-20. The foreign ministers meet every year at the forum of the IRC consisting of India, China and Russia. The Indo-Russian Inter-Governmental Commission on Trade, Economic, Scientific, Technological and Cultural Cooperation, co-chaired by the external affairs minister of India and the deputy prime minister of Russia, provides guidelines and outlines of a long-term vision for bilateral economic, scientific and cultural cooperation. It has some 10 working groups dealing with specific areas like energy, petroleum, science and technology, information technology, environmental and natural resources. The Inter-Governmental Commission on Military Technical Cooperation, chaired by the defence ministers of the two countries, provides the requisite momentum and impetus to bilateral relations in the military field. Russia is the only country with which India has established such a high-level consultative mechanism in the defence field. There are also joint fora for the nuclear, space, energy and petroleum agencies of the two countries to discuss scientific collaboration and thrash out agreements on important projects and programmes. The two countries have an Integrated Long-Term Programme of Cooperation in Science and Technology. This programme has been extended from time to time. During President Medvedev's visit to India in December 2010, it was extended up to 2020. The agenda for the strategic partnership between the two countries is being continuously widened, depending upon the need to reach an understanding or forge common positions on evolving strategic issues.

There is a striking convergence of the positions of the two countries on a number of strategic issues. On the nuclear issue, both India and Russia have traditionally been in favour of the international community making a systematic and progressive effort to reduce nuclear weapons globally with the ultimate goal of eliminating them.[16] However, in the context of the recent revival of cold war between Russia and Western powers, Russia, as much as the US, seems to have put nuclear disarmament and arms control on the back burner. It is, therefore, not surprising that the latest Summit Level Joint Statement between India and Russia is conspicuously silent on this issue. On non-proliferation, the Russian position is determined by the perception of its interest as a major nuclear weapon power. Russia sees its interest in preserving the existing nuclear order and attaches great importance to ensuring non-proliferation of nuclear weapons. It was among the first to sign the CTBT. Moreover, Russia sees itself as a committed member of the NSG, the MTCR and the Australia Club, all of which are intended to prevent the proliferation of weapons of mass destruction. After the 1998 nuclear explosions by India and Pakistan, Russia joined the P5 (the five permanent members of the UN Security Council) to call upon India and Pakistan to observe a moratorium on nuclear testing, unconditionally sign the CTBT and accede to the NPT. At the same time, Russia showed a great degree of pragmatism and sensitivity to India's security requirements. As mentioned previously, it did not join the Western countries in applying sanctions against India, continued uninterrupted, the supply of military equipment and spares to India and adhered to the commitment to supply cryogenic engines for India's space programme. Russia appreciated the declaration by India of a voluntary moratorium on nuclear testing and the Government of India's effort to develop a broad national consensus for signing the CTBT. In a speech made by him in Mumbai on 5 October 2000 to a gathering of nuclear scientists, President Putin stated that he would like to see India participate in the CTBT but at the same time recognized that India's decision should be based on its strategic vision, national interest and needs of the people.

Russia fully backed the US move in the NSG to obtain a waiver for India from its restrictions on the supply of nuclear material, equipment and technology to non-member countries. Now that India has indicated its intention to join these groups, Russia has 'expressed readiness to assist and promote a discussion and positive decision in the NSG on India's full membership in the NSG'.[17] Russia 'also took into positive consideration India's interest in full membership in MTCR and the Wassenaar Arrangement'.[18]

However, on an important disarmament issue, that is, the US decision to develop and deploy a global BMD system, India's attitude has been somewhat ambivalent, which in recent years, has cast a shadow on the Indo-Russian relationship. In the Joint Statement issued by President Putin and the then Prime Minister Atal Bihari Vajpayee, at the end of the Russian President's visit to India in 2000, 'both sides stressed the need for full implementation, in good faith, of existing bilateral and multilateral arms control treaties, including the Anti-Ballistic Missile (ABM) Treaty'.[19] Thus, India, along with Russia, adopted a clear-cut position against President Bush's publicly declared intention to withdraw from this treaty in order to pave the ground for launching a BMD system. But subsequently, when the system was formally launched by him, the then Indian Foreign Minister Jaswant Singh wholeheartedly welcomed it in the Indian Parliament. The UPA government, both by its silence on this issue and by agreeing to the provision in the Indo-US Defence Framework, signed on 28 June 2005, to 'expand collaboration relating to missile defence', continued the policy of the NDA government. Since Russia regards the development and deployment of BMD as the greatest threat to its security, it has been irked by India's ambivalence on this issue.

In the Putin–Vajpayee Joint Statement of 5 October 2000, India and Russia agreed that they 'would work together and with others towards a multipolar world based on sovereign equality of all states, territorial integrity and non-interference in their internal affairs as the only sustainable basis for the emergence of a new, equitable and just international order'.[20] The two sides also 'expressed their determined opposition to unilateral use or threat of use of force in violation of the UN Charter and intervention in the internal affairs of other states, including under the plea of humanitarian assistance'.[21] This statement was clearly directed against US unilateralism and its recourse to use of force against other countries without being authorized by the UN Security Council. It is significant that the joint statements issued since 2010, while continuing to oppose use of force or economic sanctions without the authorization of the Security Council, have not been as explicit on this issue as before. This may be because of the distinct lurch in the Indian foreign policy towards the US, following the Indo-US Nuclear Deal.

Since the late 1990s, there has been frequent speculation regarding the possibility of the formation of a trilateral alliance consisting of Russia, China and India. This idea gathered momentum after its endorsement by Primakov, the then Russian prime minister, during his visit to India in December 1998. In reply to a leading question by a correspondent he said, 'If we succeed in establishing a triangle, it would be very good'. Since then, this idea has not been espoused by any Russian statesman nor has it figured in any talks held between the leaders of India and Russia or in any statement issued by them. As a matter of fact, in the Strategic Partnership Agreement between India and Russia of 3 October 2000, it is specifically stated: 'The strategic partnership between the sides is not directed against any other state or group of states and does not need to create a military political alliance'.[22]

Indeed, these three countries have recently come together on the common platforms of SCO, BRICS and IRC, but none of these three groupings are in the nature of a military alliance, let alone being directed against the US. Their sole purpose is to provide platforms to formulate common positions on global issues and to undertake schemes of mutual cooperation. The military exercises undertaken under the aegis of the SCO have not been directed against the US or any other power outside the organization. They are mainly intended to make preparations to meet emergency humanitarian situations and to learn from each other's experience. In any case, India has not participated in these military exercises. The question of India, China and Russia forming a strategic triangle against the US does not arise, mainly because the relationship of each of them with the US is more important than their relationship with each other. By emphasizing multipolarity, multilateralism under the UN and the supremacy of international law in the declarations adopted at these fora, the intention of the member countries is to create space for themselves in the international arena in the context of the proclivity of the US to resort to unilateralism and interfere in the internal affairs of other countries in violation of international law.

That India finds these platforms of strategic value is reflected, among others, in the fact that it has sought the elevation of its status in the SCO from an observer to a full member. In the Medvedev–Manmohan Singh Joint Statement, 'the Russian Federation agreed to make efforts along with other SCO members to accelerate the process of India's entry into the Organisation'.[23] This assurance has been reiterated in subsequent Joint Statements. India this year became a full-fledged member of the SCO. In these Joint Statements, the two sides have also noted the successful interaction between India, Russia and China in the IRC format and the importance of this regional arrangement in fostering dialogue and cooperation on global and regional issues between these three major states and great civilizations of the region.

On the issue of terrorism, the Russian position is closer to India's standpoint and more in unison with its interest than that of the US and other Western countries. This is partly because both India and Russia are victims of terrorism emanating from the same source and both these countries are under pressure to preserve the unity and integrity of their pluralistic societies against the onslaught of both internal and external forces. The common position of the two countries on terrorism as reflected in their summit-level Joint Statements issued since October 2000, have the following elements. First, they have condemned 'terrorism and extremism in all its forms, irrespective of political, philosophical, ideological, religious, ethnic, racial or any other consideration that may be invoked to justify them'. Second, the two sides have condemned 'states that aid, abet and directly support cross-border and international terrorism'.[24] In the Joint Statement of October 2000, the two sides also:

> noted with concern the growth of the force of religious extremism in their neighbourhood and the objective of these forces, with official support, to destabilize the entire region. They called upon these authorities to contain and eliminate these forces and return to the path of peace and moderation.[25]

These points in the Joint Statements have been clearly addressed to Pakistan. They have not figured in the common position on the issues relating to terrorism forged with the US and its Western allies. However, in the context of the recent signs of thaw in the relationships between Russia and Pakistan, these elements find no place in the Joint Statement issued at the end of President Putin's last visit to India.

On yet another issue of strategic interest to India, that is, its candidature for the permanent membership of the UN Security Council, Russia has extended to India its categorical and unwavering support. In the Putin–Vajpayee Joint Statement of October 2000, the Russian Federation 'reiterated that it supports India . . . as a strong and appropriate candidate of the expanded Security Council'.[26] Since then, this support has been reiterated several times at the highest political level, including in the summit-level Joint Statements issued since then.

India and Russia have achieved a very high level of cooperation in peaceful uses of nuclear energy. They have to their credit notable achievement in this field, including collaborative research and development and the construction and operation of a number of nuclear power plants with Russian assistance. An important stage in this cooperation was reached with the signing in 2008 of an agreement between the two countries on cooperation for the construction of additional nuclear power plants at Kudankulam and at new sites in India. On 12 March 2010, the two countries signed the Roadmap for the serial construction in India of Russian-designed nuclear power plants. A very important stage in cooperation in this field is the signing in New Delhi on 11 December 2014 of the 'Strategic Vision for Strengthening Cooperation in Peaceful Uses of Atomic Energy between the Republic of India and the Russian Federation'. This document highlights the achievements of cooperation so far and gives a profile of activities planned for the near future. In this document, the two sides expressed satisfaction that Unit-1 of the Kudankulam Nuclear Power Plant (KKNPP) 'achieved full rated power in July 2014'. They agreed to 'take necessary steps to expedite

[the] commissioning of Unit-2 of KNPP'. They also 'welcomed the entry into force of the General Framework Agreement' for Units 3 and 4, and agreed to strive to 'complete the construction and commissioning of not less than 12 units in the next two decades'. Towards this objective, India agreed to 'expeditiously identify a second site, in addition to Kudankulam'. They did not rule out the possibility of the 'construction of further [more than 12 units] Russian-designed nuclear power plants in India'.[27]

Some of the distinguishing features of Indo-Russian cooperation in the field of nuclear energy, incorporated in the document and generally not figuring in India's civil nuclear cooperation with any other country are:

- manufacture in India of both main equipment and spares for Russian designed nuclear power plants;
- exploring opportunity for 'sourcing materials, equipment and services from Indian industry for the construction' of such power plants in third countries;
- fabrication in India of the nuclear fuel assemblies to be used in these power plants;
- examining the 'possibility of technical cooperation in mining activities' within Russian territory;
- collaborating in exploration and mining activities in third countries;
- developing a 'framework for collaboration in the field of radioactive waste management';
- and elaborating possible approaches to cooperation in spent fuel management.[28]

Finally, the two sides have underlined their 'desire for active cooperation in the scientific and technical [field] . . . and radiation technologies'. This will include joint research in fast reactors, thorium fuel cycle, high current protons, and controlled thermo-nuclear fusion.[29] To monitor the implementation of the entire range of activities outlined in this document, they have established a Coordination Committee for cooperation in the peaceful uses of nuclear energy.

It is clear from this seminal document that cooperation between the two countries in the nuclear energy field is not only one of the largest between any two countries in this world, but also unique in several ways.

In areas other than nuclear energy, Russia has for a long time been contributing to India's energy security by the supply of oil and gas and through collaboration for exploration and production in this field. By far, the most important venture in this area has been the investment by India of approximately $2.7 billion in the Sakhalin-1 offshore oil exploration project and the purchase of Russia's Imperial Energy Company for $2.5 billion. Under the Sakhalin-I project, over 1 million tons of oil is supplied to India annually. India has, for the last few years, been regularly showing interest in equity participation through the ONGC (Oil and Natural Gas Corporation Limited) Videsh in the exploration and production of new projects in Siberia, Russia's Far East and the Arctic Shelf.

There is already a long-term agreement signed in 2012 between Gazporm Group of Russia and GAIL of India, providing for the delivery of 2.5 million tons of liquefied natural gas per year for a period of 20 years starting from 2017. Since the historic announcement by Russia in 2014 of its plan to construct a pipeline for the supply of massive quantity of natural gas to China, India has shown interest in collaborating with Russia to build a gas pipeline between the two countries. Russia has not shown much interest in it mainly because of considerations related to its feasibility. In a pre-Summit media interview on 9 December 2014, President Putin indicated the Russian position thus: 'For the time being, Russian liquefied natural gas transportation seems to be the best choice'.[30] However, in the Joint Statement issued after the Summit on 11 December, the two sides agreed to 'study the possibilities of building a hydro-carbon pipeline system connecting the Russian Federation with India'.[31]

The Joint Statement has also addressed the frequent Indian request for greater participation in oil exploration and production in Russia by agreeing upon the following formulation: 'It is expected that Indian companies will strongly participate in projects related to new oil and gas fields in the territory of the Russian Federation'.[32] The other areas of cooperation in the energy field agreed upon during President Putin's visit, were greater participation in each other's power generation projects, supply of equipment, technology for enhanced oil recoveries and extraction of coal.

In 1987, India and Russia signed 'An Integrated Long Term Programme for Cooperation in Science & Technology', under which more than 500 joint projects have been taken up and several of them successfully implemented. In the Joint Statement issued during President Putin's visit to India on 11 December 2014, it was decided to 'increase collaboration in joint design, development, manufacturing and marketing of technology-driven products and scientific interaction between the two countries ... [S]uch cooperation will extend to space application, defence technology, aviation, new materials, communication and information technology'.[33] They put special emphasis on innovation, high technology sectors and their commercial application. For this purpose, their bilateral collaboration will cover such frontier areas as environmental science, energy security, alternative sources of energy, nano-technology, bio-energy, biotechnology, affordable diagnosing equipment for healthcare and agriculture, horticulture biotechnology and rare earth mineral mining, development and research.

In recent years, Russia has assisted India in the Chandrayaan-2 Joint Indo-Russian Lunar Mission, aimed at exploring lunar soil at a distance as far away from the landing site as possible, to confirm the presence of water. In 2011, India successfully launched the YouthSat jointly built with Russia. Another major area of space cooperation has been India's participation in Russia's GLONASS Satellite Navigation Programme which gives Indian agencies access to high-precision navigation signals for both military and civilian purposes. In the Joint Statement issued at the end of President Putin's last official visit to India on 11 December 2014, the two countries recognized the 'limitless opportunities for bilateral cooperation in outer space'. To this end, the space agencies of the two countries would engage more actively in 'space technology applications, space transportation, satellite navigation, space science and planetary exploration'.[34]

A major weakness in the relations between the two countries is the relatively low level of trade exchanges and investment flows. In modern times, a strategic bilateral relationship between major powers cannot be sustained without its having a significant economic content. In fact, more often than not, it is the economic content that vests the bilateral relationship with its strategic character. Economic exchanges between India and Russia remain far below their potential. Both India's exports to Russia and the total trade between the two countries declined dramatically, by more than 50 per cent, between the years 1991–92 and 1992–93. The decade of the 1990s saw a moderate increase in the two-way trade. The trade in 1999–2000 was marginally higher than that in 1991–92. In 1999–2000, India's exports reached the level of Rs 4,108 crore (Rs 41.08 billion) and the value of total trade was Rs 6,808 crore (Rs 68.08 billion).[35] There has been further growth in the two-way trade during the past decade and a half, reaching a level of approximately $6.88 billion in 2012.[36] However, the rate of increase has been much lower than that in India's trade with its other major trading partners. In fact, there was a decline in the total trade volume to $6 billion in 2013.[37] In 2009, the two countries set the target for the value of bilateral trade to reach $20 billion by 2015 and agreed to implement a set of measures to achieve this target. An increase in the two-way flow of investment, undertaking of joint projects and joint collaboration for the development of innovative technologies in the civilian sector were the measures announced for propelling the trade between the two countries to new heights.

Going by the recent trend, the achievement of this target appears to be beyond the realm of possibility. In spite of this, during President Putin's last visit to India, the leader of the two countries decided to pre-empt the 2015 target and set a target of bilateral trade turnover of goods and services at $30 billion by the year 2025.[38] They expect the level of mutual investment by then to be over $15 billion each way.[39] Expansion of two-way investment will no doubt assist in the realization of the newly set trade target. At the same time, it will be necessary to accelerate cooperation in wider sectors of the economies of the two countries in order to generate the surpluses to be traded. On the latter point, President Putin, in his press conference before the release of the Joint Statement, sounded quite optimistic. He made it a point to mention the progress made in initiating and implementing major joint projects. The construction of the world's largest butyl rubber producing plant in Gujarat with Russian assistance would be completed very soon. Another joint venture project, a bulldozer equipment assembly plant, would soon reach design capacity. Russia had offered to produce Sukhoi Superjet 100 and MC-21 airplanes in India. Progress had also been made in promoting direct trade in diamonds between the two countries. This has immense possibilities because the Russian company Alrosa is currently the largest diamond producer in the world, while India is the leading country in diamond processing.

In the Joint Statement, the two leaders also identified areas of mutual investment in the two countries. In India, the emphasis will be on promoting Russian investment in major infrastructure projects, telecommunications, power and roads. India's investments in Russia will be in industrial parks, technology platforms, pharmaceuticals, fertilizer, coal and energy. In this connection, the two leaders welcomed the initiative of a direct investment fund of $2 billion between Rosnano of Russia and suitable Indian investment partners for the implementation of high-technology projects.

A distinguishing feature of the latest Joint Statement is the call given by the leaders to private companies of the two countries to expedite the implementation of joint projects undertaken by them. A number of very important commercial contracts between Indian companies including Tatas and Essar and their Russian counterparts, both from the public and private sectors, were signed during President Putin's visit. A conscious effort to involve the private sector in economic cooperation between the two countries is a recognition of the role it is playing in the respective economies.

A decision of far-reaching implications taken during President Putin's visit was to 'encourage payment in national currencies for bilateral trade'.[40] A Working Group has been established for this purpose which will make recommendations on eliminating the existing barriers and stimulating transactions in national currencies. This is important for Russia because of the draw-down on its foreign exchange reserve due to the sanctions imposed by Western countries. This will also help India in judicious use of its foreign exchange earnings. In the process, it would strengthen both the rouble and the rupee, and together with China's initiatives for conducting trade with its major trading partners in its national currency, yuan, will go some way towards reducing the importance of the dollar as the international reserve currency.

Notes

* An earlier, shorter version of this chapter was published in Mainstream Weekly, 22 September 2012.

1. Arun Mohanty, 'Indo-Russian Strategic Partnership: A Reality Check', *Mainstream*, Volume 49, No. 16 (2011). *SIPRI Yearbook 2014* states 'Russia is still India's largest supplier of weapons amounting to 75 percent of Indian military's imports between 2009-2013'. Stockholm International Peace Research Institute (SIPRI), *SIPRI Yearbook 2014: Armaments, Disarmament and International Security* (Oxford: Oxford University Press, 2015).
2. Government of India, *Economic Survey of India, 1974–75 to 1990–1991* (New Delhi: Economic Division, Ministry of Finance).
3. The New Delhi Declaration was signed by the Indian Prime Minister Rajiv Gandhi and the Soviet General Secretary Mikhail Gorbachev during the latter's visit to India in November 1986.
4. Quoted from the New Delhi Declaration.
5. Ibid.
6. Ibid.
7. Mikhail Gorbachev, 'Address to the Council of Europe' (Strasbourg, 6 July 1989).
8. Government of India, *Economic Survey of India, 1990–2000* (New Delhi: Economic Division, Ministry of Finance).
9. Vladimir Radyuhin, 'Oil Revenues: Bonanza for Russia', *The Hindu*, 4 August 2008.

10. Ibid.
11. Data taken from http://data.worldbank.org (accessed on 28 April 2015).
12. Ibid.
13. Ibid.
14. Prime Minister's Office, 'PM's Media Statement During the Official Visit of the President of Russian Federation to India' (Government of India, 11 December 2014).
15. Ibid.
16. Joint Statement Issued by the Governments of India and Russia on the Occasion of President Vladimir Putin's Visit to India (Ministry of External Affairs, Government of India, New Delhi, 5 October 2000).
17. Joint Statement Issued by the Governments of India and Russia on the occasion of President Dmitry Medvedev's Visit to India (Ministry of External Affairs, Government of India, New Delhi, 21 December 2010). This has been reiterated in subsequent Joint Statements at the Summit level.
18. Ibid.
19. Institute for Defence Studies and Analyses (IDSA), *Strategic Digest*, Volume xxx, No. 10, New Delhi (October 2000) 1455–57.
20. Ibid.
21. Ibid.
22. Ministry of External Affairs, 'Declaration on Strategic Partnership between the Republic of India and the Russian Federation' (3 October 2000), http://mea.gov.in/Images/pdf/DeclerationStrategicPartnership.pdf (accessed on 28 April 2015).
23. Joint Statement Issued by the Governments of India and Russia on the occasion of President Dmitry Medvedev's Visit to India.
24. Joint Statement Issued by the Governments of India and Russia on the Occasion of President Vladimir Putin's Visit to India.
25. Ibid.
26. Institute for Defence Studies and Analyses (IDSA), *Strategic Digest*, Volume xxx, No. 10, New Delhi (October 2000) 1455–57.
27. Ministry of External Affairs, 'Strategic Vision for Strengthening Cooperation in Peaceful Uses of Atomic Energy between the Republic of India and the Russian Federation' (11 December 2014), http://pib.nic.in/newsite/PrintRelease.aspx?relid=113165 (accessed on 28 April 2015).
28. Ibid.
29. Ibid.
30. *Hindustan Times*, '"Good to help Pak Fight Terror": Putin', 10 December 2014.
31. Ministry of External Affairs, '"Druzhba-Dosti: A Vision for Strengthening the Indian-Russian Partnership over the Next Decade"—Joint Statement during the Visit of President of the Russian Federation to India' (Government of India, 11 December 2014).
32. Ibid.

33. Ibid.
34. Ibid.
35. Government of India, *Economic Survey of India, 1999–2000* (New Delhi: Economic Division, Ministry of Finance).
36. Calculated from data taken from International Monetary Fund, Direction of Trade Statistics database, http://elibrary-data.imf.org/ (accessed on 8 April 2015).
37. Ibid.
38. Ministry of External Affairs, 'Druzhba-Dosti'.
39. Ibid.
40. Ibid.

NINE India and China

An Uneasy but Critically Important Relationship

Historical Background

India has always attached great importance to its relations with China, not only because of the old historical legacies that bind the two countries together, but also because of China's strategic importance for India as its biggest and the most powerful neighbour. India, therefore, assiduously cultivated its ties with China after the Communist Revolution of 1949. One of the great visions of Jawaharlal Nehru was to enlist China's support and collaboration for building a stable and peaceful world based on adherence to the rule of international law, and free from the rivalry of the major powers for supremacy and from the burden of armament. It was, therefore, not surprising that India was the first non-Communist country after Burma, to recognize the People's Republic of China. India also led the movement for ending the isolation of the new China in international politics and restoring to it the Chinese membership of the UN.

One of the most disappointing experiences of newly independent India and its leader Jawaharlal Nehru was the fast deterioration in Sino-Indian relations beginning from the late 1950s. Though this was brought about by a variety of factors, the immediate trigger was developments in Tibet, starting from the Chinese invasion and reoccupation of Tibet in 1950. For maintaining amity in Sino Indian relations, which was essential for realizing Nehru's vision of the world as well as out of practical considerations, India reconciled itself to the fait accompli presented by the Chinese presence in Tibet and gave up almost all its privileges in the region inherited from the colonial past. This was done through the 1954 Agreement on Border Trade[1] which also formally recognized China's sovereignty over the Autonomous Region of Tibet and incorporated the famous Panchsheel or the Five Principles of Peaceful Coexistence. Following the Tibetan uprising in 1959 and its cruel suppression by the Chinese, the Dalai Lama fled Tibet, and sought and was given asylum in India. This was followed by the exodus of thousands of Tibetans who were also given asylum and subsequently settled down in India. The presence and activities of the Dalai Lama and his followers in India became a permanent source of tension simmering under the surface in the relations between the two countries.

The problem arising out of the Tibetan uprising was compounded by the eruption at about the same time of the border problem between the two countries. The Indo-Chinese border on the eastern side of India became a source of friction after the Chinese refusal to accept the McMahon Line delineating the border in this sector. Another major controversy relating to the border surfaced with the announcement by China in September 1957, of the completion of a road across the Aksai Chin plateau in the western sector, which India regarded as a part of its territory. During his visit to India in 1954, Zhou Enlai, the then Chinese prime minister, had unofficially proposed that the border problem between the two countries should be resolved by China relinquishing its claim in the east in exchange for India dropping its claim in the west. Nehru rejected this proposal in the belief that the huge chunk of territory occupied and claimed by China in the west was part of India's sovereign territory from which China must withdraw. This was followed by a bitter propaganda campaign unleashed by China against India, and personally, against Nehru. Nehru was shocked by China's attribution to him of hostile intentions in spite of the efforts made by him to befriend it, by China's refusal to recognize the McMahon Line, by its use of military force to occupy territory in the western sector and by its ruthless suppression of the Tibetan uprising. He, therefore, decided to follow a hard-line border policy. This led to skirmishes along the border, culminating in the Chinese invasion of India in 1962.

India's defeat in the 1962 War left a deep and enduring impact on its domestic politics, its policy towards China and towards other major powers of the world. The Indian Parliament passed a resolution enjoining upon the Indian government to recover every inch of the territory occupied by China, if necessary by the use of force. Much closer attention was paid to the building of India's military capabilities and the related infrastructure in the border area to meet future challenges from China. In its defence planning, India was required thereafter to make contingent military provisions for coping, in the event of a war with Pakistan, with a two-pronged threat, one emanating from Pakistan and the other from China.

The boundary problem remained a stumbling block in the development of relations between the two countries till almost the middle of the 1970s. The severance of the relations between China and the Soviet Union during the second half of the 1960s and the latter's general support for India also contributed to the deterioration of Sino-Indian relations. This coincided with Pakistan turning towards China after the Indo-Pakistan War of 1965, when the US stopped arms supplies to both the warring powers, and China's positive and prompt response culminating in the two countries forging a special relationship that endures till today.

China has since emerged as the largest source of military supplies and assistance for military capacity building for Pakistan. Between 2009 and 2013, Pakistan received 47 per cent of the total volume of the Chinese arms exports.[2] This has helped Pakistan in a major way to maintain near-parity with India in conventional arms. It is now well-documented that China transferred equipment and technology and provided scientific expertise for Pakistan's nuclear and ballistic missile programmes throughout the 1980s and 1990s.[3] Going by newspaper stories and published research findings, China provided the design for Pakistan's nuclear weapons and also carried out tests in its territory to verify their reliability. A significant development in this regard was the supply of 34 short-range M-11 missiles by China in 1992. China has built two nuclear reactors at Chasma in Pakistan and is currently moving forward with plans for building two additional nuclear reactors at the same site. It also built a turnkey ballistic missile manufacturing facility near Rawalpindi and helped Pakistan develop the 750 km-range solid fuelled Shaheen-I missile. Moreover, the Chinese JF-17 Thunder fighter aircraft is under serial production in Pakistan. China also plans to provide Pakistan with J-10 medium-role combat aircraft. China's other recent sales of weapons to Pakistan include F-22P frigates with helicopters, K-8 Jet trainers, T-85 tanks and F-7 aircrafts.[4] Pakistan placed an order for eight F22P frigates from China out of which four were delivered in 2009. Pakistan is also the recipient of anti-ship cruise missiles as well as submarines from China. China is helping Pakistan develop a deep sea port at the naval base Gwadar. It financed 80 per cent of this $250 million project in its first phase and is reportedly funding most of the second phase. It is speculated that China will use it for the berthing of its warship and as a vantage point for exercising influence and observation of military activities in the nearby Indian Ocean and the Gulf region.

China has extended its support to Pakistan in its dispute with India on Kashmir. On a few occasions of conflict between India and Pakistan, China has even held out an indirect threat to intervene on behalf of Pakistan. It has also supported India's other neighbours in their disputes with India and joined their chorus of protests against India's alleged hegemonic intentions in South Asia.

The principal motive behind China's assistance to Pakistan for maintaining military parity with India and behind military supplies to India's other neighbours, particularly Bangladesh, Sri Lanka and Nepal, is to undermine India's position in its neighbourhood and to prevent India from emerging as a rival Asian power. In its military assistance to Pakistan and in seeking access to military facilities there, China is also motivated by its desire of using Pakistan's geo-strategic position to reach out to West and Central Asia, where China has crucial interests at stake. In the process, China has been instrumental in placing Pakistan in a position to pose by far the most serious, direct and immediate threat to India's security.

In a major shift of India's policy towards China, the then Prime Minister Indira Gandhi took the initiative in 1975 to order India's Tibetan Special Frontier Force to draw back at least 10 kilometres from their position along the Indo-Chinese border and also despatched an Indian ambassador to China in July 1976, thereby restoring the diplomatic relationship to the ambassadorial level some 15 years after it was downgraded in 1961. When Indira Gandhi came to power again in 1980, the Chinese Foreign Minister Huang Hua visited India in June 1981, when the two sides agreed to resume talks on the border issue at the level of vice ministers annually by rotation in their capitals.

The next major initiative for improving Sino-Indian relations was taken in 1988 by the then Prime Minister Rajiv Gandhi who, in the midst of the intensified tension prevailing along the eastern sector of the border due to the military confrontation in the Sumdorung Chu Valley, decided to pay a visit to China in an attempt to normalize the relations between the two countries. This visit took place 34 years after the last visit by an Indian prime minister to China, that is, by Jawaharlal Nehru in 1954. By then, the Chinese political scene had undergone a drastic transformation. The Secretary General of the Chinese Communist Party, Deng Xiaoping, who became the supreme leader soon after the death of Mao Zedong, ushered in an era of pragmatism and openness in Chinese society, putting aside the earlier policy of pursuing ideological militancy. He needed the breathing space for attaining the goal of economic modernization that he had set before the nation. During Rajiv Gandhi's visit, the two sides agreed to set up a joint working group at the vice-ministerial level to meet annually in order to accelerate the search for a settlement of the border issue.

Since Rajiv Gandhi's visit, both China and India have made serious efforts to impart to their relationship an active and high profile. The most conspicuous manifestation of this has been the regular visits of the heads of government of the two countries to each other. Prime Minister Li Peng visited India in December 1991. President R. Venkataraman's visit to China in 1992 was followed by the visit of Prime Minister Narasimha Rao in 1993. Jiang Zemin, the paramount Chinese leader, came to India in 1996 and Prime Minister Atal Bihari Vajpayee visited China in 2003. This was followed by Prime Minister Wen Jiabao's visit to India in 2005 and President Hu Jintao's visit in 2006. Since then, the visits to each other by the heads of government of the two countries have become quite frequent. In addition, they meet at the summit gatherings of groups like G-20, BRICS and SCO.

Prime Minister Manmohan Singh visited China in January 2008 when a joint document entitled 'A Shared Vision for the 21st Century' was issued.[5] During the Chinese Premier Li Keqiang's visit to India in May 2013, the two sides issued a Joint Statement and signed several agreements and MoUs. After assuming the post of Prime Ministership, Li Keqiang made India the first destination of his foreign visit. During Prime Minister Manmohan Singh's visit to China in 2013, the two sides released a Joint Statement entitled 'A Vision for Future Development of India-China Strategic and Cooperative Partnership'.[6] The Vice President of India visited China to participate in a function on 28 June 2014, to commemorate the 60th anniversary of Panchsheel. During this visit he had meetings with top Chinese leaders to discuss issues of mutual interest and three agreements between the two countries were signed. The new Chinese President Xi Jinping visited India from 17 to 19 September 2014 at the end of which a Joint Statement by the two sides was issued. In this Joint Statement, the two sides, among others 'agreed upon regular visits at the level of Heads of State/Government'.[7]

These high-level visits and exchanges at other levels have no doubt resulted in significant improvements in the relations between the two countries. On the border issue, an agreement was signed during Narasimha Rao's visit to Maintain Peace and Tranquility along the Line of Actual Control (LAC). This was reinforced by an Agreement on Confidence Building Measures in the military field along the LAC. In 2001, measures were initiated to exchange maps that would clarify the LAC. During Atal Bihari Vajpayee's visit, it was decided to raise the level of the border talks to the political representatives of the leaders of the two countries. During this visit, China gave an indication of a movement towards recognizing Sikkim as a part of India, which it had not done since Sikkim merged with the Indian Union in 1975. It was also decided to open the traditional route between India and Tibet via the Nathu La for border trade. In order to resolve problems relating to border incidents, army commanders of the two countries have been meeting regularly at predetermined places in the border areas. In December 1992, China opened its Consulate General in Mumbai and India opened its Consulate General in Shanghai.

During the April 2005 visit of Premier Wen Jiabao, the two sides established Strategic and Cooperative Partnership for Peace and Prosperity. They also signed an 'Agreement on Political Parameters and Guiding Principles' for solving the border question. This sought to signal progress in the first phase of the Special Representatives' Talks. By now some 40 dialogue mechanisms covering diverse subjects of bilateral, regional and international issues, are operational under the Strategic and Cooperative Partnership. A mechanism called Strategic Economic Dialogue (SED) has been created and meetings are taking place under it every year. So far three meetings have taken place under it and the fourth is planned in 2015. Five Working Groups covering such subjects as policy coordination, infrastructure, energy, environmental protection and high technology are meeting under the SED and a number of MoUs have been signed reflecting the outcome of the discussions in these Groups. In the Joint Statement issued at the end of President Xi's visit to India, the SED was assigned to look into new areas such as industrial development, clean energy and sustainable urbanization. The two sides have also set up an India–China CEO Forum, the first meeting of which took place during Premier Li Keqiang's s visit to India.

Peace and tranquillity generally reign in the border areas of the two countries. Occasional border intrusions still take place, but they are more in the nature of asserting claims on the disputed territories under the other party's occupation than an indication of the intention to provoke a conflict. The two sides view these intrusions in the proper perspective and do not allow them to mar the trend of continuing normalization of relations. The incursions are followed by withdrawal to previously held positions. Till recently, protests against such intrusions were few and far between and a conscious effort used to be made not to elevate them to the level of formal diplomatic démarches.

A jarring note in the relationship between the two countries was introduced following the Pokhran-II nuclear weapon tests by India in 1998. China joined the other major nuclear weapon powers in denouncing these tests and moving the P5 (permanent members of the UN Security Council) and the Security Council to adopt resolutions to compel India to freeze and roll back its nuclear weapons programme and to sign the NPT. The tone that China adopted in reacting to the tests was harsher than that of the other permanent members. The Joint Statement of 1998 issued by the Presidents of China and the US during the latter's visit to China provoked widespread resentment in India, because it not only asked India to give up its nuclear ambitions, but also envisaged that China and the US would work together for stability and security in the South Asian region. The opinion widely shared in India was that China, being a part of the problem in South Asia, could hardly be expected to play an objective and constructive role in the region.

Positive Turn at the Beginning of the 21st Century

The political equation between India and China changed for the better with the onset of the 21st century. China got reconciled to the fait accompli of India's emergence as a de facto nuclear weapon state. It realized that any attempt by it, in collaboration with other major powers, to pressurize India to freeze and roll back its nuclear weapon programme and to accede to the NPT, was going to be of no avail. An evidence of the changed situation was China's willingness in the beginning of 2000, to have regular strategic dialogue with India, which included discussion on the nuclear issue. Before that date, China used to reject India's overtures to discuss the nuclear issue, on the ground that the latter being a non-nuclear weapon state had no locus standi to engage China in such a discussion. The other factor that brought about the change in China's attitude towards India was the impressive growth rate achieved by India during the 1990s and its moving closer to China's rate of growth as it entered the new century.

By far the most important decision taken by the two countries at the turn of the century was not to allow their bilateral differences to come in the way of their exploiting opportunities for economic cooperation to the fullest extent possible. This resulted in a phenomenal progress in the expansion of trade between them. The value of the two-way trade increased from a modest $2.21 billion in 2000 to $73.9 billion in 2011. In 2010, China became the biggest trading partner of India, overtaking the US. During Premier Wen Jiabao's visit to India in December 2010, the two sides agreed to boost their trade to over $100 billion annually over the next five years. The trade between the two countries has declined since 2011. It was at the level of $66.5 billion in 2012 and $65.4 billion in 2013.[8] This proves that growth in bilateral trade cannot be sustained in a situation of prolonged trade imbalance. Hundreds of the companies of the two countries have started operations in each other's territory, even though the two-way flow of foreign direct investment (FDI) does not yet add up to an impressive figure. However, given the dynamics of growth of their economies, the prospects for growth in FDI flows to each other, particularly from China to India, cannot but be promising.

India and China signed a Memorandum of Understanding for Exchanges and Cooperation in the field of Defence in May 2006. As a result, exchanges between Indian and Chinese military officials have increased during the last few years and joint naval exercises in the Indian Ocean have been conducted. However, in the absence of trust between the two countries, there can be no genuine military cooperation. According to a protocol between the two countries signed during President Hu Jintao's visit to India in 2006, India opened a Consulate General in Guangzhou, and China, in Calcutta. The two countries have also started cooperating frequently and closely in international economic fora and negotiations. This is particularly true of the Doha Round of Trade Negotiations and the UN climate change negotiations. In addition, they are actively pursuing their common interests in the newly established groups like the G-20 at the summit level, BRICS and SCO. It is significant that China did not come in the way of India becoming an observer in the SCO and later supported India's full membership of this group. China no doubt opposed the Indian initiative launched in 2006–07 for ASEAN+6 (including India) moving towards an Asian economic community. However, it ultimately accepted the compromise of launching in Kuala Lumpur in December 2005 the annual East Asia Summit Conference, which includes India. The Chinese President Hu Jintao, during his visit to India in November 2006, endorsed the idea of a pan-Asian economic grouping. Addressing a public meeting in Delhi, he said that China–India cooperation would be a positive step towards the establishment of an Asian economic community. However, with the proliferation of negotiations on formation of mega groupings in the Asia and Pacific region, the idea of setting up a Pan-Asian economic grouping has acquired an altogether new character.

Persistence of Negative Factors

Except the remarkable spurt in trade exchanges which have now started stagnating, there has been no qualitative change in the relationship between the two countries. China has not resiled from or brought about any significant change in any of its policies that impinge on India's vital interests. In spite of raising the level of discussions on the border issue to a notch higher and despite more than two decades of annual meetings on this subject at this level, an agreement even on the alignment of the lines of actual control in the disputed sectors, let alone on the demarcation of the border, is nowhere in sight. This has made peace and tranquillity along the border a hostage to China's sweet will. In 2003, the two sides reached an understanding on the line of control in the middle sector of the border and exchanged maps to confirm it. However, one is still waiting for the exchange of maps confirming the understanding on the line of control in the eastern and western sectors, where the real dispute lies. In these sectors, reaching an agreement on the line of control amounts to an agreement on the border alignment itself. Since such an agreement can be reached only as a part of the package for an overall solution of the boundary dispute, it is not surprising that there is no progress towards reaching an understanding on the line of control in these sectors.

In the meanwhile, China has taken a series of steps which have led to the exacerbation of the border controversy and have, from the Indian perspective, introduced unexpected and uncalled for tensions in Sino-Indian relations. China sought to block an Asian Development Bank project for the Indian state of Arunachal Pradesh, which China regards a disputed territory. China has been lodging formal protests against the visits of Indian leaders, including the Prime Minister of India, to Arunachal Pradesh and has denied visas or issued the so-called stapled visas to officials and citizens belonging to this state and the state of Jammu and Kashmir. In the summer of 2010, India was constrained to take the extreme step of suspending military ties with China in retaliation for the latter refusing a visa to the Chief of the Northern Command of the Indian Army, to visit China to participate in a high-level India-China defence dialogue. The defence ties were resumed in June 2011 when China allowed the visit of an eight-member military team to China.

In the maps issued recently, China is now showing as a part of its territory not only Arunachal Pradesh but also the part of Jammu and Kashmir ceded to it by Pakistan. It has ignored all protests by India against its road link through this territory with Pakistan and its plan to build a rail link. The Chinese protest against the visit of Prime Minister Modi to Arunachal Pradesh in February 2015 was unusually harsh. Apart from taking it to the formal diplomatic level, China characterized it as inimical to finding solution to the boundary problem. The incidents of confrontation resulting from assertion of claims and counter-claims in the Western sector are becoming more frequent and assuming threatening proportions. The timing of some of these incidents have been, to say the least, quite intriguing. The troops of the two countries came face-to-face in the Depsang region in April–May 2014, just before the much heralded visit by the new Chinese prime minister. Instead of the earlier practice of withdrawing and leaving trails behind as an assertion of claim to the disputed territory, the Chinese this time built temporary structures. The next incident in Chumar coincided with the visit of President Xi Jinping. An unusual feature of this incident was that India's show of presence in the disputed territory was sought to be deliberately obstructed and the troops deployed from both sides were unusually large in size.

Nevertheless the two sides avoided any clash or firing. They constantly kept in touch with each other, including at a fairly high military level and in both the instances the issue was ultimately resolved through the use of the established mechanism. After the May 2013 incident, the two countries signed a Border Defence Cooperation Agreement (BDCA) to improve management of the border. It is designed to reduce tension by providing more and higher levels of avenues for taking up border incidents and establishing additional channels of communication.

A reason why border incidents have become more frequent and have assumed relatively serious proportions is that with the improvement in the infrastructure in border areas on both sides, patrolling has become more frequent and method of asserting claim more high-tech. In 2006, India introduced a major road building programme for the border area. Three years later, it announced its decision to raise two new Mountain Divisions for deployment on its side of the border. Subsequently it upgraded several airstrips and advanced landing grounds. In 2013, the Government of India approved the raising of a new Strike Corps for the Eastern sector of the border, the first offensive military formation India has deployed along the Line of Actual Control. On its part, China has bolstered its own capabilities in the border area in a comprehensive manner. Through its superior roadways and long-range rail transport connectivity to the border area it can move troops and equipment with high speed. China fields 400,000 PLA soldiers in the military regions opposite India. In recent years, it has also upgraded its arsenals of ballistic missiles located in the area and built new air fields in Tibet.

The Chinese assistance to build the military might of Pakistan to keep India unsettled in the region, continues unabated. China promptly comes to Pakistan's support whenever the latter is censured by the international community for harbouring terrorist groups operating against India. Through its stand in the Security Council, China has prevented Pakistani terrorists from being blacklisted by the UN.

China is today engaged in a single-minded pursuit of establishing itself as a major military power in the world. It is busy testing and producing or acquiring the most up-to-date varieties of weapons, including stealth bombers, intercontinental missiles, aircraft carriers and submarines. It tested an anti satellite system in 2007. It has one of the most ambitious plans undertaken by any power in recent times, to expand and upgrade its navy and air force. China has embarked on the path of the accumulation and upgradation of nuclear arms and its delivery vehicles at a time when other nuclear weapon states are making progress in reducing their nuclear arsenals. Its declared objective is to interdict access of US naval forces in its vicinity and to develop a second strike capacity.

The US and its allies and Russia do not have to fear from the augmentation of the Chinese nuclear force. For, their arsenals, even after recent reductions, are far larger than and superior to that of the Chinese. Therefore, the Chinese nuclear arms build-up does not pose a short or medium term threat to the security of these nations. It actually threatens countries like India which neither have nor can develop a nuclear deterrence against China in the foreseeable future. India also cannot ignore the Chinese deployment of armed forces in Tibet, which includes nuclear weapons targeted at India, a large number of troops and a large air force, backed by state-of-the-art railways, roads and supply infrastructure. To strengthen its deterrence postures relative to India, China has recently replaced liquid-fuelled nuclear capable CSS-2 intermediate-range ballistic missiles (IRBMs) with more advanced and survivable solid-fuelled CSS-5 medium-range ballistic missile (MRBM) systems. There is no doubt that these pose a strategic threat to India's security.

Though the trade exchanges between the two countries increased nearly 30 times within a decade, India faces an ever-widening adverse balance of trade with China. The adverse balance increased from $0.69 billion in 2000 to nearly $31.4 billion in 2013.[9] Moreover, the structure of India's exports to and imports from China is reminiscent of the pattern of trade between developed and developing countries during the post-Second World War period. Whereas China is exporting mostly manufactured goods to India, the Indian exports consist primarily of raw materials. The share of capital goods in India's total exports to China remained stagnant between 2002 and 2010 at around 4 per cent; the share of intermediate goods declined during this period from 57.9 per cent to 24.6 per cent, but the share of raw materials increased from 35.3 per cent to 68.5 per cent.[10] Thus, most of the increase in India's exports to China during the last 14 years has been accounted for by raw materials. On the other hand, China's export of capital goods to India almost doubled from 28.6 per cent in 2002 to 54.8 per cent in 2009. The share of intermediate goods declined sharply from 47.7 per cent in 2002 to 36.4 per cent in 2010, whereas raw materials virtually disappeared from China's export basket to India, the share declining from 11.7 per cent to 1.3 per cent during this period.[11] There has been very little qualitative change in the situation since 2009. Capital goods are now missing altogether from India's export basket to China. The shares of raw materials and intermediate goods have declined from 20 and 21 per cent, respectively, in 2010 to 17 and 18 per cent in 2013. The share of consumer goods has gone up from 58 to nearly 64 per cent during this period. There have been only marginal variations in the shares of these four product groups in China's exports to India between 2010 and 2013.[12] The trade exchanges are basically market-driven and have no backward or forward linkages in the economies of the two countries. There has not been a single major joint-venture project undertaken by them so far.

A major problem that has emerged recently in Indo-Chinese relations is China's construction of structures on the upper reaches of the Brahmaputra lying in its territory. Transfer of water or the blockage of its flows through these structures can have a disastrous impact on the lives and livelihood of the millions of Indians inhabiting the Brahmaputra valley. Ever since this Chinese activity came to India's notice, it has been taking it up with China at the official level, demanding transparency, access to data and mutual consultation. All that China has been saying in response is that it is conscious of its responsibilities in this regard and of the interest of the lower riparian countries. It has also been asserting that the structures are basically run-of-the-river projects which should not give cause for anxiety as they do not involve diversion of water. Last year, it was reported in the media that the Chinese government gave a go ahead for building three new hydro-power dams on the river. China has not denied this report yet and has simply reiterated that any structure that is built will not adversely affect the downstream flow.

An agreement was signed during the Indian Prime Minister's visit to China in October 2013 in which the 'two sides agreed to further strengthen cooperation on trans-border rivers, cooperate through the existing Expert Level Mechanism on provision of flood season hydrological data and emergency management and exchange views on other issues of mutual interest'.[13] More or less the same formulation was repeated in the Joint Statement issued at the end of Chinese President Xi Jinping visit to India in September 2014. The Indian side is taking comfort from the part of the formulation providing for 'exchange [of] views on other issues of mutual interest',[14] which could include exchanging views on the projects. But China may not agree to this interpretation. Moreover, it is not possible to engage in any serious discussion on the matter without China providing the project details.

According to the prevailing international law, a lower riparian to a common river has the right to be consulted before the upper riparian takes up a development project in its territory that can adversely impact the former's interest. The Chinese are persistently refusing to agree to such consultation or make data available on the project. The MoU that they have signed is confined to sharing data relating to only the flow of the river which can have an impact in terms of creating a flood situation. China's obduracy on the subject can be explained only by its determination to pursue its national interest at all costs, even if it is in disregard of international law.

Another negative factor is that China has never been enthusiastic about India playing an important role in the evolving regional multilateralism in the Asia-Pacific region. China certainly does not want India to be a part of the monetary arrangement taking shape in Asia under ASEAN+3 in which China is a dominant partner. In 2004–05 when India was actively promoting the idea of a pan-Asian economic grouping, China was in the frontline opposing this initiative. Currently, it seems to be more inclined to work with the developed member countries of APEC, particularly the US, to negotiate a new generation of economic integration schemes, involving far-reaching liberalization in the exchange of goods, services and flow of investment and much higher level of protection of intellectual property rights, than working with earnestness with other countries of Asia, including India, to make the RCEP a reality.

The position that China has taken on the expansion of the Security Council also seems to be primarily designed to frustrate the effort of India to seek permanent membership of the Council. The only formulation acceptable to China on India's permanent membership of the Security Council is that it would like India to play a more active role in the UN, including in the Security Council. This formulation is hardly of any consequence. India is already playing an active role in the UN, in fact more active than China in several spheres. Besides, playing an active role in the Security Council depends critically on India becoming one of its permanent members, preferably with a veto power. And China currently happens to be the biggest obstacle to the realization of this Indian ambition. Moreover, by emphasizing the need for increased representation of small and medium powers in the Security Council, China, having already inherited a permanent seat there, wants to keep India as far away as possible from even the non-permanent membership.

Compulsions of Maintaining Good Relations with China

What attitude should India adopt towards China in the present circumstances? It is clearly against India's interest to live with a hostile China as its neighbour. For, the benefits of having close relations with China are immense both for India and China and the rest of the world, and the costs of not having such a relationship are huge. Normalizing relations with China will free vast amounts of resources that India is devoting to military build-up and the deployment of its forces along the Sino-Indian borders. It can also facilitate resolving problems and normalizing relations with Pakistan. Until now, India has been relying heavily, without commensurate benefits, on the US to resolve its problems with Pakistan. As Pakistan is in the process of veering away from the US and moving closer to China in the coming years, it would make greater sense for India to seek China's help in lessening trouble in its relations with Pakistan.

India will have to deal with China at multiple levels. It has a long-standing and complex border dispute to settle with China. It will continue for quite some time to come; to harbour Dalai Lama and a large Tibetan population which will remain a constant source of tension with China. India will also remain, at least for the next few decades, a strategic competitor of China for influence and raw materials in Asia and Africa.

India and China have been principally responsible for creating a new geography of world trade in which they are in the process of emerging as among the largest markets in the world. They may both need each other's market more than those of other countries to accelerate their economic development. Besides, both these countries are leaders in science and technology, particularly frontier technologies. In recent years, China of course has leaped to a decisive lead over India in several spheres. Their mutual cooperation in this field has great potentialities to bring economic benefits. Moreover, the only chance of sustaining the phenomenal growth in their bilateral trade lies in cooperation in the wider sectors of the economy, in which collaboration in science and technology can play an important role.

The leaders of the two countries have recognized that their relationship is of 'global and strategic significance'.[15] Improvement in their relations will also make a positive contribution to bring peace, stability and prosperity in Asia and the world. It will put them in a better position to cooperate with the international community in solving global problems in the areas of money, finance, trade, environment, proliferation of weapons of mass destruction and such trans-border problems as terrorism, pandemics, drug and human trafficking and natural disasters. Very few developments will be as important as mutual cooperation between India and China, in protecting and advancing the interests of the developing world. As the 2006 Joint Declaration stated: 'India and China share unique responsibilities to protect and promote the interests of the developing world in the emerging international order and help them benefit from the positive forces of globalization'.[16] In his Special Address under the Forum of the Indian Council of World Affairs on 18 September 2014, President Xi Jinping said: 'If India and China speak with one voice, the whole world will listen'. He also stated: 'We should put forward plans that represent the interests of the vast number of developing countries in terms of climate change, food safety, energy, internet security and other global issues'.[17]

Both India and China have crucial common interests at stake in some of the ongoing international negotiations, particularly the Doha Round and climate change negotiations. They also have a common interest in ensuring that there is a movement mainly through the issue of additional SDRs, away from the exclusive reliance on the dollar as an international reserve currency, and that any regime that emerges out of the climate change negotiations leaves enough space for their future development and that of other developing countries. The common stand of India and China on some of the issues under negotiation in the Doha Round has been a major factor in transforming the very agenda of multilateral trade negotiations. It is due to the common position of these two countries that there is a spotlight on the elimination of domestic agricultural subsidies, on the redressal of the inequities and imbalances in the existing rules and regimes governing international trade, and on the other items on the 'development agenda' of the Doha Round.

There are important factors rooted in the Chinese economy and society that are likely to prevent China from indulging in adventurism or acting aggressively in dealing with important powers in the world, including India. Henry Kissinger, in his book *On China*, has highlighted some of these factors. These include such domestic problems as low per capita income for hundreds of millions of the Chinese; regional disparity; growing interpersonal inequality; environmental degradation; and ever mounting incidents of protests and agitations by the people on issues related to land acquisition, environmental degradation and governance. To these can be added the demographic factor. By 2050, one half of the Chinese population is projected to be 45 or older, with a full quarter of China's population, roughly equivalent to the entire current US population, being of the age of 65 or older.[18] Kissinger concludes, 'a country facing such large domestic tasks is not going to throw itself easily, much less automatically, into strategic confrontation or a quest for world domination'. He is also of the view that 'the crucial competition between the United States and China is more likely to be economic and social than military'. The last prognosis seems to be applicable also to China's relations with India and, for that matter, with any country which, in the eventuality of military hostilities, has the capacity to inflict a damage on China that can retard the fulfilment of its objective of ensuring a decent living standard for its people and social harmony.

China's vastly increased integration with the global system will also be a restraining factor in its resorting to any adventure which could have the effect of isolating it from the mainstream of the world economy. This is particularly so as the Chinese see a window of opportunity in the global system at least during the next 15 years to further enhance their recently acquired formidable economic and military might. There is a view shared at the highest political level in China that this 'strategic opportunity period' should not in any circumstances be frittered away.

During this period, China's strategic goal is to build 'a moderately prosperous society in all aspects'.[19] In order to dispel any apprehension regarding their harbouring aggressive intentions against foreign powers, particularly neighbours, the Chinese leadership has gone out of its way to project the image of China's 'peaceful rise' and the objective of building a 'harmonious world of lasting peace and common prosperity'.[20]

Strategy for Dealing with China

India should, therefore, persist with the goal of multifaceted development of its relations with China, even if there is no progress in the near future towards the solution of some of the contentious issues between the two countries, like the boundary dispute, China's military assistance to Pakistan and its stand on Tibet. While keeping China engaged in the discussion on these controversial issues with a view to narrowing the differences, India should not allow these to come in the way of its effort to bring about an overall improvement in the relations or moving ahead in areas that hold out prospects for gains for both the countries. For this purpose, full advantage should be taken of the various mechanisms for bilateral dialogue that have recently been created. India should maintain and further intensify the momentum in the bilateral relations generated by high-level political visits from both sides.

The unresolved boundary dispute between the two countries has no doubt come in the way of a full blossoming of the bilateral relations and hence, in their playing a larger role in the shaping of the world order. A sense of urgency was injected into the slow-moving border talks when in the Joint Statement issued during President Hu Jintao's visit to India in November 2006, it was agreed that '[a]n early settlement of the boundary question will advance the basic interest of the two countries and shall, therefore, be pursued as a strategic objective'. The two sides also agreed that 'the special representatives shall complete at an early date the task of finalising an appropriate framework for a final package settlement covering all sectors of the India-China boundary'.[21] This has been reiterated in all the Joint Statements issued by the Leaders of the two countries in recent years. In spite of this, the border talks have not yielded any worthwhile outcome. It is unlikely that there would be any significant forward movement in the near future. For any progress on this issue, it will be necessary for both sides to cede some portion of the territories under their possession or claimed by them. In India, even though prospects have improved after the BJP-led government enjoying absolute majority in the Lok Sabha (Lower House of the Parliament), given the fractious nature acquired by Indian politics recently, it is not going to be an easy task by any means to arrive at a consensus on ceding territory. The Chinese, on the other hand, are under no compulsion to make adjustments in their claims, without which no solution is possible, as they are sitting pretty on a large chunk of the territory claimed by India, particularly on the western side. India does not have the bargaining power to compel China to approach the border talks more seriously than it has done until now and make adjustments in, what appears to India, its extravagant claims. In the ultimate analysis, any forward movement in the border talks will depend upon China's perception of India's economic and military clout and the stake that China has in bringing about a qualitative change in its relations with India. India, on the other hand, cannot afford to allow the border issue to be put on the backburner. India's posture should, therefore, be to ensure that the Chinese remain actively engaged with us on this issue. As a step in this direction, India should press for commencement of negotiation for reaching an understanding on the line of actual control in the Eastern and Western sectors of the border.

India should seek to tie up China into the widest and strongest possible bonds of economic relationship by the further expansion of mutual trade and investment in each other's economy, by undertaking joint ventures for industrial development and projects of joint collaboration in science and technology and through people-to-people contact. Growing economic, scientific and cultural ties will help in China developing a stake in the Indian economy. However, this is by no means going to be an easy task. A qualitative change in the political relations between the two countries and greater convergence of views on regional and global issues are the pre-conditions for forging durable and sustainable economic linkages. No doubt, the two-way trade registered a phenomenal increase until 2011, and a much higher target was set for further growth during the next few years. But the composition of the Indian exports and the massive and growing trade imbalance against India has effectively come in the way of further growth in trade. In the Joint Statement issued at the end of President Xi Jinping visit to India in September 2014, the two sides recognized that the existing structural imbalance in bilateral trade 'has a bearing on its sustainability'.[22] The areas in which the imbalance could be redressed were recognized. These are: cooperation on pharmaceutical supervision; speedier negotiation on phyto-sanitary measures affecting trade of agro-products; stronger links between Indian IT companies and their Chinese counterparts; and expanding trade in services like tourism, films, healthcare and IT. In the discussions under the Strategic Economic Dialogue, India has been requesting China to provide a level playing field and enhancing access for its competitive products like pharmaceuticals, automobile parts, niche engineering products, IT-enabled services, cotton textiles and home furnishing. However, progress in this regard is still awaited.

In the long run, India will be able to balance its trade with China only by enhancing the competitiveness of its economy. However, in the short and medium run, increased flow of Chinese investment in India can help in mitigating the situation. The Government of India has been seeking foreign capital on a large scale for the development of infrastructure in the country. The Chinese have the potentiality of coming to the Indian economy in a big way, both by virtue of the surplus resources at their disposal and their rich experience in building infrastructure, both domestic and in foreign countries. A Bilateral Investment Promotion and Protection Agreement was signed between the two countries during President Hu Jintao's visit to India in 2006. In the first Strategic Economic Dialogue between the two countries, held in Beijing in September 2011, the two sides reiterated their commitment to deepening investment cooperation and improving the investment environment in both countries.

India has now come to terms with the global reach of the Chinese companies and the immense financial resources at their disposal. It has, therefore, substantially diluted its reservation, largely on security grounds, on Chinese investment in India. It has been using the Strategic Economic Dialogue for urging China to invest in India and for the purpose of identifying sectors for such investment and measures for facilitating it. In the third meeting under the Dialogue, the Indian representative expressed the hope that a sizeable part of the Chinese surplus resources for outward investment could be channelled to India in areas of mutual interest. In the Joint Statement issued after Premier Li's visit to India in May 2013, 'the Indian side welcomed Chinese enterprises to invest in India and participate in India's infrastructure development'.[23]

The decision in the third meeting of the Dialogue to establish a Task Force on Investment by Chinese companies in industries and industrial zones in India, and India's approval in principle, at the time of President Xi Jinping's visit to India, of the request of the Bank of China to open a branch in Mumbai, add to the institutional wherewithal for facilitating Chinese investment in India. During President Xi's visit, the Chinese side also announced its decision to establish two industrial parks in India to facilitate Chinese investment.

The leaders of the two countries have now come to realize that the full potentialities of trade exchanges between the two countries and Chinese investment in India can be realized only within the framework of comprehensive economic cooperation. In the Joint Statement of 19 September 2014, it was agreed that 'development goals are interlinked and should be pursued in a mutually supportive manner'. The two sides, therefore, 'agreed to leverage mutual complementarities and build a close developmental partnership'. This partnership, they stated, 'will be a core component of their Strategic and Cooperative Partnership for Peace and Prosperity'. Through the Strategic Economic Dialogue, the two countries have been exploring areas of deeper economic cooperation, like industrial and infrastructure development, energy conservation, environmental protection, high-tech industry, clean energy and sustainable urbanization. In this connection, a very important step taken during President Xi's visit was the signing of a Five-Year Development Programme for Economic and Trade Cooperation, which lays down 'a roadmap for comprehensively deepening and balancing bilateral economic engagement'.[24]

The Chinese side now appears to be more forthcoming on the issue of investment in India. This was reflected in the various measures included in the Joint Statement issued at the end of President Xi's visit and more concretely in the announcement of a target of $20 billion for Chinese investment in India over the next five years. This is a small amount given the huge resources at the disposal of the Chinese and their active search for avenues for investing them. But it will be difficult to hold the Chinese at fault for being cautious in this regard due, in large part, to the faultiness in India's development path. Moreover, the lack of strategic trust between the two countries on account of the prevailing political climate of their relationship sets a limit on what can be achieved in this or in other areas.

India's obsession with national security has, on several occasions, come in the way of its launching bold initiatives for economic cooperation with China. The Indian authorities invoked security as a justification for their lukewarm attitude towards China's Kunming Initiative for sub-regional cooperation between the Yunnan province of China, the adjoining areas of India and other bordering countries like Myanmar and Bangladesh. When the Chinese agreed to open the Nathu La for border trade, both India and China worked hard to reduce it to a race to the bottom by restricting the items that could be traded and limiting the number of agents who could trade. One of the arguments given by the

Indian authorities in both these cases was that opening up the border for trade would encourage infiltration across the border of miscreants and intelligence agents from the Chinese side, which would pose a threat to India's security. The other argument advanced was that given the comparative advantage of China in the export of manufactured goods, the opening up of the border area for trade between the two countries would result in the flooding of the Indian market by Chinese goods.

Both these arguments are highly exaggerated, if not totally misplaced. China does not have to use the border route if it wants to infiltrate agents to create disruption in India. It might have done so in the past in the north-eastern region of India, but there is no evidence of this happening in recent years. Invoking the fear of the aggravation of India's security situation in the northeast as a result of opening the border for trade betrays India's lack of confidence in its own ability to manage the border and in dealing with the domestic political situation prevailing in the north-eastern states.

As regards the apprehension regarding Chinese goods flooding the Indian market, it is important to bear in mind that the recent Chinese penetration into the Indian market has been due to the competitiveness of the Chinese products and not their dumping by China. As a member of the WTO, China has the right to demand access for its competitive products to the Indian market, subject to the limitations imposed by India's trade regime, which is applicable to all WTO member countries. It is no doubt open to India to take anti-dumping and countervailing measures permitted under the WTO against imports from China. But the fact is that India has not been able to muster enough evidence to prove more than a handful of cases of alleged dumping by China in the Indian market. Besides, if China has not caused market disruption in India through the normal oceanic route of trade, there is no reason why the opening up of yet another land route would cause such disruption. India should, therefore, seek China's cooperation in broadening the scope of the border trade through the newly opened land route via the Nathu La so that it can bring prosperity to the adjoining regions of both the countries and to the two countries as a whole. Moreover, instead of cribbing about the dumping of Chinese goods, India should bring about necessary structural changes in its industries to be able to cope with the Chinese competition in the Indian as well as foreign markets, including the vast Chinese market. India should also unhesitatingly embrace all proposals—including the Kunming Initiative—which have the potentiality of linking the economies of the two countries.

The Kunming Initiative has now assumed the form of the BCIM Economic Corridor, the main purpose of which is to improve connectivity through railways, highways, personnel and information flows, tourism and energy links. After sulking on the Kunming Initiative for more than a decade, India has decided to join the BCIM Corridor scheme. In the Joint Statement of May 2013, the two sides agreed to consult the other party with a view to establishing a joint study group on strengthening connectivity in the BCIM region for facilitating cooperation. The joint study group is now in existence and has met three times, the last meeting having been held in New Delhi towards the end of 2014.

India should shed its lingering inhibition and cooperate wholeheartedly in this Chinese initiative. This will enable India to tap Chinese capital and technology for enhanced connectivity with Bangladesh and Myanmar which, in turn, will facilitate linkages with South-East Asian and East Asian countries. It also has the potentiality of reviving the Kolkata port with an important part of the Chinese territory serving as its hinterland. India should, in fact, join other Chinese initiatives for improving connectivity in the Asian region. This includes China's initiative for reviving the ancient Silk Road and for making large-scale investment for building the infrastructure for this purpose. India has very wisely decided to become the founder member and the second largest shareholder of the Asian Infrastructure Investment Bank (AIIB) launched by China. This will enable India to play a role in shaping the scope, lending principles and operational rules of the Bank. Moreover, India is likely to become an important recipient of funds under this Bank, because unlike the BRICS Development Bank, financing under the AIIB is likely to be confined to Asian countries.

The most effective means of preventing China from creating problems for India in the South Asian region is to bring about a qualitative change in India's relations with the countries in this region, particularly Bangladesh, Nepal, Sri Lanka and the Maldives. This calls for an ambitious approach to achieving economic integration with these countries by providing vastly enlarged access to their products in the Indian market, preferably on a non-reciprocal basis, and undertaking joint mega projects for their industrialization and for building their infrastructure. It will also be necessary to adopt bold and innovative approaches for resolving bilateral issues with them and for promoting people-to-people contacts. Though the prospects for moving along these lines in India's relations with Pakistan do not appear to be promising in the present circumstances, there is no reason why these should not be pursued as a long-term goal of India's relations with Pakistan as well.

During the last five to six years, China has vastly expanded its economic ties with India's neighbours. It has invested in the building of the infrastructure and in the industrial, agriculture and natural resources sectors in these countries on a scale far exceeding India's investments there. India should not be deterred by this Chinese thrust in the economies of our neighbouring countries and should continue and accelerate its own economic cooperation with them. For, there is enough space in these countries, as elsewhere in the developing world, for both India and China to play their role. Besides, by virtue of historical ties and geographical proximity, India has unique advantages over China in cooperating with these countries, which even China recognizes.

In the coming years, India and China will continue to compete for mobilizing political support; expanding access to markets; and securing energy, metals, minerals and other natural resources in Asia and Africa. This competition will intensify with the passage of time, mainly because of the rising demands for natural resources in both India and China and the exhaustible nature of most of these resources. India should, therefore, gear itself up to the inevitability of competition with China in this area.

In spite of being a latecomer, China has taken a headlong lead over India in the investment it is making for the purpose of advancing its interests in Third World countries, and the number of projects it has undertaken and contracts it has signed in these countries. This situation has come about mainly because during the crucial decades of the 1980s and 1990s, China accumulated disposable resources on a much larger scale than India could. In recent years, there has been a substantial increase in such resources at the disposal of India too, but it is still far behind China. In the circumstances, India should display greater initiative, enterprise and innovativeness in deploying resources for investment in major infrastructure, industrial and resource development projects in developing countries. There is also immense scope for making improvements on the delivery of projects, where China's record is far superior. Finally, India should use in a planned and systematic manner its soft power in Asia and Africa, particularly in areas where it has advantages over China. India's soft power mainly lies in its past and continuing cultural contacts with these countries, the presence of the Indian diaspora in these countries and India's capacity for institution building, particularly in the IT sector. In the 2006 Joint Declaration between India and China, the two sides agreed that 'they are not rivals or competitors, but are partners for mutual benefit'.[25] There is scope for India and China to cooperate with the countries of these regions, through joint projects and joint delivery of goods and services.

The two countries should seek to reach an agreement preferably in concert with other BRICS countries, on a set of guidelines for economic cooperation with these countries, the hallmark of which should be equality, respect for sovereignty and capacity building for autonomous development. Their cooperation with Asian and African countries should mark a distinct departure from the traditional pattern of North–South economic relations.

The economic resurgence of India and China has been the major factor taking the world to the doorstep of an Asian century. In the immediate post-Second World War period, the call for a new awakening of Asia was given by Jawaharlal Nehru at the Asian Relations Conference (ARC) held in New Delhi in March 1947. He had declared in that conference:

> For too long, we of Asia have been petitioners in Western Courts and Chancelleries. That story must now belong to the past. We propose to stand on our own feet and to cooperate with all others who are prepared to cooperate with us. We do not intend to be the plaything of the others.[26]

The establishment of an Asian Federation was an important part of Nehru's vision and that of other leaders of India's independence movement. Through the ARC, Nehru tried to start a pan-Asian movement, which unfortunately could not succeed because of the then configuration of global economic and political forces and the almost exclusive preoccupation of Asian countries with the struggles they were waging at that time for their national liberation and resurgence. But today, an integrated Asian market, basically driven by market forces, in which India and China are major players, is taking shape. This may turn out to be an important instrument for ushering in the Asian century. Sino-Indian cooperation is going to be of crucial importance in bringing about this outcome.

It is in this background that India had taken the initiative during the early years of this century for achieving a pan-Asian economic integration, with both India and China in it. It was felt that this would be the logical culmination of the series of bilateral FTAs that both India and China as well as other major Asian countries had negotiated or were in the process of negotiating with each other. It was felt that the merger of these FTAs into a single framework of Asian economic integration would bring much enhanced welfare gains, and order and systemic cohesion in the trade and development field in the Asian region. It would also prove a decisive step forward in taking the on-going shift in the global economic power balance from the West to the Asia to its logical conclusion. Finally, it would go a long way towards eliminating the animosity and tension that characterizes bilateral relations between several pairs of Asian countries. This Indian initiative was, however thwarted by China in the ASEAN forum. But it has now emerged in the new form of the RCEP. A decision to launch negotiations for RCEP was taken at the 19th ASEAN Summit in 2011. The negotiations, which are to be completed by the end of 2015, were started among the 16 participating countries, including India, in 2013. By now six rounds of the RCEP negotiations have been completed, the last one held in Delhi in December 2014. But there has been very little progress so far, and the modalities are still unclear.

RCEP has the very ambitious agenda of agglomerating all FTAs concluded with ASEAN and between the participating countries. Moreover, it faces problems from the sides of both China and India. It is not clear what priority China attaches to RCEP as compared to the other initiatives for negotiating regional economic integration in Asia and the Pacific. China seems to be according higher priority to integration with major developed countries than with other dynamic economies of the Asian region. One of the motives of the US behind launching the TPP negotiation was to isolate China. But the two countries now seem to have substantially closed the distance separating them on this issue. China always kept open its option for participating in the TPP negotiation. Now it has clearly indicated that it is interested in joining it if invited to do so. At the same time, at the APEC summit held in Beijing last year, China was able to secure APEC's approval to initiate the process that will eventually lead to the formation of an FTAAP. As the first step, the APEC member countries launched a collective strategic study on the issues related to the formation of this free trade area. It is not clear what shape FTAAP eventually will take but there is no doubt that it would be steered by China and, being an APEC initiative, the US will be a part of it.

India's problem with RCEP is that it is the main target of negotiation for market opening under it but there is not much scope for further market opening by India because of its obligations to protect the livelihood and other social and economic interests of its vast number of poor people and also because in the absence of restructuring of some of the key sectors of its economy, India is not in a position to withstand competition from the other participants in the negotiation. India is, understandably putting emphasis on the liberalization of services in these negotiations, but in the service sector too, it has lost some of its competitive advantage over the past decade or so. For the same reason, unlike China and several ASEAN countries, India is not in a position to participate in the negotiations under TPP or for the formation of any other economic integration grouping of which major developed countries like the US are a part. India's development imperatives do not permit it to go beyond a point in further liberalizing trade and investment and strengthening the global IPR regime, in which these latter countries are mainly interested.

India's concentration should, therefore, be in the RCEP negotiation in which it must emphasize that economic integration calls for not only trade liberalization but also bridging the development gap. For this purpose, the negotiation must address, among others, the problem of connectivity and infrastructure. India should have a frank discussion with China at the bilateral level on this issue in order to develop an understanding to work together to take the RCEP negotiation to finality before the target date and make it the model for Asian integration. This would, among others, enhance the bargaining power of both the countries in negotiations on key global issues with a view to moving towards the establishment of a more equitable world order.

During the 1980s and the early 1990s, China was generally for a status quo in the world economic order, whereas India was a leader in the struggle waged through the platform of NAM and G-77 for bringing about a change in it. From the mid-90s, the position of the two countries on this issue began to converge, as both of them started linking in a comprehensive way with the existing order and hence, developed a stake in it. Now both of them have become status quoists. At the same time, both of them see their interests in bringing about some essential changes, particularly in the international trading and financial systems, without, however, causing any upheaval. In this effort, both of them are also very keen to avoid confrontation with other major economic powers.

Both India and China have acquired significantly enhanced bargaining power to have a reasonably good prospect for serving their common interests and forcing changes in the desired direction. This broadly sets the background of their participation and cooperation in the ongoing negotiations on international economic issues. Their cooperation has been in evidence in fora like the UN (mainly in the negotiations on climate change), the WTO (in the Doha Round of Trade Negotiations), the G-20, the IMF and the World Bank, and has yielded significant results for the two countries, the developing world and the world community as a whole. They should continue and intensify their cooperation in these fora and negotiations and look for new avenues for cooperation, The areas identified by them for cooperation in international fora are climate change, Doha Development Round, energy and food security, reform of the international financial institutions and global governance.[27] Out of these, a major divergence on the positions of the two countries on climate change looms on the horizon with China signing a Joint Statement with US in which it has agreed to target for reducing the level of emission after 2020. India is obviously in no position to accept such a target for a long time to come. In addition to the issues mentioned in their Joint Statement, India and China should work together for undertaking a review of the TRIPS Agreement in the WTO, restoring to the UN the Charter functions it has been deprived of and enhancing the capacity of the UN effectively to discharge its functions under the Charter.

A major question is: How should India respond to China's rising power? There is no option for India but to get reconciled to this phenomenon and work constructively with China with a view to serving its national interests and shaping the world order. Even the US appears to have accepted China's vastly enhanced economic and military clout and decided to work with it in critical areas of its national interest and on global problems. At the joint press conference in Beijing in November 2014, President Obama not only welcomed but also supported the continuing rise of China, characterizing it as 'peaceful, prosperous and stable'. He even said that:

> a strong cooperative relationship with China is at the heart of our pivot to Asia. And if the United States is going to continue to lead the world in addressing the global challenges, then we have to have the second largest economy and most populous nation on earth as our partner.[28]

As a relatively weaker but rising power, this should be true of India as well. India should, therefore, join all those Chinese initiatives that can be leveraged for accelerating our development and for moulding the world order in our favour and that of other developing countries. In this process, we should accept the reality that commensurate with its vastly enhanced economic power, China would play a dominant, even a controlling, role in the running of the institutions built at its initiative and largely financed by it. We should, at the same time, use our own bargaining strength to shape the agenda, scope of activities and the management structures of these institutions.

Tibet is one of the most important bilateral issues bedevilling the relations between India and China. It is also one of the weak links in China's domestic policy. Tibet has enjoyed sovereignty for long spells in history. The Tibetans have a distinctive cultural identity which is fundamentally different from that of the Hans who constitute the overwhelming majority of the Chinese population. In spite of its best efforts, China has neither been able to obliterate the Tibetan cultural identity nor integrate the Tibetans in a harmonious relationship with the Chinese mainland. China, therefore, feels vulnerable and insecure on the Tibetan issue. That is why it regards a foreign country's stand on Tibet as a litmus test of its acceptance of China's sovereignty and the 'One China Policy'. China overreacts and indulges in vitriolics at the slightest indication of what it perceives as a foreign country's derogation from this policy. A mere meeting between the Head of a Government and the Dalai Lama is regarded as such a derogation and provokes an intemperate reaction. The Dalai Lama himself is sub-jected to frequent condemnations by the Chinese government, couched in uncivil and harsh language

Instead of accusing foreign countries, the Chinese government should have realized that it has itself to blame for the continuing alienation of the Tibetans. It has refused to honour its own constitutional commitment to grant autonomy to the Tibetan people. It has frequently resorted to repressive measures that have resulted in the killing of hundreds of thousands of Tibetans and their continuing exodus from Tibet, particularly to the neighbouring countries of India and Nepal. Its measures for the suppression of the Tibetans' religious freedom, including the destruction of monasteries, verge on cultural genocide. Its attempt to appease the Tibetans by bringing material benefits through ill-conceived development projects has led to ecological degradation and unsustainable exploitation of the natural resources of the region on a massive scale.

No outside country has a greater stake than India in Tibet's peace and stability and in the preservation of the Tibetans' cultural identity. The Tibetans are culturally closer to India than to mainland China and they look upon India for the growth and survival of their culture. India gave asylum to the Dalai Lama in 1959 and has since allowed him to live and function in India. The people of India revere him as they would any other Indian saint or savant. India also hosts the world's largest Tibetan community outside Tibet, numbering nearly 120,000. It would not be an exaggeration to say that but for India's support, the Tibetan issue would not have remained alive in China and in foreign countries. Going by humanitarian considerations, India has no alternative but to provide the Tibetans opportunities for education, health and employment and assist them in building and maintaining institutions for the preservation and promotion of their culture. Finally, as human rights and individual freedom constitute the very bedrock of the Indian Constitution, India cannot remain neutral when it comes to the demand for the exercise of the basic human rights and freedom by the Tibetans.

The vast majority of the Indians believe that the stand taken by the Dalai Lama on Tibet's autonomy is just and reasonable. The Dalai Lama has irrevocably and repeatedly asserted his support for 'One China', which includes Tibet. All that he has been demanding from the Chinese authorities is that they honour their constitutional obligation to grant autonomy to the Tibetan region. This has also been India's official position. India 'has recognized the Tibet Autonomous region as part of the territory of the People's Republic of China'.[29] In the years to come, until the issue of Tibetan autonomy is resolved, India has no alternative but to continue its present Tibetan policy.

India and China will continue to differ in their reactions to major developments in the world relating to human rights and democracy. Democracy and fundamental freedoms constitute important elements of the soft power of India, which it must use in the conduct of its foreign policy. Normally, there is no need for India to question the socio-economic and political system prevailing in China. However, India may have to speak out if there is a persistent and massive violation of human rights in this country. Moreover, India may have to speak in a voice different from that of China when it comes to violations of human rights in other parts of the world, as happened recently in the Gulf, the West Asian and the North African regions.

While pursuing a policy of a broad-based cooperative relationship with China, India should be aware that China is essentially driven by 'realist' considerations in the conduct of its foreign policy. To quote Robert D. Kaplan, China is an 'über-realist' power.[30] The image that it has of itself is that of the 'Middle Kingdom' which is supposed to lie in the centre of the universe, with the rest of the world lying in its periphery. So, in dealing with China, India should proceed on the assumption that China's moves abroad will be propelled by a desire to attain supremacy in Asia and a dominant position in the world. In an effort to enlarge its diplomatic space for dealing with China, India should forge closer alliances with important countries in China's as well as India's neighbourhood, particularly Australia, Japan, South Korea, Indonesia, Thailand and Vietnam. They should not be construed as adversely affecting our relationship with China. Every country, including China, tries to acquire larger diplomatic space in the conduct of its foreign policy. Moreover, India has had centuries-old civilizational and cultural ties with most of these countries and in the post-war period we established relationships with several of them much earlier than China did. As these countries are either already highly developed or among the emerging economies, it makes tremendous sense to forge strategic relations with them covering most of its important aspects, including defence.

Since 'realist' calculations play a dominant role in the conduct of China's foreign policy, India should not expect it to resile from its negative position on or seriously address the issues of concern to India, like the border dispute, military assistance to Pakistan, terrorism emanating from Pakistan and India's legitimate interest in its neighbourhood, unless there is a change in China's perception of India as a military and economic power. Thus, India will be able to forge durable relations with China only when it emerges as a stronger, if not an equal, military and economic power. For this, India must restore and maintain the dynamism displayed by its economy over a decade into the 21st century and strengthen its military power. The real challenge in the economic field is to attain inclusive growth that brings the poorest and the marginalized to the mainstream of the economy; to universalize school education and raise the quality of education at all levels; ensure universal access to primary health services; build the much needed infrastructure, particularly in the rural sector; and bring about drastic improvements in the system of governance. The sustainability of development and social cohesion in India will also depend a great deal upon the extent to which all sections of Indian society, irrespective of caste, creed, religion or sex, feel equal and secure and enjoy equality of opportunity.

In the military field, without getting involved in a nuclear arms race with China, India must factor the threat to its security emanating from that country into the building of its nuclear deterrent. India should have adequate nuclear prowess in order to make China feel threatened enough not to take it for granted. India has also a long way to go towards enhancing its conventional warfare capacity. The country also needs to build a credible defence against ballistic missiles. There is a need to expand and upgrade the Indian Navy to meet external threats to India's security and for effective projection of power, protection of the nation's coastlines and economic zones and for combating piracy. India's air power capacity also needs to be modernized and enhanced several fold. In particular, it is necessary to deploy air power in greater strength along the Sino-Indian border. Finally, India also needs to rapidly expand and upgrade its military infrastructure in general and in the border areas in particular. The extent of further militarization, which is a matter of national choice, should in the ultimate analysis depend upon its economic viability and the supreme necessity to guarantee the enjoyment of basic rights, like the rights to food, livelihood, education and health, conferred upon the Indian citizens by the Constitution of India.

Notes

1. 'Agreement (with exchange of notes) on Trade and Intercourse between Tibet Region of China and India', *United Nations Treaty Series*, Volume 299, No. 430729, April 1954.
2. SIPRI, *SIPRI Yearbook 2014*.
3. Lisa Curtis and Dean Cheng, 'The China Challenge: A Strategic Vision for U.S.-India Relations', (Backgrounder no. 2583, The Heritage Foundation, Washington DC, 18 July 2011).
4. Ibid.
5. Ministry of External Affairs, 'A Shared Vision for the 21st Century of the Republic of India and the People's Republic of China' (Government of the Republic of India and Government of People's Republic of China, Beijing, 14 January 2008), http://mea.gov.in/outoging-visit-detail.htm?5145/A+Shared+Vision+for+the+21st+Century+of+the+Republic+of+India+and+the+Peoples+Republic+of+China (accessed on 29 April 2015).
6. Ministry of External Affairs, 'Joint Statement: A Vision for Future Development of India-China Strategic and Cooperative Partnership' (Government of the Republic of India and Government of People's Republic of China, 23 October 2013), http://mea.gov.in/bilateral-documents.htm?dtl/22379/Joint+Statement+A+vision+for+future+development+of+IndiaChina+strategic+and+cooperative+partnership (accessed on 29 April 2015).
7. Ministry of External Affairs, 'Joint Statement between the Republic of India and the People's Republic of China on Building a Closer Developmental Partnership' (Government of the Republic of India and Government of People's Republic of China, 19 September 2014), http://www.mea.gov.in/bilateral-documents.htm?dtl/24022/Joint+Statement+between+the+Republic+of+India+and+the+Peoples+Republic+of+China+on+Building+a+Closer+Developmental+Partnership (accessed on 29 April 2015).
8. Calculated from data taken from International Monetary Fund, Direction of Trade Statistics database, http://elibrary.data.imf.org/ (accessed on 2 March 2015).

9. Ibid.
10. United Nations Commodity Statistics Database, http://comtrade.un.org (accessed on 5 August 2011).
11. Ibid.
12. Calculation based on data taken from United Nations Commodity Statistics Database, http://comtrade.un.org/ (accessed on 3 March 2015).
13. Prime Minister's Office, 'MoU between the Ministry of Water Resources, India and the Ministry of Water Resources, China on Strengthening Co-operation on Trans-Border Rivers' (Ministry of Water Resources, Republic of India and the Ministry of Water Resources, the People's Republic of China, 23 October 2013), http://www.pib.nic.in/newsite/erelcontent.aspx?relid=100181 (accessed on 29 April 2015).
14. Ministry of External Affairs, 'Joint Statement between the Republic of India and the People's Republic of China on Building a Closer Developmental Partnership'.
15. Prime Minister's Office, 'Joint Declaration by the Republic of India and the People's Republic of China' (Government of the Republic of India and Government of People's Republic of China, 21 November 2006), http://pib.nic.in/newsite/erelcontent.aspx?relid=22168 (accessed on 29 April 2015).
16. Prime Minister's Office, 'Joint Declaration by the Republic of India and the People's Republic of China'.
17. Indian Council of World Affairs (ICWA), Special Address by H.E. Mr. Xi Jinping, President of the People's Republic of China (New Delhi, 18 September 2014), http://www.icwa.in/pdfs/stmtdg/2014/AddressbyXiJinping.pdf (accessed on 29 April 2015).
18. Henry Kissinger, *On China* (New York: Allen Lane, 2011).
19. Dai Bingguo, 'Persisting with the Path of Peaceful Development' (Ministry of Foreign Affairs, People's Republic of China, 6 December 2010), http://www.gov.cn/ldhd/2010-12/06/content_1760381.htm (accessed on 30 December 2011).
20. Hu Jintao, UN General Assembly Speech, 2005. Also see Bingguo, 'Persisting with the Path of Peaceful Development'; Information Office of the State Council, 'White Paper: China's Peaceful Development Road' (People's Republic of China, 22 December 2005); Information Office of the State Council, 'White Paper: China's Peaceful Development' (People's Republic of China, Beijing, 6 September 2011).
21. Prime Minister's Office, 'Joint Declaration by the Republic of India and the People's Republic of China'.
22. Ministry of External Affairs, 'Joint Statement between the Republic of India and the People's Republic of China on Building a Closer Developmental Partnership'.
23. Ministry of External Affairs, 'Joint Statement on the State Visit of Chinese Premier Li Keqiang to India' (20 May 2013), http://mea.gov.in/bilateral-

documents.htm?dtl/21723/Joint+Statement+on+the+State+Visit+of+Chinese++Li+Keqiang+to+India (accessed on 29 April 2015).

24. Ministry of External Affairs, 'Joint Statement between the Republic of India and the People's Republic of China on Building a Closer Developmental Partnership'.
25. Prime Minister's Office, 'Joint Declaration by the Republic of India and the People's Republic of China'.
26. Jawaharlal Nehru, Speech at Asian Relations Conference, in *Asian Relations, Being Report of the Proceedings and Documentation of the First Asian Relations Conference, New Delhi, March–April, 1947* (New Delhi: Asian Relations Organization, 1948).
27. Ministry of External Affairs, 'Joint Statement on the State Visit of Chinese Premier Li Keqiang to India'; Ministry of External Affairs, 'Joint Statement between the Republic of India and the People's Republic of China on Building a Closer Developmental Partnership'.
28. White House Press Office, 'Remarks by President Obama and President Xi Jinping in Joint Press Conference' (Office of the Press Secretary, Federal Government of the United States of America, Beijing, 12 November 2014), https://www.whitehouse.gov/the-press-office/2014/11/12/remarks-president-obama-and-president-xi-jinping-joint-press-conference (accessed on 30 April 2015)
29. Government of the People's Republic of China, 'Declaration on Principles for Relations and Comprehensive Cooperation Between the People's Republic of China and the Republic of India', 25 June 2003; Prime Minister's Office, 'Joint Declaration by the Republic of India and the People's Republic of China'.
30. Robert D. Kaplan, 'The Geography of Chinese Power: How Far Can Beijing Reach on Land and Sea', *Foreign Affairs*, May–June 2010.

TEN The United Nations as a Foreign Policy Arena for India and China

A nation utilizes all the instrumentalities at its disposal to pursue its foreign policy objectives. The bilateral is the most direct, convenient and effective means of doing so. Then come the multilateral inter-governmental fora, both at the regional and global levels. The United Nations (UN)[1] occupies the central place among these organizations. It is, therefore, an extremely important arena for pursuing foreign policy objectives.

The basic factors determining the success or failure of a foreign policy remain the same irrespective of whether such a policy is pursued bilaterally or multilaterally through the UN. Some of these factors are: the country's military and economic strength, its political prestige and its general ability to manage its foreign policy. The last-mentioned factor includes a clear-cut formulation and articulation of policy, the ability to anticipate changes and plan in advance for coping with them, institutional underpinning for these efforts, effective decision-making procedures and diplomatic experience, and the knowledge and skill to implement foreign policy. Of course, depending upon the position of a country in the comity of nations, it can have certain advantages in multilateral fora which are not available bilaterally and vice versa. But, in the ultimate analysis, the basic factors mentioned here are the primary determinants.

Whatever the level of excellence of multilateral diplomacy, it is very seldom that a foreign policy that has failed bilaterally will succeed multilaterally. However, if played with skill and finesse, bilateral and multilateral diplomacy can reinforce each other in the pursuit of particular foreign policy goals. This is what each major nation seeks to do, in varying combinations of these two formats of diplomacy and with varying degrees of success.

There are certain issues that are uniquely amenable to being pursued multilaterally through the UN. These are issues where global linking of foreign policy is either indispensable or essential for reaping specific national advantage. The membership of the IMF, the World Bank and the regional development banks gives a nation access to much-needed financial resources and technical assistance. Membership of the WTO automatically confers MFN treatment in international trade. Membership of the UN Security Council endows a nation with political leverage in matters of international peace and security. Some of the issues where recourse to international fora for finding appropriate solutions has become indispensable are international peace and security, disarmament, international monetary and financial problems, environment, human rights and such transnational problems as terrorism, drug trafficking, natural disasters and pandemics like HIV/AIDS and avian flu.

The current process of globalization has accentuated the multilateral dimensions of foreign policy. It has made interdependence among nations a dominant feature of international life, both as a reality as well as a perception. A large number of national policies of a major nation send reverberations and even shock waves to distant lands lying beyond its borders. Besides, the phenomenon of globalization has made international issues much more complex and interrelated than ever before.

India and China in the United Nations

Both India and China have the potentialities of playing major roles in the UN by virtue of their history, geo-strategic position, land mass, the size of their population and their economic and military strength. Their resources and riches have been coveted since time immemorial. They came into reckoning once again in the final decade of the last century and the first decade of the current century, by virtue of emerging as the two most dynamic and the largest economies in the world. They are now looked upon as providing huge markets for foreign goods, services, capital and technology.

The People's Republic of China was kept outside the UN till 1971 through manipulation by the Western powers. In the initial period after the resumption of the Chinese seat in the UN till the early 1980s, China was still feeling its way around in the Organization. It exercised a great deal of circumspection and caution in getting involved in the activities and deliberations in the UN. In dealing with the UN during this period, it literally followed the edict of Deng Xiaoping: 'Hiding one's capacity while biding one's time' and 'not seeking to lead'. Its substantive contribution to discussions in the UN used to be very limited. It had not developed in depth or with nuances its positions on major economic and political issues featuring on the UN agenda. Its position used to be generally articulated in clichés couched in ideological terms. The Chinese representatives used to repeat these clichés as appropriate in various debates. They seldom made any move to participate actively in the negotiating process on issues of general interest. However, even during this period, the Chinese were very serious and purposive. They never allowed any opportunity in the UN for advancing their national interest to go by default. They assiduously went about acquiring knowledge and expertise in UN matters and equipping themselves to play a full-fledged role subsequently.

China became really active in the UN from about the early 1980s. The period between the early 1980s and the end of the 1990s coincided with China's opening up to the world, its effective implementation of the policy of both internal and external liberalization and its progress towards integrating itself with the world economy. During this period, it had redoubled the size of its national economy and accumulated huge foreign exchange reserves. China's membership of inter-governmental organizations increased from one to 21 between 1966 and 1977. During the period 1977 to 1988, it increased to 37.[2] China became a member of the IMF, the World Bank and its subsidiaries, the International Development Association (IDA) and the International Finance Corporation (IFC) as well as the Asian Development Bank (ADB), and was knocking at the door of the WTO. Between 1949 and 1970, China was party to only eight international conventions. This number increased to 103 between 1977 and 1987. In the early 1990s, China participated in 126 international conventions.[3] As of September 2011, China was a member of over 100 intergovernmental organizations, a party to over 300 international conventions and 'an active participant in building the international system'.[4]

India played a leading and, on several occasions, a pioneering role in the UN ever since its inception. It was linked with the UN system for decades, when the People's Republic of China was outside it. Before the People's Republic of China came to the UN and during the period when it was relatively quiescent in the Organization, India was visible everywhere, making statements in UN fora and moving and sponsoring resolutions on practically all issues of general and global concern. It was in the vanguard of the movement launched by non-aligned and developing countries in the UN, for the liquidation of apartheid, for decolonization, and for disarmament and development. Some of the major initiatives taken by India in these areas during that period included the call for a nuclear test ban treaty and nuclear disarmament; reaching an agreement on a target for the transfer of resources for the development of developing countries; acceptance of the principle of granting trade preferences to the products of developing countries in the markets of developed countries and, not the least, the admission of the People's Republic of China to the UN.

One of the advantages of India over China in the UN was that it had been there much longer than China. It had acquired much greater experience and a higher level of and more diversified expertise in UN matters than China. By virtue of its membership of NAM, G-77 and other groups of developing countries, India had a greater opportunity than China to interact on a continuing basis with a vast majority of UN members. This often had the effect of inspiring confidence in India among these countries and, therefore, their wanting to work together with India in pursuit of common goals. By working together in the fora of the developing countries operating in the UN, Indian diplomats and other professionals developed personal acquaintances with a large number of their counterparts from other countries as well as an identity of views with them on the issues under discussion.

Even during the relatively quiescent phase of its involvement with the UN, China in practical terms was more effective than India. In particular, when it came to pulling the wires and using the leverage of power to get specific national interests served through UN fora, China had greater achievements to its credit than India. This was mainly because China was a nuclear weapon power, which India was not, and as a permanent member of the Security Council, it enjoyed and selectively exercised its veto power. Moreover, even during that period, China was economically stronger than India and was operating a sizeable foreign aid programme.

During the late 1980s and early 1990s, when China's weight in the world economy and its involvement in the UN started increasing by leaps and bounds, there was a relative decline in India's influence in the world, including in the UN. The NAM had achieved some of its basic purposes, that is, the end of apartheid and decolonization as well as the end of rivalry between the two major power blocs for the supremacy of the world. Therefore, several issues on which India made a common front with other developing countries disappeared from the global agenda. Till the middle of the 1990s, the Indian economy was moving at a sluggish pace. Until 1998, there was no spectacular development on the military front either, which could have attracted the attention of the outside world. By virtue of the immense resources at its disposal, made possible by its high rate of growth averaging nearly 10 per cent per annum since the 1980s, China outpaced India in extending military and economic assistance to the developing world. This influenced the way China was perceived in the world and the world body, the UN. For, in the ultimate analysis, a nation's attitude towards other nations is very much determined by what they can do for it.

There is also an important psychological factor influencing the relative prestige and position of India and China internationally. This concerns the poor image that the outside world has of India because of its lingering massive poverty and poor performance in the social sector as contrasted with the image of China as a country that has succeeded in meeting the basic needs of its people by removing illiteracy, universalizing public health services and substantially achieving social equality. For, poverty is a curse nationally and a crying shame internationally.

Until the economic reforms in China starting in 1978, India was institutionally linked with the global system for decades when China was outside it. But India's linkages with the system were formal and institutional rather than substantive. India's shares of the world trade and world GNP were negligible when it emerged as a sovereign independent entity. Over the years, rather than looking up, these shares went down further. On the other hand, during the same period, China enhanced its shares substantially. From the early 1990s, India decided to link up with the global economy in a full-fledged manner. But during the last two decades, China's linkages have developed much faster and are deeper than those of India, which continues to remain at the periphery of the world economy. The following figures present a picture of the comparative weight of India and China in the global trade, world GDP and in the openness of their economies.

In 1948, almost immediately after India's independence and just before the Communist Revolution in China, India's share of world exports was 2.2 per cent. Thereafter, it started declining and stood at 0.7 per cent in 2000. Then, it started increasing slowly, reaching 1.4 per cent in 2010 and 1.73 per cent in 2013. It was still below the 1948 figure of 2.2 per cent. On the other hand, China's share of global exports was 0.9 per cent in 1948. It remained more or less at that level until 1980, after which it started increasing and reached 3.9 per cent in 2000. Thereafter, there was a phenomenal expansion in China's exports, which reached the level of 10.4 per cent of global exports in 2010.[5] In 2013, it further increased to 12.10 per cent.[6] In 1990, India's share of the world GDP at 1.2 per cent was only a little below China's share of 1.6 per cent. India's share stagnated at that level until the end of the 20th century. It started increasing after the beginning of the 21st century and reached 2.7 per cent in 2010, and then declined to 2.08 per cent in 2013.[7] On the other hand, the Chinese share has been steadily increasing since 1990. It reached 3.7 per cent of the world GDP in 2000 and was as high as 9.3 per cent in 2010, and 12.22 per cent in 2013.[8] The openness of the Indian economy, measured in terms of the share of India's trade to its GDP, has increased sharply during the last two decades, from 15.7 per cent in 1990 to 43.5 per cent in 2009 and 53.23 per cent in 2013.[9] China progressed more rapidly in opening up its economy. China's share of trade to GDP was 29.2 per cent in 1990; it peaked at 70 per cent in 2006. It has been declining since then, but was still at the level of a little above 45 per cent in 2013.[10] The decline is the outcome of a deliberate policy to steer the economy towards greater reliance on domestic demand for its growth.

India's democratic form of government, its rule of law and the fundamental rights enshrined in its Constitution and enforceable by an independent judiciary would seem to put India in an advantageous position in UN fora, as compared to China. India is no doubt in a better position than China to parade its record and defend its position in the field of human rights in international fora. Also, India's democracy should carry a greater weight, as compared to China's, in dealing with Western democracies. The upsurge of democratic sentiments witnessed all over the world since the early 1990s and more recently on display in the Arab world is no doubt a vindication of the system of governance prevailing in India. But in reality, the democracy factor has conferred very limited benefits to India in the international arena.

In spite of the clamour for a democratic system of governance in some parts of the Third World, dictatorship in one form or the other still reigns supreme in a majority of developing countries. So far as the Western countries are concerned, their commitment to democracy abroad is highly selective and suspect. Their strategic and other interests in the regions and the countries going through democratic turmoil take precedence over their desire to see democracy prevail there. Besides, the Indian democracy itself is in a bad shape. Whereas India has democratic institutions and still regularly goes through democratic processes like elections, there has been a deep erosion of democratic values which in turn is undermining democratic institutions and processes. This has led to India's credentials as a democracy being seriously questioned in international quarters.

Till the end of the Cold War, and particularly before it became a de facto nuclear weapon power, India, on the whole, had a value-based approach to dealing with major international issues, whereas China pursued a pragmatic approach. India's value-based approach to major global issues was an inheritantce from its culture and tradition and from the teachings of the leaders of India's independence movement which fundamentally influenced both the conceptualization and conduct of India's foreign policy, particularly under the stewardship of Jawaharlal Nehru. This value-based approach to foreign policy got reflected in India taking a principled stand on major global issues irrespective of its likely adverse implications at least over the short run, for its relations with major powers.

Their Positions on Disarmament Issues

India's value-based approach was brought to bear most prominently on the stand it took on global disarmament and development issues. In the field of disarmament, India remained a strong critic of the Nuclear NPT on the ground that it was discriminatory in that it divided the world into nuclear haves and have-nots. China, on the other hand, acceded to the NPT, though somewhat belatedly. India also took a very strong stand against ad hoc discriminatory regimes like the Australia Club, the MTCR and the NSG, all designed to control the export of dual-purpose equipment, substances and technologies which can be used for manufacturing weapons of mass destruction. In contrast, China joined the NSG and has been collaborating with other discriminatory export control regimes. Whereas India advocated the elimination of nuclear weapons within a time-bound framework and the immediate commencement of negotiations for achieving this purpose, China has persistently refused to join any nuclear arms control or disarmament negotiation. China supported Nuclear-Weapon-Free Zones (NWFZs) established by non-nuclear weapon states, while India was opposed to them on the ground that as long as nuclear weapon states possessed and deployed their nuclear arsenals that had a global reach, there could be no zones truly free from nuclear weapons. At the same time, India had adopted a pragmatic attitude on NWFZs, taking into account the relevant political considerations. For example, India used to vote for the UN resolutions on a NWFZ in the Middle East and abstain from those covering some other regions.

After India's 1998 nuclear weapon tests, there has been a measure of convergence in the positions of India and China on some of these issues.

India no longer opposes NWFZs and has even expressed its willingness to enter into special arrangements for collaborating with some of them. After obtaining the NSG waiver from the restrictions that its members impose on export of nuclear material and technology to non-members, India ceased to be critical of the non-proliferation regimes like the NSG, MTCR and Australia Club. It is now, in fact, seeking opportunities to collaborate with them and explore possibilities of joining them. Several important members of these groups, including the US, Russia, UK and France have publicly pledged support for India's membership of these regimes; but in view of the changed global situation, this does not figure high in their foreign policy priority and hence they are in no urgency to actively push for it. Besides, the support of China and some other member countries of the NSG is still problematic.

India's position on nuclear disarmament per se, however, has not undergone any change after 1998. It remains committed to Rajiv Gandhi's Action Plan for a Nuclear-Weapons-Free and Non-Violent World Order[11] and the urgent launching of negotiations for reaching this goal in a phased manner and within a time-bound framework. The Indian Nuclear Doctrine which was issued in a draft form on 17 August 1999 clearly states that 'nuclear disarmament is a national security objective' and that 'India shall continue its efforts to achieve the goal of a nuclear-weapon-free world at an early date'.[12] This position was reiterated in a Working Paper that India submitted to the Conference on Disarmament on 20 February 2007.[13] The suggestions made in this document include:

> the reaffirmation of the unequivocal commitment of all nuclear weapon states to the goal of complete elimination of nuclear weapons, negotiation of a Convention on the complete prohibition of the use or threat of use of nuclear weapons and negotiation of a Nuclear Weapon Convention prohibiting the development, production, stockpiling and use of nuclear weapons and on their destruction, leading to the global, non-discriminatory and verifiable elimination of nuclear weapons within a specified time frame.[14]

In the White Paper on China's National Defence, issued in 2010,[15] China reiterated its commitment 'for complete prohibition and thorough destruction of nuclear weapons'.[16] But China is not prepared to join any negotiation on nuclear disarmament. According to the White Paper, negotiations for drawing up a plan or formulating a convention for the complete prohibition of nuclear weapons can be taken up only 'at an appropriate time'. That time will come only after countries possessing the largest nuclear arsenals 'drastically reduce their nuclear arsenals'.[17]

This represented a slight modification in China's earlier position that it would join negotiation only after the countries possessing the largest nuclear arsenals reduced them to the level of China's arsenals. But, according to even this modified Chinese position, the commencement of negotiations on nuclear disarmament remains a distant dream. By its policy of not participating in any negotiations on nuclear disarmament from the very beginning, China is effectively coming in the way of the international community launching any significant initiative for the elimination of nuclear weapons.

There is a substantial degree of convergence in the positions of India and China on the non-use of nuclear weapons. Both countries are for a 'legally binding assurance on use or threat of use of nuclear weapons against non-nuclear weapon states'.[18] China would, in addition, like the non-use commitment to cover NWFZs. India has also recently expressed its preparedness to formalize its commitment not to use nuclear weapons against NWFZs. Both these countries are also against the first-use of nuclear weapons and in favour of nuclear weapon states negotiating a treaty on the subject.

On nuclear non-proliferation, there is a change in India's position after concluding the civilian nuclear deal with the US. Unlike its earlier position of characterizing the global non-proliferation system as the discriminatory and vertical proliferation as dangerous, if not more, as the horizontal one, India has stated that its 'civilian nuclear initiative will strengthen the international non-proliferation regime'.[19]

However, whereas China is a party to the NPT and has signed the CTBT and is in favour of its early entry into force, India maintains its opposition to the NPT, and there is no national consensus on signing the CTBT. India's contribution to the non-proliferation regime will, therefore, be through other measures like its voluntary unilateral moratorium on nuclear testing and its 'effective and comprehensive system of national export control which . . . meet the highest international standards'.[20] India is now increasingly joining major powers in subscribing to the goal of promoting nuclear non-proliferation.

China declared in its 2010 White Paper on National Defence that 'the authority, effectiveness and universality of the international non-proliferation regime should be upheld and enhanced'. In spite of this, there is ample evidence to indicate that China has wilfully violated the provisions of the NPT, which is the kingpin of the system of non-proliferation, by clandestinely transferring to non-nuclear weapon states, both members and non-members of the NPT, material, equipment and technology for the manufacture of nuclear weapons. Moreover, China in its 2010 White Paper put in a number of riders that will make it difficult to uphold the authority and ensure the effectiveness and universality of the non-proliferation regime. First, China believes that 'the root causes of proliferation should be eliminated'.[21] This position carries the implication that proliferation may be justified if its root causes are not adequately addressed. But this will never be possible unless nuclear weapons themselves are eliminated.

The second rider put in by China is that the 'non-proliferation issue should be resolved through political and diplomatic means'.[22] This implies that there should be no resort to sanctions in pursuit of the objective of non-proliferation. By taking this position, China ignores the fact that the UN Charter itself provides for sanctions as an enforcement measure in the last resort. On the other hand, India's rider that non-proliferation policies, including the export control system, should not 'hinder legitimate applications of science and technology for peaceful and development purposes'[23] is in accordance with the spirit of the UN Charter and the relevant provisions of the NPT.

A major difference that has cropped up recently in the positions of the two countries is on BMD. China 'maintains that the global missile defence programme will be detrimental to international strategic balance and stability, will undermine international and regional security, and will have a negative impact on the process of nuclear disarmament'.[24] China, therefore, is of the view that 'no state should deploy overseas, missile defence systems that have strategic missile defence capabilities or potential, or engage in any such international collaboration'.[25]

This position, which is also fully shared by Russia, clearly refers to the missile defence programme launched by the US administration in 2001. This programme no doubt carries the serious implications pointed out both by the Chinese and the Russians. In spite of this, the then NDA Government of India supported this programme and none of the succeeding governments have repudiated that position. This remains a serious flaw in India's disarmament policy. India should be comfortable with the Chinese position because it does not rule out a country developing and deploying a domestic missile defence system. What the Chinese are opposed to is its deployment 'overseas' and for global strategic purposes.

China, like India, is in favour of 'the early commencement of negotiations on Fissile Material Cut-off Treaty (FMCT) at the Conference on Disarmament (CD)' in Geneva.[26] China is committed to negotiations on FMCT, also as a party to the consensus that emerged at the last NPT

Review Conference which, among others, underlined the importance of FMCT as a non-proliferation measure. According to publicly available non-governmental estimates, China has a stock of 17 to 26 tonnes of weapon-grade uranium and 2.3 to 3.2 tonnes of plutonium.[27] This stockpile appears to be 'sufficient in quantities for future expansion of its nuclear arsenals, should the need arise'.[28] However, in spite of its commitment, in principle, to negotiation on FMCT, China, in practice, has adopted an ambiguous position on this subject. Instead of pushing for negotiations in the CD, it is taking shelter behind the absence of consensus there, primarily because of Pakistan's insistence that any negotiations on fissile materials cut-off should include reductions in existing stocks as well.

There are also some discrepancies between China's public position on nuclear disarmament issues and its actions on the ground. For example, in its White Paper on National Defence, 2006, China stated that 'it has never entered into or will ever enter into a nuclear arms race with any other country'.[29] In spite of this, China is pursuing by far the most active programme among all nuclear weapon powers, for the expansion and modernization of its nuclear force.

China's defence expenditure, with a double-digit average annual increase over more than a decade now, is another indication of the aggressive manner in which it is engaged in enhancing its military, including nuclear arms, capability. China's official defence budget in 2010 was $78 billion, second to the US, the world's top military spender. However, unofficial estimates put China's defence expenditure at a higher level, ranging between $100 billion to $150 billion.[30] In its annual report to the Congress, the US Defence Department estimated China's total military-related spending for 2007 to be between $97 billion and $139 billion. By 2013, China's military spending reached an estimated $188 billion, more than twice the spending of Russia.[31] China was second among the 15 countries with the highest military spending in 2013.[32] China's share of the world military expenditure in 2013 was the second highest at 11 per cent, the highest spender continuing to be the US with a share of 37 per cent.[33] The rate of growth in military spending in China was also relatively high. Between 2004 and 2013, military spending in Asia and Oceania increased by 62 per cent and China accounted for the largest share of this increase. This is in contrast to the decline in military expenditure in the US and Western Europe during the same period.[34] China's military spending more than quadrupled in real terms between 2000 and 2012.[35] In 2013, India's military expenditure was $49 billion, increasing from $33.8 billion in 2004. The same year, China's military expenditure was $171 billion, increasing from $63 billion in 2004.[36]

People's Liberation Army (PLA's) Second Artillery Force, which controls most of China's nuclear and conventional ballistic missiles, had, as of November 2013, 1,000 short-range ballistic missiles in its inventory. In addition, it had deployed new conventional medium-range missiles including CSS-5 Mod 5 anti-ship ballistic missiles. It is also enhancing its ICBM force, as well as developing a new road-mobile ICBM known as Dong Feng-41 possibly capable of carrying Multiple Independently Targetable Re-entry Vehicles (MIRVs). In 2012, China launched its first aircraft carrier, Liaoning, and in 2013, it announced a plan to develop indigenously built aircraft careers with greater capabilities. The PLA Navy places a high priority on the modernization of its submarine force. It continues the production of JIN-class nuclear-powered ballistic missile submarines. Three of them are currently operational and up to five may enter service over the next decade. During this period, China is also planning to produce its next-generation nuclear-powered ballistic missile submarines called JL-2. China has also expanded its nuclear power attack submarines. The PLA Air Force is pursuing modernization on a scale unprecedented in its history and is rapidly closing the gap with Western Air Forces across the broad spectrum of capabilities. China is attempting to procure Su-35 advance fighter aircraft from Russia, and vigorously pursuing fifth-generation capabilities within two years. It has already tested J-20 stealth fighters and advanced fighter J-31.[37] Observers of China's military rise believe that China has already achieved a credible nuclear deterrent based on a survivable second strike capability.

In its 2012 Defence White Paper issued in April 2013, the Government of the People's Republic of China stated that it will continue to pursue a long-term comprehensive military modernization programme designed to improve the capacity of the Armed Forces to fight and win short-duration high-intensity regional contingencies. In this White Paper there is a strong focus on maritime security and hence on the modernization of the PLA Navy.

China has, in the past, engaged in the deployment of tactical nuclear weapons. Some of its medium-range ballistic missiles are capable of reaching targets within a range that typically falls in the area of tactical use.[38] This would indicate that the Chinese nuclear arsenals are not only for defensive purposes, as claimed by it.

Finally, China has publicly advocated and even taken the initiative of putting forward a proposal for an international treaty banning the weaponization of outer space. At the same time, China has demonstrated that it has its own anti-satellite weapons (ASAT) system.

Both India and China are engaged in developing their missile defence systems. But, whereas India is still at a very early stage in this endeavour, China has moved far ahead, as was demonstrated by its successful missile defence intercept in 2011.

Their Positions on the World Economic Order

In the economic field, India frequently used to place itself in the role of a pioneer in the UN, working for the adoption of new norms and principles governing international economic relations and new approaches and strategies for the development of developing countries. China, on the other hand, played safe without taking any initiatives of its own. On several North–South issues, it went along with developing countries as long as their proposals or resolutions were put at a sufficiently high level of generalization, but whenever a move by developing countries involved a confrontation with major developed countries, China used to take a back seat.

Currently, both India and China have set themselves on the course of integrating themselves with the global capitalist system, though China has achieved much greater success than India in this endeavour. Both countries have developed a stake in the stability of the existing system and are working together to this end through common fora like the IMF, World Bank and G-20. India has considerably moderated its earlier role of a pioneer to bring about changes in the world order. It has joined China in becoming a status quoist power.

China has chosen not to identify itself formally with either NAM or G-77, though it closely collaborates with these groupings. China has an 'observer' status with NAM. Most of the major statements of G-77 are issued as position papers on behalf of 'G-77 and China'. When China tried to participate in the Global System of Trade Preferences (GSTP) among developing countries, it was told that it could do so only by becoming a full-fledged member of G-77, if not in general then at least within the ambit of the GSTP. China politely declined to accept this precondition, at the cost of depriving itself of the benefits of GSTP. On the other hand, even now, China keeps on reiterating that it is a developing country and, hence, entitled to the concessions and privileges that these countries enjoy in the UN system. China's refusal to join the G-77 or NAM is because it is keen to preserve its separate identity and retain its freedom of action in international fora as a major world power.

In terms of substantive interests, China no doubt still has a lot in common with developing countries, though India has more in common with them than China. China has a common stake, particularly with major developing countries like India, Brazil and South Africa, in issues figuring in the Doha Round of Trade Negotiations, in environmental issues, particularly climate change negotiations, and in international monetary and financial issues. Experience has shown that China's solidarity with other major developing countries can often make a difference in getting decisions which are in the general interest of developing countries, taken in international fora. The 1999 Revision of the Montreal Protocol on Substances that Deplete the Ozone Layer was in large part due to the common stand taken by China, India and Brazil in the negotiation on the Protocol. The common positions taken by these countries have been a decisive factor in some of the major achievements for developing countries during the Doha Round of Trade Negotiation and in coping with the recent global economic crisis. Some of these positive outcomes include advances made in the negotiations on agriculture, the Declaration on Public Health and the TRIPS Agreement made during the Doha Round and fairly large amounts of resources made available to developing countries during the period of the global financial and economic crisis.

For over a decade now, thanks to its vastly enhanced economic clout and military might, China's influence in the UN system has grown dramatically. It is now actively engaged in shaping the policies and structures of UN organizations and extracting maximum benefits from its participation in them. An index of China's growing influence is its much enhanced contribution to the regular UN budget. For the period 2013–15, China's assessed contribution to the UN regular budget was 5.148 per cent of the total. Its contribution to the UN peacekeeping budget in 2013 was 6.641 per cent. It was the fourth largest contributor to the UN regular budget, behind the US (22 per cent), France (5.593 per cent) and the UK (5.179 per cent).[39]

Today, China's engagement with the UN system is on a much wider front than before. It no longer keeps itself confined to flagging and pursuing its national interest through the debates and discussions in the UN. It also takes initiatives to influence policies and actions on issues of global interest. Besides, it is now shaping the rules of the game and the institutional structure, administration, staffing patterns and operations of UN organizations. China does so in a constructive and helpful manner, which is widely appreciated in the institutions concerned. In this, it is greatly helped by its very well-briefed and well-prepared experts and diplomats.

China now systematically 'taps into and profits from the collective international expertise'. It also 'taps heavily into the institutional network of information sharing, and exchange of best practices and technical expertise on economic issues'.[40] It frequently takes initiatives in UN organizations to get studies conducted that can throw light on its own developmental problems.

During the last few years, China has considerably enhanced its influence in the IMF and World Bank by virtue of its enhanced quotas in these institutions, its effective participation in the G-20 forum and its remarkable performance as a provider of foreign aid to developing countries. China has recently taken some bold initiatives to shape the international financial architecture. It has openly and officially challenged the supremacy of the dollar as an international reserve currency and called for its replacement, mainly by additional issues of SDR. Its proposal to include the yuan in the basket of currencies, the others being the dollar, the euro, the Japanese yen and the British pound, in determining the value of the SDR, has already been accepted by the G-20. Simultaneously, the Chinese are taking steps for making the yuan a de facto international currency. For this, they have succeeded in persuading several of their trade partners to use the yuan for settlement of trade. Yuan-settled trade was 7 per cent of the country's total foreign trade in the first quarter of 2011.[41] A survey conducted at that time by the HSBC Bank revealed that more than half of China's total trade would be settled in yuan by 2015. During the last three years, China has signed agreements with its major trading partners like Russia, Japan and Germany to settle payments for significant parts of its bilateral trade with them in yuan.

At the regional level, it took a major initiative in 2009 to multilateralize the Chiang Mai Initiative (CMI) of the ASEAN+3 by converting it into the Chiang Mai Initiative Multilateralization (CMIM). The core purpose of the CMIM is to address balance of payments and short-term liquid-ity difficulties in the region and to supplement the existing international financial arrangements. The total size of the CMIM, which became operational in March 2010, is $120 billion of which China and Japan will contribute 32 per cent each. In the middle of 2011, the countries participating in the CMIM established an ASEAN+3 Macro Research Office (AMRO), which was tasked to monitor, assess and report on the macro-economic situation and financial soundness of the member countries, assess their macroeconomic and financial vulnerability, and ensure compliance of swap requesting parties with the lending covenants under the CMIM Agreement. This development is an attempt to put in place a regional financial arrangement as a part of the evolving international financial architecture.

China's much enhanced activism in the UN and other multilateral organizations is in large part also designed to project an image of a co-operative and constructive China, in order to allay the widely prevalent apprehensions concerning a 'Rising China'. The image that China is trying to project through UN organizations and other means is very well articulated in the White Paper on China's Peaceful Development Role, issued in 2005. It states: 'It has become the national determination of China to safeguard world peace and promote common development'. It further says: 'What the Chinese people need and cherish most is a peaceful international environment. They are willing to do their best to make energetic contributions for the common development of all countries'. It also seeks to assure the rest of the world by asserting that 'China did not seek hegemony in the past, nor does it now, and will not do so in the future when it gets stronger'.[42]

Their Positions on UN Reforms

In mid-2005, when reform was the most important item on the UN agenda, China submitted a Position Paper on the subject. The Position Paper neither calls for the restoration of the Charter functions the UN has lost nor suggests any really effective and innovative measures for the enhancement of the capacity of the UN. However, the very fact that China decided to submit a detailed paper outlining its position on almost all the proposals on UN reforms under consideration at that time is of considerable significance. This is in sharp contrast to the fact that since the commencement in the early 1990s, of the most recent phase of the debate on UN reform, India has not submitted any comprehensive position paper or a blueprint on the subject. This lack of initiative from a country which has been one of the most ardent and longstanding supporters of the UN is really disappointing.

China's Position Paper gives some very interesting insights into China's general attitude towards the UN. Unlike the US and other Western countries which regard the UN as only one of the institutions underpinning multilateralism, the Chinese Position Paper underlines the unique position of the UN in the multilateral system. It states: 'United Nations plays an indispensable role in international affairs. As the most universal, representative, authoritative intergovernmental international organization, the UN is the best venue to practise multilateralism, and an effective platform for collective action to cope with various threats and challenges'.[43]

On the whole, China takes a pragmatic and open-minded view of issues on the reform agenda so as to be able to go along with the consensus that emerges on these issues. For example, it does not rule out the imposition of sanctions so long as they are 'applied with prudence and on the precondition that all peaceful means have been exhausted'. On use of force, the Position Paper underlines that 'the Security Council is the only body that can decide the use of force' and 'regional arrangements or organizations must obtain Security Council authorization to any enforcement action'.[44] Thus, China rules out an 'alliance of the like-minded' or a regional organization like NATO deciding on its own to intervene in situations of conflict. A positive feature of the Position Paper is that 'China supports the enhancement of the UN peacekeeping capacity and welcomes the Secretary-General's proposal on the establishment of strategic reserves and civilian police standby capacity'. The Position Paper does not reject the proposal to entrust the UN with 'the responsibility to protect'. However, it clarifies that its support for the proposal is subject to the qualification that 'no reckless intervention should be allowed' and that 'there should be more prudence in the consideration of each case'.[45]

China is 'in favour of turning ECOSOC [Economic and Social Council] into a high-level development forum for reviewing trends in international development cooperation and playing a coordinating role'. Moreover, the Council should play the 'leading, normative and strategy-setting role . . . in mapping out a global development agenda'.[46] However, China is silent on restoring to the UN the Charter functions in the realm of trade, money, finance and development strategies, which have been effectively transferred to the IMF, World Bank and WTO.

The position taken by China on the expansion of the Security Council comprehensively militates against India's aspiration to become a permanent member of the Council. China is silent on the expansion of permanent membership. While accepting in principle that 'increasing the representation of developing countries should be given priority', China states that 'small and medium-sized' countries 'should be given more opportunities to enter the Council on a rotating basis', and that 'all the regional groups should, first of all, reach an agreement on reform proposals concerning their respective regions'.[47] China also emphasizes achieving a consensus through full diplomatic discussions, thus ruling out a decision by voting. The acceptance of these propositions would amount to an indefinite postponement of the expansion of the membership of the Security Council.

By virtue of its superior economic and military power, China is able to bestow favours and forge strategic relationships with other countries of a kind and on a scale that India cannot afford. China, therefore, enjoys a much stronger bargaining power than India in seeking votes or support in the UN. Other member countries are keener to woo China and more circumspect about displeasing or rebuffing it than they are when it comes to India. Its superior economic and military power also enables China to be more flexible than India in dealing with sensitive and controversial international issues. For example, China led the way in establishing full diplomatic relations with Israel when India was still weighing the pros and cons of doing so. China maintains full-fledged relations with Taiwan in matters relating to cooperation in trade, finance and technology while effectively preventing other countries, including India, from having similar relations with this territory.

India and China as Arms Exporters

China is an important supplier of military hardware and technology to the Third World countries. It has been exporting arms to developing countries for decades. Between 1984 and 1989, China's export of arms to these countries was in the range of $1 billion to $1.8 billion annually.[48] Between 2006 and 2009, the total value of China's arms transfer agreements worldwide, out of which 98.6 per cent was with developing countries, amounted to $7.5 billion, yielding an average of approximately $1.9 billion per annum. The peak year during this period was reached in 2005, when the value of China's arms transfer to developing countries was $3.25 billion, equivalent to 9.69 per cent of the global total. In 2009, China's share came down to 3.3 per cent. During this period, China was the fifth largest arms supplier to developing countries, coming after the US, Russia, the UK and France, in that order, and ranking above countries like Germany and Italy.[49] In contrast, India is yet to join the rank of important arms exporters of the world. Its forays into developing countries for the purpose of military supplies are, therefore, few and far between and mostly of an exploratory nature. In 2013, China held the fourth position among the 50 largest suppliers of major weapons, whereas India's position was 39th. In total volume, China's exports were $1.8 billion, as against India's only $10 million.[50]

China's arms supply to India's neighbours complicates India's security environment in its neighbourhood. In 2013, 60 per cent of China's arms supply went to South Asia.[51] China is the largest supplier of arms to two of India's most important neighbours, Pakistan and Bangladesh. It has also supplied arms to Sri Lanka on a fairly large scale from time to time and, on a couple of occasions, to Nepal. With Pakistan, it has concluded major agreements for defence production and military technology transfer.

China, through its military supplies (some estimates put it at $2 billion to $2.5 billion) to Myanmar, has brought about a qualitative change in the latter's military capabilities. This has had an inevitable negative impact on Myanmar's domestic political process.

Between 2004–08 and 2009–13, the Chinese exports of major arms increased by 212 per cent and China's share in the volume of all arms export increased from 2 to 6 per cent. China has now firmly established itself as one of the top arms suppliers, edging out both France and UK from the first four positions.[52] China has now started competing with major suppliers like the US and Russia in the world market. One of the latest examples is its successful bid in 2012 for the supply of three F-22 frigates to Algeria.[53] From 2008 to 2012, China signed about $10 billion-worth agreements for conventional arms sales worldwide.[54]

Of late, China has concluded a large number of agreements for military supplies to countries in Central Asia, West Asia and Africa. These give China a clout in the UN which India does not have, apart from tilting the power balance in these regions in China's favour.

Their Economic Aid to Developing Countries

India, since its independence, and China, after the success of the Communist Revolution, have been providing development assistance to Third World countries on a regular basis in pursuit of their foreign policy objectives. Most of this assistance has been bilateral, even as both countries have also contributed to UN multilateral aid programmes. In 2010–12, China contributed approximately $278 million to UN operational activities, while according to the Ministry of Finance Budget Document 2014–15, India's contribution in this budget year was $27.4 million. Both their bilateral and multilateral aid programmes have been a major factor in contributing to their influence in the UN fora.

During the period 1950–74, China used development assistance as a major instrument of its foreign policy. Political interests played far more important a role in the provision of assistance during this period than the economic ones. Chinese foreign assistance was used to win international recognition and support for the new China after the Communist Revolution and for exporting socialist ideology to and buttressing socialist governments in foreign countries. After the Soviet Union got entangled in ideological confusion soon after the death of Stalin in 1953 and particularly during the earlier part of the Khrushchev era, the government of the People's Republic of China took upon itself the mantle of keeping communism alive and spreading and underpinning its own brand of socialism across the globe. For example, China provided more than ¥9 billion as aid to the Communist Party of Vietnam from 1970 to 1973.[55] The main purposes of Chinese foreign aid during that period are very clearly articulated in the following statement of Zhou Enlai, the then Chinese Premier:

> The starting point of our foreign aid is, in the spirit of proletarian internationalism, to support fraternal countries in their socialist construction and enhance the strength of the whole socialist camp, support countries in their effort to win independence, the newly independent countries in their efforts to develop their national economies by self-reliance and consolidate the fruits of their independence and enhance the anti-imperialistic forces of the peoples of all countries.[56]

The total foreign aid given by China during the period 1950 to 1974 amounted to ¥32.67 billion, which was equivalent of 0.99 per cent of its GNP. The Chinese foreign aid reached ¥4.77 billion, equivalent to 1.71 per cent of its GNP in 1974.[57] A major infrastructure project financed during this period was the Tan-Zam Railway line in Africa.

The early part of the second phase, that is, 1975–90, of the Chinese foreign assistance, coincided with the commencement of the liberalization of the Chinese economy. With the changes in its development policy and strategy, China made important adjustments in its aid policy. Economic factors took precedence over political considerations. The Chinese foreign aid became more discriminatory and a great deal of emphasis was put on reciprocity and mutual benefit. The combined effect of the shift of emphasis from political to economic factors, the quest for mutual benefit and the virtual discarding of the ideological perspective in the conduct of international relations led to a sharp decline in Chinese foreign aid during the second phase. The volume of aid declined from ¥4.77 billion in 1974 to ¥1.56 billion in 1990. The decline in the Chinese aid as a percentage of its GNP, from 1.71 per cent in 1974 to 0.08 per cent in 1990, was really precipitous.[58]

In the third phase of the Chinese foreign aid, beginning from 1991 and continuing till now, the government adopted an integrated approach to providing foreign aid, taking into account both economic and political factors, environmental considerations, the objective of obtaining natural resources for China's fast growing economy and the new strategy of projecting an image of a benign, cooperative and helpful China in the face of apprehensions regarding 'Rising China'. An outcome of this comprehensive approach was a sharp increase in the volume of aid. China's foreign aid increased from ¥1.68 billion, equivalent to 0.08 per cent of its GNP in 1991, to a whopping ¥7.47 billion in 2005. However, on account of the very rapid rate of growth of the Chinese economy, this much-increased aid in volume, declined further as a percentage of the GDP to 0.04 per cent in 2005. Between 2004 and 2009, financial resources for China's foreign aid increased by 29.4 per cent on an average.[59] During the last several years, the rate of growth in the resources for foreign aid has been much higher than the rate of growth of the economy.

An important feature of Chinese aid in this phase was the establishment in 1993 of a Fund for Joint Venture and Cooperative Projects and the entry in 1995, of the Chinese EXIM Bank into this arena for providing concessional loans to recipient countries. These loans have been provided mostly for complete projects in the area of infrastructure and civilian construction. The Chinese concessional loans are made available at the rate of 2 to 3 per cent with a repayment period of 16 to 20 years and a grace period of five years. By the end of 2009, China had provided such loans to 76 foreign countries, supporting 325 projects. Complete projects accounted for 40 per cent of the total Chinese aid. Among the number of completed projects by the end of 2009, the largest number, that is, 670 out of the total 2,025, came under the heading 'public facilities' which included such demonstrative structures as conference halls, sports stadia, theatres, cinemas and civilian buildings to accommodate offices.[60]

The Chinese government, through its successive White Papers on Foreign Aid issued recently, has projected its foreign aid as an important dimension of its peaceful and responsible role as a rising global power. In its 2014 White Paper on Foreign Aid, it has stated that its objective is to 'provide assistance to other developing countries within the framework of South-South cooperation to help, especially the least developed countries, to reduce poverty and improve livelihood'. The White Paper specifically mentions that 'China has pro-actively promoted international development and cooperation and played a constructive role in this aspect'.[61]

According to the information provided in this White Paper, during the three years period, 2010–12, China appropriated a total of US$14.41 billion for foreign assistance which covered 121 countries, including 13 in Asia and 51 in Africa. It trained a total of 49,148 persons from other developing countries.

During the third phase, Africa emerged as the largest recipient of the Chinese aid, accounting for 45.7 per cent of the total aid, with Asia coming next with 32.8 per cent.[62] In 2005, China lent some $8 billion to Nigeria, Angola and Mozambique. This was more than three times the total loan of $2.3 billion provided by the World Bank to the whole of Africa during that year. The amount of China's aid in the form of loans to Africa in 2006 was three times that of the total aid extended by all member countries of the OECD, and 25 times the aid from America's EXIM Bank during that year.[63]

China has provided considerable amount of resources for debt relief to the heavily indebted poor countries and to least developed countries having diplomatic relations with China. These debt reliefs have been announced from time to time in major conferences. By the end of 2009, China had signed debt relief protocols with 50 developing countries, cancelling matured debts totalling ¥25.58 billion.[64] During 2011–13, China gave debt reliefs to nine least developed and heavily indebted poor countries, all of them from Africa.[65]

India has also sought to win friends, influence people and thereby serve its national interest by its development assistance to other developing countries. However, the resource crunch has been a major constraint to India's development assistance, except during the last decade. The balance-of-payment crisis which India got into from time to time, resulted in the relatively smaller size of India's aid programme and its disruption and discontinuity, which reduced its impact and thus the economic and political capital that India could get out of it.

From the early 1990s, there was a dramatic improvement in China's foreign exchange reserve position. At the end of 2013, its foreign exchange reserves touched the level of $3.8 trillion, against India's foreign exchange reserve of $267.7 billion.[66] In addition to the huge magnitude of resources at its command, China is capable of delivering its projects and programmes according to the specifications and within or even ahead of the time limits set by it. This gives China an additional edge over India.

A distinguishing common feature of the foreign aid provided by both India and China is that it has been free from conditionalities of a political nature. In extending their aid, both countries have adhered to the principle of non-interference in the internal affairs of the recipient countries. Unlike the Western countries, India and China have not used their aid to achieve non-economic objectives like democratization, promotion of human rights and good governance. This absence of conditionalities has made their aid more welcome and acceptable than that from Western countries. China's policy in this regard is reiterated in its 2014 White Paper on Foreign Aid where it is stated: 'While providing foreign assistance, China adheres to the principle of non-imposing any political conditions, not interfering in the internal affairs of the recipient countries and fully respecting their right to independently choosing their own paths and mode of development'.[67]

In highlighting the distinguishing features of their foreign aid, both India and China claim that their assistance is primarily designed to build the self-development capacity of the partner countries. They are doing so by training local personnel, building infrastructure and developing the domestic resources of the recipient countries. On the other hand, the North–South economic relationship has been exploitative in nature and has enhanced the dependency of the South on the North. However, the fact remains that not all the projects undertaken by India and China through their aid are designed for capacity building in the partner countries. Both countries have gone in for projects that involve prospecting, extraction and processing of resources with a view to their transfer for meeting the increasing demand for resources for fuelling growth in these countries. However, India has undertaken relatively fewer projects in this category, mainly because it cannot dispose of the resources on the scale on which China can in order to invest in such projects. On the whole, as compared to China, a larger proportion of the Indian aid has financed capacity and institution building projects. The Indian Technical and Economic Cooperation (ITEC) programme, launched in 1964, is almost entirely devoted to this purpose. As many as 68,780 personnel from developing countries were trained under this programme between 1991 and 2011. This compares favourably with the total number of 120,000, trained by China since the beginning of its foreign aid programme. During the last three years, India has on an average been providing over 8,000 training slots every year for trainees from developing countries.[68] As of 2011, the total aid provided by India under ITEC since its establishment amounted to $2 billion. Like China, India's EXIM Bank also provides soft loans to developing countries for complete projects as a part of its foreign aid programme. As of February 2015, the total amount of line of credit opened by the EXIM Bank of India stood at $11.58 billion.[69] The amount of credit extended by it in 2013–14 was $1.77 billion and in 2014–15 (up to 28 February 2015) it was $1.62 billion.[70] Of this, 54 per cent went to Africa and 35 per cent to South Asia, mainly to India's neighbouring countries.[71] However, a greater proportion of India's aid than that of China is provided as grants. For example, the Chinese aid to Sri Lanka in 2010 was entirely in the form of loans, whereas the Indian aid had a grant component amounting to about $20 million.[72] The situation has changed somewhat during the last three years when grants constituted 36.2 per cent of China's total assistance.[73]

Both India and China claim that their foreign assistance projects are tailored to the needs of the recipient developing countries. In the past, the developed countries also used to make such claims. But, because of the overwhelming dependence of the recipient countries on the developed donor countries, the latter were able to impose their priorities in providing assistance. The UN system has been a worse offender in this regard. We are all aware of the discredited conditionalities of the structural adjustment programmes of the IMF and World Bank. Other UN bodies have been imposing their so-called global priorities, which have not been very different from those pursued by developed countries through their bilateral aid programmes. The foreign aid provided by India and China has by and large been free from this stigma.

In recent years, there has been a shift of emphasis in the foreign aid programmes of both India and China towards Africa. This is partly because of the dynamism displayed recently by the economies of several African countries and the much enhanced voice of these countries in UN fora. This continent also happens to be very rich in natural resources which are much in demand in both India and China.

India has been geographically and historically closer to Africa than China. India, therefore, has the advantage of long cultural and economic links with Africa. Trade routes between India and Africa were established centuries ago. Another advantage that India enjoys is the presence of an almost 2 million-strong Indian diaspora in Africa whose members are engaged in teaching, business activities and industrial development in African countries. In spite of these advantages, when China decided to move into Africa in a full-fledged manner in pursuit of its economic and political interests, it did so with a bang, soon leaving India far behind. An index of China's march in Africa is that in spite of being a late starter in trading with African countries, China's overall trade volume with Africa in 2008 was $108 billion against India's $46 billion. The value of India–Africa bilateral trade jumped from $5.3 billion in 2001 to $12 billion in 2005 to $63 billion in 2011. The rate of growth during the period 2005–11 was 31.8 per cent.[74] During January–November 2010, the China–Africa trade volume increased to $114.81 billion, representing a year-on-year growth of 43.5 per cent.[75]

China is today Africa's largest trading partner, its major import source, the second largest overseas construction project contract market and the fourth largest investment destination. In 2012, the total volumes of China–Africa trade reached $198.49 billion. From 2000 to 2012, the share of China–Africa trade, of China's total foreign trade volume increased from 2.23 per cent to 5.13 per cent. In 2012, the proportion of mechanical and electrical products as a part of China's total export to Africa was 45.9 per cent. In August 2013, over 2,000 Chinese enterprises were investing in more than 50 African countries and regions in expanding sectors of development including agriculture, and mining and building industries. By the end of 2012, China had signed bilateral investment treaties with 32 African countries.[76]

The private sector of India has played an important role in initiating and undertaking economic development projects in African countries. But here also, during the last 14 years, Chinese companies have been much more active in Africa than Indian enterprises. However, the former cannot be described as 'private' in the strict sense of the term. For, though Chinese companies active in Africa enjoy considerable autonomy in decision making on operational matters and their portfolios are diversified, they are still essentially under government control and work in tandem with the government in pursuit of the geo-strategic interest of China in Africa. The same cannot be said about Indian firms, which are guided principally by the profit motive.

In recognition of the importance of Africa, both India and China have set up summit-level fora for cooperation with Africa. The Forum of China–Africa Cooperation (FOCAC) was set up in 2000 and has provided a platform for regular consultations and dialogue between China and African countries. In the November 2006 meeting of the Forum held in Beijing, President Hu Jintao announced a number of proposals constituting a vision for a new Sino-African Strategic Partnership. These included:[77]

- Doubling the resources earmarked for foreign aid to Africa during the next three years

- Providing during the next three years, a sum of $3 billion as concessional loans and $2 billion as concessional export credit
- Establishing a Sino-African Development Fund with a total funding of up to $5 billion in order to encourage and provide resources to Chinese enterprises to invest in Africa
- Constructing an African Union conference centre
- Training 15,000 Africans in various professions.

The fourth meeting of the Forum on China–Africa Cooperation was held in 2009. In the action plan adopted at this forum, the Chinese government offered, among others, the following:[78]

- A provision of $10 billion of preferential loans to African countries, mainly intended to support infrastructure and social development projects
- Active implementation of projects covered by China's $30 million contribution to the Food and Agriculture Organization's (FAO's) Special Programme for Food Security
- An increase in the size of the China–Africa Development Fund to $3 billion to support the expansion of investment by Chinese business firms to Africa
- Establishment by Chinese financial institutions of a special loan window of $1 billion to help the growth of small and medium enterprises in Africa.

In addition to these, China pledged zero-tariff treatment to over 95 per cent of the exports to China by all least developed countries that have diplomatic relations with China.[79] An overwhelming majority of these countries are from Africa.

In a similar move, India also set up an Indo-African Forum for Development Cooperation in 2008. A major announcement made by the Prime Minister of India at the India–Africa Forum Summit Conference, held in New Delhi in 2008, was the extension of duty-free and preferential access to the Indian market for products of 49 least developed countries which included 33 countries from Africa. According to this scheme, 85 per cent of the product lines covering export from these countries was to be provided duty-free access and 9 per cent preferential access. At the second meeting of the forum at the summit level in June 2011, the Prime Minister of India announced the following measures:

- A provision of $5 billion over the next three years for providing development support to African countries
- A provision of $700 million for establishing 80 new institutions in Africa

- A provision of $300 million for the Ethiopia–Djibouti railway line
- An ambitious programme for providing training facilities to African candidates and experts.

In an attempt to extend the benefits of IT to Africa, India has launched a Pan-African e-Network project. The objective of this project is to connect all members of the African Union by a satellite and fibre optic network in order to support e-governance and e-commerce, resource mapping and to provide meteorological, educational and health services. So far, 48 African countries have been brought within the Pan-African e-Network. The telemedicine component of the project is being implemented in 11 African countries. Seven Indian educational institutions and 12 super-speciality hospitals are involved in the project. Under the tele-education component, three Indian universities, three regional universities in Africa and 24 learning centres in as many African countries are linked.[80] India has also announced the establishment of an India-Africa Virtual University, which will be undertaken by the Indira Gandhi National Open University (IGNOU).

Institution-building activities by India in Africa include the establishment of a diamond centre in Botswana, a vocational training centre for small and medium enterprises in Zimbabwe, a plastic technology centre in Namibia, an entrepreneurship development centre in Senegal, an Institute of Telemedicine in Ethiopia, an Institute of Educational Planning and Administration in Burundi, an Institute of Information Technology in Ghana and an Institute of Foreign Trade in Uganda.

In addition, 10 vocational centres, five human settlement institutes for supporting low-cost housing and two institutions concerned with coal are to be set up. Human capacity building is a major component of India–Africa economic relations. There are commitments for establishing an India–Africa University for Life and Earth Sciences and a couple of industrial clusters with capacity-building components. The India–Africa Food Processing Cluster and India–Africa Integrated Textiles Cluster are two major projects that may take off soon. The Food Processing Cluster is a US$24 million project. The integrated textile cluster will be developed on the basis of the value chain concept for the growth of textile and clothing industry in African countries.

During the last three years, China's engagement with Africa has expanded by leaps and bounds. China–Africa trade volume exceeded $200 billion in 2013. According to the Chinese customs data released towards the end of 2014, 2,500 Chinese companies have established themselves in Africa over the last two decades. During this period there has, however, been rumblings of complaints regarding China's use of its aid for acquiring natural resources, including land, the poor quality of the Chinese-built infrastructure, and the use of migrant labour from China in the projects assisted by it. In 2013, Ghana deported thousands of Chinese workers in a crackdown on illegal mining in the country, and in early 2014, workers in Chinese projects in Chad and Niger went on strike in protest against their being paid unequal salaries.[81] In his visit to Africa in May 2014, the new Chinese Premier rejected accusations against Chinese assistance but admitted that some African countries suffered from growing pangs of their rapidly expanding economic relationship with China. He announced that China would increase its credit line for African countries by $10 billion, bringing the total to $30 billion for the period 2013–15. At the time of his visit, China also signed a $2 billion deal with the African Development Bank, thus making a departure from its erstwhile policy of relying overwhelmingly on bilateral deals in the continent. A positive aspect of this deal is that the contracts for projects under it are open for suitable bidders other than the Chinese companies.[82]

In spite of the shift of emphasis to Africa, China continues to be active in carrying out major projects in south-east Asian countries that are of strategic importance to it. For example, as of 2011, China emerged as the highest donor for Cambodia, overtaking both Japan and the EU, with an overall commitment of $257 million. In Vietnam, an agreement was reached in 2004 to set up three projects to build economic corridors linking Vietnam's provinces with the adjoining Chinese provinces. China is also financing hydropower projects in Vietnam. In Thailand, a canal is being built at the cost of $20 billion across the Kra Isthumus to allow ships to bypass the Strait of Malacca. China also emerged as the largest loan-giver to the Philippines, which totalled $2 billion in 2007. One of the largest Chinese-funded projects in the Philippines is the $1 billion North Rail line.[83] China signed a $6 billion refinery deal with Brunei in November 2011.[84]

Even in India's close neighbourhood in South Asia, China is outperforming India practically in every country except Bhutan. In all these countries, the Chinese are concentrating on infrastructure building and construction of public buildings which are demonstrative of Chinese involvement and presence in these countries. One of the biggest Chinese projects in Nepal is the proposed Lhasa–Xigaze–Khasa rail link across the Sino-Nepal border. In addition, Chinese assistance has focused on hydropower, roads and tourism projects. China has also built a hospital and a polytechnic institute in Nepal. China has invested heavily in energy and transportation projects in Nepal, including a $1.6 billion hydropower plant and a $1.9 billion road-rail project to connect Lhasa to Kathmandu. Other transportation projects include the Pokhara regional international airport and a number of roads, bridges and container depots.[85] A state-owned company, Three Gorges International Corporation, has pledged an amount of $1.6 billion to build dams in Nepal.

In 2011, China advanced a loan of $1 billion for the implementation of a slew of projects in Bangladesh. Among the on-going projects are deep sea ports in Chittagong and Sonadia Island.[86] China has invested $226 million for a water plant and $559 million for a fertilizer factory in Bangladesh, and it also plans to build a road and rail link through Myanmar to connect Kunming with Chittagong.[87]

In Sri Lanka, Chinese companies are funding a large number of mega projects, with close to 26,000 semi-skilled and unskilled Chinese workers involved in these projects.[88] Among the major projects that have either been completed or are in the process of being completed with Chinese assistance are a 35,000-seat cricket stadium, a large convention centre, a $209 million international airport and a nearly $2 billion sea port in Hambantota.[89] The other projects mentioned in Saman Kelegama's paper are a Special Economic Zone in Mirigama, a 1,000-acre Tapioca Farm, a coal-fired power plant, the Colombo–Katunayake Expressway, the Palai–Kankasanthurai rail line and Jaffna Housing Complex for the army.

In Afghanistan, China has made a $3.5 billion investment in the Aynak copper field, which includes a captive 400 MW power plant and a rail connection from Tajikistan to Afghanistan. Chinese companies have also ventured into Afghanistan's telecommunication sector in collaboration with the Afghan Ministry of Communication. China has written off all matured debts owed to it by Afghanistan. In a 25-year pact signed between Afghanistan and China, China's National Petroleum Company is to develop Afghanistan's energy resources, transport infrastructure and refining capacity. The company has already kicked off production at the Amu Darya oil field in northern Afghanistan under this pact.

China's economic engagement with Pakistan is extensive, on a very large scale, and of crucial economic and strategic significance. To cite only a few of the projects falling in this category, China has invested $200 million to upgrade the Gwadar deep sea port and is currently mining for lead and zinc in south-west Pakistan.

India and China in UN Peacekeeping

Both India and China are among the most active UN members participating in UN peacekeeping operations. Of the two, India remains the more active participant. For the past several years, India along with Bangladesh and Pakistan, has been among the largest contributors of troops to UN peacekeeping. As of December 2012, China ranked 15th among the 115 UN member countries participating in UN peacekeeping operations.[90] In 2013, a total of approximately 1,900 Chinese peacekeepers were participating in UN operations around the world, mostly in sub-Saharan Africa and the Middle East.[91] China maintained its position as the highest participant among the permanent members of the Security Council. In terms of contribution to the UN peacekeeping budget, its assessed contribution for the year 2013–15 was 6.64 per cent, the sixth largest among all contributors. India's assessed contribution for this period was only 0.0016 per cent.[92] China's contribution in the 1990s was only 0.9 per cent.

UN peacekeeping operations have recently become highly diversified. They now include post-war rehabilitation and peace building. They call for contributions of not only military troops, but also providing logis-tical support, police and civilian personnel, assisting in the maintenance of law and order, training the local police force and administrative personnel and conducting elections. Both India and China are participating in all these activities. Till very recently, the Chinese were reluctant to send combat troops and concentrated on despatching technical teams of engineers, doctors and unarmed police forces. In the White Paper on China's National Defence issued in 2010, the Chinese emphasized the non-combat role of their peacekeepers. They claimed that their peacekeeping personnel 'built and repaired over 8,700 km of roads, 270 bridges, cleared over 8,900 mines, transported over 600,000 tonnes of cargo across a total distance of 9.3 million km and treated 79,000 patients'.[93] As a country which regarded the UN as a major forum for conducting its foreign policy and, during the Jawaharlal Nehru era, as an embryonic form of world government, India started participating in UN peacekeeping operations right from its beginning, as a part of its contribution to promoting the ideals of peace and cooperation through the UN Charter. It was actively involved in the conceptualization and operationalization of the UN peacekeeping system. It participated in a big way in some of the major peacekeeping operations that were undertaken during the first decade and a half after the establishment of the UN.

For example, the Indian battalion was the largest single unit under the UN command of the peacekeeping operation in the Congo.

The main reason for India's involvement in the earlier peacekeeping operations was its acceptability to the parties involved in the conflicts, due to its impeccable credentials as a non-aligned country and Jawaharlal Nehru's stewardship of the foreign policy of India. India's involvement in peacekeeping slowed down from 1964 until the end of the Cold War. During this period, the UN launched a total of six peacekeeping operations but Indian troops did not participate in any of them. This was partly due to India's preoccupation with security along its borders with China and Pakistan after the 1962 War with China and the 1965 War with Pakistan, and partly because the government that came to power in India after Nehru attached relatively lower priority to the UN in general and to UN peacekeeping in particular.

There was a dramatic increase in UN peacekeeping operations after the end of the Cold War because of the much enhanced possibility of achieving big power unanimity in the Security Council in favour of UN interventions in conflict situations in the world. For example, the UN carried out only 13 peacekeeping operations during the 42 years coinciding with the Cold War, from 1945 to 1987. It carried out the same number of peacekeeping operations during the period of only five years between 1987 and 1992, that is, on the eve of and after the end of the Cold War. The total expenditure incurred by the Organization during 1947 to 1986 was far short of $1 billion, whereas the expenditure incurred during 1987 to 1992 was $8.3 billion.[94]

The increase in the number of UN peacekeeping operations provided both India and China vastly expanded opportunities to contribute to them. Another important change during that period was a shift in the UN's involvement, from inter-state conflicts to intra-state conflicts. In the beginning, this presented a dilemma for both India and China. This is because both of them were of the view that intervention in a conflict situation within a country, involving the use of force under Chapter VII of the UN Charter, without the consent of the government in power, amounted to the violation of state sovereignty and the principle of non-interference in domestic affairs enshrined in the Charter. Though they still adhere to this position in principle, on the whole they have now taken a pragmatic view of the matter. They have not only decided not to come in the way of UN involvement in peacekeeping in situations of intra-state conflict, but have actually participated in such operations in a selective manner. Today, Indian and Chinese troops can be seen in UN contingents despatched for managing situations of intra-state conflicts in a large number of countries in Africa and Asia. In the meantime, their positions on the principle of non-intervention in the domestic affairs of member states now stands significantly compromised by their endorsement of the concept of the 'right to protect', which was an important element in the package of UN reforms adopted by consensus at the 2005 summit-level session of the General Assembly.

Before it acquired its membership of the UN in 1971, Communist China had a negative attitude towards the Organization, including its peacekeeping operations. It had seen in the denial of its legitimate claim to UN membership, an attempt by the Western powers to force it into international isolation. China, therefore, saw the UN as an instrument used by the Western countries to serve their national interests. It was also of the view that these countries systematically manipulated decisions and affairs in the UN to suit their convenience. China also found itself at the receiving end of the bargain in the 1950–53 UN peacekeeping operation in Korea.

Even after assuming its seat in the UN, China continued to oppose the launching of peacekeeping operations and did not participate in them till almost the end of the 1980s. A change in China's negative attitude towards UN peacekeeping was noticed in May 1981 when it voted for the extension of the UN peacekeeping force in Cyprus. Later that year, China agreed to pay its share towards the expenditure on peacekeeping operations, which it had refused to do since joining the UN. The next important stage came when it became a member of the UN Sub-Committee on Peacekeeping Operations in 1988. However, in spite of these indications of support, China's actual participation in peacekeeping started only in 1989. In November 1989, China decided to despatch five Chinese military observers to serve in the UN Truce Supervision Organization in the Middle East, and 20 Chinese civilians to serve as members of the UN Transition Assistance Group to help monitor the independence process in Namibia. In 1992, it despatched an engineering corps to the UN Transitional Authority in Cambodia. In 2001, it established a Peacekeeping Affairs Office in its Ministry of Defence. In 2002, it joined the UN Stand-by Arrangement System for Peacekeeping Operations. China also established a training programme for peacekeepers in China under the PLA.

Recently, there has been a spurt in Chinese participation in UN peacekeeping operations. Chinese peacekeeping deployment increased twentyfold from 2000 to 2008. It has increased further since then. China has contributed in various forms including combat troops, to peacekeeping in Western Sahara, Liberia, Ivory Coast, Congo, Sudan, Lebanon, Kosovo, Haiti and East Timor. In 2012, China for the first time deployed an armed infantry unit to a UN peacekeeping operation. It was a guard unit to provide security to PLA engineers and medical personnel operating in the UN peacekeeping mission in South Sudan.[95] A Chinese contingent joined the UN peacekeeping mission in Bomako in December 2013.

Most of the purposes that India and China seek to serve through their participation in UN peacekeeping operations are identical. Their main purpose, as highlighted in their public statements, is to demonstrate their commitment to the objectives of the UN Charter and to contribute to the maintenance of global peace and security. Moreover, through their participation, both nations have sought to build a good self image among other countries of the world and to obtain support for their causes in the UN. Their participation has also enabled them to exert a more positive influence in UN policy in general and UN peacekeeping in particular.

Second, both of them have found it extremely useful to be present on the ground with their troops and other means of influence, in the trouble spots of the world where their vital interests are involved. This is particularly true of West Asia, Africa, South-East and North-East Asia. Reduction of tension in these areas, brought about by UN peacekeeping operations, is generally in their geo-strategic interest, which is further advanced by demonstrating that their own participation in peacekeeping has directly contributed to it. Their influence in these regions is further enhanced by the opportunity that their participation in peacekeeping provides for playing a mediatory role from behind the scene.

Third, through their participation in UN peacekeeping operations, both the countries have gained valuable experience for increasing the capabilities of their armed forces by field testing of equipment and methods, in gaining experience of operations at the ground level in different circumstances; in enhancing the skills of their troops; in promoting modernization and professionalism as well as in assessing the capabilities of other nations participating in peacekeeping side by side with them. Lastly, there is the obvious financial gain for the participating troops who receive salaries and allowances by the UN, which are much higher than what they get from their own governments.

At the same time, both countries have sought to serve their specific foreign policy objectives through their participation in UN peacekeeping. China has done so more systematically, and sometimes blatantly, than India. This is mainly because of the leverage that China enjoys by virtue of having a veto on decision making for launching peacekeeping operations.

There are several instances of China having used its veto power to pressurize a country where a peacekeeping operation had been proposed to be launched, to snap its ties with Taiwan and embrace the 'one China' policy. This happened in 1977 when China rejected a move to send ceasefire observers to Guatemala, which recognized Taiwan, and in 1999 when it vetoed the extension of the UN peacekeeping mandate to the former Yugoslav Republic of Macedonia because of its ties with Taiwan.

India has used its contributions to UN peacekeeping operations as a qualification for seeking permanent membership of the Security Council. It is generally recognized as a legitimate argument to use to buttress one's claims to be a permanent member of the Council. Moreover, India is using this argument ex post, in the sense that its participation in UN peacekeeping operations so far demonstrates its commitment to the UN. There is no evidence of India having participated or intensified its participation in an effortt to strengthen its case for permanent membership.

A factor playing an extremely important role in the recent intensification of the Chinese involvement in UN peacekeeping operations is China's desire to dispel the fear among other countries, particularly its neighbours, that a 'Rising China' poses a threat to them or to world peace and security. Participation in peacekeeping affords an opportunity to China to showcase the sincerity of its commitment to building a 'harmonious world' and playing the role of a responsible great power. Since the PLA is the visible symbol of the threat that China's military might and economic strength can pose to the rest of the world, particularly to its neighbouring countries, Chinese authorities are making an extra effort to let the PLA be seen as a force actively engaged in enforcing and building peace in different parts of the world

Notes

1. The term 'United Nations' embraces the principal organs of the UN, their subsidiary bodies and the specialized agencies, including the IMF and the

World Bank. The WTO is not formally associated with the UN, but for the sake of analysis in this chapter is treated as a part of the UN system.

2. Figures taken from Samuel S. Kim, 'Thinking Globally in Post-Mao China', *Journal of Peace Research*, Volume 27, No. 2 (1990) 191–209.
3. Ibid.
4. Information Office of the State Council, 'White Paper: China's Peaceful Development'.
5. World Trade Organization, Statistics Database, http://stat.wto.org/Home/WSDB-Home.aspx?Languatge=E (accessed on 22 August 2011).
6. Calculated from data taken from International Monetary Fund, Direction of Trade Statistics Database, http://elibrary-data.imf.org/ (accessed on 6 March 2015).
7. Data accessed from http://data.worldbank.org (accessed on 30 April 2015).
8. Ibid.
9. Ibid.
10. Ibid.
11. Action Plan for Ushering in a Nuclear-Weapon-Free and Non-Violent World Order (for full text, see Annexure 1 to the letter dated 20 May 1988, from the Permanent Representative of India to the UN addressed to the Secretary General).
12. Ministry of External Affairs, 'Draft Report of National Security Advisory Board on Indian Nuclear Doctrine' (Government of India, 17 August 1999), http://mea.gov.in/in-focus-article.htm?18916/Draft+Report+of+National+Security+Advisory+Board+on+Indian+Nuclear+Doctrine (accessed on 30 April 2015).
13. Working Paper on Nuclear Disarmament presented by India at the UN Conference on Disarmament (CD/1816, 20 February 2007), http://meaindia.nic.in/cdgeneva/?pdf06010?000 (accessed on 22 February 2015).
14. Pranab Mukherjee, 'Statement by External Affirs Minister of India Shri Pranab Mukherjee on the Civilian Nuclear Initiative', 5 September 2008.
15. China's authoritative position on disarmament was last enunciated in detail in the 2010 White Paper on China's National Defence. Information Office of the State Council, 'White Paper on China's National Defense in 2010' (People's Republic of China, 31 March 2011), http://www.china.org.cn/government/whitepaper/node_7114675.htm (accessed on 30 April 2015). After that, the next biennial White Paper on National Defence for 2012 was issued in April 2013. But this White Paper, in its changed format, does not contain any section or material on disarmament. It is, therefore, assumed that the position on disarmament as stated in the 2010 White Paper remains valid unless contradicted by subsequent policy statements.
16. Information Office of the State Council, 'White Paper on China's National Defense in 2010'.
17. Ibid.

18. Ministry of External Affairs, 'Working Paper on Nuclear Disarmament' (CD/1816, 20 February 2007), http://meaindia.nic.in/cdgeneva/?pdf0610?000 (accessed on 30 April 2015); Information Office of the State Council, 'White Paper on China's National Defense in 2010'.
19. Ministry of External Affairs, 'Statement by External Affairs Minister of India Shri Pranab Mukherjee on the Civil Nuclear Initiative' (Government of India, 5 September 2008), http://www.mea.gov.in/in-focus-article.htm?18806/Statement+by+External+Affairs+Minister+of+India+Shri+Pranab+Mukherjee+on+the+Civil+Nuclear+Initiative (accessed on 30 April 2014).
20. Ibid.
21. Information Office of the State Council, 'White Paper on China's National Defense in 2010'.
22. Ibid.
23. Ministry of External Affairs, 'Working Paper on Nuclear Disarmament'.
24. Information Office of the State Council, 'White Paper on China's National Defense in 2010'.
25. Ibid.
26. Ibid.
27. Data taken from Jing-dong Yuan, 'Chinese Perceptions of the Utility of Nuclear Weapons: Prospects and Potential Problems in Disarmament' (Proliferation Paper No. 34, French Institute of International Relations, Paris, Spring 2010).
28. Ibid.
29. Information Office of the State Council, 'White Paper on China's National Defense in 2006' (People's Republic of China, Beijing, December), http://www.china.org.cn/english/features/book/194421.htm (accessed on 30 April 2015).
30. Yuan, 'Chinese Perceptions of the Utility of Nuclear Weapons'.
31. SIPRI, *SIPRI Yearbook 2014.*
32. Table 4.3, in ibid.
33. Ibid.
34. Ibid.
35. Ibid.
36. SIPRI, *SIPRI Yearbook 2014.*
37. The information in this paragraph on China's military capabilities and modernization is from US Department of Defense, 'Annual Report to Congress: Military and Security Developments Involving the People's Republic of China 2014' (Office of the Secretary of Defense, Federal Government of the United States of America, Washington DC, 2014).
38. Yuan, 'Chinese Perceptions of the Utility of Nuclear Weapons'
39. United Nations, 'Implementation of General Assembly Resolutions 55/235 and 55/236: Report of the Secretary General' (Annex to the UN General Assembly document A/67/224/Add1, 27 December 2012), http://www.

un.org/ga/search/view_doc.asp?symbol=A/67/224/Add.1 (accessed on 30 April 2015).

40. Stephen Olson and Clyde Prestowitz, 'The Evolving Role of China in International Institutions' (paper prepared for the US–China Economic and Security Review Commission, The Economic Strategy Institute, Washington DC, January 2011).
41. Biswajit Dhar, 'Quiet Ascendancy of the Yuan', *LiveMint*, 7 July 2011.
42. Information Office of the State Council, 'White Paper: China's Peaceful Development Road'.
43. 'Position Paper of the People's Republic of China on the United Nations Reforms', 7 June 2005, http://www.fmprc.gov.cn/mfa_eng/wjdt_665385/2649_665393/t1188610.shtml (accessed on 30 April 2015).
44. Ibid.
45. Ibid.
46. Ibid.
47. Ibid.
48. Data taken from Stockholm International Peace Research Institute (SIPRI), *SIPRI Yearbook: Armaments, Disarmament and International Security* (Oxford: Oxford University Press, several years).
49. Richard F. Grimmett, 'Conventional Arms Transfers to Developing Nations, 2002–2009' (Congressional Research Service Report for the United States Congress, 10 September 2010), http://www.fas.org/sgp/crs/weapons/R41403.pdf (accessed on 5 September 2011).
50. Table 5.2, in SIPRI, *SIPRI Yearbook 2014*.
51. Ibid.
52. Ibid.
53. Ibid.
54. US Department of Defense, 'Annual Report to Congress'.
55. Fu Daopeng, 'Studies on the Official Development Aid' (PhD thesis, Finance and Science Research Institute of the Ministry of Finance, Government of China, 2003).
56. Zhou Enlai, 'Government Report to the First Session of the Third National People's Congress', as it appeared in *The People's Daily*, 31 December 1964.
57. Daopeng, 'Studies on the Official Development Aid'.
58. Ibid.
59. Information Office of the State Council, 'White Paper on China's Foreign Aid' (People's Republic of China, Beijing, 21 April 2011), http://www.eu-china.net/web/cms/upload/pdf/nachrichten/2011-04-21Chinas-ForeignAid-WhitePaper.pdf (accessed on 30 April 2015).
60. Ibid.
61. Ibid.
62. Ibid.

63. Figures cited in Sohu.com, 'American Media, China's Aid Gains its Popularity in Africa, China Displayed the Great Nation Image' (28 June 2007).
64. Information Office of the State Council, 'White Paper on China's Foreign Aid'.
65. Information Office of the State Council, 'China's Foreign Aid (2014)' (People's Republic of China, Beijing, July 2014).
66. Data accessed from http://data.worldbank.org (accessed on 4 May 2015).
67. Information Office of the State Council, 'China's Foreign Aid (2014)'.
68. Based on figures given in the Annual Reports of the Ministry of External Affairs, Government of India, for the years 2012–13, 2013–14 and 2014–15.
69. EXIM Bank of India, http://www.eximbankindia.in/ (accessed on 4 May 2015).
70. Ibid.
71. Sachin Chaturvedi, 'India's Development Partnership', in *Development Cooperation and Emerging Powers: New Partners or Old Patterns*, eds Sachin Chaturvedi, Thomas Fues and Elizabeth Sidiropoulos (London: Zed Books, 2012).
72. Government of Sri Lanka, 'Foreign Financing', in *Annual Report 2010* (Colombo: Ministry of Finance and Planning, March 2011) 244–87.
73. Information Office of the State Council, 'China's Foreign Aid (2014)'.
74. Confederation of Indian Industry (CII) and World Trade Organization (WTO), India–Africa: South–South Trade and Investment for Development', https://www.wto.org/english/tratop_e/devel_e/a4t_e/global_review13prog_e/india_africa_report.pdf (accessed on 4 May 2015).
75. Zhou Hong, 'China as Development Co-operator', in *Development Cooperation and Emerging Powers: New Partners or Old Patterns*, eds Sachin Chaturvedi, Thomas Fues and Elizabeth Sidiropoulos (London: Zed Books, 2012).
76. All the facts and data in this paragraph are from Information Office of the State Council, 'White Paper: China-Africa Economic and Trade Cooperation' (People's Republic of China, Beijing, August 2013).
77. Hu Jintao, Address at the Opening Ceremony of the Beijing Summit of the Forum on China–Africa Cooperation (11 April 2006), http://za.china-embassy.org/eng/zfgx/zfhzlt/t279014.htm (accessed on 6 January 2012.
78. Forum on China-Africa Cooperation (FOCAC), 'Sharm El Sheikh Action Plan (2010–2012)', 9 November 2009, http://www.focac.org/eng/dsjbzjhy/hywj/t626387.htm (accessed on 4 May 2015).
79. Information Office of the State Council, 'White Paper: China's Peaceful Development'.
80. Pan-African e-Network Project, 'Implementation Status–at a Glance', http://www.panafricanenetwork.com/Portal/ProjectDetails.jsp?projectidhide=7&projectnamehide=Implementatin%20Status (accessed on 4 May 2015).
81. Javier Blas, 'China Changes Tack on Africa with $2 Billion Multilateral Investment', *Financial Times*, 18 May 2014.
82. Ibid.

83. Parama Sinha Palit and Amitendu Palit, 'Strategic Influence of Soft Power: Inferences for India from Chinese Engagement of South and Southeast Asia' (Policy Series no. 3, Indian Council for Research in International Economic Relations (ICRIER), New Delhi, August 2011).
84. US Department of Defense, 'Annual Report to Congress'.
85. Emily Brunjes, Nicholas Levine, Miriam Palmer and Addison Smith, 'China's Increased Trade and Investment in South Asia (Spoiler Alert: It's The Economy)' (report prepared for the US Government Office of South Asia Policy and part of Workshop in International Public Affairs, Robert M. La Follette School of Public Affairs, University of Wisconsin–Madison, 2013).
86. Ibid.
87. Ibid.
88. Saman Kelegama, 'China-Sri Lanka Economic Relationship: An Overview', *China Report*, Volume 50, No. 2 (2014) 131–49.
89. Brunjes et al., 'China's Increased Trade and Investment in South Asia'.
90. Jacques Lecarte, 'China's Role in U.N. Peacekeeping Operations' (Library Briefing, Library of the European Parliament, 22 April 2013).
91. US Department of Defense, 'Annual Report to Congress'.
92. United Nations, 'Implementation of General Assembly Resolutions 55/235 and 55/236'.
93. Information Office of the State Council, 'White Paper on China's National Defense in 2010'.
94. United Nations, 'An Agenda for Peace: Preventive Diplomacy, Peacemaking and Peacekeeping (report of the United Nations Secretary-General pursuant to the statement adopted by the Summit Meeting of the Security Council, 31 January 1992).
95. US Department of Defense, 'Annual Report to Congress'.

ELEVEN China's Tryst with Globalization

Impact of the First Generation of Economic Reforms

When China, along with the rest of the world, was confronted with the challenges of the new era of globalization beginning from the end of the 1980s, it had already gone through a decade of far-reaching changes in its economic policy. Reforms were first introduced in China's agriculture in 1978 and subsequently extended to other sectors of the economy, particularly industry and foreign trade. The main thrusts of the reforms were greater reliance on market forces, devolution of decision making at the enterprise level, introducing elements of competition in the economy and opening it to foreign competition. Some of the essential preconditions for the success of the liberalization policy had already been created during the Mao Zedong era. These included thoroughgoing land reforms carried out almost as an integral part of the communist revolution, which paved the way for an egalitarian society, universal literacy and access to primary health services for all, and the decentralization of economic management and governance system which came concomitantly with the nationwide domination and omnipresence of the Communist Party of China.

The economic achievements of China even during the first decade after the reforms were indeed phenomenal. In spite of the brakes applied on economic growth from time to time in order to maintain macroeconomic balance, China's GNP doubled well before the end of the 1980s. This period also witnessed the doubling of per capita income. The average annual rate of growth during the decade was 9 per cent in real terms, with agriculture registering a growth of 6.3 per cent per annum and industry 12.6 per cent.

The reform in agriculture was followed by a veritable explosion in agricultural production. As a result, China's food grain production increased during the decade from a little over 300 million tonnes to 435 million tonnes. The spurt in the production of other agricultural products, vital raw materials, energy resources and industrial goods was equally impressive. The production of coal increased from 620 million tonnes to 1,080 million tonnes, of crude oil from 106 million to 138 million tonnes, of electricity from 300 to 618 billion kWh, of steel from 37.12 to 66.04 million tonnes and of cement from 80 to 203 million tonnes. At the turn of the decade, China emerged as the world's largest producer of food grains, cotton, meat, textiles, cement and machine tools; and the fourth largest producer of steel, chemical, fibres and non-ferrous metals. This formidable pace of growth was maintained while keeping the inflation rate down to a little over 1 per cent in 1990.

Next to agriculture and industry, the sector that displayed the most remarkable dynamism was foreign trade. The volume of exports increased from $18.1 billion in 1980 to $62.1 billion in 1990. The average annual rate of growth in exports was 15.2 per cent during 1985–89 and 24 per cent in 1990. China's share of international trade increased from 0.97 per cent in 1978 to 1.7 per cent in 1988. The share of foreign trade in China's GNP jumped to 30 per cent in the beginning of the 1990s from the modest level of 9 per cent in 1979. The unprecedented expansion of exports was accompanied by a qualitative change in China's export structure. Manufactured goods, consisting mainly of readymade garments, consumer electronics, office and telecommunication equipment, toys and machinery accounted for 70 per cent of the total exports. Capital goods comprised 34 per cent of China's total exports. China also achieved remarkable success in attracting foreign private capital. Commitments made for FDI amounted to $51.4 billion involving the establishment of some 41,000 units with foreign participation. The contracts signed for 1991 alone involved a total investment of $12 billion.

One of the most remarkable phenomena that appeared on the Chinese economic scene during this period was the Township and Village Enterprises (TVEs). These employed 100 million people and contributed 30 to 40 per cent of the industrial value added in 1989. They exported goods and services worth $10 billion, which was 30 per cent of the total manufactured export. They also effectively prevented urban migration in the wake of the agricultural revolution that rendered surplus vast numbers of the rural labour force.

What added up to the economic miracle of the 1980s were the agricultural revolution, the dynamism and vigour displayed by the TVEs, the rapid growth of the export sector and the extraordinarily high rate of domestic savings. The growth in exports was attributable mainly to the ability of the Chinese government to attract investors of Chinese origin from Hong Kong and Taiwan. The agricultural revolution would not have come about but for the land reforms during the Mao Zedong era. High literacy and universal access to health services were also central to the success of both the agricultural revolution and the TVEs.

The Second Generation of Economic Reforms

In order to meet the challenges of globalization during the 1990s, China introduced further far-reaching changes in its economic policies, including unilateral liberalization of trade and investment, and restructuring of the economy. It decided to eliminate uncompetitive and outmoded economic structures and go in for an unprecedented opening up of the economy to foreign investment and supply of goods and services. China's determination to face globalization headlong derived from its confidence in the strength that the economy gained during the 1980s. The second generation of economic reforms which started in 1993, included further decentralization of decision-making at the enterprise level, a greater role for market forces, heavier reliance on export-led growth and the introduction of dual exchange rates and dual pricing systems. An attempt was also made to make the banking system, rather than the government budget, the main source of funding investment.

These policies resulted in the continuation and acceleration of China's dramatic economic performance witnessed during the 1980s. The two decades after the reforms saw a quadrupling of China's GDP and a three-fold increase in per capita income. Production of food grains increased from 435 million tonnes in 1980 to 495 million tonnes in 1998. The number of people living below the poverty line declined from 300 million in 1978 to only 30 million in 1998. This was the largest decline in poverty witnessed anywhere in the world in recent times. In percentage terms, the decline was from 31 per cent of the total population to only 7 per cent.

China's foreign trade touched the figure of $400 billion in 1999. The trade surplus increased to $43.4 billion in 1998 and foreign exchange reserves were at $154.7 billion in 1999. There was a massive build-up of infrastructure, mainly in the south and the east. By 1993, investment in infrastructure went up to 6.5 per cent of the GDP. The actual investment in infrastructure in the Eighth Five-Year Plan (1991 95) was $170 billion. The bulk of the expenditure on infrastructure was financed jointly by the central government and the provincial governments concerned. The contribution of foreign aid and foreign private investment to infrastructure building was only 7.3 per cent in 1994.

However, during the closing years of the 20th century, it appeared that the advantages of the first two generations of reforms were on the verge of being exhausted. This was reflected in the relative sluggishness of economic growth and the slowdown of the rate of growth of exports. There was also an accentuation of both regional and per capita income disparities. While the southern and eastern provinces had progressed by leaps and bounds, the northern and western provinces had lagged behind. Abject urban poverty was almost non-existent in China before 1968, thanks to the social security guarantees provided by the state-owned enterprises (SOEs). But by the end of the century, while the social security system in the rural areas was threatened because of the virtual dismantling of the commune system, the poorer section of the urban population was being marginalized because of the withdrawal of the social security guarantees as a part of the reform of the SOEs. The unemployed from the rural areas were rushing towards urban conglomerates which did not have enough opportunities to offer and, therefore, decided to follow a policy of shutting out the migrants. The official unemployment figure for China quoted in 1997 was only 3.1 per cent. But this did not include urban unemployment caused by the SOEs laying off workers and disguised rural unemployment. The unofficial estimate of unemployment was as high as 25 to 35 per cent at that time. Moreover, the reforms introduced in some important sectors were progressing rather slowly. This was particularly true of the reforms in the financial sector and of the SOEs.

There was a fierce debate raging in China at the turn of the century as to whether the reform process should be slowed down if not reversed or continued with greater vigour. Those who believed in the latter course of action ultimately won the debate and China decided in the late 1990s in favour of deeper reforms and greater opening up of the economy. The new generation of reforms emphasized strategic restructuring of the economy; greater enhancement in the role of the market, all-round improvement in quality, standards and competitiveness; modern management; building up of the legal system and firmer control by the central government over macroeconomic policymaking.

In agriculture, following the achievement of self-sufficiency in the production of major food crops, there was already a trend of withdrawal of land from these crops for producing higher value-added items or returning the land to forests and pastures. In pursuance of this policy, China had started importing food grains on a regular basis and had planned to import 10 to 20 million tonnes per annum over the next few years. Greater emphasis was laid on the development of aquaculture, livestock and on the processing of food grains. High priority was also attached to the application of science and technology, particularly biotechnology to revolutionize agricultural production.

The important measures already under implementation for the reform of the SOEs were to be pursued vigorously and systematically. These included permitting enterprises to go bankrupt, pursuing a policy of mergers and acquisitions, converting them into joint stock companies, infusing additional resources for their technological upgradation, management reforms, moving further in the direction of reducing their social burdens and restructuring their assets and debts in order to make them financially viable.

For redressing regional imbalances, China embarked upon a very ambitious 'Look West' policy, which covered 10 provinces in the west and the north. This policy was regarded as essential for maintaining national unity, safeguarding social stability and consolidating border security. A major component of the policy was the investment of hundreds of billions of yuan for building infrastructure in the provinces. As in the south and the east, in the west and the north also, the central and provincial governments were to bear the main burden of providing resources, mainly through the banking channels. A part of the funds was expected to come from the Chinese private sector. Though some projects were open for participation by foreign entities, their contribution was not expected to be very significant.

Accession to WTO

It was in this setting that China decided to renew and accelerate its effort to accede to the WTO. China formally made a move to enter the GATT in 1986, almost a decade after launching its economic liberalization plan. The Chinese move was generally welcomed by the major member countries of GATT because China's economic reforms conformed to their policy prescriptions and they were impressed by the rapid economic progress made by it since the introduction of the reforms. They hoped that China's entry into GATT would nudge the country towards deeper and wider economic reforms and thereby strengthen its ties with the Western countries. The major Western members of GATT also regarded their burgeoning ties with China as a means of maintaining power balance with Russia.

The progress towards China's accession to GATT had slowed down during the early 1990s. The Clinton administration laid down some minimum requirements for Chinese accession. These included the adoption of a uniform system of trade laws throughout the country, greater transparency of the trade regime, an official pledge by China to transform itself into a full-fledged market economy, elimination of all non-tariff barriers and safeguards in the event of a surge in US imports from China following the latter's entry into GATT. The Chinese found these proposals largely unacceptable. There was, however, a dramatic shift in the Chinese position once the globalizers in the top hierarchy of the Chinese Communist Party won the internal debate on the future course of liberalization in China.

Premier Zhu Rongji led a big delegation to Washington in 1999 and presented a package accepting far-reaching measures of liberalization, including substantial reduction in tariffs, elimination of non-tariff barriers across the board and opening up of the Chinese market for key agricultural and manufactured imports from the US and for investment in a number of service industries. Soon after the US–Chinese agreement, China reached an agreement with the EU, which extracted further concessions for liberalization by China, particularly in the service sector. China formally acceded to the WTO after the completion of all formalities in December 2001.

The Chinese leadership saw the main purpose of accession to the WTO as a means of locking in and further accelerating the sweeping internal liberalization that had been set in motion in the 1990s. The accession was thus both a consequence and a cause of domestic liberalization. For, full advantage of domestic liberalization could be taken only if it was accompanied by external liberalization which, in turn, would pave the way for further domestic liberalization. Moreover, in its effort to reform the SOEs, the Chinese authorities had come across formidable domestic opposition which, they thought, would be overcome by a treaty-bound commitment for reforming these entities. Finally, China's far-reaching concessions under the WTO Protocol of Accession were an act of faith in the dynamism and the potential for further expansion of the Chinese economy. The Chinese were convinced that once, by virtue of their accession to the WTO, they became automatically entitled to MFN, access for their competitive products in the markets of developed countries and the shares in these markets for their products would vastly expand. At that time, this was particularly true of low labour-cost simple manufactures like textiles, toys and household goods. Their gamble paid off and the development on the trade front during the post-accession period amply vindicated the faith of the Chinese leadership in the strength of their economy.

China thus regarded its accession to the WTO as a means of riding the crest of globalization and emerging as a major player in the international trading system. The Chinese leaders also thought that the accession would mark the coming of age of the Chinese economy and provide an international seal of approval that it had been transformed from a state-run to a market-driven system. Moreover, they wanted to use the accession for further pushing the domestic economic reforms underway, particularly phasing out inefficient units in the auto, chemical, pharmaceutical and heavy industries, and building them up as international leaders. They also believed that the WTO membership would open the window for them for privileged access to foreign markets, capital and technology. It would bring stability to their external economic relations. Assurances of the enhanced access to foreign markets on a long-term stable basis would be a springboard for expanding industrial capacity and taking the risk of industrial restructuring and rationalization. Among the immediate advantages would be the extension of the MFN treatment as a matter of routine rather than on the basis of annual bilateral bargaining. And by virtue of its access to the WTO's Dispute Settlement Body, protection from unilateral action would be available. In an effort to expedite China's accessions to the WTO, the Chinese leaders made several concessions to the US and EU, going beyond their obligations under the relevant WTO agreements. China's assumption of obligations far exceeding those called for under WTO regimes was a reflection of its confidence, derived from the strength of its economy, in its ability to cope with the changes of unprecedented dimensions that it had decided to unleash autonomously in order to be on the right side of the process of globalization. The main argument used by the Western countries to extract concessions going beyond the provisions in WTO regimes was that as a non-market economy, China had to assume additional obligations as a price for membership.

Thus, in agriculture, China agreed to remove all export subsidies, whereas the obligation under the Agreement on Agriculture was to reduce it by only 36 per cent (24 per cent for developing countries). China agreed to reduce by 2004 its overall average tariff on agricultural products to 17 per cent and establish tariff rate quotas for importing wheat, corn, cotton, barley and rice from the US. China gave a minimum access guarantee amounting to 4 per cent of its total consumption of agricultural products concerned during the base period, and rising thereafter, thus putting it at par with developed countries under the Agreement on Agriculture. The minimum access guarantee obligation for developing countries is only 1 to 2 per cent of their total consumption. These commitments implied hefty increases in the imports of items like cotton, wool and soyabean, involving large-scale job loss and loss in farm production running into billions of dollars. In spite of this, China accepted these commitments, mainly in the backdrop of the decision that it had already taken for further liberalization in the agricultural sector.

In the manufacturing sector, China agreed to reduce tariffs to an average of 9.4 per cent overall and eliminate all quantitative restrictions and licensing requirements by the year 2005. The reduction agreed upon in the duty on the import of automobiles was really drastic, from 100 per cent in 1998 to 25 per cent in 2006. The duty on auto parts was to be reduced to 10 per cent by the end of the phase-in period. In addition, China agreed to a basic level quota for auto imports amounting in value to $56 billion, which would grow at 15 per cent annually until quotas were eliminated in 2005. As in the agricultural sector, in the auto sector too China agreed to these far-reaching changes because it had already decided to go in for a thorough restructuring of the sector, according to which most of the small-sized auto manufacturing companies would disappear and production would concentrate in two to three conglomerates to be set up as joint-venture enterprises in collaboration with transnational auto giants capable of competing in the world market. Similarly, China had also decided to close down the non-competitive and inefficient units of its chemical and pharmaceutical industry and concentrate on those holding promise for the future.

In the service sector, China agreed to phase out all geographic restrictions for paging and value-added telecommunication services in two years, mobile and cellular phone services in three years, and domestic wireless services in six years. It agreed to permit a 40 per cent share to foreign investors in all telecommunication services and 50 per cent share in value-added and paging services. In insurance, China agreed to eliminate all geographic limitation for future licensing over a period of five years and allow US entities access to key cities in two to three years. The foreign companies willing to come to this sector would be allowed 50 per cent ownership of joint ventures. Reinsurance business would be completely open to foreign participation upon China's accession to the WTO. For banking services, both geographical and economic restrictions were agreed to be withdrawn and full market access was to be provided within five years. China, however, did not undertake any commitment to allow foreign equity participation or acquisition of banks.

Thus, China agreed to forego the flexibility provided in the GATS whereby member countries are free to specify in their respective schedules the extent of access they intend to provide and the conditions they want to lay down. In the service sector again, as in other sectors, the opening up was seen as a part of the process of forcing Chinese companies to restructure and rationalize and, in the process, attract foreign private capital in order to expand and emerge stronger.

The most far-reaching concession given by China was trading and distribution rights to foreign firms, to be exercised almost all over the country without being obliged to have local partners, for practically all goods and services, including wholesale trade, transportation, maintenance and repairs. These concessions were to be phased into the Chinese economy within three years. This was also one of the most important steps taken by China in its bid to qualify as a free-market economy.

On investment, China agreed to eliminate export performance, local content and foreign exchange balancing requirements from its laws, regulations and other measures. In addition, it agreed that it would no longer condition importation or investment approvals on these or other requirements such as technology transfers.

China made extraordinary concessions to the US with regard to anti-dumping and safeguard measures. For 15 years after China's accession, the US was allowed to continue its national methodology for applying anti-dumping measures against Chinese products, and China self-abrogated its right as a member of the WTO to invoke the technical and legal criteria laid down in the relevant WTO agreement. Similarly, for 12 years from the time of accession, the US retained its right to unilaterally apply restraint measures against Chinese imports in case of a surge in these imports, without China being able to invoke the legal standards laid down under the WTO Safeguard Agreement.

In its agreement with the EU, China was barred from having recourse to several of the Articles under the WTO Agreement on Subsidies and Countervailing Measures. China also agreed to publicly declare its intention to join the plurilateral Agreement on Government Procurement (GPA) as soon as possible. It thus gave up the option available to WTO member countries to stay out of this agreement. Pending its accession to the GPA, China committed itself to extend MFN treatment to foreign entities in sales to and purchases by state-owned enterprises.

Textile and clothing was the only sector in which China received concessions from its most important interlocutor, the US. The US agreed to eliminate its quotas on Chinese textile imports by 2005, which was also the time limit for the completion of the integration of the Multi-Fibre Agreement (MFA) into the WTO. However, the US retained its right to apply its current safeguard measures against imports from China, which would include that of textiles and clothing until the end of 2008, that is, three years after the integration of the MFA into the WTO. For China, even this qualified concession given by the US was of great significance because it anticipated one of the largest gains out of the membership of the WTO to accrue in the textile sector. This turned out to be true, as there was an exponential growth in China's exports of textiles and clothing to the markets of the developed countries after the integration of the MFA into the WTO.

Implementation of the Protocol of Accession

China displayed a remarkable degree of seriousness in implementing its commitments under the Protocol of Accession to the WTO. The Chinese reviewed and either scrapped or revised over 3,000 laws and regulations to ensure their conformity with WTO disciplines. In 2004, the Constitution of the People's Republic of China was revised in order to incorporate in it the concepts of property rights and human rights. China also revised its patent laws in order to provide for the protection of intellectual property rights in line with the provisions in the TRIPS Agreement. It undertook a huge programme for aligning national technical standards with international standards. By 2005, 1,416 national standards which were not consistent with the commensurate international standards had been scrapped.

According to a survey by the US–China Business Council, the most important measure of liberalization that the respondents singled out was trading and distribution rights. To implement its commitment for liberalizing trading rights, China first put in place a registration system which provided for trading rights to be made automatically available through a registration process. This provision was reflected in China's revised Foreign Trade Laws issued in April 2004. Thus, almost immediately after China's accession to the WTO, foreign companies were given the freedom to import and distribute their products throughout China without the requirement to tie up with any local intermediary.

The Protocol made an exception for the importation of goods like petrol and sugar which were still kept reserved for state trading enterprises. Moreover, for goods subject to tariff rate quotas, such as grains, cotton, vegetable oils and fertilizers, China reserved a portion of the quota imports for state trading enterprises. Moreover, even after the notification of the revised trade laws, China continued to restrict the import and distribution of products covered by copyright such as books, newspapers and journals. As this was a contravention of China's commitment on trading rights, the US challenged it in the WTO and, following consultations, China agreed to remove those restrictions by March 2011.

In fulfilment of its commitment under the Protocol, China reduced duties on some 5,000 items. The reductions of most tariff restrictions were completed by the end of 2005. The average tariff rate in China came down from 15.6 per cent in 2001 to 9 per cent in 2006. Tariffs on all IT products covered under the WTO IT Agreement were eliminated. The average tariff on manufactured goods came down to 9.4 per cent and that on agricultural products to 14.5 per cent. All the reduced tariffs were bound at the applied rates.

As regards non-tariff barriers, all licensing requirements and quotas were eliminated by 2005. After pressure from the US, tariff rate quotas on selected agricultural products were expanded in line with the obligations under the Protocol.

China also complied with its obligation under the Protocol to eliminate all subsidies prohibited under Article 3 of the WTO Agreement on Subsidies and Countervailing Measures. China also committed that it would not make import or investment approvals, conditional upon whether there are competing domestic suppliers, or impose other performance requirements. To implement this commitment, China made changes in its legal system to eliminate local content requirement for foreign investment. However, under both subsidies and investment measures, China still allows some of the earlier practices to continue. This has become a bone of contention with its major trading partners.

On the whole, the US has reasons to be satisfied with the positive impact on its exports to China, of the liberalization measures undertaken by the latter under the terms of the Protocol of Accession to the WTO. In the 10 years since 2000, the year before China joined the WTO, till the end of 2009, the export of US goods to China increased at the rate of 33 per cent per annum, and that of services at 21.2 per cent.[1]

Even more important for the US was the fact that China remained a stable market for US exports during the recession of 2008–09. The extent of benefit from the liberalization of trading rights can be gauged from the fact that US multinational corporations operating in China increased their local sales of goods and services by 48.6 per cent per annum during the decade, reaching the level of $98.4 billion in 2008.[2]

During this period, US exports of crops and livestock to China increased by 75.8 per cent per annum, reaching a total of $11.6 billion in 2009; of chemical products, by 31 per cent per annum reaching the level of $9.7 billion in 2009; of medical equipment and supplies, by 64.7 per cent, reaching a level of $553 million; and of pharmaceutical and medicines, by 58.1 per cent, reaching the level of $662 million.[3]

According to a survey conducted by the US–China Business Council in 2006, 49 per cent of the US companies covered by the survey gave to China a grade of 'excellent' or 'good' in the implementation of the WTO obligations, 38 per cent of the respondents said that the Chinese had done a fair job and 54 per cent of them said that profits from China had increased by a fair margin in 2005 as compared to 2000. Two-fifths of the respondents reported that their China operation earned higher profits than their global average.[4]

According to the latest US–China Business Council Survey, 68 per cent of the respondents noted that their China operations had earned better profit margins than their global operations; 85 per cent reported increased revenue from their China operations during the economic slowdown in 2009.[5] In the view of EU businessmen, China scored 8 out of 10 in its effort to comply with WTO obligations, measured in terms of expansion of exports, investment flows into China and doing business in the Chinese domestic market.[6]

While moving promptly to eliminate barriers to cross-border trade and aligning the domestic laws, rules and regulations to conform to its international obligations, China accepted few obligations that would have required the state to give up or substantially reduce its firm grip on the key sectors of the economy. Moreover, it decided to go slow in the implementation of its obligations that went beyond the cross-border flow of goods and services—in the areas of intellectual property rights, investment, subsidies and the liberalization of the service sector. This was intended to buy time to build domestic industrial strength, develop indigenous technology and strengthen, rationalize and consolidate state-owned enterprises. The Chinese modified or removed the measures inconsistent with their WTO obligations in these areas only when pressurized to do so by major trading partners, particularly the US and the EU. These trading partners were so busy reaping the fruits of the

Chinese liberalization in other areas, particularly the right to trade, that before 2005 they took very few cases of Chinese non-compliance to the Dispute Settlement Mechanism of the WTO. In most cases, the Chinese repealed the measure whenever a case was pressed through consultations and before it reached the stage of scrutiny by a WTO panel; and in some cases soon after the panel passed a verdict against China.

Throughout the period of the implementation of its obligations under the WTO and thereafter, China followed a well-planned and systematic policy of using tax incentives, subsidies, price controls, high-level policy prescriptions and administrative guidance to encourage the development of key domestic industries, mainly in the public sector, to close down inefficient and redundant units, to rationalize the existing structure, to accelerate mergers and to infuse funds to introduce new technology in these industries. China also used these policies to give preference to domestic industries over foreign suppliers and to make foreign entry conditional upon transfer of technology or minimum equity participation. Some of these policies no doubt constituted infringements of China's obligations under the Protocol of Accession or were otherwise inconsistent with the WTO. The industries concerned included iron and steel, chemicals, pharmaceuticals, automobiles and auto parts, telecommunication, forestry, paper, non-ferrous metals and semi-conductors.

In his '2011 National Trade Estimate Report on Foreign Trade Barriers',[7] the United States Trade Representative (USTR) has illustrated a number of policy measures that discriminated in favour of key industries and were designed to direct foreign investment towards high-end manufacturing, high technology, modern service industries, alternative energy sector and energy-saving and environmentally friendly industries. These measures also restricted foreign investment in industries that are resource-intensive, highly polluting or use obsolete technology. The following were some examples of such measures and policies:

- Under the provisions on the Mergers and Acquisitions of Domestic Enterprises by Foreign Investors issued by China in 2006, foreign mergers and acquisition of domestic enterprises that would result in actual control of domestic enterprises in a key industry with potential impact on national economic security or that would give control of a famous Chinese trademark or traditional Chinese brand to a foreign investor required the approval of the central government.
- In December 2006, the government issued the 'Guiding Opinion Concerning the Advancement of Adjustments of State Capital and the Restructuring of State-Owned Enterprises', which identified a

large list of sectors deemed critical to national economy. It stated that 'pillar' and 'backbone' industries such as automotive, chemical, construction, electronic, information, iron and steel, equipment manufacturing, non-ferrous metal, science and technology, and survey and design must remain under relatively strong state control.

- According to another law that came into effect in May 2009, it was stipulated that where state-owned assets were transferred to a foreign investor, the transfer must not harm the national security or public interest of China.
- In August 2010, the State Council of China issued directives that promoted consolidation of enterprises in several industries, most of which were state-owned. These include automobiles, steel, cement, aluminium, rare earths and machinery manufacturing industry.
- Moreover, in 2006, China announced an indigenous innovation policy that was geared to promote domestic technological companies at the cost of foreign enterprises.[8]

China's energy sector is largely insulated from global markets. Price controls apply to coal, natural gas, oil, electricity and nuclear and non-renewable energy. Foreign makers of electric cars, wind turbines and solar panels are shut out of domestic projects. The state-owned enterprises in these sectors are protected from international competition by export restrictions and import control.[9]

The steel industry in China has emerged as an international leader, in large part due to the supportive measures adopted by the state. In July 2005, the government issued a Steel and Iron Industry Development Policy which prescribed the number and size of steel producers in China, their location, the type of products that would be produced and the technology that would be used. It provided for a de facto technology transfer requirement in spite of China's commitment under the WTO Protocol not to condition investment rights or approvals on the transfer of technology. In June 2010, the government published the 'Opinions on Strengthening Energy Saving and Emission Reduction and Accelerating Structural Adjustment in the Iron and Steel Sector'. The objectives of these Opinions were: controlling the growth of the steel industry, eliminating outdated capacity, promoting energy savings and emission reduction, technical innovation, accelerating mergers and disciplining access to iron ore. Later that year, the government published a list of 762 steel plants that were required to close down in order to improve the country's energy efficiency. In large part due to these measures, China's steel production has grown very rapidly, at a rate faster than that in the domestic steel consumption. China became the largest steel-exporting country in 2006. Its steel production reached a record of 567 million metric tonnes in 2009 and another record of 627 metric tonnes in 2010.[10]

In May 2004, China issued a new automobile industrial policy that discouraged manufacturers in China from using imported parts in the assembly of vehicles. In 2006, the US and some other countries initiated a dispute settlement proceeding on this policy directive in the WTO, which ruled in their favour. In September 2009, China repealed the challenged measures.[11]

Through discriminatory Value-Added Tax (VAT) policies, China encouraged the development of its domestic integrated circuit industry. The US lodged a protest against it in the WTO in March 2004, which resulted in the elimination of this tax. In the case of fertilizers also, China has used its VAT policy to the benefit of domestic fertilizer production. In 2001, China began exempting VAT on all phosphate fertilizers except DAP (diammonium hydrogen phosphate), of which the US was an exporter.[12]

Barriers to trade and investment in services have come down more slowly than those applicable to goods. Several of the service industries are being protected, mainly by high and discriminatory capital requirements and equity restrictions. China imposes restrictions in a number of service sectors to prevent or discourage foreign suppliers from gaining or further expanding market access. This is particularly true of those domestic sectors that are politically and culturally sensitive.

For telecommunication equipment, China adopted policies to discourage the use of imported components. There has been no new market entry in basic telecommunications over the past decade. In 2008, there was a consolidation in this sector, which reduced the number of national operators from six to three—namely, China Mobile, China Telecom and China Unicom. China appears to apply an economic needs test to new entrants in this sector to avoid unhealthy competition.[13]

The import and distribution of books, newspapers, journals, sound recordings, videos, films and television programmes remain highly restricted. Investment in the audio-visual sector is also restricted by keeping the foreign capital investment below 49 per cent.

In August 2005, the State Council issued a directive stating that private capital cannot be used to establish or operate a news agency, a newspaper, a publishing house, a radio or TV station.[14]

In the educational and training services, China permits only non-profit activities that do not compete with the government-supervised nine years of compulsory education. China also bars foreign companies and organizations from offering educational services via satellite networks. Foreign universities are permitted to enter but they can carry out only non-profit educational activities.[15] China did not undertake any commitment in the area of legal services. This is in large part due to the highly underdeveloped stage that the legal services in China are in. China's major interlocutors, particularly the US and EU, did not press for commitment in this area perhaps because they did not see much chance of their legal firms or experts rendering their services in that country.

Insurance companies can be established only as joint ventures, with foreign equity kept at 50 per cent. China applies a 33 per cent equity limit for joint ventures in security services. It permits foreign equity participation up to a maximum of 49 per cent for basic telecommunication and 50 per cent for value-added telecommunication.

In September 2010, the US requested consultation under the WTO over China's restriction on electronic payment services by foreign suppliers. Consultations were held in October 2010 but remained inconclusive. In February 2011, the US requested the establishment of a dispute settlement panel on its complaint.

Major exporters to the Chinese market, particularly the US and EU, have complained against widespread violations and weak enforcement of intellectual property rights in China, particularly with regard to movies and software. The main problems from the point of view of the US interest are retail and wholesale counterfeiting; piracy of books, journals, business software and copyright surfacing over the internet and very feeble criminal, civil and administrative measures to enforce intellectual property rights. The US government in 2007 took three cases in this area to WTO panels which gave findings favourable to the US in two. China did not appeal against the panels' rulings and subsequently took corrective measures.[16]

The Third Amendment to China's Patent Law passed in 2008 went into effect from 1 October 2009. Patent holders from Western countries have raised objections to some of the provisions of the new law, particularly disclosure requirements for genetic resources, remuneration to be paid to the inventor and the scope and procedures relating to compulsory licensing.

China has submitted to the WTO only one of its annually required notifications on subsidies. This notification did not include subsidies provided by provincial and local governments nor any commitment to withdraw them.

US companies have complained that even a decade after joining the WTO, China maintains significant non-tariff barriers to trade. These include 'regulations that set high threshold for entry into service sectors such as banking, insurance and telecommunication; selective and unwarranted inspection requirements for agricultural products; and the use of questionable sanitary and phytosanitary measures to control import volumes'.[17]

China is seeking to encourage the deployment of domestically owned technical standards in an effort to reduce dependence on foreign technology. This is natural for a large country and a large market like China. What is important is that these standards should be based solely on scientific criteria and should not be a tool of trade or industrial policy and that they should conform to international standards. The Western suppliers of goods and services in these sectors have complained that this is not the case and that China is seeking to encourage domestically owned technical standards mainly with a view to reducing dependence on foreign technology.

The USTR in his report has complained that China has promoted unique national standards which act as a barrier to foreign imports in the sectors concerned and which are not in conformity with international standards in these sectors. In 2011, China issued rules on technology safety, testing and labelling which has the effect of restricting imports of genetically modified crops to China. In 2003, China attempted to establish a new wireless standard in the name of information security. When the US protested against it, the Chinese government indefinitely suspended the implementation of this standard.

Even after its accession to the WTO, China has continued to impose restrictions of various kinds, including quotas, duties and licensing requirement on exports of raw materials and agricultural products. China applies quotas and duties on the export of antimony, oxide, coke, magnesium carbonate, rare earths, silicon, tin and zinc. Most of the raw materials under restraint are in short supply globally and China happens to be the world's leading producer of several of them. Restrictions imposed by China have the effect of artificially increasing the prices of finished products manufactured by foreign countries and also give Chinese producers an unfair advantage in downstream production. The Chinese, on the other hand, have argued that the restrictions imposed by them are intended to reduce energy consumption and combat food inflation.

China controls about 97 per cent of the global rare earths market. In July 2010, it sharply reduced by 72 per cent compared to the previous year, its export quota on rare earth metals, causing world prices of some of the rare earths to rise dramatically. In September 2010, China reportedly 'imposed a temporary de facto ban on all exports of rare earths to Japan'.[18]

In June 2009, the US and EU filed a complaint in the WTO challenging the restrictions on Chinese exports of raw materials. The WTO panel's verdict on the complaint, which was against China, was given in July 2011. The panel recommended the Dispute Settlement Body to request China to bring its measures into conformity with its WTO obligations. China is reported to have taken corrective measures.

In the Protocol, China undertook to initiate negotiations for joining the WTO AGP 'as soon as possible'. It did not take any action to implement this commitment until mid-2006 when some initial discussions were held with major stakeholders. The latter found the Chinese offer very limited and highly conditional. In December 2009, China submitted its formal application for accession. Negotiations on this application have been going on since then and China is yet to accede to the GPA. China's government procurement policy implicitly discriminates in favour of domestic enterprises. There is a strong lobby of key domestic industries and ministries in China which views government procurement as a tool for promoting domestic industry.

The active phase of China's compliance with its obligations under the Protocol of Accession to the WTO came to an end in 2006. During this period, China succeeded in putting in place one of the most liberal trade regimes in the world. Moreover, 'the ideas of market economy and trade and investment liberalization have been integrated into popular thinking. More importantly, the Chinese public now widely accepts core WTO concepts such as transparency, accountable governance and national treatment'.[19]

Post-Accession Policies

After 2006, China has not shown any enthusiasm for further liberalization of its trade regime. It has in fact rejected all suggestions for unilateral liberalization. At the same time, there is no evidence of a planned retreat to protectionism. The Chinese economy is by now far too integrated with the global economy for the Chinese authorities to think of any reversal of the policy of liberalization. The inflow of FDI is still increasing at an exponential rate in spite of complaints regarding the Chinese imposing various restrictions and conditions on such inflows. Multinational corporations of major economic powers still find it more profitable to do business in China than in other emerging economies and they are committed to stay there.

The Chinese do not want to unfold a new programme of unilateral liberalization simply because they do not think it is necessary for them to do so or that it is going to serve their national interest. According to their perception, they have fulfilled most of the commitments undertaken under the Protocol. Now, for making any significant trade concessions, they naturally expect reciprocity, which is simply not forthcoming from those who are pressurizing the Chinese to take initiatives for trade liberalization. Second, for the last few years, the Chinese leadership has been according much higher priority to coping with the widespread social unrest in the country, which is perceived to be a consequence of the policy of liberalization. Lastly, China's vastly increased economic clout may be another reason for its being tough in trade negotiations. The Chinese are aware of the new bargaining strength they have acquired in the world economy, as an increasing number of countries are now dependent on them for their market, investible funds and technology. The Chinese naturally want to extract the maximum advantage out of this enhanced bargaining power.

In several other ways, the Chinese continue to remain engaged with the world economy as never before. They are now more active than before in international economic fora, including the WTO. In the Doha Round of Trade Negotiations, they are taking interest mainly in rule-making, particularly those relating to anti-dumping and countervailing measures, safeguards and technical barriers to trade. They have become both a major victim as well as an important user of anti-dumping measures. In other sectors of the negotiations, they have decided to work in concert with major emerging economies like India, Brazil and South Africa. On agriculture, which is a central issue in the negotiations, they are happy to go along with the G-20 developing countries in WTO, which have decided to pursue a common position in these negotiations.

Experts and policymakers of Western countries have argued that since Chinese interest lies in further liberalization of world trade, they have more at stake in the successful conclusion of the Doha Round than other emerging economies and developing countries and, therefore, it is in their interest to take initiative by offering further liberalization in order to give a push to the Doha Round. The Chinese have, however, decided not to break ranks with these countries and accept the unreasonable position of the developed countries to seek further liberalization without offering any significant reciprocal concessions, particularly in the areas of agriculture, services and early harvest for the least developed among the developing countries.

In the next few years, China will remain under considerable pressure to better implement its commitments under the terms of its accession to the WTO, particularly those relating to domestic measures. Many more complaints are likely to be filed in the WTO and China is likely to adopt corrective measures where the WTO panels' verdicts would go against it. This is going to happen mainly in the field of TRIPS, TRIMs, services, Agreement on Sanitary and Phytosanitary Measures and that on Technical Barriers to Trade. The Chinese are also likely to come under a great deal of pressure for complying with their obligations relating to the transparency of their trade laws and policies and trade-related domestic measures.

Major developed countries would also continue to insist on China adopting unilateral liberalization measures and eliminating those which, though not inconsistent with the WTO, constitute a hindrance to their increased access to the Chinese market. For example, these countries would like China to further reduce its applied tariffs, reverse export controls on raw material and agricultural products, align its national standards with international ones, and undertake further commitments for liberalization of services, particularly by relaxing its present restrictions on equity participation and capitalization requirements. China will be called upon to offer better terms and conditions in the ongoing negotiations on the accession to the Government Procurement Agreement and to conclude these negotiations speedily. China's response to these demands is likely to be cautious and strictly on the basis of reciprocity, except in some of those borderline cases where measures being currently applied are adjudged to be inconsistent with China's WTO obligations.

Some experts, policymakers and corporate leaders from Western countries would like China to adopt measures designed to bring about a change in the socio-economic system of the country. In their view, China can qualify to become a market economy only after these measures are implemented. These include restructuring and privatization of state-owned enterprises and banks, liberalization of credit allocation and the bond market, permitting private property rights, including legal titles to rural land and market pricing for social goods and utilities like education and health services, land and water. In the present social situation in the country, it is very unlikely that any of these demands would commend themselves to the Chinese government.

For the first five years after China's accession to the WTO, its major trading partners exercised restraint in taking China-related cases to the WTO's DSB. China's over-all approach to the WTO's dispute settlement procedure has been constructive and disciplined. Most of the disputes were settled through consultations at the political level and in each of these cases China made important concessions. However, after the end of the phase-in period, the US and EU in particular have lodged a slew of complaints with the WTO, and in a majority of them the verdicts have gone against China. China has generally eliminated or amended the measures under dispute in response to the verdicts, without going to the WTO Appellate Tribunal.

China itself has recently started using the dispute settlement mechanism to safeguard its trading interests. However, instead of directly lodging complaints, China's policy has been to participate as a third party to a dispute lodged by other WTO members. Currently, China is participating in 20 such cases. In 2006 and 2007, China was subjected to the largest number of anti-dumping enquiries lodged against any single country. It was at the receiving end of one-third of the WTO anti-dumping trade disputes, up from 15 per cent in 2001. The commodities that China has been accused of dumping include light industry goods, chemicals, textiles and leather products.[20] In view of its growing shares of world trade and output and the controversial nature of a large number of its domestic economic measures, China is likely to be involved in many more disputes in future both as a user and a target.

Impact of Accession to WTO

It is not possible to establish a direct co-relationship between China's implementation of its obligations under the Protocol and the rate of growth of its economy. All that can be said, and that too with some qualifications, is that the accession to the WTO was a factor responsible for sustaining and accelerating China's very high rate of growth achieved during the period of liberalization. The real GDP of China increased by 9.85 per cent per annum between 1978 and 1995, by 9.82 per cent between 1978 and 2007 and by 9.77 per cent between 1995 and 2007.[21] China's GDP had doubled between 1999 and 2005. It doubled again during the five years after its joining the WTO, surpassing $2 trillion in 2006. In 2010, the total output reached $5.88 trillion, over 16 times that of 1978. This output was 9.3 per cent of the world output as compared to 1.8 per cent in 1978.[22] China surpassed Japan as the second largest economy of the world. According to a projection made by *The Economist* in December 2010, China is likely to surpass the US as the number one economy of the world in 2019.[23] China's per capita GDP in 2010 was approximately $4,400. The share of this per capita income was 46.8 per cent of the global average, representing almost a doubling as compared to the share of 24.9 per cent of the global GDP in 2005.[24]

The phenomenal progress in the external variables of the Chinese economy can perhaps be attributed more directly to its accelerated liberalization policy as a result of its accession to the WTO. China's earlier progress along these variables was indeed very impressive, but there is definitely an evidence of acceleration during 2000–10. China's annual average rate of growth in trade between 2001 and 2005 was nearly 29 per cent. The total trade volume reached a record level of $1.4 trillion in 2005 compared to $620.79 billion in 2002.[25] During this four-year period, China's imports increased by an annual average rate of 28.6 per cent, and between 2000 and 2006, its exports increased by 23.3 per cent.[26] The country's total trade volume grew from $20.6 billion in 1978 to $2.974 trillion in 2010.[27]

China's overall trade as a percentage of GDP increased from 44 in 2001 to 72 in 2006. The trade GDP ratio reached the level of 74 per cent in 2007 and then came down to 56 per cent in 2009 due to the global financial and economic crisis.[28]

The phenomenal rate of growth in China's GDP as well as trade remains dominated by foreign capital and reliant on the international market.[29] The inflow of FDI into China rose rapidly in the early 1990s. It plateaued at around $40 billion per year thereafter and then took off rapidly following China's entry into the WTO in 2001. The major sources of FDI in China have been its closest neighbours—Hong Kong, Taiwan and Macau.[30] The total FDI flow in 2008 reached the level of $110 billion, up from $55 billion in 2002. This represented a manifold increase from the FDI flow of only $4.3 billion in 1982.[31] The flow was $230 billion between 2002 and 2005.[32] The FDI between 1979 and 2010 exceeded $1 trillion.[33] China has been the second largest recipient of FDI (next to the US) in the world since 2000.[34]

Enterprises financed by foreign investment were responsible for 40 per cent of China's recent economic growth[35] and accounted for more than 60 per cent of Chinese exports in 2005.[36] In 2010, they accounted for 68 per cent of China's trade surplus.[37] The FDI was mostly in the manufacturing sector, but in recent years, it has also started playing an important role in the services sector, accounting for nearly 40 per cent of the total FDI flow. Over 90,000 enterprises based on foreign investment have established themselves in various service sectors, with a total investment amounting to $160 billion.[38]

Soon after its accession to the WTO, China adopted a very vigorous policy of outward investment. Between 2001 and 2005, the country's outward investment, mainly designed to secure energy, raw materials and foreign market, had doubled.[39] From 2000 to 2010, China's annual non-financial direct overseas investment grew from less than $1 billion to $59 billion.[40]

China's foreign exchange reserves reached the level of $875 billion in March 2005. This jumped to about $3 trillion by 2010.[41]

A very significant change that has occurred since China's accession to the WTO is its emergence as the manufacturing hub of the world. China is now referred to as the 'world's principal factory' or the 'centre of gravity of world manufacturing'. The share of manufacture in GDP increased from 19 per cent in 1990 to 37 per cent in 2005 and its share in the country's total exports increased from 65 per cent to 84 per cent during the same period.[42]

Earlier, the bulk of Chinese manufacturing export consisted of light industry products like textiles and clothing, footwear, toys and transport equipment, but since China's accession to the WTO, there has been a significant increase in the technological sophistication of the Chinese manufacturing industry, including its manufactured export. The share of high-tech manufacture increased, while the share of unskilled labour-intensive products went down during 2001–06. In 2006, the share of high-tech products reached the level of 32 per cent of China's total exports and 43 per cent of its total imports.[43] China is now the biggest exporter of computers, computer electronics and other IT goods to the US.[44] FDI has played a very important role in stimulating China's high-tech exports. Foreign multinational corporations bring high skill-content and high value-added inputs to China, assemble them into final products and export them to foreign markets. In 2008, China's total high-tech exports increased to $415.6 billion (29.1 per cent of the total Chinese exports). According to another estimate, foreign manufacturing investors have been responsible for more than 96 per cent of all Chinese advanced technology exports since 2002.[45] Foreign investment enterprises were responsible for 82.5 per cent of this increase.[46]

China succeeded in carrying out a drastic restructuring of some of its leading industries. These include the motor vehicles; telecommunications; and chemical, pharmaceutical and IT industries. As a result, these industries recorded dramatic expansion and emerged as 'leaders' or 'pillars' not only in the Chinese economy but also at the global level. For example, during the period 2001–09, the production of motor vehicles increased from 2.34 million to 13.79 million (more than six times); that of cars, from 0.7 million to 7.48 million (more than 10 times); that of mobile phones, from 80 million to 619 million (more than seven times); that of microcomputers, from 8.77 million to 182.15 million (more than 20 times); and that of chemical raw medicines, from 0.76 million tonnes to 2 million tonnes (nearly three times).[47] China's automobile market will nearly triple in size to 40 million units and account for half of the world production by 2020.[48]

As a result of the drastic rationalization and restructuring of the state-owned enterprises, there was a significant reduction in their share of the national economy. These enterprises were omnipresent on the industrial scene some 25 to 30 years ago, but there are now fewer than 120 centrally-controlled SOEs, and their number is still shrinking.[49] An important part of the space occupied by them has been taken over by private firms, which run into tens of millions today, but they are still comparatively very small. 'A reasonable range for the genuinely private share of production is 30–35 per cent'.[50] The state economic sector, including government-owned industrial enterprises and banks, account for about 35 per cent of the Chinese economy.[51] The state enterprises in the core sectors continue to dominate much of the heavy industry and key services industry of China. Even after the reforms of the SOEs, they continue to be under state control. Where SOEs have been converted into shareholding companies, the state continues to hold majority shares. The reformed SOEs have taken up commercial activities and have introduced some form of private orientation, but are still state-controlled and directed.

From the middle of the first decade of the 21st century, the SOEs 'began to wax again'.[52] In late 2006, the Chinese State Council formally set aside the core of the economy for SOEs. The order issued by it stated:

> The State should solely own or have a majority share in enterprises engaged in power generation and distribution, oil, petrochemicals and natural gas, telecommunications and armaments. The state must also have a controlling

stake in coal, aviation and shipping industries ... Central SOEs should also become heavyweights in sectors including machinery, automobiles, IT, construction, iron and steel, and non-ferrous metals.[53]

If to this list is added the state-dominated banking, insurance and the rest of the financial sectors, the media and railways, few really important industrial sectors would remain outside the pale of state domination. Besides, there are thousands of provincial and municipality-controlled SOEs. The reversal of policy towards SOEs was confirmed by Wu Bangguo, a high official in the Party hierarchy, when he said in his annual parliamentary address on 10 March 2011, 'We have made a solemn declaration that we will not ... carry out privatization'.[54]

The mere diversification of the shares of the SOEs does not amount to their privatization or a significant change in state control. A large majority of the firms listed on domestic stock markets are specifically designated as state-owned. For example, companies like China Mobile and Chinalco, even after divesting a part of their shares, are still centrally controlled. No doubt, some SOEs operate within the market, but these markets are state controlled. Besides, the SOEs receive state support in a variety of ways. Regulatory protection is the most powerful subsidy many SOEs receive. They have immediate call on free loans, which are technically owned by the state. They also as a matter of course receive hefty power and other input subsidies not available to genuinely private firms. As regards capital, all large financial institutions are state-owned.[55]

Some of the SOEs are of a staggering size. For example, China National Petroleum and China Mobile earned more profit in 2009 than the top 500 Chinese firms combined. The sectors that SOEs dominate accounted for 80 per cent of the capitalization of the domestic stock exchange at the end of 2010. The Chinese national banks are among the largest in the world, as are the Chinese state-controlled telecom companies. The Chinese steel industry is grotesquely oversized in the world economy.[56] The total non-state investment in China appears to have been below $13 billion since 2005, which is less than 6 per cent of the total investment made by the four largest state controlled investors, that is, China National Petroleum Corporation, China National Petrochemical Corporation, China Investment Corporation and Aluminium Corporation of China. As of December 2010, these four companies accounted for half of the Chinese investment.[57]

China has been remarkably successful in designing industrial policies and conditions for joint ventures in order to use FDI for technology transfer to create national champions in prominent industrial sectors. These include high-speed rail transport, IT, auto assembly and the currently emerging civil aviation sector. China has struck deals with foreign enterprises, which have enabled them to overcome their cash crises and even make short-term profits, but at the same time obliged them to part with technology which, in the long run, has undermined their competitiveness vis-à-vis the Chinese in their own country as well as in other countries.[58] After accession to the WTO, China, on one hand, rationalized its auto industry by reducing the number of units and reaching out to indigenous suppliers and, on the other, sought the assistance of foreign automotive investors in meeting the more stringent quality, safety and anti-pollution standards in order to enable the industry to expand its exports in Europe and North America. The Airbus, on its website, reported that over half its fleet worldwide contained components produced by Chinese companies.[59]

The period of the phasing in of the WTO commitments coincided with China's state-supported 'go global' policy. This has had a relatively recent origin, starting from 2005. Among other factors, 'China's WTO accession precipitated a profound sense of China's exposure to globalization and with it a greater awareness of the importance of outward investment'.[60] This led to a more active encouragement of the 'go global' policy. By the end of 2007, the annual volume of China's overseas FDI had grown to around \$25 billion. By 2008, it doubled to more than \$50 billion. The stock of Chinese cross-border investment was approximately \$170 billion by that time. More than 7,000 Chinese firms ran a total of more than 10,000 investment projects abroad, as of 2007.[61]

The super-active role of the Chinese Outbound Foreign Direct Investment (OFDI) has caused concern, based mainly on political considerations, in some of the recipient countries. There have been instances of Chinese OFDI being blocked on national security grounds. Examples include the abortive bid of the China National Offshore Oil Corporation to buy American oil company Unocal Corporation in 2005 and China Harbour Engineering Company's bid in 2006 for the Vizhinjam port development project near Thiruvananthapuram, Kerala.[62]

China is taking full advantage of the cash shortage of Central and East European countries to acquire assets in these countries. In a paper entitled 'Scramble for Europe', the authors have painted a quite panicky picture of China's economic incursion into Europe. They have said:

> Its transportation firms are acquiring, leasing or managing harbours, airports and logistical and assembly bases across the continent. Its development

banks are financing projects in Europe's periphery much like they do in Africa. Its purchase of public debt is anxiously sought by deficit European Union member states.[63]

The authors continue, 'China buys or builds infrastructure projects in Europe, snaps up ailing companies or collects assets from quasi-insolvent states and gets a foothold in the distribution sector'. It is often advanced technology in which China is interested when it acquires European companies. China invests in sectors in which it is at a comparative disadvantage and when it wants to boost its own technological development.[64]

China is concentrating on the Mediterranean and the south-east European states which are most in need of Chinese cash. Portugal, Italy, Greece and Spain claim 30 per cent of China's investment in Europe. Central and East European countries claim another 10 per cent.[65]

China's 'go global' policy is motivated by a variety of factors. There is, first, a desire to find an alternative to holding US debts. Second, OFDI is found helpful in establishing the infrastructure needed to integrate China into the global trading system. Third, it is intended to meet the increased domestic demand, generated by the high rate of growth, for raw material and commodities like iron, oil, cement, timber and other resources not in abundant supply in China. China consumes 20 to 25 per cent of the global supply of iron, steel, aluminium and copper.[66] And lastly, as a part of its effort to rebalance its economy, China is using OFDI to shift some of its heavy industry to foreign lands. Chinese firms have already started building refineries and smeltering and other heavy industries in foreign countries.[67]

In spite of the rapidly increasing flow of Chinese FDI to foreign countries, it will be an exaggeration to conclude that Chinese firms are buying up the world. China's role as a global investor remains minor in terms of both global FDI flow and total FDI stock. From 2000 to 2007, the average Chinese OFDI accounted for less than 1 per cent of the global flows annually and was far below the share of the OECD countries. China's OFDI in 2007 was comparable with those of relatively smaller OECD countries like Austria and the Netherlands and fell far short of the flow from a country like the US, which was 14 times larger. China's OFDI stock in 2007 was $70 billion, compared with $25 billion from India. The US FDI stock that year was about 30 times that of China. Moreover, China's net FDI position is still pronouncedly negative, with an inward FDI stock in 2008 of $876 billion compared with an outward stock of $170 billion.[68]

In the coming years, China's OFDI is going to be influenced by its compulsion to rebalance its economy. The emphasis in the rebalancing is going to be on increasing household disposable income and domestic consumption. In any case, external consumption demand growth is likely to flatten and the lower wage countries are going to increasingly claim a part of the current market share of Chinese low-end products. Therefore, China's manufacturers would try to capture a larger share of the global value chain. This will require upgrading the sophistication of Chinese manufactures and competing for the most lucrative portion of the value chain. This would be a powerful incentive for Chinese firms to go abroad. This also implies that the outbound shift will be more to the developed OECD countries than to developing countries.[69]

Discontents of Globalization

China's embrace of globalization and liberalization has no doubt brought about extraordinary improvements not only in the economic power of the country, but also in the living conditions of its people. As the Chinese White Paper on China's Peaceful Development states:

> The first step was to double the GDP of 1980 and ensure people's basic living needs. The second step was to redouble the 1980 GDP and achieve initial prosperity by the end of the 20th century. The goals of these two steps have been met.[70]

But in the process, a number of imbalances have appeared in the Chinese economy. These have caused a great deal of concern and led to the adoption of several remedial measures. This is how these imbalances are summed up in the White Paper:

> Unbalanced development still exists between the urban and rural areas and among different regions; the structural problems in economic and social development remain acute; and economic growth, which exceedingly depends on resource input, is increasingly constrained by resource shortages and environmental problems ... China's capacity for independent innovation is weak and it is at the low end of the value chain in both international division of labour and trade. The standard of living of the Chinese is not high, and China's social security system is inadequate, lagging far behind those of developed countries.[71]

There is also a problem of over-investment and under-consumption in China. It is estimated that 75 per cent of China's industries is plagued by over-capacity.[72] The manufacturing capacity that has been created during the last two decades far exceeds the domestic demand for the products of these industries and can be sustained only by exports to foreign markets. Most of these markets are likely to become protectionist because of the weak demand conditions. The Chinese authorities are aware of this problem and a policy decision has been taken to make a gradual shift from foreign to domestic demand. This was reflected in China's Eleventh Five-Year Plan. However, the pace of the shift is going to be determined less under outside pressure and more by domestic economic and social conditions.

While riding on the crest of globalization and exploiting its opportunities more than any other country in the world has managed to do, China has, of late, started facing the adverse consequences of the globalization process. The discontents of globalization that have emerged on the Chinese economic and social scene have a striking resemblance with those afflicting the Indian economy and society. There is evidence of growing income and regional disparity. The Chinese Gini co-efficient was 47.0 in 2008, which was 10 points higher than that prevailing 15 years ago. China was more unequal than India, which had a Gini co-efficient of 36.8, Indonesia (34.3) and the Philippines (44.5).[73] That year, China had a hundred billionaires, second only to the US. This was a sharp rise from the figure of three billionaires in 2002 and 10 as late as in 2005.[74]

The gap in incomes between China's urban and rural areas is greater than in any other country in the world.[75] The unprecedented expansion of infrastructure in China has been mostly in the urban areas. The share of infrastructure investment in the rural sector declined from 10.6 per cent in 1979 to 2.8 per cent in 1992 and was only 1.7 per cent in 1994.[76]

After the 1990s, there has been a large-scale migration of the rural population to the urban areas. This was facilitated by the elimination of food rations and of free education and health services, which had for some time acted as a constraint to migration.[77] In the last 20 years, some 200 million rural labourers have relocated to urban areas in search of work and other necessities of life.[78]

As a result, rural population, as a proportion of the total population, declined from 80 per cent before the introduction of the agricultural reforms to 60 per cent in 2008. This means that in spite of the phenomenal progress in manufacturing, China, like India, can still be regarded as an agricultural country. This is in spite of the steady decline in government expenditure on agriculture as a percentage of the total national expenditure. This expenditure declined from 10.5 per cent during 1976–80 to 5 per cent during 1981–85, and 3.3 per cent in the year 1985–90. Recently, because of the loss of jobs in the coastal special export zones and the government's renewed attention to improving the condition of life in the rural areas, there is an evidence of reverse migration to these areas. According to an estimate, from mid-October to mid-December 2008, more than 10 million migrant workers returned home after losing their jobs in the coastal areas. This became possible partly because they still retained their lease on land and their village home to return to.[79] However, this does not indicate that this return to the rural areas would become a generalized long-term phenomenon. On the contrary, in the Twelfth Five-Year Plan, Chinese authorities have set the goal of expanding urbanization to cover over 50 per cent of the population. Independent sources have projected that over the next 20 years, some 360 million people will move from the rural to the urban areas, raising China's urbanization rate to 70 per cent, as in many developed countries.

Earlier, in the rural areas, the state used to guarantee entitlement to food, clothing, shelter, education, health services and decent burial. These still exist nominally, but have deteriorated considerably without the institutional support of the communes. By 1980, more than 90 per cent of the Chinese population was covered by the state healthcare system. The dissolution of the communes led to a medical 'free fall' for the rural population.[80] Jiajun Wen Dale states, '[T]he Maoist era brought health to the Chinese people, while the reform era has almost liquidated its achievement for quick money'.[81] Raymond Lotta, in his article in the *Economic and Political Weekly*, has stated, 'in China, the less well-off increasingly go without healthcare altogether'.[82] The main difference between the situation in China and that in India with regard to the provision of education and health services is that whereas in China the services were universalized decades ago and still remain in place in spite of the decline in their quality and coverage, in India, they have never been universalized and quality education and health services continue to be elitist in character and the privilege of a few.

There was an explosion in enrolment in primary and secondary education in the rural areas during the Maoist era and the character of school education had been transformed as a result of the participation of peasants and workers. A new 'popular model' of education had developed and new sets of textbooks in local languages and drawing from local legends and knowledge had become available. All this changed during the reform era. School education has now become increasingly commercialized with the entry of a very large number of private operators.

Education has got increasingly alienated from its local roots and skyrocketing tuition fees have made it unaffordable for a large section of the rural population.[83]

In addition to direct monetary investment in agriculture and rural infrastructure, the government earlier used to provide other forms of support for the welfare of the rural people, like maintenance of waterworks, flood control and drought management. Most of these services have now deteriorated and some of them have even disappeared in the reform era because of the withdrawal of these support measures and the migration of rural workers.[84] Fragmented village communities have lost their collective power and fallen prey to the unchecked bureaucratic power of the rural party cadre and their corrupt behaviour.

The two major factors that account for China's high-speed state-driven growth are low labour cost and high savings. The low wage rate was one of the important factors behind the Chinese success in attracting private foreign capital and for the competitiveness of Chinese manufactured goods in foreign markets. Lotta, in his article, has asserted that 'China's growth is based on the exploitation of wage labour and peasant' labour.[85] The increase in production in enterprises financed through foreign investment was overwhelmingly due to an increase in productivity rather than that in the employment of wage labour. In 2010, these enterprises employed 3 per cent of Chinese labour but generated 22 per cent of its output.[86]

Until a few years ago, the Chinese authorities paid scant regard to the environmental consequences of the country's industrial growth. This is perhaps true of most developing countries and a large number of developed countries as well. But given the vast size of the Chinese economy and the massive scale of its industrialization, the environmental degradation in China has far-reaching consequences both for the Chinese people and the world at large. By all accounts, high growth has led to a very large-scale degradation of the environment in China. Five out of the 10 most polluted cities in the world are in China.[87] The Chinese government itself has recognized this and is now paying increasing attention to the environmental dimensions of economic growth.

Finally, the widening social polarization has triggered off large-scale strikes, protests and other forms of confrontation with authorities in China, centred mainly on the issue of corruption, forcible land takeover by the state, environmental damages and unavailability of essential public goods.

The discontents of globalization have led to a rethinking of the development strategy and economic reform policy of the Chinese government at the highest level of the Party hierarchy. The resultant shift in government policy is reflected in the removal of rural taxes, enactment of a law to make primary education free for all rural children and initiating efforts to rebuild the cooperative healthcare system. In order to deal with the rising social tensions in the agrarian sector, the government has cancelled the national agricultural tax, pushed local authorities to eliminate or reduce levies on peasantries, raised prices of farm products and provided subsidies.[88]

This shift in the policy at the macro level was reflected in China's Eleventh Five-Year Plan covering the period 2006–10, which focused on technological innovation, growth driven by domestic demand, improvement in the infrastructure and industrialization of the relatively less-developed provinces and strengthening of local research and development capabilities. There are compelling economic and political reasons justifying the continuation of this shift in the Twelfth and subsequent development plans. But it is doubtful whether there will be a revival and expansion of the rural economy or a return to the commune system, even in a reformed or modernized version. China has gone too far in its pursuit of globalization to afford to revise its policy of liberalization in any substantial way. Its economy is too deeply and extensively linked with the global economy to revert to a policy of national self-sufficiency and mercantilism. At the same time, China has demonstrated that while moving at full speed towards globalization, a large country can selectively de-link from the global economy in order to build very large-sized and powerful 'pillars' and 'backbone industries', which are essentially state-controlled.

The main thrust in China's Twelfth Five-Year Plan, which commenced in 2011, is to further increase the GDP with a view to reaching the per capita level of medium developed countries, bringing about general prosperity and attaining a higher level of modernization, mainly through innovation. In order to redress the imbalances, China's future economic growth 'will be driven by the combined forces of consumption, investment and export instead of investment and export only'.[89] It will 'also be driven by the combined forces of primary, secondary and tertiary sectors instead of the secondary sector alone'.[90] The primary sector is brought in to underline the environmental factor, particularly the desirability of going back to the nature and preserving natural resources. The tertiary sector has been added in order to underline the objective of enhanced service provision in order to increase the standard of living of the people. These changes in the emphasis in the Twelfth Plan open up important opportunities for countries like India, which are in the process of developing economic relations of a significant dimension with China.

At least during the next few decades, China will continue to be one of the most important players in the process of globalization. It will continue to remain a formidable competitor for countries like India in foreign markets and for foreign capital. It is likely to further liberalize its economy and give greater play to market forces, at its own pace and strictly within the confines of its development strategy, in its quest for recognition as a market economy. At the same time, it has started taking measures for correcting the imbalances that have cropped up in its economy due to the excesses of globalization.

There has been an over-investment in China's manufacturing sector resulting in the creation of huge excess capacity. This has occurred mainly in a bid to claim the largest possible share of the consumer demand in developed countries. An accompanying factor has been huge investments made by foreign companies in order to use China as a manufacturing hub to cater to this demand. The consumer demand in developed countries suffered a jolt due to the global recession of 2008 and 2009, and remains depressed because of the slow and faltering recovery of the US and European economies. There is, therefore, going to be a significant reduction in China's export dependence for its development. Some of the latest figures already provide pointers in that direction. For sustaining growth, China has declared its policy to substantially enhance dependence on domestic demand. Because of the divergence in the patterns of domestic and foreign demands, it would be necessary to bring about changes in the structure of production in China. China is very likely to curb its manufacturing ambitions sustained by foreign demand and increasingly to produce goods that can meet the domestic demand. Moreover, China's production for exports and its dependence on FDI and foreign technologies are going to be highly selective, with concentration on the production of sophisticated and technology-intensive goods and services. This may open up space in foreign markets for consumer goods from developing countries like India, and also for the diversion of FDI from China to these countries. But for this to acquire any significant dimension, the recovery in the economies of developed countries would have to be robust and stable. This seems doubtful because of the very slow pace of recovery in the US and the sovereign debt crisis in the Eurozone, triggering widespread apprehension of a double dip recession.

One of the principal goals of China's development strategy is to further increase per capita income and reduce income disparities. The government is going to adopt policies that can put larger incomes at the disposal of those sections of the Chinese population whose standard of living is still modest. This will, above all, call for tax concessions and subsidies, and the state playing a much greater role in the provisioning of essential services, particularly health and education. This is likely to create huge domestic demand for goods and services in the supply of which developing countries like India would have competitive advantage. But, for this potentiality to be realized, China would be required to further open up its economy for imports from these countries. It would need to bring about changes in the government procurement policy and selective import restrictions. For example, the currently prevailing curbs on the import of pharmaceuticals and IT products and services from India would need to be lifted. Finally, in order to reduce excess capacity in the manufacturing sector, with the critical environmental consideration in mind, China is likely to transfer some of its manufacturing activities to foreign countries, particularly developing countries. This is likely to open up opportunities for enhanced Chinese investment in countries like India.

Notes

1. John Frisbie, 'China's Implementation of Its World Trade Organization Commitments: An Assessment by the US-China Business Council' (testimony for the US–China Business Council Trade Policy Staff Committee Hearing, 6 October 2010).
2. Ibid.
3. Ibid.
4. Wang Yong, 'China in the WTO: A Chinese View', *China Business Review* (September–October 2006).
5. Frisbie, China's Implementation of Its World Trade Organization Commitments'.
6. T. P. Bhat, 'Five Years of China in WTO: An Assessment' (Working Paper No. 2007/06, Institute for Studies in Industrial Development, New Delhi, April 2007).
7. Office of the United States Trade Representative (USTR), '2011 National Trade Estimate Report on Foreign Trade Barriers' (March 2011), https://ustr.gov/sites/default/files/uploads/gsp/speeches/reports/2011/nte/NTE%20Final%20Printed%203.29%20mmw.pdf (accessed on 5 May 2015).

8. Razeen Sally, 'Chinese Trade Policy After (Almost) Ten Years in the WTO: A Post-Crisis Stocktake' (Occasional Paper No. 2/2011, European Centre for International Political Economy, Brussels, 2011).
9. Ibid.
10. Office of the USTR, '2011 National Trade Estimate Report on Foreign Trade Barriers' 61–92.
11. Ibid.
12. Ibid.
13. Ibid.
14. Ibid.
15. Ibid.
16. Ibid.
17. Ibid.
18. Ibid.
19. Yong, 'China in the WTO'.
20. Bhat, 'Five Years of China in WTO'.
21. Dic Lo and Yu Zhang, 'Globalization Meets its Match: Lessons from China's Economic Transformation', *Economic and Political Weekly*, Volume 43, No. 52 (27 December 2008).
22. Information Office of the State Council, 'White Paper: China's Peaceful Development'.
23. *The Economist*, 'The World's Biggest Economy: Dating Game', 16 December 2010, http://www.economist.com/node/17733177 (accessed on 5 May 2015).
24. Information Office of the State Council, 'White Paper: China's Peaceful Development'.
25. Yong, 'China in the WTO'.
26. Ibid.
27. Information Office of the State Council, 'White Paper: China's Peaceful Development'.
28. Sally, 'Chinese Trade Policy'.
29. Raymond Lotta, 'China's Rise in the World Economy', *Economic and Political Weekly*, Volume 44, No. 8 (21 February 2009).
30. Robert E. Scott, US Investments in China, Testimony before the US China Economic and Security Review Commission at the Hearing on 'Chinese State-Owned Enterprises and US–China Bilateral Investment' (30 March 2011).
31. Sunanda Sen, 'Finance in China after WTO', *Economic and Political Weekly*, Volume 40, No. 6 (5 February 2005).
32. Yong, 'China in the WTO'.
33. Information Office of the State Council, 'White Paper: China's Peaceful Development'.
34. Sally, 'Chinese Trade Policy'.

35. Scott, 'US Investments in China'.
36. Sally, 'Chinese Trade Policy'.
37. Scott, 'US Investments in China'.
38. Sally, 'Chinese Trade Policy'.
39. Ibid.
40. Information Office of the State Council, 'White Paper: China's Peaceful Development'.
41. National Bureau of Statistics, China.
42. Ajit K. Ghose, 'The Growth Miracle, Institutional Reforms and Employment in China', *Economic and Political Weekly*, Volume 43, No. 22 (31 May 2008).
43. Geethanjali Natraj and Anjali Tandon, 'China's Changing Export Structure: A Factor-Based Analysis', *Economic and Political Weekly*, Volume 46, No. 13 (26 March 2011).
44. Lotta, 'China's Rise in the World Economy'.
45. Theodore H. Moran, 'Foreign Manufacturing Multinationals and the Transformation of the Chinese Economy: Faustian Bargain to Trade Technology for Access' (Testimony before the US–China Economic and Security Review Commission, 30 March 2011).
46. Scott, 'US Investments in China'.
47. National Bureau of Statistics, China.
48. John Reed, 'China's Car Market to Triple by 2020', *Financial Times*, 13 January 2011.
49. Derek Scissors, 'The Fall and Rise of Chinese State Owned Enterprises' (Testimony before the US–China Economic and Security Review Commission, 30 March 2011).
50. Ibid.
51. Lotta, 'China's Rise in the World Economy'.
52. Scissors, 'The Fall and Rise of Chinese State Owned Enterprises'.
53. Zhao Huanxin, 'China Names Key Industries for Absolute State Control', *China Daily*, 19 December 2006.
54. Quoted in *The China Post*, 'China Vows no Western-Style Political Reforms', 10 March 2011.
55. Scissors, 'The Fall and Rise of Chinese State Owned Enterprises'.
56. Ibid.
57. Ibid.
58. Moran, 'Foreign Manufacturing Multinationals'.
59. Ibid.
60. Daniel H. Rosen and Thilo Hanemann, 'China's Changing Outbound Foreign Direct Investment Profile: Drivers and Policy Implications' (Policy Brief no. PB09-14, Peterson Institute for International Economics, Washington DC, June 2009).
61. Ibid.

62. Siddharth Srivastava, 'Delhi Divided over Chinese 'Threat', *Asian Times*, 8 November 2006; *The Economic Times*, 'Costlier Land, Infrastructure to Hike Vizhinjam Port Cost by 60%', 28 January 2012.
63. François Godement, Jonas Parello-Plesner and Alice Richard, 'The Scramble for Europe' (Policy Brief, European Council on Foreign Relations, London, July 2011).
64. Ibid.
65. Ibid.
66. Lotta, 'China's Rise in the World Economy'.
67. Rosen and Hanemann, 'China's Changing Outbound Foreign Direct Investment Profile'.
68. Ibid.
69. Ibid.
70. Information Office of the State Council, 'White Paper: China's Peaceful Development'.
71. Ibid.
72. Lotta, 'China's Rise in the World Economy'.
73. Robert Weil, 'A House Divided: China after 30 Years of "Reforms"', *Economic and Political Weekly*, Volume 43, No. 52 (27 December 2008).
74. Ibid
75. Lotta, 'China's Rise in the World Economy'.
76. Jiajun Wen Dale, 'Chinese Rural Reforms: Crisis and Ongoing Debate', *Economic and Political Weekly*, Volume 43, No. 52 (27 December 2008).
77. Ghose, 'The Growth Miracle'.
78. Lotta, 'China's Rise in the World Economy'.
79. Dale, 'Chinese Rural Reforms'.
80. Ibid.
81. Ibid.
82. Lotta, 'China's Rise in the World Economy'.
83. Dale, 'Chinese Rural Reforms'.
84. Ibid.
85. Lotta, 'China's Rise in the World Economy'.
86. Scott, 'US Investments in China'.
87. Lotta, 'China's Rise in the World Economy'.
88. Ibid.
89. Information Office of the State Council, 'White Paper: China's Peaceful Development'.
90. Ibid.

TWELVE Perspectives of India and Japan on Disarmament and Security Issues

The Indian Perspective

When the first atom bombs devastated the cities of Hiroshima and Nagasaki during the Second World War, the reaction in India was one of unqualified horror and revulsion. Mahatma Gandhi characterized the atom bomb as the diabolical use of science. Jawaharlal Nehru described it as 'an evil thing'. There was, therefore, no question at that time of India seeking to ensure its security through the acquisition of nuclear weapons.

After taking a conscious decision neither to become a member of any military alliance nor to enter into a bilateral security arrangement with any nuclear weapon power, India had no alternative but to pursue its security through the path of the elimination of nuclear weapons. India, therefore, made several moves to stop the nuclear arms race and achieve nuclear disarmament. Jawaharlal Nehru was the first statesman in the world who took the initiative, as early as in 1954, for the cessation of nuclear weapon tests. India was one of the leading countries in the early 1960s to move a resolution in the UN General Assembly for preventing the proliferation of nuclear weapons. What India had in mind while taking this initiative was to prevent both vertical and horizontal proliferation. Unfortunately, the outcome of the efforts of the international community in this area, that is, the NPT, was far removed from India's original purpose, as it provided for the prevention of only horizontal proliferation. It also legitimized the possession of nuclear weapons by those who already had them. India was, therefore, obliged to part company with the others and not sign the NPT.

At the First Special Session of the UN General Assembly Devoted to Disarmament (SSOD-I), held in New York in 1978, India played a leading role in getting a consensus document adopted which embodied the most unqualified and categorical commitment ever achieved by the UN member states on nuclear disarmament. At SSOD-II, held in New York in 1982, India sought to get nuclear weapons delegitimized by putting forward a proposal for negotiating a convention on the non-use of such weapons. India also took the initiative at that Conference for a freeze on the production of fissile material and nuclear weapons pending their elimination. After 1982, India kept on moving resolutions on fissile freeze and non-use of nuclear weapons practically at every session of the General Assembly until the mid-1990s.

India could not make any headway in persuading the nuclear weapon powers and their allies to accept its proposals designed to achieve nuclear disarmament. It did not find Japan on its side in any of its initiatives. Japan consistently voted against the Indian resolutions in the General Assembly and joined its Western allies in blocking Indian initiatives on nuclear disarmament in the Conference on Disarmament. The last, and by far the most important, initiative taken by India to safeguard its security through nuclear disarmament was Rajiv Gandhi's 1988 Action Plan for Establishing a Nuclear Weapons-Free and Non-Violent World Order. This initiative also failed to elicit a positive response from the Western powers and Japan.

After China exploded its nuclear weapon in October 1964, the then Government of India sent an emissary to the US to explore the possibility of the latter providing a nuclear umbrella to India. The US expressed its inability to oblige. India's failure to secure a nuclear umbrella in 1964 was a major reason behind its keeping the nuclear weapon option open by not signing the NPT. When Rajiv Gandhi's initiative also failed and soon thereafter India came to know that Pakistan had already started assembling nuclear weapons and was actively seeking to acquire delivery vehicles for them, it was left with no option but to acquire its own nuclear deterrence. The May 1998 nuclear explosions were, in a sense, a formal declaration by India of its intentions to do so. Thus, India resorted to a minimum nuclear deterrence after 50 years of agonizing and after the failure of all its efforts during this period to seek security through alternative means, particularly the nuclear disarmament path.

Japan's Reaction to Pokhran-II Tests

Japan's reaction to these tests as well as to those subsequently conducted by Pakistan, was unusually harsh. It regarded the tests as 'extremely regrettable' and a challenge to the efforts of the international community to seek a world free from nuclear weapons. Japan applied a freeze on grant aid and Yen loans to India for new projects. It also announced that it would cautiously examine loan projects and programmes for India by international financial institutions. Japan was not content with just suspending economic aid; it joined its major allies in mounting a veritable campaign against India at several international fora, including the G-8 Summit held in Birmingham in May 1998, at the Conference on Disarmament in Geneva in June 1998, and at the UN Security Council in June 1998. Japan had sponsored the resolution passed by the UN Security Council which, among others, called upon India and Pakistan to halt and roll back their nuclear weapons programmes and join the NPT. The initiatives taken by Japan both unilaterally and jointly with other major powers caused a great deal of disquiet and consternation in India and severely strained Indo-Japanese relations. The relations remained hostage to the nuclear issue for about three years, from 1998 to 2000.

Given Japan's stake in South Asia, its concerns with the nuclear explosions by India and Pakistan were quite legitimate. Undoubtedly, the nuclearization of South Asia had serious implications for the security situation in the region. The geo-strategic location of South Asia makes the region of critical importance to Japan. South Asian countries, particularly India, have command over the routes to West Asian oil supplies on which Japan is heavily dependent. India as well as Pakistan can play a very important role in keeping the sea lanes in their vicinity open, which are so vital for Japan's commerce. Besides, South Asia, particularly India and Pakistan, is potentially a huge market for Japanese goods and services and an important destination for its investments. The dynamism displayed by the Indian economy for more than two decades and the impressive rates of growth recorded by other South Asian countries, have given Japan and its multinational corporations a great stake in South Asia, particularly in the context of the continuing stagnation of the Japanese economy.

As Japan and other major powers see it, a conflictual situation prevails in South Asia because of the historical animosity and unresolved problems between India and Pakistan. India and Pakistan have, in the past, fought three declared wars and an undeclared one over Kargil. Their forces are arrayed against each other in close proximity and in a confrontational mode. Their common borders are by no means entirely peaceful and tranquil. Outside powers, including Japan, therefore perceive the possibility of the eruption of another conventional war between the two countries. After the acquisition of nuclear weapons by India and Pakistan, there is, according to these powers, a great danger of such a conventional war escalating into a nuclear war. This would not only spell disaster for the peoples of the two countries but also imperil peace and stability in Asia as a whole, where Japan is a dominant power.

The extraordinary hue and cry raised by Japan over the May 1998 nuclear explosions by India and Pakistan was also rooted in its national security consideration. Having opted for the US nuclear umbrella, Japan has a security interest in preserving the existing nuclear order. It perceived the nuclear tests carried out by India and Pakistan as a threat to this order.

Moreover, like other major powers, Japan regarded the nuclear tests by India and Pakistan as a setback to its non-proliferation objective. Japan had reasons to be specially concerned in this regard because of the apprehension that the Indian and Pakistani tests would trigger wider proliferation of nuclear weapons, including by North Korea, which would pose a direct threat to Japan's security. Besides, because of the Hiroshima and Nagasaki experience, there is greater abhorrence of nuclear weapons among the Japanese people than among the peoples of other countries. Any government in power in Japan is obliged to respond to the public sentiment on the nuclear issue.

The Japanese Perspective

Japan's attitude and policies towards security and disarmament issues have been shaped mainly by its experience of being the only victim of nuclear warfare and the imperatives of the Cold War which characterized international relations soon after the end of the Second World War. After its defeat in the war, Japan accepted the tutelage of the US and joined the Western alliance led by the latter. Having cast its lot with the Western power bloc, Japan perceived a threat to its security emanating mainly from the other power involved in the Cold War, that is, the Soviet Union. China's emergence as a nuclear weapon state after it exploded its first nuclear weapon in 1964 and the development of North Korea's nuclear capability later were the other elements that went into the shaping of Japan's nuclear threat perception. Japan had to take measures to safeguard its security against these threats. On the other hand, in response to the strong anti-nuclear sentiment in the country, the Japanese Parliament had adopted the Three Non-Nuclear Principles—not to manufacture nuclear weapons, not to possess them and not to allow their introduction into Japan. Having consciously decided to forego the nuclear option, Japan opted for the US nuclear umbrella or the US extended deterrence, including nuclear deterrence, to safeguard its security. Since then, Japan has perpetually faced the dilemma of reconciling its objective of moving towards a nuclear weapon-free world with its reliance on, and hence support for, nuclear deterrence. To quote a Japanese scholar, 'Japan's record on international disarmament initiatives remains mixed, reflecting the conflicted domestic politics of disarmament versus extended nuclear deterrent'.[1]

By agreeing to come under the US nuclear umbrella, Japan endorsed the notion of the possession, stockpiling and proliferation of nuclear weapons by a few privileged countries. This made Japan not only approve but also indirectly become a party to the principal nuclear arms race in which the two superpowers with their respective allies were engaged during the Cold War. Even worse, this made Japan subscribe to the discriminatory nuclear world order that came to be established in the post-Second World War period. This order was based on the legitimacy of the possession of nuclear weapons by a few and the denial of such possession to others, even if they had strong security compulsions to acquire nuclear weapons. Moreover, implicit in the Japanese reliance on US extended deterrence was the notion that the recognized nuclear weapon powers were inherently more responsible, mature and rational than those which would acquire such weapons after the NPT came into force. There is no logical or empirical basis for dividing the world in this fashion.

Japan opted for the US nuclear umbrella mainly as a deterrent. For, it knew that because of the very nature of nuclear weapons, no nuclear weapon state was going to risk the life of its own population, nay the entire human population, by waging a nuclear war in order to protect one of its allies from a nuclear threat.

Lastly, in opting for the US extended deterrence, Japan clearly took the view that its mighty economic power did not constitute enough guarantee for its security and that in the ultimate analysis, military security took precedence over other forms of security. India, when it exercised its nuclear option, was motivated by the same fundamental national security considerations that compelled Japan to opt for the US extended deterrence.

Extended nuclear deterrence is not available to all countries. Its availability very much depends upon the geo-strategic location of the country concerned, its economic clout, its conventional weapon capability, and above all, its sharing common security and strategic interests and objectives with the country providing the extended deterrence. India apparently did not fall in this category. Therefore, at one stage when it tried to come under the US nuclear umbrella, while still retaining its independence of judgement and action in matters of foreign policy, it was cold-shouldered by the US.

An inevitable consequence of Japan's reliance on US extended deterrence was its obligation to align its security and disarmament policies almost entirely with those of the US. This has been a principal factor responsible for India and Japan having different perspectives on disarmament and security issues. For example, though Japan subscribes to the goal of moving towards a nuclear-weapon-free world, like its Western allies, it regards it only as a long-term or ultimate objective. It is not prepared to accept a time-bound framework for the elimination of nuclear weapons or to support the idea of the commencement of negotiations for a convention banning the use, production and possession of nuclear weapons. In the report of the Tokyo Forum,[2] the proposal for a deadline for eliminating nuclear weapons was viewed with utter disdain. The report referred to the so-called 'artificial disarmament deadlines' as a 'theology'.

Like the US and its other allies, Japan also does not accept non-use or no-first-use of nuclear weapons as a means of de-legitimizing these weapons before their elimination. The Tokyo Forum report, in the paragraph entitled 'No First Use', dismisses the idea as merely a 'pledge' and goes to great lengths to demonstrate its impracticality. The report ponderously proclaims that 'actions are far more important than words and pledges'.[3]

Japan is in favour of a gradualist step-by-step approach towards achieving nuclear disarmament. It regards Article VI of the NPT as the preferred route for moving towards it. That is one of the reasons why Japan has been taking a very active part in all NPT Review Conferences. After the May 2010 Review Conference, Japan took the initiative of convening a Meeting of Foreign Ministers of 10 Like-Minded Countries[4] on Nuclear Disarmament and Non-Proliferation. The avowed purpose of this initiative was 'to take forward the consensus outcomes of the 2010 NPT Review Conference and jointly to advance the nuclear disarmament and non-proliferation agenda as mutually reinforcing processes'.[5] These foreign ministers met first in New York on 22 September 2010, and second, in Berlin on 30 April 2011. At the end of each of these meetings, they issued a statement on disarmament and non-proliferation. In the New York Joint Statement, issued after their first meeting, the Ministers regarded the NPT as 'the essential foundation for the achievement of nuclear disarmament'. They also came out in favour of 'universal adherence to the NPT and called upon all states not party to it to accede to it immediately as non-nuclear weapon states'.[6]

From India's standpoint, Article VI of the NPT, which is couched in best endeavour terms and which has led only to the adoption of nuclear arms control measures to manage the nuclear world, is not the route that can take the international community to a nuclear-weapon-free world. One cannot legitimize the possession of nuclear weapons by a few privileged nations and at the same time claim that one is for a nuclear-weapon-free world. Moreover, experience shows that this approach has been a major factor responsible for the proliferation of nuclear weapons. For, if a few privileged states are permitted to possess nuclear weapons to safeguard their security, it is unrealistic to expect that other nations would not resort to the same device in order to safeguard their security.

According to Japan and like-minded countries, the goal of a nuclear weapon-free world can be attained by adopting step-by-step partial measures of nuclear disarmament such as the INF Treaty, the Strategic Arms Limitation Talks-I (SALT-I), SALT-II, START-I and START-II. Reacting to the approval by the US Congress of the New START Treaty between the US and Russia, the then Japanese foreign minister, in a statement issued on 23 December 2010, welcomed the step and expressed the hope 'that this development will lead to advancing nuclear disarmament involving countries possessing nuclear weapons, other than the United States and the Russian Federation'.[7] The hint was obviously to the desirability of China adopting similar measures.

Japan perceives an umbilical link between non-proliferation and nuclear disarmament. The New York Joint Statement stated, 'We agree that an effective non-proliferation regime enhances the possibility for nuclear disarmament'. The 10 Foreign Ministers also stated that 'non-proliferation and nuclear disarmament are mutually reinforcing'.[8] Therefore, from the Japanese perspective, strict adherence to the NPT, and its strengthening and universalization among non-nuclear weapon powers are crucial steps towards making progress in nuclear disarmament. Other measures to be pursued in this regard are the signing of and adherence to the CTBT and negotiations of a Fissile Material Cutoff Treaty (FMCT).

When India had earlier advanced the idea of a comprehensive test ban treaty and freezing the production of fissile material and nuclear weapons, following the US line, Japan had opposed them. Japan started supporting CTBT and FMCT only after the US reversed its own position on these proposals. The US changed its position mainly because it had by then accumulated massive stockpiles of nuclear weapons and fissile material and also because after the cessation of the principal nuclear arms race between the US and the then USSR, following the end of the Cold War, there was little justification for testing nuclear weapons to develop new weapon systems or expanding the existing arsenals of the two super powers.

Thus on the FMCT, Japan, like the US, came closer to the Indian position. But on the CTBT, India changed its earlier position and publicly opposed it. This was mainly because it wanted to keep open its option of testing if any of the countries from which it faced a direct threat to its security, that is, Pakistan and China, resumed testing. However, the NDA government had indicated that it had no objection in principle to signing the CTBT, but would need to build a national consensus to be able to do so. There is no indication so far that succeeding governments have changed this position.

Again, following the US lead, as reflected in President Obama's speech in Prague on 1 April 2009 on the elimination of nuclear weapons, Japan came to believe that diminishing the role of nuclear weapons in security strategies could contribute to nuclear disarmament. The Joint Statement issued after the Second Meeting of the 10 Foreign Ministers, held in Berlin on 30 April 2011, underlined the need to reduce the role of nuclear weapons in security strategies, concepts, doctrines and policies. For India, reducing the salience of nuclear weapons in the security doctrine of nuclear-weapon states is a good confidence-enhancing measure. But it cannot by itself be regarded as a nuclear disarmament measure.

Japan believes that nuclear weapon-free zones can enhance global peace and stability by reinforcing the nuclear non-proliferation regime and can thus contribute to the goal of achieving nuclear disarmament. Until its nuclear explosion in 1998, India used to dismiss nuclear weapon-free zones as an illusion. For, it is not possible to have such a zone when it is open to nuclear intrusion or attack by nuclear weapon powers outside the zone. After the 1998 nuclear explosions, the NDA government had declared its willingness to sign on a selective basis, protocols for collaborating with nuclear weapon-free zones. There is again no indication from any of the succeeding governments of any change in this position.

Until May 1998, Japan's attitude towards the development and deployment of BMD was different from that of India. Japan had, for all practical purposes, joined the US in its endeavour to develop a global BMD system. The Tokyo Forum Report had generally come out in favour of BMD. It stated, 'There may be times when missile defences can play useful roles in countering coercion and strengthening alliance cohesion'. The report had also sought to justify missile defence on the ground of the principle of a state's 'inherent right of self defence'.[9] India, on the other hand, used to regard BMD as a major destabilizing factor for international security. In the opinion of India and several other countries, mainly China and Russia, BMD would consolidate the hegemony of the countries possessing the system over the rest of the world, and would trigger a new spurt in the nuclear arms race. India believed that the best way to seek self defence from nuclear weapons was to eliminate them, rather than developing a new weapon system to counter them. Weapons are weapons irrespective of whether they are for offence or defence. The development of a new weapon system, even though it was for defence, was bound to compel rival powers to develop a similar system or more and new offensive weapons to counter them. However, after declaring itself to be a nuclear weapon power, India's position on BMD underwent a change. When the global BMD system was formally launched by the Bush administration in 2001, the then Indian Foreign Minister openly supported it in the Parliament. Since then, the Government of India has generally kept silent on this issue while remaining engaged in research and development activities for enhancing its own defensive capability.

In the National Defence Programme Guidelines (NDPG) issued by the Japanese government in December 2010, it was stated that Japan would continue to develop its nuclear defence system in cooperation with the US. It may be recalled that after North Korea's 1998 Taepodong-I missile test, Japan began undertaking research and development activities in missile defence in collaboration with the US. In the NDPG 2004, Japan decided to make the US–Japanese missile defence programme an exception to Japan's self-imposed three principles on arms export. In December 2005, the Japanese cabinet decided that Tokyo would develop jointly with the US more advanced next generation missile interceptors.[10]

Because of the experience of suffering nuclear devastation during the Second World War, the Japanese people expect their government to pursue the goal of nuclear disarmament with a missionary zeal. The Government of Japan, therefore, has traditionally been very active in the field of disarmament. The Japanese delegation to the CD regularly presents working papers intended to facilitate disarmament negotiations.

Japan is similarly active in other disarmament fora, particularly in the First Committee of the UN General Assembly which deals mainly with disarmament issues, and the NPT Review Conferences. Japan sponsors a large number of resolutions in the First Committee on a regular basis. Top officials from the Foreign Office in Tokyo address the CD and the General Assembly at regular intervals, outlining Japan's position on disarmament issues.

After the nuclear explosions by India and Pakistan in May 1998, the Japanese government took the initiative of setting up the Tokyo Forum. In September 2008, Japan, in collaboration with Australia, took the initiative of setting up an International Commission on Nuclear Non-Proliferation and Nuclear Disarmament (ICNND) which has been meeting from time to time and pronouncing its views on emerging disarmament and non-proliferation issues. By all indications, Japan intends to continue what it considers to be its leadership role in the disarmament field. While reacting to the approval by the US Senate of the New START Treaty, the Japanese foreign minister, in his statement on 23 December 2010, promised that 'Japan, in cooperation with the United States, will also display further leadership in the international community towards realizing the goal of a world without nuclear weapons'.[11] In the NDPG issued in early 2011, it was stated, 'To address the threat of nuclear weapons, Japan will play an active role in international nuclear disarmament and non-proliferation efforts'.[12]

In its various initiatives, Japan mainly seeks to advance and bolster the positions of the US and its allies on disarmament and security issues and present these positions in new garbs by dressing them up from time to time with new arguments. In this context, Japan's initiatives have also been frequently deployed to thwart the efforts of non-aligned and other like-minded groups that have different perspectives on these issues. It is significant that Japan has not joined any of these like-minded groups, like the New Agenda Coalition, the Rio Group and other groups of non-nuclear weapon states, which are not a part of NAM but whose position on nuclear disarmament is very close to that of NAM. The difference in the viewpoint of these groups from that of Japan is reflected, for example, in what the Rio Group said in its statement issued after the May 1998 nuclear explosions. It attributed the nuclear explosions by India and Pakistan in large part to the failure of the international community to move towards the goal of elimination. It also said that it was unrealistic to pursue the goal of non-proliferation in isolation from the objective of the elimination of nuclear weapons.

When Japan issued its NDPG in December 2010, there had been a change of government for the first time in 50 years from the Liberal Democratic Party (LDP) to a coalition led by the Democratic Party of Japan (DPJ). An important plank of the political platform of DPJ was to downgrade the US extended nuclear deterrence in Japan's security priority. It was, therefore, expected that the 2010 NDPG would reflect a change in this direction. However, there was no modification in Japan's nuclear stance under the new government. The NDPG 2010 stipulated that 'as long as nuclear weapons exist, the extended deterrence provided by the United States, with nuclear deterrent as a vital element, will be indispensable'.[13] This continued reliance on US extended deterrence also signified the continuation of Japan's policies on disarmament and security issues.

Japan's reaction, reflected in the NDPG 2010, to President Obama's 2009 Prague speech declaring the new US administration's intention to take concrete steps towards a world without nuclear weapons, was a reiteration of Japan's dependence on US extended deterrence and its belief in a gradualist approach to nuclear disarmament. What Japan found most significant in the speech was its acknowledgement 'that the abolition of nuclear weapons would not be achieved in the near future' and the declaration of the US intention 'to maintain nuclear deterrence as long as nuclear weapons exist'. These factors were singled out at the very beginning of the NDPG's reference to President Obama's speech. Japan's reaction also showed its nervousness about what may happen to US extended deterrence during the course of the pursuit of the goal of the elimination of nuclear weapons. It was underlined in the NDPG that, 'to address the threat of nuclear weapons, Japan . . . will continue to maintain and improve the credibility of US extended deterrence, including nuclear deterrent as a vital element, through close cooperation with the USA'.[14] In response to Japan's concern about the continuing strength of the US security guarantee under the US extended deterrence, the two countries agreed in July 2009 to establish an official framework to conduct periodic dialogues, including on the issue of the extended nuclear deterrence. The rest of the comments in the NDPG on Obama's speech highlighted those elements which were in conformity with Japan's approach to nuclear disarmament, that is, the reduction of the role of nuclear weapons in US security strategy, signing of the New START Treaty and Obama's promise to pursue the ratification of the CTBT by the US Congress.

China is a major security concern for both India and Japan. It poses a potential direct threat to India's security. It has committed aggression against India along the border, which still remains undemarcated. Chinese troops are deployed menacingly close to its border with India. Chinese medium-range missiles, including the latest version, are deployed in the Tibet region, from where they can easily reach targets in India. Chinese intercontinental missiles also pose a potential threat to it. Moreover, China is the only nuclear weapon power today which is still feverishly engaged in developing or acquiring weapons designed to strengthen and expand each of its triad of nuclear war-fighting machinery—land-based, airborne and sea-launched. China is a major security concern for India also because of its not-so-benevolent engagements in the security situation in South Asia. Through its military cooperation with India's neighbours, China has been exercising considerable influence in the shaping of the balance of power in South Asia. It is really a part of the problematique of security that prevails in the region.

China poses a potential threat to the security of Japan also. Its recent activities in the defence domain have caused concern to Japan. This was reflected in Japan's NDPG of both 2010 and 2011. In the NDPG 2010, Japan expressed concern over China's modernization of its military force, in stronger terms than in the previous NDPGs. It also indicated its intention to respond to the situation by increasing its own activities on the ground and outlined some of the concrete measures of force enhancement and redeployment that it was going to take in this regard. In the NDPG 2010, it was stated 'military modernization by China and its insufficient transparency are of concern for the regional and global community'.[15] Masako Toki in his policy brief stated: 'It seems that Japan is transforming its strategic orientation from a reactive post-World War-II defence orientation to a more pro-active defence posture'.[16]

While developing their respective capabilities to meet threats to their security emanating from any source, including China, both India and Japan have made it clear at the highest political level that it is not their intention to build an alliance either bilaterally or with other powers, directed against China.

The security situation in Asia Pacific, particularly in the areas surrounding Japan, has deteriorated rapidly during the last three years coinciding with Prime Minister Shinzo Abe being in power. Japan's deteriorating security environment has been very clearly and graphically depicted in the government's White Paper, 'Defense of Japan 2014', brought out by the Japanese Ministry of Defence in December 2013.[17]

The general picture presented in the Overview Chapter reads as follows:

> Opaque and uncertain factors such as issues of territorial rights and reunification remain in the vicinity of Japan ... there are clearer trends for neighbouring states to modernize and reinforce their military capabilities and to intensify their military activities. Therefore, the security issues in the Asia Pacific region including the area surrounding Japan, are becoming more serious.[18]

More specifically, the publication notes that 'North Korea's nuclear weapons development considered in conjunction with the enhancement of its ballistic missile capabilities, poses a grave threat to Japan's security'.[19] Regarding China, the document notes that this country 'is enhancing its asymmetric military capabilities to deter military forces of other countries from approaching and advancing to its surrounding regions', which is referred to as Anti-Access or Area Denial Strategy.[20] Further, China has been strengthening its military forces broadly. It has been rapidly expanding and intensifying its activities in the seas and air space, including the East China Sea and South China Sea. Here, reference is made, among others, to China's commissioning of an aircraft carrier, its development of J-20 and J-31 next-generation fighter aircrafts and a forty-fold increase in its national military budget over the past 26 years.

The document underlines that China has adopted the so-called 'assertive measures including attempts to alter the status quo by coercive measures'. In this connection, pointed attention is drawn to China's action last year to obligate aircraft flying in the East China Sea Air Defence Identification Zone, which includes the disputed Senkaku Islands, to abide by the rules set forth by the Chinese Ministry of Defence, and to the fact that if any aircraft does not follow the prescribed instructions, the Chinese armed forces would take defensive emergency measures against it. The document also refers to the unilateral commencement by China in May 2014, of oil drilling in the disputed territory in the South China Sea which triggered confrontation between the Chinese and Vietnamese vessels in which many vessels sustained damages due to collisions.[21]

In view of these developments, the Japanese government under Prime Minister Abe has adopted a more pro-active policy to deal with threats to its security. In December 2013, it set up a National Security Council and at the same time formulated the first ever National Security Strategy for Japan. In July 2014, the Government of Japan approved a Cabinet decision to interpret Article 9 of the Japanese Constitution, which confines its military cooperation with outside countries to peace-time intelligence, surveillance and reconnaissance activities, in order to take wider measures in the exercise of Japan's right of collective self-defence. This flexibility in the interpretation of the Article is designed, according to the NDPG 2014, to enhance Japan's deterrence response capabilities by conducting tailored activities swiftly and sustainably based on joint operations, and for this purpose, developing Japan's defence capabilities adequately, both in quality and quantity. The change is designed to enable Japan's Self Defence Forces (SDF) to use force in situations that constitute the exercise of right to collective self-defence under international law.

There is a great deal of speculation as to what this flexibility would amount to in actual situations. However, in view of the sacrosanctity of Article 9 of the Constitution in the mind of the Japanese people, the government has adopted a very cautious approach. A message has gone out that the use of military force to defend a country with which Japan has alliance, will be resorted to 'only if there is an imminent threat to its people's life, freedom and human rights'.[22] Some of the outer limits of operation by the SDF under this flexibility have also been defined. These are: not getting involved in a combat situation within other nations' borders, and expeditionary and strategic capacity being kept under strict limitation. A few concrete measures taken under this flexibility are reflected in the NDPG 2014. These include organizing approximately half of the SDF's divisions and brigades into rapid deployment units, increasing the number of destroyers and submarine units, and strengthening the Air Self-Defense Force. The data provided in the NDPG 2014 shows that there was an increase for the first time in Japan's defence-related expenditure during the years 2013 and 2014. This expenditure, which had declined continuously from the peak of ¥4.93 billion in 2001 to ¥4.64 billion in 2012, started increasing from 2012, reaching the level of ¥4.78 billion in 2014.

India–Japan Security Cooperation

There is no reason why the differing perspectives of India and Japan on disarmament and security issues should be allowed to cast a shadow on their bilateral relations or come in the way of their cooperation on these and other issues. The two countries should recognize that the policies they are pursuing in the nuclear field are designed to safeguard their security interests as perceived by their peoples and as generally endorsed by their parliaments. In view of Japan's Hiroshima and Nagasaki complex, India should show an understanding of the messianic zeal with which Japan seeks to pursue non-proliferation. India should also show an understanding of the circumstances that led Japan to seek the US extended deterrence. Japan, on its part, should appreciate India's security imperatives and hence its compulsion to go in for minimum nuclear deterrence. Japan should also recognize that it is unrealistic for it or any other major power to expect or compel India to roll back its nuclear weapon programme and to join the NPT in its present form. There are indications that Japan is increasingly veering around to a realistic and pragmatic view of India's nuclear status, even though it has not given up the goal of universalizing the NPT. India should also not expect Japan to accord formal recognition to its nuclear status. Hardly any major country is going to give India such a recognition. In fact, it is both tactless and beneath its dignity for India to beg for such recognition. None of the recognized nuclear weapon states went about seeking such status. They received official recognition as nuclear weapon powers long after it became a fait accompli.

A measure of convergence has come about in the positions of India and Japan on nuclear issues after the Pokhran-II tests. As a matter of fact, India's acquisition of nuclear weapons has placed it in a better position to play a constructive role in the field of disarmament and non-proliferation. There are reasons to believe that the Government of India and a fairly large section of the security community in the country are of the view that after the Pokhran-II tests, India does not need to carry out further tests in order to acquire a minimum deterrence. This should facilitate developing a consensus in the country on India signing and ratifying the CTBT. This brings India quite close to the position of Japan on the Treaty. Moreover, as India has opted for a minimum nuclear deterrence, it has no reason to accumulate huge amounts of weapon-grade fissile material. India is, therefore, in a position to participate seriously and effectively in the negotiation on FMCT. Finally, the schemes in force in India for controlling the export of dual-purpose technologies, substances and equipment, which can be used for the production of weapons of mass destruction, are among the most effective in the world. In May 2005, India put these export control measures within a statutory framework by enacting a legislation called the Weapons of Mass Destruction and their Delivery Systems (Prohibition of Unlawful Activities) Act, covering wide-ranging export controls of sensitive dual-purpose technologies and products. Later, India also announced that it was harmonizing its export control regime with the guidelines of the NSG and the MTCR.

Moreover, India follows a policy of not transferring reprocessing and uranium enrichment technologies to other countries. India's efforts and actions in this area have been duly recognized by the major nuclear weapon powers and their allies, including Japan. It was one of the major reasons why they agreed to the NSG granting a waiver to India. Japan played a positive role in supporting the Indo-US Nuclear Agreement in the IAEA and in getting the waiver from the NSG. With the encouragement of the US and other friendly countries, India is now trying to seek membership of various export control regimes. It has also been holding consultations on it with Japan, whose response so far has not been discouraging.

India is the only country possessing nuclear weapons that has committed itself to the elimination of such weapons within a time-bound framework. The right goal to pursue will be for India, with its minimum nuclear deterrence, and Japan, with its US extended deterrence, to work together for building an international security system based on a new paradigm in which nuclear deterrence of any kind has no place. No doubt, the path to this goal is hazardous and full of pitfalls, but the effort to build such a system is very much worthwhile. If such a system can be put in place, it will enable both India and Japan to get rid of the dependence on nuclear weapons for seeking security, along with all the evils it bodes for their polity, economy and society. Instead, they will be able to seek their security in a non-violent nuclear weapon-free world, which is in keeping with the aspirations of and age old values cherished by their peoples.

It is encouraging that since the beginning of this century, both countries have become increasingly aware of their common security interests in the widest sense of the term, in Asia and globally, and of the growing convergence of their perspectives on disarmament and security issues. It is because of this that after remaining in suspended animation for three years from 1998 to 2000, Indo-Japanese relations were revitalized, with the visit to India of the then Japanese Prime Minister Yoshiro Mori in August 2000, when the two countries took the initiative of defining the contours of their bilateral partnership on a much broader canvas, including regional and global issues. It was also from that time that security started figuring as a very important item on the agenda of Indo-Japanese relations. In July 2001, the first Comprehensive Bilateral Security Dialogue between the two countries was held in Tokyo to discuss security and defence policies. The dialogue was institutionalized as an annual event. The visit by the Japanese Prime Minister Junichiro

Koizumi to India in April 2005 marked the beginning of the process by which the prime ministers of the two countries started meeting annually in either of the countries. At the next summit meeting held in Tokyo in December 2006, a Joint Statement entitled 'Towards Indo-Japan Strategic and Global Partnership' was adopted, which outlined the detailed roadmap for building a multilayered network of bilateral relations. Another important landmark in the relationship was reached in October 2008 when the prime ministers of the two countries signed a Joint Declaration on Security Cooperation. In this Declaration, the two parties reiterated 'their common commitment to pursuing disarmament and non-proliferation as partners seeking a peaceful nuclear weapon-free world and working together against proliferation'.[23] They decided to create a comprehensive framework for the enhancement of security cooperation between the two countries. To that end, it was agreed to hold on a regular basis, a strategic dialogue at the foreign ministers' level, a meeting at the defence ministers' level, military-to-military talks, exchange of visits by senior military officers, meeting between the foreign secretary of India and his Japanese counterpart and dialogue on disarmament and non-proliferation at the director-general or joint secretary level. After the new ruling coalition headed by the DJP came to power in 2009, the new Japanese Prime Minister Yukio Hatoyama kept up the tradition of the annual summit by paying a visit to India at the end of December 2009. During that visit, both countries signed an Action Plan to strengthen bilateral security cooperation. Moreover, the signing of the CEPA in February 2011 opened a new chapter in the economic relationship between the two countries.

On the security side, the first maritime exercise by India, Japan and the US was held in April 2007 in the Pacific Ocean off the Boso Peninsula in central Japan. This was followed by a five-power joint military exercise including India and Japan in the Bay of Bengal in September 2007.

After the signing of the Indo-US nuclear deal and the NSG waiver, India started consultations with a number of countries in order to negotiate agreements on civil nuclear cooperation. Such agreements have so far been concluded with France, Canada, Argentina, Kazakhstan, Namibia, Mongolia, South Korea, and recently, Australia. India and France finalized a civil nuclear deal in 2010 under which the French company Areva is to set up six nuclear reactors in India, each with the capacity of generating 1,650 megawatt of energy. It has also been agreed that several parts of the nuclear reactor will be manufactured in India. Work for building the first reactor in this series is yet to begin. Like the

US, the French have also been concerned about the implications for their suppliers, of the Civil Liability for Nuclear Damage Act, 2010, enacted by the Indian Parliament. The French are hoping that any deal that would be struck between India and the US would also apply to them. With Russia, India has an on-going civil nuclear cooperation under which one nuclear reactor has recently become operational and others are either at the stage of planning or negotiation. During his visit to India on 11 December 2014, President Vladimir Putin made a bid for supplying nuclear reactors for the creation of the entire nuclear energy production capacity that India has in mind over the next 20 years. His offer was for as many as 20 reactors, though the Indian side agreed to 10 to begin with. During President Obama's recent visit to India, the Governments of India and the US reached an understanding on issues related to nuclear liability and finalized the text of an Administrative Arrangement that will allow them to move towards commercial negotiations on setting up reactors by American companies in India. It is reported that US has dropped its insistence to monitor the full fuel cycle in the reactors supplied by its companies, subject to the condition that the aggregate data provided to the IAEA under the special agreement with it will be shared with the US and will provide the basis for consultation. India has also clarified to prospective suppliers that a civil suit action for damage will be permissible only against operators. Moreover, India will create an insurance pool of Rs 1,500 crore (Rs 15 billion) which will take care of liabilities, if any.

It is in the interest of both India and Japan to move ahead and cooperate in the civil nuclear field. There is vast scope for cooperation in the areas of research, development and construction of fast breeder reactors as well as in reprocessing, drawing upon each other's expertise and experience. Besides, multinational corporations from France and the US like Areva, General Electric and Westinghouse, which can supply nuclear reactors, have financial and technological interlocking with the Japanese firms Toshiba and Hitachi. The former cannot supply nuclear reactors without the collaboration and approval of the latter. And Japanese firms need the permission of their government to get involved in the ventures. The Japanese multinational corporations themselves are also interested in supplying reactors to India in collaboration with their European and US partners. Tapping the vast Indian market for civilian nuclear supplies has become particularly important for them in the context of the continuing stagnation in the Japanese economy.

These companies are, therefore, putting pressure on their government to speedily conclude an agreement with India on civil nuclear cooperation.

It is, therefore, not surprising that the initiative for the two countries negotiating a civil nuclear cooperation agreement came from the Japanese side, when it was broached by the then Japanese Foreign Minister Katsuya Okada during his visit to India in 2010. The negotiations started soon thereafter. However, they remain inconclusive even after several rounds of talks. The biggest problem encountered in the negotiations is reconciling Japan's objective of accessing the Indian market for its nuclear supplies, with the growing anti-nuclear sentiments in the country, which became stronger after the Fukushima disaster.

After the disaster, an overwhelming section of the public opinion in Japan came out in favour of halting the country's nuclear energy programme, even though it was meeting some 30 to 35 per cent of its energy requirement. This ultimately led to the government taking a decision to shut down all nuclear power plants. However, after a time interval and at Prime Minister Abe's initiative, there has been a revival of interest in Japan's nuclear power programme. Two reactors have already been reactivated and more are likely to be operationalized in the coming years, even though Japan is unlikely to go back to its earlier heavy reliance on nuclear power.

The revival of interest in nuclear energy in Japan has led to the demonstration of greater interest on the part of the Government of Japan to conclude the on-going negotiations on a civil nuclear agreement. As already pointed out, this new vigour has also been partly generated by the realization that Japan may lose out heavily in commercial terms if the deal is not signed very soon. It would fall behind even its neighbour South Korea with which India signed a civil nuclear cooperation agreement during the Indian President's visit to South Korea in July 2011.

The issues that separate the two countries in their effort to arrive at an agreement are:

(*a*) Japan insists that India should sign the CTBT, but India does not want to go beyond its commitment to maintain its officially announced moratorium on testing;

(*b*) Japan expects India to accept restrictions on its basic right to reprocess fuel, whereas India's position is that it must retain this right while providing assurance that this will be exercised under IAEA safeguards and for peaceful purposes only; and (*c*) India also finds unacceptable Japan's insistence that India accept inspections over and above what it has agreed to with the IAEA in its special protocol with the Agency.

Japan's demands are clearly more stringent than those made by any other nuclear weapon power, including the US. It also goes beyond the relevant provisions in the Indo-US nuclear deal which is the basis for the waiver provided by the NSG. Given this Japanese position, the prospects of reaching an agreement do not appear to be bright. However, if the US companies, General Electric and Westinghouse, decide to go ahead and build nuclear reactors in India on the basis of the clarifications made and assurances given by the Government of India to the US during President Obama's visit to India in January 2015, the Japanese government may find a modus vivendi to allow its companies to collaborate with the American companies. This may eventually pave the way for a civil nuclear agreement.

Since Mr Shinzo Abe became the prime minister again in 2012, the relationship between India and Japan has become particularly warm and their bilateral cooperation, which had already been placed at a multi-dimensional strategic level, gathered further momentum. Prime Minister Abe visited India in June 2014 after which a Joint Statement was issued between the two countries. The Indian Prime Minister hardly lost any time after assuming power in Delhi in paying a return visit to Tokyo in August–September 2014, at the end of which they issued the Tokyo Declaration.

In the Joint Statement, the two leaders reviewed the progress in the regular Foreign Ministers' Strategic Dialogue and consultations between the Secretary-General of the National Secretariat of Japan and India's National Security Advisor. They also 'reaffirmed their shared commitment to the total elimination of nuclear weapons' as well as their commitment to work towards the commencement and the eventual conclusion, of negotiations on FMCT.[24] In both the Joint Statement and Tokyo Declaration, the two countries reaffirmed their resolve to work together for India to become full members of the NSG, MTCR, Australia Group and Wassenaar Arrangement.

On a civil nuclear agreement, their objective of striking a deal continued to elude them. They, therefore, remained content with underlining the importance of cooperation in this area, highlighting the priority they attached to a deal, and welcoming the substantial progress made since their last meeting. They concluded by directing their officials to exert further efforts towards an early conclusion of an agreement on the subject.

During the Indian Prime Minister's visit to Tokyo, some important decisions were taken and statements made which lend new dimensions to security cooperation between the two countries. First, it was decided to elevate the Strategic and Global Partnership between the two countries to Special Strategic and Global Partnership. Second, a Memorandum of Cooperation and Exchange in the field of defence was signed. This has important implications for the security of both the countries in the context of the evolving security situation in Asia. Third, it was decided to put the bilateral naval exercises between the two countries and Japan's continued participation in the Indo-US Malabar series of exercises on a regular basis. And finally, it was decided to explore the possibility of elevating the present trilateral dialogue between India, Japan and the US to foreign ministers' level.

In the Joint Statement of January 2014, the two Prime Ministers 'underscored the importance of over-flights and civil aviation safety in accordance with the recognized principles of international law and the relevant standards and recommended practices of the ICAO'.[25] This clearly has a reference to China's unilateral embargo on overflights over the zone defined by it. The leaders also 'reiterated the commitment of [their countries] to the freedom of navigation, unimpeded commerce and peaceful settlement of disputes based on the principles of international law'.[26] This statement indirectly refers to the unilateral actions recently taken by China in the South China Sea. These may not be to the liking of China. But as a matter of principle and in its national interest, it was necessary for India to have joined Japan in issuing these statements. During President Obama's recent visit to India, India adopted a similar common position with the US as well.

India and Japan also announced highly ambitious programmes, projects, objectives and targets in the economic field in the Tokyo Declaration, which have important implications for cementing the security relationship between them. The Japanese side has made announcements for doubling its investment and the presence of Japanese companies in India during the next five years. It also announced its intention to accelerate Japan's involvement in the modernization of India's infrastructure, particularly through the development of industrial corridors and dedicated freight corridors and of the Indian railways. It was Japan's extensive current and planned activities in this area that led the Prime Minister of

India to state that 'no country has done more for modernizing India's infrastructure than Japan'.[27]

Finally, it is also of considerable significance from the strategic point of view that the two countries in the Tokyo Declaration reaffirmed 'their commitment to actively engage in RCEP negotiations and make RCEP a modern, comprehensive, high quality and mutually beneficial economic partnership agreement'.[28] They decided to cooperate further towards concluding the agreement.

It is difficult to predict the extent to which these objectives and targets in the economic field will be realized. A lot will depend on India's own capacity to implement these projects and the general, social, economic, and law and order conditions prevailing in the country.

Notes

1. Masako Toki, 'Japan's Defence Guidelines: New Conventional Strategy, Same Old Nuclear Dilemma' (Policy Brief, James Martin Centre for Non-proliferation Studies, Monterey, 1 March 2011).
2. The Tokyo Forum was set up at the initiative of Japan after the May 1998 nuclear explosions by India and Pakistan. It submitted its report in July 1999. The report was published by the Ministry of Foreign Affairs of Japan under the title: 'Facing Nuclear Dangers: An Action Plan for the 21st Century' (Tokyo Forum Report, 25 July 1999), http://www.mofa.go.jp/policy/un/disarmament/forum/tokyo9907/index.html (accessed on 6 May 2015).
3. Ibid.
4. These 10 countries are Australia, Canada, Chile, Germany, Japan, Mexico, the Netherlands, Poland, Turkey and the United Arab Emirates. Almost all of them are close allies of the US and depend on US extended nuclear deterrence for their security.
5. Ministry of Foreign Affairs of Japan, 'Joint Statement by Foreign Ministers on Nuclear Disarmament and Non-Proliferation' (New York, 22 September 2010).
6. Ibid.
7. Ministry of Foreign Affairs of Japan, 'Statement by the Minister for Foreign Affairs of Japan on the Approval of the New START Treaty by the U.S. Senate' (23 December 2010), http://www.mofa.go.jp/announce/announce/2010/12/1223_01.html (accessed on 6 May 2015).
8. Ministry of Foreign Affairs of Japan, 'Joint Statement by Foreign Ministers on Nuclear Disarmament and Non-Proliferation'.
9. Ministry of Foreign Affairs of Japan, 'Facing Nuclear Dangers'.

10. Toki, 'Japan's Defence Guidelines'.
11. Ministry of Foreign Affairs of Japan, 'Statement by the Minister for Foreign Affairs of Japan on the Approval of the New START Treaty by the U.S. Senate'.
12. Ministry of Defense, 'National Defense Program Guidelines for FY 2011 and Beyond' (approved by the Security Council and the Cabinet on 17 December 2010, Government of Japan), http://www.mod.go.jp/e/d_act/d_policy/pdf/guidelinesFY2011.pdf (accessed on 6 May 2015).
13. Ibid.
14. Ibid.
15. Ibid.
16. Toki, 'Japan's Defence Guidelines'.
17. Ministry of Defense, 'Defense of Japan 2014' (Government of Japan), http://www.mod.go.jp/e/publ/w_paper/2014.html (accessed on 6 May 2015).
18. Ibid.
19. Ibid.
20. Ibid.
21. Ibid.
22. Ryo Sahashi, 'The Political and Diplomatic Hard-Yards Still to be done on Collective Self-Defence', East Asia Forum, 6 July 2014.
23. Ministry of Foreign Affairs of Japan, 'Joint Declaration on Security Co-operation between Japan and India' (Tokyo, 22 October 2008), http://www.mofa.go.jp/region/asia-paci/india/pmv0810/joint_d.html (accessed on 6 May 2015).
24. Ministry of External Affairs, 'Joint Statement on the Occasion of Official Visit of the Prime Minister of Japan to India (January 25–27, 2014)' (Government of India, New Delhi, 25 January 2014).
25. Ibid.
26. Ibid.
27. Quoted in *Business Standard*, 'Japan has Committed $35-bn Investment in India: Modi', 1 September 2014.
28. Press Information Bureau, 'Tokyo Declaration for India–Japan Special Strategic and Global Partnership' (Prime Minister's Office, Government of India, 1 September 2014).

THIRTEEN India and the Indian Diaspora

Changing Salience

India has attached varied degrees of importance and meted out various kinds of treatment to the Indian diaspora at different phases during the post-independence period. During the 1950s and the better part of the 1960s, establishing a special relationship with the diaspora was not a priority of India's foreign policy. The advice given by Jawaharlal Nehru, the first prime minister of India, to Indian diplomats was generally to follow a 'hands-off' policy with regard to the diaspora. The diaspora, on the other hand, was advised to live up to its loyalty to the host country. Only cultural links with the home country were emphasized on appropriate occasions. Seldom did the political and the economic, let alone the strategic purpose of the diaspora from the perspective of the mother country, come into play.

This policy was partly derived from the fact that the earlier migrants from India came either from the unprivileged classes of agricultural labourers or from traders. The first category of migrants—agricultural labourers—had no constituency in India and hence their suffering in the countries of migration did not evoke much sympathy in the home country. They were left very much to their own fates. The traders, who migrated from India mostly during the colonial era, and later in the post-colonial period, also did not attract much attention to their conditions in the host countries. Since their migration was seen as being motivated by self-interest, aimed at seeking better living conditions and prosperity in foreign lands, the home country did not feel that it had any moral obligation towards them.

The behaviour of the earlier migrants in these countries was also one of the factors prompting Indian leaders and policymakers not to be seen as associated with them. During the colonial period, a section of the diaspora in African countries sided with the colonial rulers, and played the role of comprador bourgeoisie. This alienated them from the local people who were fighting for their country's independence. Second, the early migrants, particularly the traders, tried to maintain a cultural distance from the native people—avoiding intermarriages or other forms of cultural assimilation with the local community. This also led to the alienation of early migrants from the mainstream of the local society. This state of alienation prevailed for a long time after the end of colonialism and still continues, though to a lesser extent than before.

Perhaps the only exception was the Indian diaspora in South Africa with whom Mahatma Gandhi worked and experimented with his method of *satyagraha* (passive resistance). On Gandhiji's return to India, this experiment was converted into history's biggest mass movement based on truth and non-violence. The historical association of the Indian diaspora in South Africa with this movement vested it with a hallow of respectability and gratitude in India.

The migration from India of professionals with a middle-class family background started on a modest scale from the early 1960s, mainly to the US, Canada and Europe. This migration also did not draw much attention of Indian policymakers because it was on a minuscule scale and was also seen as being prompted by the self-interest of the migrants. The situation, however, started changing in the 1970s and the early 1980s, when migration on a much larger scale started taking place from India to West Asia, mainly the Gulf countries. The hefty increase in the oil prices in two successive instalments in 1973 and 1976 resulted in the accumulation of high levels of surplus resources in the Gulf countries. This triggered new economic activities which in these sparsely populated countries could be sustained only by the import of cheap labour. The South Asian countries, including India, with large Muslim populations, became the most important source of such labour. The new wealth accumulated in the Gulf countries generated demand for labour, not only in the infrastructure, trading and some manufacturing sectors, but substantially in the service sectors as well—for maids, nurses, school teachers, accountants and bookkeepers. The South Asian countries were the cheapest and otherwise most acceptable source of supply of labour for providing these services. The migration from India to West Asia during this phase was, therefore, both of low-skilled and skilled and trained workers.

In the beginning, this burgeoning Indian diaspora in West Asia did not attract much attention of Indian policymakers. But later, as they were perceived as becoming economically and politically important, Indian policymakers started taking an increasing interest in them. This class of the Indian diaspora maintained and continuously nurtured its links with India. They paid regular visits to the home country, and made a visible impact on the urban and rural scene back home by investing a part of their remittance for improving the living conditions of their families left behind. They even started exercising some electoral influence. It was, therefore, not surprising that at the time of the first Gulf War in 1990–91, when the people of the Indian origin had to be evacuated from Kuwait and were brought to camps in Amman before repatriation, politicians from India paid visits to these camps to send a message back home about their concern for the evacuees. Since a fairly large proportion of the displaced Indians in these camps were nurses from Kerala, one of the then senior union ministers belonging to that state was among those who visited the camps mainly for political and electoral purposes.

Gradually, the Indian missions in the Gulf countries consciously started establishing and maintaining contact with Indian migrants to these countries, without in any way putting themselves on the wrong side of the local authorities. They tried to extend assistance to some of those who were in trouble, particularly because of the unscrupulous behaviour of Indian and local agents who facilitated their migration. However, there was still no coherent policy of the Government of India to control illegal migration to Gulf countries, to guide the migrants both during the pre-migration and post-migration phases and to rescue those in distress.

During this period, Indian policymakers continued to follow a 'hands off' policy as far as migrants to the US, Europe and regions outside West Asia were concerned. This attitude of Indian diplomats is best summed up by a remark attributed to a senior diplomat posted in the Indian High Commission in London. When asked how much interest he was taking in the affairs of the people of the Indian origin in the UK, he is reported to have said, 'I am accredited to the St James Court here, and not to the local Indians'. In a public speech delivered in the campus of the Columbia University, New York in October 1978, the BJP stalwart and the then Foreign Minister, Atal Bihari Vajpayee, described NRIs as *Bharat se bhaga Bharatiya* (The Indians who fled away from India). Though this was said in a jocular vein, it did reflect the then prevailing attitude of Indians back home towards NRIs, particularly those in developed countries like the US, which was far from positive.

During the Gulf War, India faced an acute balance-of-payment crisis. It was left with foreign exchange reserves adequate to meet only two weeks' import requirements and had come very close to the point of declaring itself bankrupt. At the official level, with the full support of the political leadership, attempts were made to import oil, the most critical import requirement, on credit. Some foreign governments with comfortable foreign exchange reserves were approached to transfer a part of their surplus to the Reserve Bank of India (RBI) in order to bolster India's payment position and thereby prevent the flight of short-term capital. At the political level, some very important cabinet ministers seriously entertained the idea of being able to persuade important Indian business houses and NRI businessmen to transfer to India a part of their foreign exchange resources held abroad. Indian business houses functioning from London and New York as well as prominent businessmen in Hong Kong were directly contacted by these political leaders, at times against the advice of senior officials. But when the moment of reckoning came, these leaders drew a blank. Not a dollar was transferred from the reserves of these businessmen to the RBI for enabling the country to tide over the foreign exchange crisis at that time.

In fact, NRIs contributed to the aggravation of the crisis by withdrawing in an indecent hurry their short-term deposits in Indian banks. From the point of view of the mother country, these Indians apparently did not meet its expectation at the moment of distress. The NRIs concerned, on their part, thought that they were only cutting their losses. Those who were in a position to help wanted a quick quid pro quo, which the nation either could not afford or did not think it proper to pay.

The relationship between India and the Indian diaspora started changing in a dramatic fashion from the second half of the 1990s. In this, the adoption in 1991 of a full-fledged policy of liberalization of the Indian economy and dominance of Indians in the global IT revolution played a very important role. The buoyancy in the Indian economy, clearly evident in the second half of the 1990s and continuing till recently, restored the faith in it of a large section of the diaspora. It was, therefore, not surprising that the Resurgent India Bonds and the India Millennium Deposits floated for NRIs after the nuclear explosion in May 1998 were oversubscribed. No doubt, the terms offered, that is, the high interest rate and 87 per cent foreign exchange return guarantee, played a very important role, but the dynamism of the Indian economy and a sense of pride in the nation after its overt demonstration of having become a de facto nuclear-weapon power were also major factors.

The new migrants from India during the late 1980s and 1990s, mainly to the US and Canada and to other developed countries, added a sense of distinctiveness to the Indian diaspora. Indian migration to the US quadrupled between 1970 and 1996. The new diaspora, as these migrants have come to be called, constitutes a highly skilled group of professionals who are among the highest earning ethnic groups in their respective countries of migration. They are mostly middle-class elites who are reared in the global marketplace and are highly committed converts to the values of liberal democracy and economics. Globalization has played an important role in shaping their attitude towards the mother country. One of the consequences of globalization has been the blurring of the cultural identity of the Indian diaspora, as of other migrant ethnic groups, in the countries of their residence. This has engendered a strong urge among the diaspora to go back to their cultural roots, as a defence mechanism.

The Indian diaspora has acquired a higher status and respect in their countries of residence both because of their own contributions in varied fields as well as on account of the higher status acquired by the mother country in the comity of nations by virtue of the dynamism displayed by its economy and the remarkable achievements in frontier areas of technology. On the other hand, the mother country has also started basking in the glory of the pioneering role of the new diaspora in the expansion and sophistication of the IT industry in advanced countries and of its notable contributions in other areas of knowledge. The international fame and stature acquired during this period by prominent NRIs like Amartya Sen, Jagdish N. Bhagwati, Bhikhu Parekh, Meghnad Desai, Raghuram Rajan, Indra Nooyi and the late Kalpana Chawla has given currency to the phrase 'the global Indians'. These personalities have contributed to a considerable enhancement of the overall image of the NRIs in the mother country. In his speech on the occasion of Pravasi Bharatiya Divas in 2006, the Prime Minister of India Manmohan Singh called for the celebration of 'the global Indians'. The acquisition of this global identity by this section of the Indian diaspora provides them greater flexibility today than before to play a larger role in India's development. There is now a growing reciprocity between the diaspora and India. India now regards them as an asset while they look upon India as a source of intellectual and cultural inspiration as well as a land of opportunities.

The new diaspora is also playing a crucial role in influencing the foreign policy of the countries of their residence, in favour of India. For example, the Indian diaspora in the US played a very important role in mobilizing local support for the Indo-US Civilian Nuclear Deal. This was publicly recognized by the Prime Minister of India in his speeches on Pravasi Bharatiya Divas. In this speech at the 2007 Pravasi Bharatiya Divas, he said, 'And I thank the Americans of Indian origin for the stellar role that they played in ensuring that this legislation was passed through the US Congress'.[1]

At the same time, the new diaspora has increasingly come to influence India's policies, including foreign policy, in the direction of its ideological preferences and to its advantage. Devesh Kapur, the author of a recent publication on the Indian diaspora, has gone to the extent of postulating that 'the more India cultivates its diaspora, the more its foreign policy becomes hostage to the well-being of its diaspora'.[2]

These developments have brought about a remarkable shift in the relationship between India and the Indian diaspora. India has now come to acquire a higher stake than ever before in the performance, status and treatment meted out to the Indian diaspora in the host countries. This has led to a distinct policy shift in the mother country from relative indifference to greater attention and care of the Indian diaspora. The beginning of this policy shift was heralded by the appointment of a High-Level Committee on the Indian Diaspora by the Ministry of External Affairs in September 2000. The Committee in its report made a series of recommendations, including the following:

- The issue of Persons of Indian Origin (PIO) Card;
- Annual celebration of Pravasi Bharatiya Divas;
- Award of Pravasi Bharatiya Samman;
- Grant of dual citizenship within the rubric of the Citizenship Act, 1955;
- Establishment of a dedicated mechanism which would provide consultancy services to overseas investors and be a single-point window for getting various clearances for making investment;
- Devising a transparent, fair and fast-track mechanism to process clearances for philanthropists among the members of the diaspora who want to contribute to India's development;
- Creation of a data bank of the members of the diaspora worldwide to facilitate their interaction with India.

The Committee also addressed the problems of overseas blue-collar workers in a number of recommendations. These included:

- Creation of a welfare fund for overseas workers in distress in the country of migration;
- Negotiating a standard labour export agreement with the host countries;
- Greater role to missions abroad to monitor and supervise employment contracts and conditions of workers;

- Establishing mechanisms for pre-departure counselling and provision of legal assistance locally;
- Instituting training programmes for human resource development and skills upgradation for potential and actual migrants.

The government, during the last decade or so, has implemented most of the recommendations made by the High-Level Committee and in some areas, has taken additional measures. In a few cases, the progress in the implementation of the recommendations has been tardy.

In the following section, some of the steps recently taken by the Indian government towards building a relationship with the Indian diaspora are discussed in some detail.

Follow-Up on the Recommendations of the Committee on Indian Diaspora

Ministry of Overseas Indian Affairs

By far the most important step taken with regard to the diaspora has been the establishment of the Ministry of Overseas Indian Affairs (MOIA) in 2004. The ministry incorporates the former NRI division of the Ministry of External Affairs, now redesignated as the Diaspora Services division, and the Office of the Protector General of Emigrants, which earlier used to function under the Ministry of Labour. In addition, it has constituted a new Financial Services division. The creation of the new ministry is in recognition of the fact that the welfare of the overseas Indians needs continuing mainstream attention.

Pravasi Bharatiya Divas

The Pravasi Bharatiya Divas has been celebrated regularly since 2003 to bring the Indian diaspora closer to the mother country and to highlight and seek the latter's contribution to India's development. Pravasi Bharatiya Sammans are awarded on this occasion. The prime minister of India has inaugurated the Pravasi Bharatiya Divas every year since 2003. In their inaugural speeches, the prime ministers have taken advantage of the occasion to bring out the unique features of the Indian diaspora, project India's achievements to overseas Indians assembled for the occasion and to invite them to contribute towards meeting the challenges of India's development. The two distinguishing features of the diaspora highlighted by the prime ministers have been its pluralistic make-up and its near ubiquitous character. On pluralism, in his 2008 speech, the Prime Minister remarked:

> The Indian diaspora is a pluralistic community just as India is. It holds within its fold peoples of different languages, faiths and religions. I call this multicultural identity Indianness. The idea of India transcends the narrow barrier of a religion, language, caste or class, both within and outside the Indian nation.[3]

He further added, 'We can show our troubled, divided and embattled world a new pathway of living together, inspired by our modern idea of unity in diversity'.[4] On the near universal presence of the Indian diaspora, the Prime Minister had this to say in his 2007 speech:

> We are one family. The whole world is our home. That is why I have often said that while the sun has set on many great empires of the world in the past, the sun will never set on the world of the Indian diaspora.[5]

In projecting India's achievements, he emphasized its open society and open economy, its commitment to the rule of law and the respect for all fundamental human freedoms, its high rates of growth, its success in lifting millions above the poverty line and its advancement in science and technology.

Voting Rights to NRIs

On the 2010 Pravasi Bharatiya Divas, the Prime Minister announced that the government was taking steps to grant voting rights to some 10 million NRIs. The government has since got an amendment to the Representation of People Act, 1950 enacted by the Parliament, which provides for the registration of Indian passport holders living abroad in the electoral rolls in the constituency that their address mentioned in the passports comes under. A notification was issued on 3 February 2011 to amend the Registration of Electors Rules, 1960, allowing overseas electors to participate in the country's election process.

Overseas Citizens of India and Persons of Indian Origin

The Government of India has granted dual nationality to a group of overseas Indians in order to enable them to exercise some rights and privileges. For this, the Overseas Citizenship of India (OCI) Scheme was launched in August 2005 by amending the Citizenship Act, 1955. The scheme provides for the registration as OCI of all persons of Indian origin who were citizens of India on or after 26 January 1950, or were eligible to become citizens of India on that date and who are citizens of other countries except Pakistan and Bangladesh. The scheme was introduced in the financial year 2006–07. Until 31 March 2014, a total of 1,525,890 PIOs had been registered as OCIs.[6] The privileges under the OCI are confined to undertaking on par with resident Indian citizens, activities of a professional and business character. It does not confer any political right.

On 6 January 2015, the President of India signed the Citizenship Ordinance which provides for the merger of the OCI and the PIO schemes. Under it, the PIOs will now be entitled to the same privileges that were currently being enjoyed by the OCIs. These include life-long visa, exemption from appearing before the local police, and right to buy property in India.

PIO University

In one of his speeches during the Pravasi Bharatiya Divas, the Prime Minister had promised the establishment of a world-class university for children of PIOs, whom their parents would like to leave behind for education in the Indian cultural environment. On a closer examination of this proposal, it was found that it would not be possible for the government to set up and run a university which in its admission policy would discriminate in favour of a particular section of students, that is, the children of PIOs. It has, therefore, been decided to give up this project and consider other means of providing facilities for the admission of such children.

Overseas Indian Facilitation Centre

An Overseas Indian Facilitation Centre (OIFC) has been set up as a non-profit trust in partnership with the CII. The Centre is currently in its seventh year of operation since its inception in May 2007. It is a one-stop shop for serving the interest of the overseas Indian community and has the mandate to promote overseas investment in India and facilitate business partnership by giving authentic and real-time information; and to establish and maintain a Diaspora India Network by creating a database of overseas Indians who will act as Knowledge Diaspora and whose resources could be accessed using the Information and Communication Technology (ICT) platform. The Centre compiled a regulatory and investment handbook under the title 'Homeward Bound' for overseas Indians, which was released during the 2011 Pravasi Bharatiya Divas.

India Development Foundation of Overseas Indians

This is a non-profit trust registered under the Societies Registration Act. It provides a window for overseas Indian philanthropy in India's social development. The objective is to facilitate philanthropic activities by overseas Indians through innovative projects and instruments such as microcredit for rural entrepreneurs and self-help groups, economic empowerment of women, primary education and technology intervention in rural healthcare delivery.

Global Indian Network of Knowledge (Global-INK)

A trend in recent years has been to create knowledge network among institutions and professionals in the country of origin and the members of the diaspora. Many developing countries having a significant diaspora abroad are today making attempts to forge links with them through networks and alliances. Unfortunately, progress in such networking in India has been rather slow. The task of developing the network was entrusted to Tata Consultancy Services. The possible outcome of the project being developed was the germination of ideas on development, identification of approaches and challenges to development and articulation and mapping out of solutions to development problems through innovation and technology interventions. The latest position is that a Diaspora Knowledge Network is being developed under the Management of the OIFC which will draw upon the knowledge and expertise of global Indians who are outstanding in areas of environment, healthcare, innovation and science and technology.

Indian Centre for Migration

The earlier ICOE has now been renamed as the Indian Centre for Migration (ICM). It is a kind of a think tank of the MOIA. Its function is basically to promote employment of Indian migrants in foreign countries. To this end, it commissions studies on international labour markets; identifies emerging overseas employment opportunities; projects India as a supplier of skilled, trained and qualified workers; and adapts or develops training material. The ICM is a society set up under the Societies Registration Act and has its own governing board and executive directorate. Its functions include building and maintaining a database of emerging employment opportunities, identifying labour supply gaps in overseas markets, initiating programmes for skill development and providing pre-departure orientation programmes.

Human Resources Mobility Partnerships

For promoting migration to developed countries, the Government of India has recently signed or is in the process of negotiating Human Resource Mobility Partnership Agreements (HRMPAs) with a number of developed and emerging economies in Europe. By March 2014, an HRMPA was signed with Denmark; the negotiation for such an agreement with the Netherlands had been concluded; and those with Australia, Switzerland, France, Sweden and the EU had been initiated.

Bilateral Social Security Agreements

For protecting the interest of migrants to developed countries, the Government of India has signed Bilateral Social Security Agreements (SSAs) with a number of developed countries in Europe and the Republic of Korea. As of March 2014, SSAs had been signed with 18 countries. The main purpose of this agreement is to ensure that Indians who migrate temporarily for work are not required to pay double security contributions or pay such contributions out of which they cannot get any benefits because of possible relocation before the benefits can accrue.

Overseas Blue-Collar Workers

The Government of India has accepted and implemented almost all the recommendations of the high-level committee relating to the welfare of the migrants to the Gulf area and Malaysia. These include the following:

- As of March 2014, bilateral cooperation agreements had been signed with seven countries, six in the Gulf and Malaysia, in order to enlist the commitment of the host governments to ensure better protection and welfare of Indian emigrants. These agreements generally contain a Declaration of Mutual Intent to enhance employment opportunities and to cooperate for the protection and welfare of workers. Generally, a joint working group is set up under the agreement, which meets from time to time to look into specific problems.
- The government has set up an Indian Community Welfare Fund (ICWF), placed at the disposal of Indian missions abroad, which is utilized to mitigate the problems that overseas Indian workers face, such as extortion by agents, non-payment or delayed payment of salaries, poor living and working conditions, physical abuse, problems in resettlement on return and vulnerability against emergency.

The scheme has recently been extended to all Indian missions across the globe.

- An Overseas Workers Resource Centre (OWRC) has been set up to provide information and assistance relating to all aspects of overseas employment to prospective migrants and the family members of overseas workers.

Pravasi Bharatiya Kendra

The high-level committee had recommended the construction of a Pravasi Bharatiya Bhawan to serve multiple purposes—as a permanent exhibition place to depict the history and the present status and contributions of the Indian diaspora, a focal point for interaction with and between overseas Indians, a research and documentation centre and a cultural centre. The Bhawan is also expected to have an auditorium and guest rooms. This ambitious project, now under the nomenclature Pravasi Bharatiya Kendra, has been taken in hand. The project started on 1 May 2011, and was to be completed by the end of 2014.

Prime Minister's Global Advisory Council of Overseas Indians

The idea behind setting up this Council in 2010 was to draw upon the knowledge and the expertise of a select group of overseas Indians to seek advice on the development problems facing the country. Meetings of the Council are convened on the eve of the Pravasi Bharatiya Divas.

Remittances by Indian Migrants

One of the important ways in which the benefits of the new relationship between India and its diaspora has been reflected recently is the dramatic increase in the volume of remittances by the diaspora to India. There is also a significant shift in the provenance and composition of these remittances. In 1991, remittances to India from overseas Indians were a modest $2.1 billion. The figure increased to $12.3 billion in 1996–97, and then jumped to $22 billion in 2003–04. The remittances doubled in three years between 2000–01 and 2003–04. In 2005–06, Indians living abroad transferred $24.6 billion to India.[7] Between 2000 and 2004, India headed the list of countries receiving workers' remittances. In 2005, it was overtaken by China, which remained marginally ahead of India in 2007 as well. From 2008 to 2014, India has retained its position as the top recipient of workers' remittances. The total remittances to India during

2012 and 2013 were $68.8 billion and $69.9 billion respectively. In 2014, it was estimated to reach $71 billion.[8]

The economic significance of these remittances should not be underestimated. They were 4.1 per cent of the country's GDP in 2005, rising from only 0.7 per cent of the GDP in 1990–91. In 2009, they accounted for 3.6 per cent of the GDP. In 2005–06, the remittances were higher—by about $3 billion—than the much touted earnings from India's software exports. The remittances were more than the amount spent by the state and central governments combined on education and twice that spent by these authorities on health.[9]

As regards the origin of the remittances, in 2006, North America was the most important source. According to RBI figures, 44 per cent of the remittances that year originated in North America, 24 per cent in the Gulf region and 13 per cent in Europe. In contrast, in 1990–91, 40 per cent of the remittances originated in West Asia and 24 per cent in North America.[10]

The 1990s witnessed a major shift in the pattern of migration from India. The number of migrants to the US, particularly IT workers, doubled during this period. The growth of IT-enabled services in India was an important factor in this regard. This fostered strong business connections between India and Indian IT professionals abroad. Indeed, even in the Gulf countries, the proportion of professionals to the total migrants increased significantly during the decade.[11] The migration of IT workers and the growth of IT-enabled services in India were important factors in contributing to the dramatic increase in the remittances since the mid-1990s. In spite of the sharp rise in inward remittances, unlike in the case of China, there are very few instances of investment by the Indian diaspora in major ventures in India, like green field industries, infrastructure and science and technology for bringing new products to the market.

The diaspora's contribution to India's development is now being seen not only in financial terms, but much more in terms of 'the vast reservoir of technical, managerial and entrepreneurial skills' represented by them and in terms of their knowledge, expertise and ability to network and open the way to resources and markets in their countries of residence.[12]

India has provided special savings investment schemes and instruments for NRIs to bring capital in various forms to the home country. These include bonds floated at highly attractive terms, tax benefits on investment in India and freedom to open non-resident local as well as foreign currency accounts. NRIs have also been permitted to move capital freely between their home and host countries. Portfolio investments have also been facilitated for them by making income from their investment in India repatriable. Largely as a result of these incentives and schemes, starting from the 1990s and continuing until now, the skilled Indian diaspora has remitted and invested substantially through foreign banking channels and the stock market.

As regards the remittances, a lot depends upon where they are concentrated and how they are invested. The available figures show that the diaspora's investments in India are mostly in urban areas, in conspicuous consumption, in real estate and in private education and private healthcare. For example, according to an estimate, in the urban area of Delhi, 20 per cent of all properties worth over Rs 1 crore (Rs 1 million) were bought or funded by NRIs.[13]

Some studies show that the diaspora's remittances and investments have contributed to widening the regional disparities and the gap between urban and rural areas. Moreover, the concentration of remittances in the southern and western states of India has also had the effect of amplifying inter-state inequalities. Since most of the expertise of the new diaspora is in the skill-intensive service and capital-intensive manufacturing sectors, the bias in favour of these sectors has been re-enforced.

Diaspora's Contribution in Social Sectors

A principal challenge before the country today is to make development inclusive. The Eleventh Five-Year Plan was premised on the twin objectives of faster and inclusive growth. This strategy has been continued in the Twelfth Five-Year Plan. A key element of the strategy of inclusive growth is to provide to the mass of the people access to basic facilities such as health, education and clean drinking water. It is also essential to improve the delivery of core public services to the people. The government has no doubt substantially increased the budget allocation for key social sectors, but it still falls far short of the needs. It is, therefore, important to adopt a conscious policy to harness the skills, experience and resources of the diaspora for building the capacity of the Indian economy in the social sectors and providing social services on an equitable basis, particularly in the areas of education and health. NRIs should be made to realize that this is where the main challenge of development in the mother country lies and this is how they would, in the long run, get the maximum quid pro quo for their contribution to India's development. It was, therefore, appropriate that the theme of the Pravasi Bharatiya Divas of 2006 was 'building a partnership between the diaspora and India's social development'.

For the last few years, the diaspora's contribution to social sectors of development in India has been confined to individual efforts and initiatives, mainly by NRIs in the US. There have been some notable interventions in these sectors which deserve to be mentioned.[14]

In the field of education, two NRIs from the US provided substantial financial support to the NGO Pratham, which has made a pioneering intervention in the field of education, designed to mainstream out-of-school children into the government school system. Pratham was established as a public charitable trust in 1994 by the Commissioner of the Municipal Corporation of Greater Mumbai, the United Nations Children's Fund (UNICEF) and several prominent citizens of the country. Its main achievement has been to bring thousands of out-of-school children, mostly from the slums of Mumbai, to the government school system by organizing bridge courses for them. By now, Pratham has expanded its activities to cover other aspects of school education, like improving the level of learning and direct delivery of pre-school and remedial education. Its Annual Status of Education Report (ASER) is looked upon as a valuable source material for researchers and as a guide for policymakers.

Another NRI initiative in the field of education is the Digital Equalization Programme (DEP), which is a computer-aided learning programme that bridges the educational and digital divide in India by preparing children in government schools to compete in the digital economy. Targeting children in Grade VI and above, the DEP provides computer and internet education to teachers and students and helps teachers to be more effective by implementing project-based learning methods. DEP has, until now, trained over 56,525 teachers and 870,000 children in 3,207 schools across India.[15]

In the field of health, there is the celebrated example of Dr Naresh Trehan who decided to migrate to India, and assembled a team of doctors and established a centre to provide world-class treatment for heart diseases and heart-care facilities. Now, Dr Trehan is so much a part of the Indian public scene, particularly of the health service landscape, that people have forgotten that he came to India as an NRI. He has now established an entire complex of top-class healthcare centres and institutions called Medanta—The Medicity, in Gurgaon, a suburb of Delhi.

Another important example in the field of healthcare was the initiative by an NRI, Gullapalli N. Rao, who left his job as an ophthalmologist in Rochester, New York, to establish a non-profit trust called L. V. Prasad Eye Institute in Hyderabad in October 1996. The institute, which is now recognized as one of the best eye care centres in India, has been and is still being helped by NRIs in various ways, including planning and development, collaborative support in research and teaching and financial support for adding to the infrastructure.

A major NRI initiative for poverty reduction in India was the establishment of the non-profit institution, SKS Microfinance, in late 1997 by Vikram Akula. Akula is said to have raised a sum of $50,000 in the US in order to launch the initiative. In 2005, SKS was converted into a profit-making company. It has provided loans to millions of poor women borrowers across the country. It is now providing other financial services like insurance and essential goods and services which the poor need, at low cost. Some figures can be cited to demonstrate the phenomenal progress made by SKS in fulfilling its mission to alleviate poverty. Its total number of branches increased from 276 in 2007 to 2,379 in 2011. During this period, the total number of districts in India covered by it increased from 103 to 378; the total number of staff, from 2,381 to 22,733; the total number of members benefitting from it, from 0.6 million to 7.3 million; and the total funds disbursed by it from Rs 452 crore (Rs 4.52 billion) to Rs 7,831 crore (Rs 78.31 billion).[16] Since then there has been a trend of decline in these figures, perhaps due to the changes in the management structure of the company. Nevertheless, the scale of its operation was still quite impressive as shown by the figures at the end of 2013 when the number of branches was 1,261, districts 298, staff 10,809, members benefitting over 5 million and amount disbursed was Rs 2,359 crore (Rs 23.59 billion).[17]

In 2001, two NRIs, Ramesh and Swati Ramanathan, founded Janaagraha, a non-profit organization based in Bangalore, to work with citizens and the government to improve the quality of life in Indian cities and towns. Janaagraha started as a movement to enable citizens' participation in urban governance. It has now evolved into a robust institution for citizenship and democracy.

There are several other initiatives that are not recorded, but which are serving extremely useful purposes in the field of social development. For example, an NRI group has offered services on the internet and through the distant mode to digitize government records, particularly land records.

These individual or group initiatives by the diaspora are laudable, but in order to have an actual impact on the social situation in India, these would have to be multiplied manifold. A very important consideration in this regard is the extent to which these initiatives are designed to contribute to resuscitating, revitalizing and building institutions capable of bringing about systemic changes.

Emerging Issues and Suggestions for New Initiatives

Correcting Bias towards New Diaspora

One of the deficiencies of the recently adopted policies in favour of the diaspora is that they suffer from a bias towards the new diaspora—those who migrated during the last two decades. The old diaspora, which migrated during the colonial period and settled down long ago in countries of their residence and yet, have maintained continuous cultural and emotional contact with the mother country, feel a sense of neglect. India has a moral obligation to satisfy the yearnings of the old diaspora with regard to the mother country and to intensify and strengthen the cultural links with it. The old diaspora may not be in a position to transfer riches or knowhow to India on the scale the new diaspora can. But they nevertheless constitute a strategic asset. They have an important contribution to make in enhancing India's prestige and strengthening its position in the comity of nations. No doubt, some of the measures adopted recently have brought the old diaspora closer to the mother country. These include the celebration of the Pravasi Bharatiya Divas, the institution of the Pravasi Bharatiya Samman, the issue of PIO cards and the recent move to open Indian Cultural Centres in many more countries. But more needs to be done to bring the old diaspora closer to the mother country.

Assistance to Diaspora in Distress

An important issue that arises in this connection is whether India's growing clout in the international arena can be utilized to assist members of the diaspora, particularly the old diaspora, when they are in trouble or are denied their legitimate rights in countries of their residence. Major powers like the US, the UK and France have often rushed to the rescue of their diasporas in distress or helped them otherwise by virtue of their economic and military clout. India still has a long way to go in building its economic and military strength before it acquires such a strategic leverage. However, the strategic space India has been able to gain recently has put it in a better position to come to the assistance of its diaspora than was the case only a few years ago. This is reflected in a changed stance in this regards. The real differences that can be discerned are the following:

- India is no longer following a hands-off policy vis-à-vis the interests of the Indian diaspora;
- India is in a position to send signals, at least to some countries, that they will have to pay a price—sometimes a heavy one—if they wantonly ignore India's concern about its diaspora; and
- There are more instances than before of India being able to send signals that it is concerned about its diaspora when it is in a difficult situation, and that it has the will to take all possible diplomatic and other measures to alleviate its condition.

However, it must be realized that one has to be very cautious and selective in sending such signals. The possibility of sending them and their effectiveness when sent very much depend upon the position of the diaspora in its country of residence and India's relations with that country. In any event, undue haste in sending such messages must be avoided.

Problems Posed by Splintered Nationalism

Politically, the PIOs are citizens of their countries of residence. But culturally, they are a part of the larger Indian nation. The challenge that policymakers face is how to maximize the assets of the diaspora for the mother country in spite of their splintered nationalism. This dilemma is faced by all diasporas, and not only by the Indian one. The extent to which a diaspora can be used as an asset for the mother country depends very much upon the historical, social, cultural and ethnic make-up of the diaspora. The easiest case is of the diaspora that migrated in the earlier phase of the colonial period and who have now independent States of their own, which are generally controlled and run by them. The obvious examples are Mauritius and Surinam. In these cases, the diaspora is a great asset for the home country in the very wide sense of the term. However, there is another group of countries like Fiji and Guyana, where the Indian diaspora, though constituting a majority of the population, finds itself in a precarious political position. In their case, the mother country must be very circumspect and cautious in using them for its purpose. The general rule in the case of this group of countries, as well as for the vast number of countries where the Indian diaspora consists of recent migrants, is that the inherent limitation in using their potential for the benefit of the home country must be recognized. In any event, a diaspora can never be expected to serve as a fifth column for the mother country. Their role should be brought into play only within the framework of cooperative arrangements between the host and the mother country. Where such arrangements are not possible and there is a conflict of interest, the diaspora has to choose the host country over the home country; otherwise it would put its welfare and destiny in jeopardy. In fact, a situation should not be allowed to arise where the diaspora is forced to choose between its loyalty to the host country and that to the home country.

Free Flow of Labour across the Globe

A major consequence of globalization is the compulsions it has created for a much enhanced cross-country flow of labour. Developing countries like India, with their large and expanding pool of skilled and semi-skilled workers, are likely to benefit most from this increased labour flow. There has, no doubt, been a sizeable increase in recent years in the migration of workers from these countries. But several countries, particularly in the Western world, where there is an increased demand for migrant workers, have put all kinds of obstacles to labour inflows. As a result, much of the inflow taking place in response to this demand is of a clandestine nature. To take advantage of the opportunities for international labour mobility and to protect the interest of its migrant workers, India has no doubt concluded a number of bilateral human resources mobility and migrant workers' protection agreements. In addition, India should take the initiative for negotiating new regimes and bring about changes in the existing regimes for liberalizing the movement of labour across borders and for bringing about improvements in the conditions of migrant workers. Going by the trend of the negotiations on services within the framework of the Doha Round of Trade Negotiations, this is going to be a difficult task. Prospects for liberalization of services under Mode IV, that is, movement of labour for seeking employment abroad, do not appear to be bright. Therefore, a time may come very soon when developing countries like India would have to make—as they have done with the issue of domestic agricultural subsidies of developed countries—progress in this sector a litmus test for the success of the entire Doha Round. But in that event, these countries should be prepared to accept larger scale movement of labour to their own territories from other developing countries, particularly from neighbouring least developed countries.

Autonomous Research Institution for Diaspora Research

For universities and research institutions in India, there awaits a large research agenda for further work on the issues of Indian diaspora. The most important item on this agenda is to carry out desegregated studies in order to fully understand the problems and potentialities of the diaspora. It is necessary to desegregate the diaspora in terms of their historical origin, place of residence, ethnic composition, the degree of their keenness to establish links with the mother country and the extent of the progress made in this direction. On the diaspora's contribution to India's development, it will be necessary, among others, to study the composition of foreign remittances and the diaspora's investment portfolio in India. For these purposes, the government may consider supporting the establishment of an autonomous research institution on the Indian diaspora at the central level, with linkages to universities and research institutions in both India and the host countries. Alternatively, the government may sanction the creation of chairs for diaspora studies in selected universities and research institutions both in India and abroad. The ICM is not equipped to meet the challenge of research in diaspora affairs. First, it is narrowly focused on employment. Second, it is designed to play basically a promotional role. And lastly, the way it is constituted and functions, it can hardly be regarded as an autonomous research institution, which is the need of the hour.

Notes

1. Prime Minister's Inaugural Address at the Pravasi Bharatiya Divas (New Delhi, 7 January 2007).
2. Devesh Kapur, *Diaspora, Development and Democracy: The Domestic Impact of International Migration from India* (Princeton: Princeton University Press, 2010) 209.
3. Prime Minister's Inaugural Address at the Pravasi Bharatiya Divas (New Delhi, 8 January 2008).
4. Ibid.
5. Prime Minister's Inaugural Address at the Pravasi Bharatiya Divas (New Delhi, 7 January 2007).
6. Ministry of Overseas Indian Affairs (MOIA), *Annual Report 2013–14* (New Delhi: Government of India, 2014).
7. Reserve Bank of India, 'Balance of Payment Statistics', Reserve Bank of India Bulletin of December 1997, January 1999, January 2000, January 2001, December 2002, December 2004, January 2005, February 2006 and November 2006.
8. World Bank, World Development Indicators (several years), http://data.worldbank.org/datacatalog/world-development-indicators (accessed on 19 January 2015).

9. Data taken from the Reserve Bank of India. Quoted in Muzaffar Chishti, *The Rise in Remittances to India: A Closer Look* (Washington DC: Migration Policy Institute, February 2007).
10. Chishti, *The Rise in Remittances to India.*
11. Ibid.
12. Prime Minister's Inaugural Address at the Pravasi Bharatiya Divas (New Delhi, 8 January 2008).
13. Chishti, *The Rise in Remittances to India.*
14. The examples and some of the details of the initiatives by NRIs in the social field, discussed in this section, have been taken from a study on the contribution of the Indian diaspora in the US to India's development, conducted by Muzaffar Chishti in 2004–05, at the time the Director of the Emigration Policy Institute of New York University, when he was based as a visiting professor at the Council for Social Development (CSD). His study has not been published in full, but he presented its main findings in a seminar held at CSD in 2005. The details regarding these initiatives have been updated on the basis of the latest information available on the websites of these organizations.
15. American India Foundation, 'Education', http://aif.org/investment-area/education/ (accessed on 20 January 2015).
16. SKS Microfinance, 'Financial Info', http://www.sksindia.com/financial_info.php (accessed on 27 August 2011).
17. Ibid.

Index